Cinematic Realism

Bicycle Thieves (Vittorio De Sica, 1948)

Cinematic Realism

Lukács, Kracauer and Theories of the Filmic Real

Ian Aitken

EDINBURGH
University Press

Edinburgh University Press is one of the leading university presses in the UK. We publish academic books and journals in our selected subject areas across the humanities and social sciences, combining cutting-edge scholarship with high editorial and production values to produce academic works of lasting importance. For more information visit our website: edinburghuniversitypress.com

© Ian Aitken, 2020, 2022

Edinburgh University Press Ltd
The Tun – Holyrood Road
12 (2f) Jackson's Entry
Edinburgh EH8 8PJ

First published in hardback by Edinburgh University Press 2020

Typeset in 11/13 Ehrhardt by
IDSUK (DataConnection) Ltd

A CIP record for this book is available from the British Library

ISBN 978 1 4744 4134 6 (hardback)
ISBN 978 1 4744 4135 3 (paperback)
ISBN 978 1 4744 4136 0 (webready PDF)
ISBN 978 1 4744 4137 7 (epub)

The right of Ian Aitken to be identified as author of this work has been asserted in accordance with the Copyright, Designs and Patents Act 1988 and the Copyright and Related Rights Regulations 2003 (SI No. 2498)

Contents

Acknowledgements	vi
Preface	vii
Introduction: Representation, Perception and Cinematic Realism	1
1. Bergson, the Image and Time	45
2. Introduction to Lukács: Essence, Phenomena and Temporality	72
3. 'On the Phenomenology of the Creative Process' (Lukács 1914)	94
4. 'Thoughts towards an Aesthetic of the Cinema' (Lukács 1913)	113
5. *The Specificity of the Aesthetic* (Lukács 1963)	133
6. Husserl, *Epochē* and *Lebenswelt*	157
7. Introduction to Kracauer: Abstraction, Redemption and Modernity	180
8. 'Photography' (Kracauer 1927)	191
9. 'Introduction: Photography' and 'Basic Concepts', from *Theory of Film* (Kracauer 1960)	217
10. 'The Historical Approach' and 'The Historian's Journey', from *History: The Last Things Before the Last* (Kracauer 1968)	254
Bibliography	290
Index	304

Acknowledgements

I would like to take this opportunity to thank the various and numerous colleagues with whom I have discussed aspects of this book over the last three years. I would also like to acknowledge the support of the School of Communication and Academy of Film of Hong Kong Baptist University. Particularly, I would like to thank Eva Man and Huang Yu, for helping to arrange my sabbatical at Edinburgh University during September to December 2019. This sabbatical enabled me to bring this book to fruition. I would also like to acknowledge the support of the School of Languages, Literature and Culture at Edinburgh University during my sabbatical. The manuscript for this book was delivered to Edinburgh University Press during the period of virus lockdown, and I would like to thank my wife and children for providing me with support and peace of mind during this unsettling time. As I now head into retirement, leaving Hong Kong after spending fifteen years there and returning to my native Scotland, I am aware that I will miss the people of Hong Kong, and wish them well in their struggle against the virus, and for freedom and democracy. I hope to return on a regular basis.

Preface

This book has grown out of my previous writings on cinematic realism. As I reviewed those writings, going back to the 1980s, I do not think that my core beliefs concerning cinematic realism have changed overmuch. The same concern with philosophical realism, the philosophy of perception, phenomenology, and even classical Marxism and the Frankfurt School, still permeate this present work. In my book *The Major Realist Film Theorists* (2016), a long Introduction attempted to set out the key characteristics of what I first called 'intuitionist cinematic realism', and then 'phenomenal cinematic realism'. This provided the starting point for the focus on phenomenology in the current book. I had become convinced that Bergsonian conceptions of time had influenced the writings of Georg Lukács, and that certain Husserlian notions, particularly that of the *Lebenswelt*, had significantly influenced the writings of Siegfried Kracauer. The structure of the present book has evolved from that. The long Introduction attempts to set out a model of cinematic realism based on a philosophical realist and 'externalist' position, and takes the matter further on from the considerations covered in the Introduction to *The Major Realist Film Theorists*. This is followed by an introductory chapter on Bergson, which serves as a foundation for the following four chapters, which cover the work of Lukács. In these chapters, and amongst other matters, I follow Lukács's intellectual move from Platonism to phenomenology. The same structure is then repeated for Kracauer: an introductory chapter on Husserl is followed by four chapters on Kracauer's theory. The objective was to explore these pieces of writings in as much depth as possible, and, so, the focus on them is relatively intense. I decided not to write a 'Conclusions' to the book, as this would impose an artificial closure on writings which are full of and vibrant with connotation and possibility. Indeed, it is not possible to bring closure to the subject of either cinematic realism or realism in general, and I intend to keep pursuing both.

INTRODUCTION

Representation, Perception and Cinematic Realism

This Introduction will begin with an account of the relation between representation and reality. The purpose of this is not to provide a comprehensive account of that relation, but to furnish a platform for an exploration of cinematic realism. What follows is, therefore, a schematic outline of an enduring area of philosophical enquiry. In the writings of Henri Bergson, which will be considered in the first chapter of this book, 'reality' is principally defined as that which is displayed within states of consciousness concerning a known material reality external to those states but which those states are also part of. Here, the phrase 'known material reality' refers to phenomenal reality as revealed by the senses, our more abstract conceptual knowledge of material reality as revealed by the intellect, and a material reality that can be imagined, given current understandings, even though those understandings may be limited (for example, certain aspects of quantum mechanics). Bergson is not overly concerned with what might exist outside of known material reality: what is frequently referred to as an unknowable 'external reality'. External reality is that which lies outside of our conceptual schemes and cognitive–sensory capacities, and, consequently, it is a reality that cannot be engaged with directly.

Nomenclature can, however, become easily disordered, because the phrase 'external reality' is often used as a substitute for the phrase material reality, and to indicate a fundamental binary opposition between that externality and 'internal' reality, or consciousness. In this Introduction, however, the phrase material reality will be used to indicate known and potentially knowable material reality, whilst the phrase external reality will be used to indicate a potentially always unknowable material reality. Known and potentially knowable material reality, together with unknowable external reality, form the totality of reality, and this totality means that the idea that only known or potentially knowable material reality constitutes reality is an 'idealist' and 'anthropocentric' one (Trigg 1989: xxiv). Reality, as a totality, is not anthropocentric; and this also means that it is 'metaphysical' to us, in the sense that it is connected not just to our materiality, but beyond that (56); and this also means that, ultimately, 'realism is a metaphysical, not empirical question' (xxiv). 'Metaphysical realism' contends that reality cannot be reduced to the way that humans perceive and conceptualise it.

As atoms cluster to form cells, and then an organism, the cognate–sensory apparatus of that organism is formed. This apparatus is 'internal' to the organism, and its principal purpose is to process the sense data it receives from outside the 'skin'[1] of the organism in order to understand and react to what is outside (Rowlands 2003: 173). The nature of this understanding and reaction has been a crucial issue within philosophy, because it raises the question of whether the perceptual experience which is the outcome of such internal processing is entirely the product of that dispensation, or whether it is also influenced, to one extent or another, by what is outside the skin of the organism. At one level, this may amount to a distinction between idealism and realism. However, and as will be argued shortly, at another more complicated level, it can also amount to a distinction between different forms of realism.

This Introduction is concerned not so much with the general idea of idealism, as with the more specific concept of 'internalism', and not so much with the general idea of realism, either, but rather with the narrower notion of 'externalism'. One approach to the question just raised concerning the causes and character of perceptual experience is to argue that the organism's consciousness, including its perceptions, consists of 'representations' of what is external to the internal apparatus, where the term representation means something known – consciousness and perceptual experience – that stands for something unknowable in itself because it is external to the apparatus. The notion of representation is a contentious one, and one that can be defined in several ways. Within certain academic disciplines, including film studies, a conception of what is sometimes referred to as 'pure' representation contends that a conscious experience of something, including perceptual experience of that thing, is a mental representation of that thing, and that such a representation is distinct from what is represented. The material reality that the organism perceives in conscious experience is not that reality per se but an account of that reality as internally manufactured representation. According to this view, 'all our thoughts and feelings are caused by processes in the brain' (Searle 1989: 19). What we become aware of is the output from an internal information-processing system which generates that output (43). According to this argument to pure symbolic representationalism, the organism can only know representations of material reality, and not material reality 'itself', because a barrier, or 'veil' of perception, exists between the consciousness of the organism and the external world, preventing direct contact with and knowledge of that world.[2] Nevertheless, the very notion of a 'veil', whilst indicating that something is 'veiled off', still implies the existence of a reality that exists outside the veil; and this position on representationalism is sometimes referred to as 'representational realism'. The position on pure representationalism is not necessarily an idealist or solipsistic one, although, of course, it can be. In the latter cases there is neither a veil nor an external reality, only an internal reality. In contrast, in representational realism, there is not just an embrace of the mental, but an admission of something that exists outside the skin.

The notion of the veil of perception, and idea of representational realism, raise the question as to whether the representation is entirely different from whatever in material reality is represented, or whether that representation is shaped to some degree by what is represented. What might be called a 'hard' (or pure) representational–realist stance emphasises the former, so that:

> for instance, perception, such as colour vision, is . . . explained in terms of processes occurring in several neuronal systems in the neocortex. And emotions, such as fear, are . . . explained in terms of processes in the central amygdala[3] and other components of the limbic systems.[4] (Bunge 2006: 80)

If, on the other hand, the representation is shaped to some degree or other by what is represented, then experience of material reality at the level of consciousness, including phenomenal experience, will be a combination of coding organised by the cognitive–sensory apparatus that is determined by internal processes, and coding that is also determined by what is outside the brain (80). In the latter case, the coding is not fully representational in the symbolic sense of the term, because it is not entirely different from the object that exists beyond the barrier of perception.[5]

Another way of saying this is that what is happening inside the skin also projects outside the skin towards physical reality, so that the veil becomes more permeable, and, as a consequence, the 'skin', or veil, occurs *outside* the corporeal organism, in order to comprehend material reality, or meet material reality half-way (Devitt 1997: 68). This notion of a projection outwards is the basis of the externalist position, which will be set out in detail later in this Introduction. Adopting the terminology of one author, let us imagine a sliding scale, and call that part of experience that is entirely coded by the brain, and situated at one end of the scale, 'representational', and that in which the coding is also shaped by material reality, 'phenomenal', with an impossibly pure phenomenalism situated at the other end of the scale (Rowlands 2003: 185).[6] In the case where phenomenal experience holds, a pure or hard notion of representation does not. Any experience, can, therefore, be said to possess both representational and phenomenal aspects, or properties. Within a purely symbolic representational account of consciousness, including perceptual experience, however, this is not admitted, because, within such an account, the 'phenomenal properties of experience reduce to the representational properties of that experience', and to the point where the notion of phenomenal properties can no longer apply (185).

A softer representationalist position would be based on the premise that the phenomenal properties of experience do not reduce to the representational properties of that experience because those phenomenal properties are influenced by something that is outside the internal system of coding that generates the representational properties. This also raises the issue that the characterisation of 'soft representation', or even the idea of representation itself, might not be best suited to account for this latter scenario. The concept of representation is controversial for several reasons. First, the symbolic representation of one thing as another can imply either that what is represented is primary or secondary, or that the representation is primary or secondary. Either way, there is the prospect of creating a hierarchy. So, for example, the phrase 'film is a representation of reality' could be taken to mean either that film is secondary to reality, or that the act of representation takes priority because it embellishes a disordered reality.

Whilst, however, there is, in theory, the possibility for either representation or the thing represented to be considered as primary or secondary, the process begins with the thing represented and ends with the representation, and, within a representationalist paradigm, it is this termination point – which is also the point of substantive access – that lends priority to representation. The problem here is that reality becomes, ipso facto, secondary to representation, which, after all, is only part of the world. Second, within a representationalist paradigm, the hegemony of representation may lead to or imply an acceptance of determinism, and to idealism and solipsism as well. This is because, where representation means something standing for something else entirely, and where that something is generated internally, it could be posited that internal processes determine how the world appears, and how the organism, as automaton, is ultimately directed to function. In other words, the organism is determined by those internal processes that generate the representations. Therefore, the idea of representation in experience, as well as in film, may be associated with idealism, solipsism and determinism.

The emphasis here is on innate structures, rather than on 'input' to those structures from outside the skin, and here 'a thin account of input entails an excessively rich account of the inner state' (Hamlyn 1990: 34). Where input is insufficiently theorised, emphasis falls on the internal mechanisms. Within 'apparatus' film theory the real is out of reach, and, so, what matters is to reveal the operation of systems of representation in order to offset determinism through ideological and other forms of positive manipulation operating through those representations. But this position still espouses the secondary nature of reality and contains an overly deterministic conception of agency. Accordingly, as an exploration of cinematic realism, this Introduction will present a more adequate account of input and move the emphasis away from internal processes.

One other way of understanding what representation is and is not is to consider the notion of the 'representational function'. This function emerges from a prior premise that there is no way of knowing how the cognitive system or physical brain states produce mental states unless those states are reduced to the level of physical conditions. Saying that a mental state is a brain state, and that the two cannot be distinguished, would, however, amount to an act of 'reductive materialism' that few would accept (Hamlyn 1990: 41). According to Wittgenstein, not only is a mental state not the same as a brain state, but also there is no possibility of a direct match between brain states and mental states (Wittgenstein, referenced in Hamlyn 1990: 47), and this means that, at this level, the notion of representation fails: the mental state is not a representation of the brain state; it is influenced in some unknown way by the brain state, but is also influenced in some unknown way by something else, and is something else. If the mental state is only indirectly influenced by the physical brain state, it could also be indirectly influenced by something else, and that can only be input.

The 'representational function', as opposed to symbolic representation, occurs when the cognitive–sensory apparatus produces an image for us in order that we can use it in some way in relation to input (Hamlyn 1990: 49). This is not only internally generated representation, but also externally generated representation: something 'appears' which is designed to capture and absorb what is outside the skin, as well as to accommodate the workings of the apparatus within the skin. The mental state, or appearance, is 'there' because we have an interest in it, an interest born of both internal and external factors. Data input is received by the apparatus, and what comes out as mental state and perception is information related to interest, and what interests any organism is its relation to its environment, not its relation to its internal cognitive processes. The idea of 'representational function', therefore, unlike the notion of symbolic representation, refers to the production of information, as consciousness and perception, that is based on the interaction between the organism and the environment. The focus, now, is on the relation between the environment, organism and apparatus, rather than just on the relation between apparatus and organism (50–1), and, now, a 'thicker' account of input has been established, and one which will be developed further. The notion of the representational function also accords with Wittgenstein's claim, previously referred to, that there is no direct connection between brain states and mental states, as would be the case if the mental state was a representation of the brain state.

This notion of the representational function also accords with the philosophical realist notion of convergence. With a focus on inner central processes, experience may be so different from external reality that it is not worth considering the latter. This is counter to a realist stance, which holds that experience is not entirely determined by innate processes, that such experience does 'converge' with reality to one extent or another, and that external reality is worth considering because it exists. The realist convergence stance is predicated on two central principles: that reality exists independently of mind, and that mind and reality can converge (Trigg 1989: xxiii). Of course, mind is part of overall reality, but what is meant here is that reality is not the product of mind and is distinct from any one mind. This externalist-convergence stance, and a substantial account of input, has been put forward in Putnam's 'twin-earth' thesis and Block's 'inverted-earth' scenario. Here, if somebody on one 'earth' with familiar representations of the characteristics of that world is taken to another world with different characteristics, that person's representations change, and that change will be caused by the characteristics of the second world. 'This new embedding would, eventually, come to dominate, and . . . representational contents would, accordingly, shift' (Putnam and Block, referenced in Rowlands 2003: 186–7). In the 'twin-earth' thesis, the two worlds in question are different, and it is this difference that leads to the change in representational content. However, if the point is taken further, it can be argued that any change of environment or context will induce a shift in representational content, and a hard, symbolic, representationalist stance then breaks down.

A hard conception of representation can be used to posit a clear division between mind and material reality in which the experience of material reality is effectively constituted by human mental activity by virtue of the existence of the barrier of perception, and by the – clearly mistaken – notion that material reality is what is outside the skin; and it has been argued that this conception is 'virtually definitive of much twentieth-century thought' (Rowlands 2003: 4). There is a certain logic to representationalism, based on the fact that, as beings who construct what reality is through the cognitive–sensory apparatus, we are unable to step outside of that apparatus, so that there is no *'reality itself* (whatever that might be), but reality-as-we-picture-it . . . reality-as-we-think-it = our reality, is the only reality we can deal with' (Rescher 1973: 167). However, the conception of known and knowable material reality laid out earlier contends that we are part of material reality, and this means that the distinction made between 'reality itself' and 'reality-as-we-picture-it' is problematic. If 'reality-as-we-picture-it' is causally shaped by 'reality itself', reality outside the skin, and if internal and external are part of one reality, then it is not just 'as-we-picture-it'. 'It', at least in part, bears the imprint of the reality that exists outside the skin. Our anthropocentric experience of reality is part of the larger reality, and not fundamentally different from that, and, as such, the latter can, potentially, be known to an extent. In this sense, the conceptual schemes which we inhabit are not static, but, on the contrary, are constantly investigating the larger reality, and absorbing more and more parts of it into the parameters of our conceptual schemes. This notion of expanding conceptual schemes is exemplified in Harré's notion of the constantly enlarging human *Umwelt* (human environment) as 'accelerating extension': the everyday reality of existence, and the growth of knowledge, consists in such accelerating extension into reality, rather than an incremental 'convergence' upon certain truths (Harré 1986: 303).[7] It may be the case that, according to a 'convergent-realist approach', successive theories are, in some cases, better and better approximations to a fixed but partially unknown reality, but, in relation to theory in general, it is not so much a case of getting closer and closer to the truth as increasing the sphere of knowledge about the world: not an accelerating convergence, but an accelerating extension (302).

If anthropocentric reality is part of the larger reality, then no fundamental 'cut' should be made between the two. In relation to what has been discussed previously, this also means that a division should not be drawn between what is inside and outside the 'skin': that is, between inner states and input to those. This position is the basis of Putnam's theory of 'internal realism', which rejects notions of a division between internal cognitive and perceptual processes, and external material reality. Putnam argues that the attempt to make what he calls the 'cut' between inside and outside, between subjectivity and objectivity, external reality and internal representation, cannot be made (Putnam 1987: 27). Instead of the cut, Putnam's model of internal realism proposes a suture of inside and outside, and a continuum of the 'relatively subjective' and 'relatively objective' (29). Putnam also, however, refers to the theory of internal realism as an 'internalist perspective', because the world can be posited only from '*within* a theory or description' (Putnam 1992a: 49). This seems paradoxical.

Putnam describes himself as an 'internalist philosopher' and distinguishes himself from what he calls 'externalist' philosophers, but his conception of externalism is not the one that is pursued within this Introduction. By the phrase externalist philosophy Putnam refers to the notion that it may be possible for a conceptual scheme to draw the definite distinctions that exist in nature. Putnam rejects the possibility of such a 'God's-Eye View' (Conant 1992: xlv). There may be definite characteristics in nature, but those are confronted from within conceptual schemes so that no 'God's-Eye View' is ever humanly possible. Putnam writes within a tradition of Pragmatist analytical philosophy, and, accordingly, emphasises the way that meaning is defined within the conceptual scheme of 'a particular community of users' (Putnam 1992b: 52), particularly in relation to intellectual principles such as 'canons and principles of rationality', and 'rational assertibility' criteria (90). These principles facilitate prospective convergence with the reality that is experienced within a conceptual scheme. As a Pragmatist, Putnam rules out absolutes, such as 'The Way the World Is', and this means that he does not pursue 'metaphysical' questions about the nature of external reality. In this sense, he is close to the cinematic realist theorists who are considered in the remainder of this book.

This Introduction is not concerned with these theorists, however, but with general questions of realism and representation, and what must be said in relation to this is that Putnam's model of 'input' hits the barrier wall of the conceptual scheme, and does not project outside that wall, even though his wall is, in a sense, outside the corporeal skin, and embedded within a community of 'users'. As will be argued, Putnam's conception of 'externalism', and denial of metaphysical realism, is a misnomer. The externalism being considered in this Introduction is a form of metaphysical realism, in that it acknowledges that:

> The aim of any conceptual system will be to draw the distinctions which actually exist in nature. Unless we wish to be conceptual idealists, it is quite wrong to think of nature, reality, things-in-themselves, or however we wish to characterise what there is, as having no definite characteristics before we apply our conceptual schemes. (Trigg 1989: 111)

If we *did* have a God's-Eye View, we would see 'the distinctions which actually exist in nature' and the 'definite characteristics' of that nature. But because we do not have a God's-Eye View, we cannot. However, the fact that we approach reality from within conceptual schemes and multiple perspectives does not mean that, within those schemes and perspectives, we cannot engage with reality. Ultimately, Putnam's pragmatism leads him to a conception of input that is limited to an unsustainable communal 'skin'. Putnam's 'canons and principles of rationality' create an 'explanation space' within a communally based conceptual scheme, and all the input comes from within that.

Putnam frames his account of internal realism in terms of truth claims within which some interpretations are more 'useful' than others, thus conflating truth and use. Putnam also rejects the correspondence theory of truth, whereby a theory is taken to be true if it corresponds to reality, and welcomes the 'demise of a theory that has lasted for two thousand years' (Putnam 1992a: 74), asserting that:

> the suggestion which constitutes the essence of 'internal realism' is that truth does not transcend use . . . What makes . . . a theory or conceptual scheme – rationally acceptable is, in large part, its coherence and fit' in terms of its own inner formations. (Putnam 1992a: 115, 54–5)

Truth is what has come to be accepted as useful and practical to believe within a community, and that judgement is also guided by the rational principles that Putnam foregrounds. If truth is merely what has come to be believed to be useful within a particular community, this could lead to relativism, but Putnam argues that the rational principles he champions set limits upon this, so that 'Internalism is not a facile relativism which says that "anything goes"' (54).

It seems unwise for anyone to claim that they can – now that the metaphysical mists have finally cleared – sound the death-knell of a 'two-thousand-year-old theory'. What will be argued here is that a conception of truth such as is offered by the theory of internal realism is ultimately untenable because, first, it is far too alterable and relativistic, and truth is surely a concept that should not be too easily allied to mutability and contingency; second, an internal-realist conception of truth is inherent to the theoretical scheme that mobilises it, and this is too inward-looking; and, third, such a conception is insufficient to account for input into the theoretical scheme from that which is outside the theoretical scheme, and *that* position can be found acceptable only if what is outside the conceptual scheme is declared to be irrelevant. In fact, and contrary to Putnam, it will be argued that 'there is no plausible alternative' to the correspondence theory of truth, and that Pragmatist, coherence-based conceptions of truth are open to the charge of 'serious regress and epistemological objection' (Schmitt 1995: 147).

As with Pragmatist approaches in general, Putnam seeks to bracket out what is outside of our conceptual schemes, including abstract levels of causality and an associated 'craving for absolutes' (Putnam 1992b: 131); and this also rules out a philosophical-realist approach that is concerned with both internal conceptual schemes and external reality. What is ruled out in the theory of internal realism is, consequently, metaphysics, and philosophical realism is a form of metaphysical realism, or ontological realism, because it postulates a reality that goes beyond us. Some of what is 'beyond us' can be imagined, but some cannot, and an acceptance of the latter is what makes philosophical realism a form of metaphysical realism. The idea that reality should not be conceived of unless it can be 'known' is, as argued, an idealist and anthropomorphic one, and, consequently, also an anti-metaphysical one (Trigg 1989: xxiv). Nevertheless, philosophical realism holds that, whilst external reality is independent of consciousness, it remains knowable by consciousness to an extent (Sayers 1985: xiv) because consciousness and reality are ultimately one: 'both distinct and yet also united' (3). Internal realism, on the other hand, and under an impetus to be 'human-centred' and deploy a 'realism with a human face', to use Putnam's vocabulary, does not so postulate.

Putnam's 'canons and principles of rationality' guide the activity of a putative theorist, operating within the parameters of a theoretical scheme, and attempting to interpret what is happening within what is available to that theoretical scheme. Translated into ordinary-life terms, a person should use rationality and coherence factors in order to understand the world with which they interact. Both the pragmatic individual and the Pragmatist philosopher bracket out the abstract and exist within a milieu of close use-values, and, whilst these may be comfortable positions to adopt, they come at the cost of bracketing out a level of thought that has its place within the one, ultimate, reality, as a meaningful stratum of knowledge. This becomes clear when the fundamental level of perceptual experience is considered, a level that underlies the pragmatic community, and whose regard undermines the internal-realist conception of truth. At the basis of perceptual experience there is the reception of information from outside the skin by the internal cognate–sensory apparatus. That information is then coded by the apparatus and the result is a mental state.

Whilst it is not known how that state comes into being, it is, unquestionably, the product of an interaction between internal processes and external factors. If that mental state then evolves into other mental states, some of which involve interaction with other organisms/people, it follows that all mental states are influenced by these external factors and must correspond to aspects of those factors. If this were not the case, existence would be difficult. The theory of internal realism weakens because it cannot accommodate the relation between mental states and external, material reality, even though that relation is undeniable. The theory deploys a weak account of input. To dispense with the 'real' is to say that 'reality' is what is experienced by human beings within a state of consciousness peculiar to human beings, and this is tantamount to saying that reality is consciousness, even though consciousness must have been partly caused by aspects of material reality, and is also part of that same, one reality. Just as 'internalism' is not enough, internal realism is not enough, because it only generates a model of communal-based input and excludes input from external, material reality. Just as a focus on internal systems leads to an insufficient conception of input, a focus on anthropomorphism, and inter-subjective anthropomorphism, does the same, because it brackets out what lies beyond the human. The need for a theory of input remains, including in relation to film.

Putnam's theory of internal realism focuses on the way that 'signs' acquire meaning within the conceptual scheme of a certain community of users, and on how representation is aligned with reality, although, and as argued, a reality for a particular scheme of users, rather than one beyond that. In the past, scholars within film studies have tried to understand this link between representation and reality, and, also, the fact that it seems sensible to go beyond a hard representationalist position in relation to a visual medium such as film, through, first, an engagement with semiotic theory, and, when the 'arbitrary' Saussurean symbolic basis of that theory proved too restrictive, taking up the 'trichotomatic' model of signs developed by Charles Sanders Peirce. Peirce's 'trichotomy' of signs consists of (a) the Icon: the sign that physically resembles what it signifies (as in a photograph or portrait); (b) the Index: something that indicates something else but does not resemble it (a weathervane does not resemble the wind but indicates aspects – in this case, the direction – of the wind); and (c), the symbol: something that has a more-or-less completely abstract and 'conventional' relationship to that which is signified.

If we take this model, and relate it back to the notion that material reality may alter the internal properties of the cognitive–perceptual apparatus so that those properties have phenomenal as well as representational aspects, and also relate that to Putnam's notion of a suture between 'inside' and 'outside', and advocacy of a union of the 'relatively subjective' and 'relatively objective', we can say that, in Peirce's model, the icon and the index have more of external reality in them than the symbol, in that icon and index are shaped by aspects of reality. The icon is shaped by an existing physical resemblance; the index (in this case the weathervane), by a physical force that directs it in a particular direction (Peirce claims that the index 'refers [to] an Object . . . by virtue of being really affected by that object') (Bordwell and Carroll 1996: 106). And yet, even the Peircean symbol must be distinguished in this respect from the entirely 'arbitrary' symbol associated with semiotic theory, because Peirce's symbol is not wholly symbolic; not completely conventional. Peirce claims that the symbol is formed in part through 'habit', and, whilst this could presume an inborn determination, if it is also 'acquired', as Peirce suggests, this could presuppose a source for such acquisition that lies outside the apparatus (106).[8] If a symbol is caused through habit, the question of 'what causes the habit?' could lead beyond the symbolic and conventional. Leaving aside this qualification of Peirce's notion of the symbol, however, and turning to the issue of perceptual experience, the fully arbitrary symbol can be defined in terms of the following, for present purposes: the symbol is entirely distinct from what it represents and, in terms of perception, is a representation of reality for,med entirely by internal processes. Icon and index, on the other hand, as suggested, are not entirely distinct from what they represent, and, in relation to perception, are, therefore, not formed only by internal processes.

The Peircean concepts of iconicity and indexicality provide a certain model of input from external reality, but only in the vaguest terms. For example, the weathervane, as index, situated within phenomenal experience, indicates the direction of the wind by virtue of being affected by the physical force of moving air that directs it in a certain direction. Peirce, remember, asserts that the index, as sign, 'refers [to] an Object . . . by virtue of being really affected by that object'. The weathervane is a 'sign' of the wind's presence, but, as a sign, it reveals only an immediate, observable and empirical affect. The Peircean index, as sign, has little explanatory power, and little possibility of indicating abstract levels of causation and reality: the weathervane does not tell us what causes the wind, or, in a fuller sense, what wind *is*. In other words, this indexical sign cannot furnish a suitable model of input from the one reality to the representation formed during perceptual experience. This is hardly surprising, given that Peirce's theory of signs is inseparable from his general philosophy, which film scholars have studied far less. That philosophy is associated with Pragmatism, as is that of Putnam, and, as with Putnam, in his general philosophy, Peirce was concerned to argue that the value of a concept was related to its practical consequences, and that high levels of abstraction should be better excluded from philosophical enquiry. In this sense, Peirce's position is comparable to Putnam's notion of internal realism, as is made clear from the following quotations, the first from Peirce, the second from Putnam:

> To attain perfect clearness in our thought of an object, then, we need only consider what conceivable effects of a practical kind the object may involve – what sensations we are to expect from it . . . Our conception of these effects . . . is then for us the whole of our conception of the object. (Peirce, cited in Putnam 1992b: 219)
> The Peircean idea of truth . . . as a coherent system of beliefs . . . will ultimately be accepted by the widest possible community of enquirers. The dictionary says truth means agreement with reality; but what does it mean for our beliefs or thoughts or ideas to agree with reality, and what does it matter anyway? (Putnam 1992b: 221, 220)

The Pragmatist conception of truth is based on coherence and utility, and this is at odds with the correspondence notion of truth, which is premised upon the conviction that an idea is true if it corresponds to – possibly inchoate – things in the world. The sense is put, in terms of scientific truth, in the following:

> Scientific Realism is a semantical thesis, it is the view that the intended and proper sense of the theories of science is as literal descriptions of the physical world, as saying what there is and how it behaves. It is the view that if a scientific theory is in fact true then there is in the world exactly those entities which the theory says there is . . . I understand scientific realism to be the view that the theoretical statements of science are, or purport to be, true generalised descriptions of reality. (cited in Devitt 1997: 39–40)

Following the position adopted within philosophical realism, such a theory would also possess an 'epistemological depth' which matched the 'ontological depth' of reality, and such depth implies the sort of abstract domains which Pragmatism wishes to bracket out (Keat and Urry 1975: 29). Peircean iconicity and indexicality, like Pragmatism more generally, do gesture towards the issue of external input in a way that stands against a purely symbolic conception of representation, but the limitations inherent in the schema mean that, in order to understand the issue of perceptual experience, and cinematic realism, the better, this Introduction will now consider an intellectual paradigm which may have more propitious outcomes: 'externalism'.

Philosophical realism encompasses a spectrum of intellectual positions, including – but to a limited extent – the ideas of Putnam. Within that spectrum, and also within the philosophy of mind, the designation 'externalism' has been given to schools of thought which maintain that consciousness, or the mind, is the product not only of what occurs within the cognitive–sensory system but also of what occurs outside that. Externalism links consciousness and representation to an environment. Recent externalist thought encompasses different positions, including 'content externalism', 'active externalism', 'architecturalism', 'vehicle externalism' and 'environmentalism' (Rowlands 2003: 5). That body of thought is, however, united by the general contention that 'mental phenomena . . . are not confined to what is going on inside the skins of mental subjects . . . [but are] . . . extended out into the world, distributed upon that world' (6). What is central to externalism is that a substantive theory of input from the one reality to representation is developed. This Introduction will now explore two externalist positions; first, and briefly, vehicle externalism; and, second, and in more depth, a form of environmentalist externalism.

In 'vehicle externalism', a distinction is made between the content and vehicle of a conscious experience. The vehicle of that experience, internal physical structures within the cognitive–sensory apparatus, may influence the content of that experience, but that content does not necessarily need to be limited to or by that influence; and, if that is so, that content may also be influenced by something external to that (156). The basic premise of vehicle externalism is that consciousness, or mental states, is/are 'broad or context-bound', and that the phenomenal content of those states are affected by outward context (Jackson and Petit 1988: 381). The vehicle of the mental state remains 'inside the skin', whereas the mental content of that state is influenced by something in addition to and beyond that vehicle – beyond the skin. The phenomenal experience remains within the mind, within the head/skin, but it has been affected by something outside it. Material reality is full of '*external information-bearing structure*[s]' which the cognitive–sensory apparatus seeks out, and, not only do these external structures inform the apparatus, not only does the apparatus need this information, but the more information-bearing structures there are in the environment, the less processing may need to be done by internal processes (Rowlands 2003: 171). Vehicle externalism is a complex theoretical position which can be treated only in brief outline here. At the heart of that position, however, and as argued, is the realist desire to resist 'internalism' and establish a strong theory of input. This notion of the perceiver actively seeking information within the external environment is also taken further in the perceptual 'environmentalist' and 'ecological' account of visual perception put forward by James J. Gibson.

Gibson was one of the pioneers of a school of externalism that sought to link cognitive processes to the body and environment, thereby rejecting Cartesian dualism (which implies a division between mind and body) and internal representationalism. In the account of perception associated with Gibson, the mind is considered to be dependent upon or even identical with the body's interaction with the environment, and perception is, consequently, considered to be not only 'a process in the brain, but a kind of skilful activity on the part of the animal as a whole' (Noë 2004: 2). Like other externalists, Gibson attempted to develop an alternative model to a representationalist one that insisted that animals – including human beings – are aware of their surroundings only indirectly, through internal mental constructs (Heil 1983: 222). Gibson's 'key insight' was to avoid such internalism and representationalism through connecting internal processes to external informational structures situated within the ambient 'optic array' of light, and then by connecting that array to physical objects within the environment (Costall and Still 1987: 9). Gibson called his approach to perception 'ecological' because it linked organism to environment in this manner:

> I now believe that we must take an ecological approach to the problems of perception . . . We are told that vision depends on the eye, which is connected to the brain. I shall suggest that natural vision depends on the eyes in the head of a body supported by the ground, the brain being only the central organ of a complete visual system. (Gibson 1986: 1)

Instead of positing only the internal mental processing of the environment, Gibson's model attempts to account for how internal perceptual processes interact with and are influenced by the external world. Such an account of interaction and influence, of course, requires the rejection of the notion of a total symbolic transformation of external reality within perception (102).

Gibson provides an account of experience based on the role played by light within the phenomenal horizon, and the relationship of that light to physical objects. The visual perception that human beings experience derives from only a small section of the electro-magnetic spectrum that surrounds them: the visible light frequency band of that spectrum. This is the human visual field. Within that field, and according to standard scientific thinking, light rays strike the eye, bringing information about the material environment. Photo-receptor cells in the retina then convert the light into electro-chemical signals, which are relayed to the brain, which then interprets what is seen. The result is the mystery of consciousness, including sense experience. It is true that what we experience is this mental state, and not the physical objects from which light rays are reflected, and this experience is also 'in our heads' and not outside our heads: 'we could never get outside our sense-experiences to discover whether or not there is something outside them to correspond to something within them' (Hospers 1978: 510). Nevertheless, and following the premise of externalism, and of realism in general, it is assumed that our sense-experiences are influenced by 'something outside them', and that this something is 'material objects [that] exist externally to us and independently of our sense experience' (Hirst 1967: 77).

There are two ways to proceed from this point in relation to perception. From a representationalist point of view, what matters most is the processing that takes place within the organism, and, here, a radical separation is often made between the first stage of the perceptual process, stimulus, which comes from outside; and stages two, three and four, sensation, perception and cognition, which are regarded as internal. The logic for this separation is that because we cannot step outside our sense-experience to comprehend the source of the stimulus, the focus should be on what is internal. The standard theory of perception is linear and unidirectional in essence: information – sense data – is received, and then processed into representations. Gibson, however, proposes a more interactive and holistic process, based on the premises that our knowledge of the physical world is mediated by the characteristics of electro-magnetic radiation and its interaction with physical objects; that the physical world affects electro-magnetic radiation in characteristic ways; and that this mediation and affect furnish a source of reliable information about the world. Within an interactive approach such as this, stimulus affects sensation, and then perception and cognition, but cognition and perception then refer back to sensation and stimulus, so that there is not just a unidirectional 'flow from the empirical source' towards the brain (Bloomer 1976: 17).

Gibson's model of perception is, accordingly, based on interaction between brain, body and environment, seeing the three as part of one 'whole system', albeit with the 'brain at the centre'. The animal, moving through an environment, receives stimulant information from that environment. This is then processed, and consciousness emerges. But as the animal continues to move through the environment, new stimuli appear, and the cognitive–sensory system requires and is affected by the information contained in that. Gibson contends that the perceiving subject makes the information about the environment contained within the optic array available to it through active mobility. Perceiving organisms are not static creatures, but actively explore their environment. According to Gibson, everything which persists must also change, constituting an evolving dialectic of persistence and change. What an animal perceives, therefore, are persisting and changing aspects of its environment as it moves through that environment (Costall and Still 1987: 93). Additionally, the optic array is also transformed for that animal as the animal moves through the environment and receives information from different perspectives within the optic array about that environment. This means that the animal actively 'samples' the array as it moves through it, appropriating the information that it feels is of interest: 'we look around, walk up to something interesting and move around it so as to see it from all sides, and go from one vista to another' (Gibson 1986: 1). This also means that the information in the array is 'embodied in structures external to organisms' and is not just inside the skin of the organism.

Perception is an active and motivated search for information about 'patterns of invariance' situated within the optic array that enable the organism to interact with its environment and build up a cumulative and conversant knowledge of the world. These patterns of invariance also signal the 'affordances' of the world for the observer: the invariance is the affordance of what is sought for because it provides familiarity with the world and a sense of certitude. An invariance is also, according to Gibson, a cluster of variables, and it is such clusters, rather than the individual variables within them, that provide more appropriate evidence regarding the real: 'An affordance is an invariant combination of variables, and one might guess that it is easier to perceive an invariant unit than it is to perceive all the variables separately' (134–5). The animal searches for meaningful connections and relationships stemming from the environment, and this search is accompanied by the imposition of pre-existing 'internalised' mental models which have the same objective (Bloomer 1976: 56). As the organism moves through the environment, it seeks out invariant combinations of variables in a process that is continuous, because 'perceiving is a stream' (Gibson 1986: 240). For Gibson, there is no radical dualist separation between perceptual processes and material reality, between inside and outside, and, in a rearticulation of the familiar phenomenological mantra, he insists that perception 'involves awareness-of instead of just awareness' (239).

From the beginning, Gibson was predisposed to develop a holistic and realist theory of visual perception. In his later work, however, he also specifically criticised cognitive-based approaches to visual perception, and cognitivism in general. He was particularly averse to the so-called 'programme analogy', in which the computer programme, or software, is related to the mind, or brain, and computer hardware to the body (Searle 1989: 28–31); and, in a reference to what he took to be the then established position on this issue, he asserts that he does not accept the 'usual analogy between the brain and a computer' (Gibson 1972: 78). Gibson, of course, was by no means alone in rejecting the programme analogy, and most of those who also rejected that did so on the basis of either a realist imperative, or on the grounds that the analogy has the effect of diminishing a sense of human agency. Gibson's rejection of the programme analogy is based on the grounds of both realism and a pro-agency stance, and this refusal also leads to a concomitant refutation of a sensation-based model of perception, in which external stimulus is said to reach the retina as 'sensation' and is then transformed by cognitive processes within the brain into a represented perceptual image. One consequence of this sort of model is that it comprises a relatively under-theorised conception of input. In contrast, Gibson promotes an 'information-based' theory of 'direct' visual perception:

> the theory here advanced assumes the existence of stable, unbounded and permanent stimulus-information in the ambient optic array. And it supposes that the visual system can explore and detect this information. The theory is information-based, not sensation-based. (77)

This entails a more theorised conception of external input. Input does not arrive at the eye as a jumble of inchoate sensation, but as information-rich and structured sensation, 'stable, unbounded and permanent'.

Gibson's emphasis on an information-based theory of perception should not, however, be confused with an 'information-processing' model of perception, which is often related to the programme analogy. Gibson makes a distinction between two types of information, and two ways in which that information can be said to be treated. With 'afferent-input information', information is conceived of as a collection of miscellaneous 'signals' to be transmitted from receptors to the brain, where it is then manufactured into perception, and the only information for perception consists of these 'neural inputs to the brain' (79). Here, the 'signals' have little semantic content in themselves. In 'optic-array information', on the other hand, the light reaching the optical system contains a great deal of information to begin with, because that information refers to, and is affected by, the physical external environment. This information does have semantic content. Perception does not occur only as a result of internal cognitive structures in the brain, but as a result of an interaction between the brain and the 'retino-neuro-muscular system as an activity of the whole system' in relation to the environment; and, 'the information does not consist of signals to be interpreted but of structural invariants which need only be attended to', or 'picked up' (79). The 'whole system', therefore, consists of the brain, the ocular system, the body, the optic array and the external physical environment; and the primary purpose of the system is to 'attend to' and 'pick up' information present in the array, an operation that does not overly require higher-level cognitive functions. Gibson, therefore, emphasises the role of exploratory sensing, rather than analytical interpretation, and he does so because he thinks that such sensing is what the animal mainly does when interacting with the world.

Perception occurs as a result of an ocular system, connected to a brain, and a body 'with its feet on the ground', seeking information from an ambient array of light within an environment. In daylight, the 'medium of air' within that environment is saturated with this ambient, reflected light, which is affected by the surfaces of objects within the environment, and from which it is reflected (80). As light rays strike these objects, scatters of photons are generated, until a rich variegated texture of interacting optical patterns is created (Gibson 1986: 66). When viewed from a point of observation, what is revealed is the perspective of the ambient optic array for that observer from that point of observation, and the array also corresponds to, and is structured by, what is present in the environment, from that perspective (Gibson 1972: 81). Any object has an unlimited set of potential points of observation (Gibson imagines a 'sphere' of such points surrounding the object), and, therefore, an unlimited set of perspectives of structures, which are 'afforded' by the optic array, and that can appear at such points of observation. All these perspectives also make up the 'family' of perspectives in the array unique to that object. The features of the object that make it different from other objects will also have corresponding features within the family of perspectives, features that are 'invariant under perspective transformation' (82). So, as the perspectives undergo transformation, as the observer shifts position, certain features of those perspectives persist from perspective to perspective, thus providing consistent information about the persisting features of the object and helping the observer to manœuvre through the environment.

The implications of this 'hypothesis' concerning the mediating role of the optic array are significant, because 'this hypothesis provides new reasons for realism in epistemology', and this is because the invariants, picked up by the visual system from the optic array, correspond to aspects of the object, and there is, therefore, an ontological, or realist–epistemological, relation between object, structures in the optic array, what is received by the visual system, and what the output of that system is. If there is correspondence 'between the structure of the environment and the structure of the ambient light at a stationary point of observation', 'direct perception', rather than symbolic internal representation, occurs, because the 'sampling of ambient array by the ocular system' results in an active 'pick-up' of what is afforded to the ocular system, rather than an internally produced representation of that affordance (Gibson 1972: 82–3). This is what Gibson means by the phrase 'direct perception', and this is also the basis of his notion of the visual sense as a 'perceptual system', and one that does not rely overmuch on cognitive processes within the brain.

The notion of the manifold, ambient optic array implies that there is a vast amount of information available to the perceiving subject concerning the environment that the subject finds itself in, and, because of this, that subject may not, in the end, as suggested, have to do too much internal processing. This is because the array is 'specific' to an environment. What has been called Gibson's 'law of specificity' connects the ambient array to definite surrounding surfaces, and this means that the perceiving subject can have confidence that the array provides appropriate information about an environment (Costall and Still 1987: 9). This account of the existence of information-bearing structures external to the perceiver, which the perceiver can access, and which refer to a definite physical environment, constitutes a considerable shift away from an internalist, representationalist theory of perceptual knowledge (Rowlands 2003: 170–1). Gibson rejects the notion of visual perception as a representational 'photographic process of image registration and image transmission' to the brain, with resultant symbolisation of the environment (Gibson 1972: 84). Instead, he focuses on the agency involved in the activity of sample-taking that occurs within the relation between the visual system and the optic array. Sample-taking, for example, by head movement, is necessary to perceive the environment, because the animal cannot perceive the environment in its totality (83). The visual system is exploratory in character, collecting information in successive samples over the course of time, samples taken from different observation points which reveal dissimilar perspectives of the ambient array, as the animal moves along a path in space and through the course of time (81). However, according to Gibson, we are not aware of this sequencing, but only of the presumed 'total scene', because the ocular system builds up the cluster of invariants over time in order to 'specify' that scene (84). The objective is to find a coherent and understandable order of things within what Gibson calls the overall 'layout' of the environment, and this means that the samples must form a totality.

Gibson's model of ecological optics depends upon the idea that a substantial amount of 'external specifying information', is available in the optic array which the ocular system can 'hunt' for (87). When that amount is reduced, as by, for example, a dimming of the optic array within the environment, the hunt for that information is correspondingly diminished, and, then, 'all sorts of internal processes begin to occur' in compensation (87). Normal, or optimal, visual perception occurs when the hunt by the ocular system for extensive external specifying information takes place, and, when that occurs successfully, there is less need for higher-level cognitive processes to come into play. This, as part of his overall model of 'ecological optics', leads Gibson to conclude that the:

> availability of information in ambient light and the possibility that it can be picked up directly have implications for epistemology. They lend sophisticated support to the naïve belief that we have direct knowledge of the world around us. They support direct realism. (89)

Gibson is not arguing that inner cognitive processes do not play a role in the process of visual perception but wishes a new balance to be struck. In place of the dominant cognitivist model, in which the focus is on internal structures, he presents a model which asserts that, within visual perception, internal processes mainly support the hunt for extensive external specifying information, and aid the transformation into perception of information carried in an optic array which has an ontic relation to physical objects. This is the basis of Gibson's claim for direct realism in understanding visual perception. The obvious criticism of Gibson's approach to visual perception, and one that will be addressed later, when cognitivist approaches are considered, is that he did not pay enough attention to central cognitive processes. But Gibson chose to do that because his project was to establish a model of visual perceptual realism, and this, it will be argued, is at odds with cognitivism.

Another influence on Gibson's thought is the notion of the *Umwelt*, which, it seems, Gibson derived from the principal exponent of that idea, the philosopher Rom Harré. *Umwelt*, whose literal translation from the German is 'environment', is a concept which Harré borrowed from biology, within which field the term refers to the aspects of the environment that are available to a certain species by virtue of that species' perceptual and physical resources and limitations. Harré then extends this concept to the notion of the human *Umwelt*: that is, to the environment that surrounds and is available to human beings, given their perceptual and physical resources and limitations (van Langenhove 2010: 6). Harré also makes a further distinction between *Umwelt* and the notion of *Umgebung*: the environment in general (or the immediate environment and its surroundings; close to *Umfeld* – 'surroundings', or *Einstellung* – 'setting'). This distinction allows him to define *Umwelt* in terms of the 'ambient world': 'the ambient world, or milieu, proper to a given species, as it exists for that species'. This is then reconceptualised by Gibson as the world of the optic array. According to Harré, within an ambient milieu:

> a species and its milieu are a mutual elaboration, in which the animal is not like a machine reacting to a situation with an automatic response, but rather like a bicyclist reacting to a signal with an appropriate action, stopping at a red light, for example . . . [and, here] . . . the reality of *Umwelt* lies below the dichotomy between subject and object, which is not in an oppositional relation. (Harré 2015: 6)

The information contained in the environment, therefore, becomes the 'system of significations for a milieu', and a 'milieu concretely experienced by the members of a certain society' who move within it (6). Here, *Umwelt* is also, consequently, defined in terms of human sensory capabilities, what is given to a human being by virtue of those capabilities; and the fundamental link, therefore, that which Harré defines as existing 'below the dichotomy between subject and object', is between those capabilities and the environment from which they seek information. This focus on 'mutualism', the idea of the *mutuality* between organism and environment, and the impossibility of separating the two, is yet another articulation of the proposition that representationalism, and the Cartesian dualism related to it, are to be rejected (Costall and Still 1987: 9).

The influence of the idea of *Umwelt* on Gibson reinforces Gibson's general realist theory of visual perception.

In addition to writing on perception more generally, Gibson also wrote on the image, photography, film and, most substantially, the 'picture'. Gibson defines a picture as a surface that is treated in such a way that it makes a limited optic array, an array which consists of an arrangement of *'persisting invariants of structure that are nameless and formless'*, available from one point of observation (Gibson 1986: 270–1). The important factor here is related to the apparently self-contradictory concept of a *'formless* invariant' which displays 'invariants under transformation', in what is none the less a still image. Gibson argues that, even though, in a still image, no transformations appear to take place (because it is, precisely, an immobile image), as they do all the time in quotidian experience of the *Umwelt*, in fact, the still image does display such transformations (271).

Formless invariants are clusters of variables which do not have physical form because they do not physically exist but are 'supposed' during the act of perception. In a still image, the invariables evoke a sense of the overall unity of a representation, just as, in experience of the *Umwelt*, perception also supposes such a unity, when only part of an object is available to a perceiver engaging with that object from a singular perspective. In terms of the image, a photograph of a house may show the house from a certain viewpoint – the front – and, consequently, is not able to show the sides and rear of the house. But what is understood is the invariant model of a standard house – the house that always does have sides and a rear – and the invariant which is sought for is, therefore, both invariant (because, for the sake of argument, all standard houses have the same or similar structure) and *formless*.[9] This also means that 'form perception . . . must entail some [formless] invariant detection'; when we look at a photograph we take in these formless invariants, as well as the form that fills the picture, and both of these amount to 'information for the persistence' of the (in this case) house (271). Gibson develops his argument by giving the example of a child seeing a cat half-hidden by a chair. The child 'perceives a partly hidden cat, not a half-cat, and therefore he is prepared to see the same thing in a drawing' (272).

Gibson, in alignment with theorists discussed previously in this chapter, argues that this means that 'the term *representation* is misleading. There is no such thing as a *literal* re-presentation of an earlier optic array. The scene cannot be re-established; the array cannot be reconstituted' (279). Even a photograph cannot preserve all the information in the pro-photographed scene, because that information is 'unlimited'. Gibson argues that the concept of representation is simply 'wrong' because a photograph cannot replicate 'past seeing'. What the photograph does do is 'record', or 'register', some information (280). A picture is both an abstraction of and extraction from the optic array within the ambient *Umwelt*; it is a means of presenting information available within the array and employs formal techniques to that end. The information in a picture is not, therefore, a simulacrum of the array, although there is a relationship between the organisation of information in the picture and external reality, based upon the fact that this organisation is related to invariances within the optic array. Two critiques of the notion of representation arise here. First, representation is not entirely symbolic, but, like an index, is affected by the object it refers to. Second, 're-presentation' is impossible because the fullness and specificity of the original 'cannot be reconstituted' (279). This means that, when we see a photograph, what we see is, at least mainly, a presentation.

Gibson's main emphasis in *The Ecological Approach to Visual Perception* is on the still image, but he also mentions film in a chapter entitled 'Motion Pictures and Visual Awareness'. According to Gibson, film differs from photography in the sense that transformations always occur. It is not an arrested optic array: 'Its structure undergoes change, disturbance or transformation. It is not frozen in time' (292). The photograph exists in a 'frozen world', yet the human eye was developed in order to register change and transformation, and this means that film, not still pictures, should be considered to be the 'basic form of depiction . . . Moviemakers are closer to life than picture makers' (293).[10] In this sense, what a photograph does is 'artificial', an 'unnatural stoppage of the flow', 'for no event can be stopped in mid-flight' (294); and, 'perception is a stream' (240). In film, the pictorial optic array is segmented so that it can reproduce the kind of 'subordinate and superordinate happenings' (mainly, 'background' and 'foreground' happenings) that exist in the optic array (301). Gibson begins his account of film by employing the phrase 'moving-pictures' (he does not think the term 'film' is appropriate any more, given the appearance of television, which does not use film stock, or still frames that appear to move when projected at 24 frames per second). However, he then proposes the phrase 'progressive picture', and distinguishes that from the 'arrested picture' (still image). Film, or the 'progressive picture', provides a changing optic array of limited scope to a point of observation located in front of the picture which matches the field of view of an observer in a natural environment (302). Gibson does not take his account of film much beyond this because his focus is upon the still image. Nevertheless, consequences for film arise from this, which will be addressed later in this Introduction.

As will be argued, Gibson's emphasis on the optic array, and the active, mobile subject appropriating information based on self-interest, is close to Bergson's thought, and provides a means of understanding the latter's theory of the image. To conclude, however, it will be necessary to return to what has been described as Gibson's 'key insight': to replace an internal conception of perception with a 'law of specificity connecting informational structures in the ambient array to the surrounding surfaces of objects' (Costall and Still 1987: 9). As one supporter of Gibson puts it:

The manipulation and transformation of external structures is, *ipso facto*, manipulation and transformation of information via the structures that carry it. As a result of such transformation information is made available to the organism that was, otherwise, not directly available. Such information can often be indispensable . . . [and] . . . any decision to deny . . . this . . . would seem to amount to nothing more than an internalist prejudice. (Rowlands: 2003: 172–3)

How does this relate to film? A simple film is imagined, showing a small tree, moving in the wind, over the course of two minutes. When the film was shot, the camera was situated directly in front of the tree, which was filmed from that central point of observation, at eye level. The two-minute-long film consists of 120 seconds, times 24 still frames: that is, 2,880 still frames in total. When these frames are then projected at 24 frames per second, the outcome is the moving film, or 'progressive picture'. This projection transforms the 2,880 still frames into something different – a moving picture – and the fact of the 2,880 still images becomes irrelevant, in terms of experience. What is experienced is not an illusion disguising the 'fact' that there are 2,880 still images, and nor is it a representation. Under projection, a change occurs which results in the experience of a qualitatively different state, or object. The film is an object of perception in itself, and, so, cannot be an illusionary presentation of 2,880 still frames. The 2,880 frames are also themselves made up of a multitude of atoms, and so do not constitute the 'real', or underlying, film in any definite way.

For Gibson, the experienced film is not a representation: 'the term representation is misleading. There is no such thing as a literal re-presentation of an earlier optic array. The scene cannot be re-established; the array cannot be reconstituted' (Gibson 1986: 279). A film cannot preserve all the information in the pro-photographed scene because that information is 'unlimited'. The concept of representation here is 'wrong' because film cannot replicate either 'past seeing' or a former optic array. What the film does do, and to repeat, is 'register' some information about that array. The pro-filmic environment was open to be engaged with from a variety of perspectives, and not only the one from which filming took place, so that there was no unitary environment to begin with. When the film is then seen later, in the present, when it is projected on to a screen, such seeing will also be from a certain perspective, as even a stationary viewpoint will be subject to the varying attentional interests of the spectator (280).

What is experienced when viewing the film, is a perceptual response to a new, and limited, optic array. The film is full of information-rich structures and patterns of variance and invariance. When the film was shot, structures of variance and invariance in the environment reflected photons, and some of these made their way into the camera, where a lens and photo-sensitive chemicals designed to replicate normal visual perception created an image that then became fixed. Our putative film contains 2,880 of these frozen images, and, when projected at 24 frames per second, a 'progressive' image appears. The information contained in the mobilised still images is projected on to the screen through a beam of light. What reaches the screen is a wave of electromagnetic radiation that consists of photons. Photons are in constant movement, but, in this case, those which constitute the visible light spectrum are also guided by the stroboscopic motion generated by the projector. In the phenomenon of stroboscopic motion, a series of brief distinct units moving at a certain frequency is perceived as continuous, and this is also aided by the phenomenon referred to as 'persistence of vision', whereby the eye has a tendency to perceive things as continuous, or as overlapping, rather than as discrete and separate (the need for such a tendency, in order to understand the environment better, is fairly obvious). The photons are arrayed on the screen in patterns that have their origins in the mobilised still images, just as photons are reflected in 'patterns of invariance' from material reality. The optic array emanating from the screen then directs photons into our eyes, after which, internal processes of various sorts help create a perceptual experience that is the film.

There is, therefore, and following Gibson, a structural correspondence between the pro-environment, the optic array reflecting from that pro-environment, the formation of the image on the film stock, structures of variance and invariance generated when the film is projected, and the perceptual experience of those during the act of spectatorship. As Gibson argues, this account of what he calls 'ecological optics' lends 'sophisticated support to the naïve belief that we have direct knowledge of the world around us ... [and] ... support[s] direct realism' (Gibson 1972: 89). The structures, and their perceptual transformation, have a consistency and coherence across different viewing experiences. This is reinforced by the fact that those structures are directed at the point of view of a centrally stationary spectator. All of this reinforces coherence, and realism.

In everyday experience, the environment does not change much, but what does change are the transforming perspectives within the optic array which emerge as an observer moves through that environment. In a simple film, such as the one imagined, the filmic environment that is experienced does not change much either, and nor, additionally, does the viewpoint of the observer. That viewpoint is at eye-level, and is – biologically – binocular, radiating from a central-point perspective and enabling the spectator to have, at least, the potential to see the entire filmic horizon. This means that there will only be a small degree of 'perspective transformation' taking place. However, there will still be changes in patterns of variance and invariance, caused by a change of lighting conditions, and movement within the filmic environment (the tree blowing in the wind). There will also be movement across the flow of time, though much of that will be imperceptible. Such a film, however, does not tally with our everyday experience, because we do not adopt a static viewpoint in everyday life, and because, as we move through the environment, we encounter a great deal of perspective transformation within the array, which is then transformed into a corresponding experience.

In a more complex, edited film, however, the situation is different. In such a film, the filmic environment and array will change frequently, whilst the point of observation of the observer none the less remains relatively static, although the spectator is still able to gaze around the images, as they flow past. What such a film delivers are many perspectives in transformation, and this means that the film is closer to normal perceptual experience. What a film such as this does is present a simulacrum of normal perceptual experience for the observer: a sort of practice run and preparation for our actual engagement with the far more testing external environment, one which it is in our interests to manœuvre through successfully. Watching a film, therefore, can be defined as a reinforcement of our normal relation to the world. This also implies that film should be 'realistic'. What film offers, according to this account, is a kind of psychological 'reward', because the world of film presents a coherence that is missing from everyday experience, and that coherence is also experienced by the 'God's-Eye View' of the privileged spectator.[11] What film offers is an encouragement and endorsement of our ability to negotiate the world successfully.

Film not only links representation and reality; it also links past and present. In the simple film referred to, in which no edits take place, when the film sequence was shot, the camera acted like the observer situated at a point of observation. Indeed, there was a person standing immediately behind the camera, adopting the same viewpoint. What is *seen*, at this point, in terms of the observer, is the perceptual transformation of the optic array. The experience of that transformation may persist in the memory of the camera person, but some aspects of that experience have also been registered on the film stock, across all frames. That was what happened in the *past*, at the point at which the optic array and its transformation was registered, in part, and permanently, on the film stock.[12] What happens in the *present* takes place during the viewing experience of that film stock when it is put into motion through projection. What is happening *now* is that a register of the transformed optic array is experienced within immediate perception. I watch the film of the tree blowing in the wind. Structures of variance and invariance of light emanating from the screen are carried by light to my visual and cognate systems. The result is perceptual experience of the film. No doubt, I will perceive the film differently to how it was perceived by the camera person, shortly after the pro-filmic event was first captured. But, despite such differences, there will still be a core of persistence connected to the transformed array, just as visual perception is informed by persistence occurring within the optic array. A difference, however, is that there is less immediate *interest* here: no struggle for survival, as might be the case with the need to manœuvre through the real world successfully. Manœuvring through the film world is, as argued, more like an assessment of possible realities, with no real consequence attached. The perceptual experience of the film that occurs, the transformation of the array that takes place, is a more disinterested one, with no requirement on the part of the spectator to take any action or make any decision, although, and as argued, the experience may offer encouragement and endorsement of our existing ability to negotiate the world.

The account of representation, perception and cinematic realism given in the previous pages of this Introduction turns upon a general critique of representationalism and suggests that what we have access to is not just a 'copy' of reality but something that contains something of reality. As will be seen, this critique is crucial to the theoretical systems of Bergson, Husserl, Kracauer and Lukács, the study of which makes up the bulk of this book. It has also been argued elsewhere that, relatively recently, film studies have taken an 'ontological turn' (Elsaesser, in Nagib and Mello 2009: 17), based upon a presumed dichotomy between representation and presentation. Much of this new work draws on phenomenology, and, also, on the Pragmatist analytical tradition. Other work draws on phenomenology too, and links that to intellectual traditions drawn from various strands of philosophical aesthetics. What most of this work has in common, however, is a desire to theorise film as possessing its own degree of reality, or *a* reality, rather than to conceive of film as a symbolic representation of something else: a representationalist trope which dominated the 'apparatus theory' of the 1970s and 1980s, and still dominates much of the cognitivist tradition which rose to prominence in the 1990s, and remains influential today. Here, the 'reality effect' is presumed: the filmic techniques and 'codes' that convince us to believe that a representation is real. The debate, therefore, is between film as representation or as 'presentness'. As will be argued, however, the notion of presentness is as problematic as the notion of representation.

For the purposes of this Introduction, we can say that there are three stances that can be adopted towards the notions of representation and presentation, as these notions relate to film. First, film is entirely representational. This, conventionalist, position acknowledges the gulf that exists between reality and representation, but, for the most part, accepts that 'external reality' does exist. Second, film is partly representational and partly shaped by what is represented. This, realist (or representational–realist), position argues that the gulf between representation and reality is not absolute. Third, film is not representational at all because it is a 'thing-in-itself' that does not refer to anything of which it is a copy. This, 'phenomenalist', stance emphasises consciousness, and the world that appears within consciousness, including film, which is, consequently, a presentation. Both conventionalism and phenomenalism bracket out external reality without necessarily denying the existence of the latter. Conventionalism argues that reality is represented, and that film is a representation, whilst phenomenalism contends that what appears in phenomenal experience is an 'object' with its own reality, and that film is such an object. In the case of phenomenalism, the issue of *causation* does not really arise, only how things are. In the case of conventionalism, a limited form of causation is considered: the formal techniques which form the representation. For realism, on the other hand, what things are must be linked to what caused them in a broad sense, and, so, for realism, the issue of causation, and the relation between cause and representation, is central.

There are important evaluative issues here which have influenced film theory since the 1960s. To say that film is a representation is to endow it with a primary value in relation to traditional aesthetics – film as 'art' – but only a secondary value in relation to what is represented (a *mere* representation, or copy). To say that film is an object-in-its-own-right is to endow it with a primary value in relation to traditional aesthetics (because it is an 'art object'), and a primary value in relation to the object itself (because it is a present object). To say that film is partly representational and partly ontic in character is to endow it with a primary value in relation to traditional aesthetics, a primary value in relation to what is represented, but a secondary value in relation to the object itself. Here, in this latter case, the film is not just there to be described and analysed; it is also linked to a network of causal factors. The idea of film as representation is still very much in vogue today. The idea of film as possessing an ontic character remains a difficult one, is still somewhat unpopular, and is pursued by a few theorists, including the present author. The idea of film as presentation, that film is a thing-in-itself, has become increasingly influential because it dispenses with the notion that film is a secondary copy of something that is primary. Much film theory related to this is influenced by phenomenology. It will, however, be argued in this Introduction that there are major problems associated with the – admittedly de rigueur – idea of film as presentation, and with the phenomenological notions that support this; whilst, later, in Chapter 6 of this book, it will be argued that, in contradistinction, certain aspects of phenomenology can be productively associated with a realist theory of film.

One of the first major works to relate phenomenology to film is Allan Casebier's 1991 book *Film and Phenomenology: Toward a Realist Theory of Cinematic Representation*. Here, Casebier engages with various Husserlian concepts, including the 'natural attitude', the '*noema*', and the idea of '*Repräsentation*' (as opposed to 'representation'), and attempts to apply these to film. All of these ideas will be discussed in greater depth in Chapter 6 of this book, but, for now, and for present purposes, the essence of Casebier's stance is that what is perceived – the *noema* (content of a perception) – is a reality in itself, and not a copy of something else, and this is because it is engaged with within experience. The *noema* is a *Repräsentation*: something that 'appears' and 'is', and which also represents. This is distinct from a representation: something that is *only* a copy of something that is. (Husserl deliberately uses the 'ä' character to distinguish his term from that of representation, and Casebier follows this.) Following Husserl, Casebier also relates this idea of something that 'is' to a type of consciousness and intellectual approach that can address that, and which can also be described as 'realist' (Casebier defines himself as a realist). In this type of consciousness, 'apperception', the indirect inference of attributes and qualities beyond the given, takes place alongside direct perception of the given. What we have is an existent, the *noema*, which appears in consciousness, and a mode of consciousness which attends to that existence, perceives it directly, and 'apperceives' attributes and qualities attendant on it and inferred beyond the given. It is that mode of consciousness that enables the *Repräsentation* to 'appear'. Casebier cites (and paraphrases) Husserl:

> The Repräesentation is, in contrast to mere noticing, a fundamentally different 'mode of being conscious of a content', and indeed precisely that mode which stamps the content as a repräesentant of an object, [of] which [the] object itself is no part, no fragment, and also no non-independent moment of [not part of] the 'representing' act. (Casebier 1991: 34)

The *Repräsentation* is attended to within an aware and knowledgeable 'mode of being conscious' and is distinct from the object: 'the object itself is no part' of the *Repräsentation* and exists outside of that *Repräsentation*. Yet there is a strong link between the mode of consciousness and the object: the *Repräsentant* is 'of an object'. This is a realist position because it goes beyond pure representation and references the object in external reality.

This Introduction is not concerned with setting out the overall position elaborated in *Film and Phenomenology*, but, rather, with relating the ideas discussed above in Casebier's book to the perspective on externalism elaborated earlier. Following this, we can say that the *Repräsentation* of the object has a phenomenal existence for us that is influenced by both internal representational coding and information reaching the cognitive–perceptual system from the environment, information that reveals that environment in a substantive manner; and this means that it is not a pure representation, although it does possess representational elements. If it was to be considered as a pure representation, it would not be fundamentally or significantly shaped by material reality but would be a completely abstract coding of that reality. If the notion of pure representation were to be applied to film, it would amount to a 'highly relativistic conception of cinematic representation' in the tradition of semiotic theory (36). Casebier rejects such application and bemoans the fact that 'contemporary film theory and criticism is permeated with an idealist [and, accordingly, relativist and representationalist] epistemology' (47).

Casebier also critiques the idea of 'coding' in relation to film: an idea that was championed within apparatus theory. For Casebier, the term 'code' refers to a set of generalisations from instances, generalisations – and simplifications – that putatively demarcate a repeated and identifiable series of instances. A common trope to be found in cognitive science is that the multiplicity of sense impressions reaching the sensory–cognate system is 'encoded' in some way so that the result is perception, the internal coding reducing the multiplicity into a limited set of generalisations, which is then expressed more broadly in perception. In film, the term could be applied to, for example, a temporal length of shot that seems to be repeated within a sequence, so that one can say that, within that sequence, each of the shots lasts for 20 seconds. This would be a temporal coding, but the same would apply to other such instances of identifiable repetition and difference. We can point to that and isolate it, but Casebier asks what that could possibly mean, other than at a basic level? The problem is that this sequence of 20-second-long shots is embedded within a filmic becoming that is a totality and is experienced as a totality within which the manifold relations pertaining will always be too complex and numerous to be 'coded' in anything like a systematic and orderly manner, no matter how many attempts are made to do so. This sort of code is relatively easy to designate, but others may be less so. For example, in a sequence of film images of out-of-shot eyeline matches involving two characters (where the characters' gaze is directed outside the frame of the shot) – the classic Hollywood shot–reverse shot system – the temporal ratio might vary between, say, an average of 4.5 seconds, and 5.5 seconds (possibly depending on which of the two characters is the more important). Whatever the generalisation sought, however, it will always amount to an imposed reduction and simplification of the phenomenal manifold that is the film, and, will, ultimately, also have only a meagre semantic significance. Casebier calls the manifold aspect of the film experience a 'total relevance factor', one that prevents the targeted application of systematic codes, or reliable and effectual systematic generalisations from individual instances (55). Casebier is reacting to the failure within apparatus theory to apply codes– such as those articulated by Roland Barthes and others in relation to literature – successfully to film. Film is a thing-in-itself, experienced as a totality, and one that is also shaped by material reality, as well as by representation. Casebier's conclusion is that the notion of representation is not particularly relevant to film, because representation implies coding, and no definite, discrete codes are meaningfully identifiable within the complex phenomenon that is the filmic experience (58).

Casebier argues that film is a type of 'object', by which he does not mean the physical apparatus of film. Film, as object, clearly cannot be the still images on a piece of celluloid, because this is not what is experienced when a film is viewed. Neither can film as object be the 'apparatus' list of camera device, chemical interaction, film strip, projector/projection and screen: a list that could also extend to other factors. Film, as object, must be the 'cinematic experience' itself. According to Gilles Deleuze, the film, or cinematic experience, as he puts it, is identifiable as the 'movement-image' and 'time-image'. This is also the sense in which Casebier calls film an 'object'. At the beginning of *Cinema 1: The Movement-Image*, Deleuze seeks to overturn Bergson's conceptualisation of cinema as 'false movement':

> Can we conclude that the result is artificial because the means are artificial? Cinema proceeds with photogrammes – that is with immobile sections – twenty-four images per second . . . But it has often been noted that what it gives us is not the photogramme: it is an intermediate image, to which movement is not appended or added; the movement on the contrary belongs to the intermediate image as immediate given . . . cinema does not give us an image to which movement is added, it immediately gives us a movement-image. It does give us a section, but a section which is mobile, not an immobile section plus abstract movement. (Deleuze 2018: 2–3)

The movement-image is the 'object' that is given in perception, intermediate between the 'photogrammes' and our sensory–cognate systems. Deleuze, as he must, accepts that the photogrammes themselves do not actually move. They remain still, 'immobile sections'. But what is given in the cinematic experience is the movement-image: a mobile section.[13] The means may be 'artificial', or mechanical, but the result is what is experienced: what has been called a 'proximal perceptual object' (Ponech 2006: 356).[14] The movement-image possesses movement which appears as actually occurring during the act of perception (Currie 1995: 47). If a particular movement-image appears during an act of perception, it must also reappear in roughly similar form in other acts of perception, experienced by other observers, because it is generated by the apparatus in relation to the perceptual apparatus in the same way for all observers. The movement-image is inter-subjective.

The idea of the cinematic experience as involving an 'intermediate' movement-image can be squared with the account of externalism given earlier. The cinematic movement-image, like the perceptual image,[15] is a representation, but not a pure representation, because it carries information that comes from both the ambient *Umwelt* and material reality: when the film was shot, and, as argued earlier, the camera lens, the instrument of human intellect, acted much like the human eye, as it was designed to do, and was made subject to the same laws of optics as the eye. The image is then fixed in the film through a chemical process, as opposed to it passing, as is the case with visual perception. The fact that it is fixed in a frame of the film strip means that what is also fixed there is information concerning the ambient array and material reality. Externality is embodied in the image; 'frozen' in the image, although in a coded representational form. However, and citing Gibson, such a frozen world is not natural, because, in material reality, of which human beings are a part, nothing is frozen, and everything moves. Through means of the apparatus, and at the point of projection, the initial experience of or encounter with the *Umwelt* becomes a transformed movement-image, and what is reanimated is the initially animated external and internally coded information embedded in the frozen image.

The fact that the 'photogrammes', or 'immobile sections', do not move, does, however, bring up the issue of illusion, because the still images are perceived as moving, even though they do not, and, therefore, the perceived movement can be said to be 'illusory' and chimerical. In studies of visual perception, film is often taken to be the exemplar of illusory motion, or 'apparent motion', because such an illusion of movement is often engendered when still images are displayed in succession at a specific rate. Here, the stroboscopic process affects various cognitive processes in the brain so that an optical illusion of movement is produced. The reality is that still images are displayed in rapid succession and remain still images; the illusion is that they become moving images. There is a considerable amount of literature on visual illusion, the most important of which may be E. H. Gombrich's *Art and Illusion* (1960) and R. L. Gregory's *Eye and Brain* (1990), the latter of which has had a robust influence on the relatively recent application of cognitivist theory and methodology to film studies. Within this literature, illusion can be regarded as a normal function of the cognitive–sensory system, and this is the case, for example, with two-dimensional pictures, which create an illusion of three-dimensional space which the picture does not have; and film, where the stroboscopic effect produces an illusion of movement that the individual frames do not have (Gregory 1991: 2).

However, the notion of illusion can also carry negative connotations, in terms of a 'malfunction' of the normal cognitive–sensory system (2), or when the idea is associated with falsehood, and opposed to reality, or truth. Film studies has not, generally, been concerned with the issue of visual illusion per se, apart from when that has been associated with the experimental film; but it has been concerned with the issue of how illusory, representational, secondary and false, or not, film may be in relation to reality. Is film an illusion that masks some other reality? Is it a representation of some other reality? Is it secondary in value to that other reality? Does it depict that other reality in a false manner? Does the fact that the actual strip of still images produces the visual illusion of apparent motion somehow devalue what appears because it is illusory? Does the fact of semblance and simulacrum mean that it is cognitive processes within the brain/mind that ultimately produce the representations which we take to constitute the film, and, if that is the case, does this not support a cognitivist, rather than realist, agenda? These are questions which arise more and more frequently in contemporary film theory, and, consequently, the issue of illusion is a central one, because it is related to such questions.

Bergson asserts that what he calls the 'cinematographic illusion' presents a false notion of the real character of time and movement, and, here, the idea of illusion is linked to a charge concerning the fundamental untruthfulness to reality of the film medium: a charge that may seem counter-intuitive, given the visual realism of the medium. There is, for Bergson, only one reality, a reality of constant change and movement. When such movement is divided up into combinations of 'positions' and 'instances', the reality of movement is lost, and what replaces that are what Deleuze, addressing Bergson, calls 'immobile sections' (*coupes immobiles*). The immobile section refers to a spacetime section that is drawn out of the flux, whereas Bergson wants to insist upon the fact that movement and time are different from space and always in flux. Bergson is talking about a way of misunderstanding that reality that misses what he takes to be the real character of that reality as constant movement, a misunderstanding that delivers a distorted sense of reality: this way of understanding 'implies the absurd proposition that every movement is made of immobilities' (Bergson 1983: 308).

Bergson refers to this way of misunderstanding reality, a misunderstanding that has a long lineage within human thought, as the 'cinematographic illusion', and, as Deleuze points out, 'it is strange that Bergson should give the oldest illusion such a modern and recent name' (Deleuze 2018: 2). In fact, however, Bergson is talking not only about an entrenched and historical mode of mistaken understanding, as Deleuze suggests, but also about how the intellect itself works. Deleuze refers to the individual film frame as an immobile section, so that, just as assigning a period and place to movement in the world via the intellect leads to a conception of an immobile section of spacetime, so, the photographed assignation of space and time does the same in a concrete manner. Photography, and cinematography, fix movement into immobile sections. However, Deleuze, the advocate rather than adversary of film, argues that the movement-image is not an immobile section; it is a 'section which is mobile' (3). Bergson thinks that the 'movement-image' *is* an immobile section; and this is what Deleuze challenges. Deleuze, like others, also feels that, despite Bergson's critique of the 'cinematographic illusion', the latter's overall philosophy furnishes the foundation for a philosophy of film. There is, therefore, a need to confront Bergson's 'critique of the camera' (Marcel L'Herbier, cited in Douglas 1999: 209).

For Bergson, the cinematographic illusion generates a misguided account of time and duration, in terms of both conceptual thought and the material, filmic 'photogramme'. In terms of film, in the beginning, there is the manifold movement of reality. The cinematic apparatus breaks that down into immobile sections, and then, through projection, returns a new synthesis that moves. But that synthetic movement is not the same as the initial, manifold movement; it is a reconstituted form which abridges and misrepresents that movement.[16] As mentioned, Bergson relates this to the way that the intellect works. Reality is a manifold in flux: 'movement is reality itself' (Bergson 1946: 169). And, through the use of fixed concepts and symbols, the intellect first fragments that flux, and then produces a synthetic conceptual explanation of sections of the flux that cannot comprehend a manifold that can, anyway, primarily be accessed through intuition. The intellect 'substitutes for the continuous the discontinuous', and so does film (222):

> Such is the contrivance of the cinematograph. And such is also that of our knowledge. Instead of attaching ourselves to the inner becoming of things, we place ourselves outside them in order to recompose their becoming artificially. We take snapshots (near instantaneous views/*des vues quasi instantanées*), as it were, of the passing reality . . . the mechanism of our ordinary (*usuelle*) knowledge is of a cinematographic kind. (Bergson 1983: 332)
>
> *Tel est l'artifice du cinématographe. Et tel est aussi celui de notre connaissance . . . Nous prenons des vues quasi instantanées sur la réalité qui passe . . . le mécanisme de notre connaissance 'usuelle' est de nature cinématographique.* (Bergson 2016: 231)

Bergson does not reject intellect entirely but wishes to foreground the role played by intuition in comprehending the movement that is reality itself. Even so, in relation to film, his critique of '*notre connaissance "usuelle"*' raises the possibility that, as Deleuze puts it, 'for Bergson, the cinema is only the projection, the reproduction of a constant universal illusion' (Deleuze 2018: 2).

Bergson's argument that the movement that appears through cinematic projection is a false movement is based on the premise that a general and 'impersonal' movement has replaced a multiplicity of actual, individual movements related to, for example, real persons being filmed, and that this, in consequence, constitutes an 'artificial recomposition':

> *Le procédé a donc consisté, en somme, à extraire de tous le mouvements propres à toutes les figures un movement impersonnel, abstrait et simple, le mouvement en général pour ainsi dire, à la mettre dans l'appareil, et à reconstituer l'individualité de chaque movement particulier par la composition de ce movement anonyme.*
>
> The method consists of extracting from all the movements related to each figure an impersonal, abstract and simple movement, that is to say,

a general movement, which we place in the apparatus, and we combine the individuality of each particular movement by means of the composition of this anonymous movement. (Bergson 2016: 230–1)[17]

The immobile section can, therefore, be related not only to the individual film frame, but also to the larger sections of the film, which necessarily embody 'artificial recompositions' of duration. Bergson accepts that there *is* movement here:

> *Le movement existe bien ici, en effet, il est dans l'appareil . . . [it is] . . . l'invisible mouvement de la bande cinématographique.*
> It is true that the movement exists, it is in the apparatus . . . it is the invisible movement of the cinematographic strip. (230)[18]

However, that movement is a false representation of real movement.

As argued, Bergson's point goes beyond the cinema, which he uses as a relatively untheorised support for his general critique of the 'usual' modality of intellect as one that fragments and artificially reconstructs '*la vraie nature de la vie, la signification profonde du mouvement évolutif/*'the true nature of life, the profound significance of the evolving movement' (7). It is true that Bergson's immobile sections of film, and Deleuze's mobile sections of film, do not represent duration as duration occurs in the world, and it is also true that a spatialisation of duration occurs here. But if we take a general model of phenomenology, engagement with the true nature of duration is by no means the only valid pursuit that takes place within the *Lebenswelt*, and, in fact, constitutes only a fraction of the activity that takes place. From an externalist position, these immobile/mobile sections also carry ontic information about the world: information that is derived from the ambient *Umwelt* from which the images of film are initially lit (Gibson 1972: 87). The fact that, as Bergson admits, there is movement present, also means that it cannot be the case that there is an illusion that such movement is present. Under projection a change occurs to the still images in the film strip which results in the experience of a qualitatively different state, or object: Deleuze's movement-image. The film is an object of perception in-itself, and, so, not an illusion of something else, or, for that matter, entirely a representation of something. The film is a mobile/immobile section that spatialises duration, carries ontic information, is present as an object of perception, and also possesses representational properties.

As will be considered in depth in the following chapter of this book, Bergson made a distinction between the 'represented' and 'present' image. The present image possesses 'a certain existence which is more than that which the idealist calls a representation, but less than that which the realist calls a thing – an existence placed halfway between the "thing" and the "representation"'

(Bergson 1991: 9). Bergson's theory of the image is complex, but, briefly, the present image exists in the manifold of reality, whilst the represented image, what appears to us in perception, can only exhibit the 'skin' of the present image. Bergson's theory of representation is, consequently, based upon two central premises: first, that representation cannot fully represent the reality of image or thing; and, second, that representation is not entirely different from those realities – that is, is not wholly symbolic. This means that perception, and the film image, are partly representation and partly ontic. If Deleuze's movement-image can be said to exhibit the skin of a present image, the present image that has been seen before will be seen again, and by many different observers; that skin is an entity that is 'given', and is not just a representation.

One issue that is related to factors of representation and presentation is that of the 'transparency' or 'opacity' of the photographic image, whether in still photographs or film. If photographic images are conceived of as 'transparent', they open on to a world, so that 'we see the world *through* them' (Walton 1984: 251). When a photographic image is printed, it consists of two aspects. First, in initial printing, it consists of an image embedded in photosensitive film stock as a negative image, and, then, as a positive print, it consists of an image embedded in ink (or equivalent) on paper (or equivalent). Second, however, it appears as an image which bears the causal trace of an earlier optic array, and the objects in the world that determined that array at the point in time and space at which the photograph was taken. The transparency thesis, at least in most rudimentary formulation, is based upon the notion that, when a photograph is viewed, what is essentially looked for is this causal trace: we want to 'see through' the photograph to the object photographed, and this is all that we want (McIver Lopes 2006: 38). This way of 'indirect seeing' is grounded in a – supposedly – uncomplicated and elementary desire to encounter the thing seen. But the question then arises as to the value of that allegedly unexacting way of seeing.

Because the transparency thesis accepts the causal connection between image and scene, it can be taken to be a realist formulation. However, the sense of the transparency thesis just given implies a rudimentary, and perhaps inadequate, way of seeing, particularly in relation to the notion of representation. It is argued that a way of seeing that looks for representations attempts to grasp the 'intentional' 'thought' that is 'embedded in the representation', whereas 'photography is [merely] a mechanism for capturing appearances', and this rules out, or at least mediates, the search for intentional thought (Scruton, cited in McIver Lopes: 36).[19] Here, far from insisting, from a realist perspective, that the photograph is not entirely representational, and is, therefore, realist, it is argued that the photograph is not representational, is realist, and that a way of seeing that is based in an elementary desire to encounter the thing seen is not an aesthetic way of seeing. Only that which is representational can be counted as art.

Where the transparency thesis was accepted as indicating a way of indirect seeing that seeks accurate information about the thing seen, this criticism had to be deflected. An 'aesthetics of transparency' was suggested, based around the notion that the photograph did not merely reproduce the object, and that the purpose of viewing the photograph was not just to grasp the object, not only to comprehend the 'appearance of the photograph's cause', although that would have been legitimate within a realist aesthetic stance (36). Some traditional aesthetic categories were then brought to bear. As photographed, the object can appear differently to how it would in a face-to-face engagement with it, because the photograph can highlight certain aspects of the object that are unavailable in face-to-face observation. In a formulation that is similar to that put forward by Siegfried Kracauer (see Chapters 7–10 of this book) photographs can afford 'revelatory, transformative, defamiliarizing or confessional seeing when they show us objects as having properties that they could not be seen to have face-to-face' (41). We still 'see through' the photograph to the objects photographed, but the objects photographed are then seen in ways different to the way that they would be seen in face-to-face engagement, and, in addition, we can also note the formal attributes of the surface of the photograph: its play of light and shade, texture and so on. The transparency thesis based on the view of the photograph merely as an 'instrument . . . for seeing through' is rejected, and an aesthetics of transparency establishes an aesthetic basis in indirect seeing through the photograph, and direct seeing of the surface of the photograph. This stance brings the issue of representation back into the frame. If the object photographed can afford 'transformative seeing', that may stem from aspects intrinsic to the object itself (that would be the Kracauerian sense). However, it may also stem from the 'formative' (to use Kracauer's terminology) photographic treatment of the object, and, in the latter case, the object photographed is 'represented', to an extent.

But there is another way of understanding the issue, and that is to consider the photograph as an entity encountered within experience, rather than as a transparency. What we experience when looking at a photograph is an object of experience. The 'object', or entity, *is* the photographic experience; and one in which the experience of surface and world depicted are part of the overall experience. The two cannot be separated, and one cannot be 'seen through' the other. The realist aspect of the photograph, its causal trace to what was photographed, is part of that experience. But this does not mean that the primary aspect of the experience of viewing the photograph consists in an interest in comprehending the causal link of the photograph to individual objects photographed in some elementary empirical, and apparently valueless manner. Rather, the issue is one of experience of the totality of the object. If we return to Gibson, there are two principal aspects of totality involved. First there is the search for 'formless invariants'. In a scene from Vittorio De Sica's *The Bicycle Thieves*, in which the two central protagonists, a father and son, are walking through a rainstorm in the city of Rome, the scene shows only part of the two characters because their legs are obscured by an object in the foreground of the image. Part of a table-like object is also discernible on the far left.[20]

As we view this image, we grasp the formless invariants of legs-joined-to-bodies and full table, even though we cannot see these directly: we are *indirectly seeing* the protagonists through the photograph, and *directly imagining* the formless invariants involved. This is not so much an interest in 'seeing the object' in a fuller sense, as it might be in everyday phenomenal experience, as it is part of a much more extensive process of understanding the totality of meaning of the object encountered within experience. This means that the transparency thesis cannot be correct. Photographs are not transparent; they are manifold objects of experience, and the causal trace to thing photographed is also manifold, and not linear. When we view a photograph, we experience an object of experience as a thing-in-itself, not a transparency, and that experience encompasses features which we peruse as a unity. That unity goes beyond the singular objects depicted (which are 'seen through') to encompass a range of significations that are related to representation, presentation and input. In the case of *The Bicycle Thieves*, it is the world of an impoverished post-war urban Italy, and the existence of the poor in that world. There is an ontic link to that which is photographed; to the capture of the optic array by the camera, and to what determines that array; there is representation in the staging and organisation of the scene, and there is a presentation which sparks a manifold of connotations. Ultimately, there is a *presentation*, into which ontic and representational aspects intervene. And there is also the indeterminate bank of knowledge brought to bear, concerning the film, the director, the type of film and so on. Rather than the notion of transparency, we can consider the photographic experience, like the cinematic experience, as affording the 'skin' of a 'present image' (see the following chapter of this book). The object that we experience is the 'skin', or 'envelope', of a manifold, and allows us intuitive access to that manifold. This is not the same as seeing through one thing to one other thing.

The ontic and representational aspects of the photograph are part of the presentation that is afforded by the experience of viewing the photograph. However, what we see is the surface of the photograph, as light rays are reflected from it into our eyes. We cannot, literally, see *into* the photograph, because light rays are not reflecting from inside the photograph, and, therefore, in this respect, the transparency thesis seems misleading. This point is also made through the idea of the 'opacity' of the image. If the image is 'opaque', then it is a present thing, rather than a showing vehicle:

> The idea of seeing involves that of being in *unmediated* or direct contact with an object . . . We see an object only if rays of light pass uninterruptedly from it to our eyes . . . [this] . . . rules out seeing through photographs,

or indeed seeing through any other kinds of picture (Gaut 2010: 91) . . . when we really see something: we do so only when rays of light from the object pass directly into our eyes. So, we do not see through any pictures: all pictures are opaque. (97)

Here, in a way that indirectly echoes the work of Gibson and Harré, seeing involves the direct transmission of light to the eye from an ambient environment. When this occurs, what we see is the movement-image as object, as defined in this Introduction; the picture is 'opaque', and present to us. However, this need not rule out the idea of either representation or realism, as both presentation and representation are caused by what is external to both. Referring to the model of environmental externalism set out earlier, it can be argued that light rays reflected from patterns of invariance in the optic array are received directly by the eye. The resulting image is not entirely presentational, but it is more presentational than representational because it is shaped more by information directly reaching the eye than by internal representational coding. Given that, the perceptual image of the phenomenal horizon, including the picture embedded within that, can be said to be opaque, rather than transparent. However, from a realist perspective, there remains a problem with the notion of opacity.

Take the following: 'the rays of light that impinged . . . onto the negative in the camera are different from those that impinge on my eye when I look at . . . [the] . . . photograph. The term 'different' can mean different things. It is the case that two separate ambient environments are involved here. However, if we take the externalist view that the optic array carries informational structures, then those structures will not be entirely different from when the photograph was taken and when it was viewed, in part, because the photograph was intentionally constructed in order to replicate – to an extent – visual perception. The rays of light will be different, but the information they carry may not be. As argued earlier, Gibson's 'law of specificity' asserts that the optic array is specific to an environment. When that array becomes 'fixed', in a photograph, its informational structures become available when viewed in a different optical environment. To consider the photograph to be opaque and reflective at the point of perception of it is not enough. Just as there cannot be pure representation, or transparency, there cannot be pure presentation, or opacity, either. Causality, and, consequently, realism, must enter the equation. Let us return to the model that was given earlier, in relation to film, rather than photography.

There is, evidently, a difference between when the film was shot and when it is viewed later. Nevertheless, both cases have at least one thing in common: notions of representation are not enough to account for their relation to reality, because there is no such thing as a literal 're-presentation' of an earlier optic array. 'The scene cannot be re-established; the array cannot be reconstituted' (Gibson 1986: 279). A film cannot preserve all the information in the pro-photographed scene because that information is unlimited. What the film does is register some information about that array. The pro-filmic environment was open to engagement from a variety of perspectives, not only the one from which filming took place; there was no unitary environment or *singular* environment to begin with. When the film is seen later, such seeing will also be from a certain perspective. When the film was shot, objects in the environment generated structures of variance and invariance in the optic array, and *some* photons carrying information about these structures made their way into the camera, where a lens and photo-sensitive chemicals designed to replicate visual perception created an image that then became fixed. When these frozen images are projected, in the present, the movement-image appears. In projection, another optic array reflects photons into our eyes, but that array carries some of the information fixed from the first array. There is, therefore, a correspondence between the pro-environment, the optic array reflecting from that pro-environment, the formation of the image on the film stock, structures of variance and invariance generated when the film is projected, and the perceptual experience of those during the act of spectatorship. This formulation is what, according to Gibson, lends 'sophisticated support to the naïve belief that we have direct knowledge of the world around us . . . [and] . . . support[s] direct realism' (Gibson 1972: 89). Opacity, therefore, like the phenomenal 'thing-in-itself', is not enough, and so the notion of presentation is also not enough.

It has been argued elsewhere that 'cinematic representation' can be traced back to Plato's allegory of the cave: the 'first appearance of cinematic representation in philosophy' (McGregor 2018: 229).[21] In the cave, prisoners chained in position see shadows projected on to a wall before them, shadows which have their source in events taking place behind them, which are illuminated by a fire, and which they cannot see. The prisoners only have access to the projected and reflected shadow-images, and, thus, take these to be real. These shadow-images move, and can, therefore, be conceived of as a form of cinematic representation, with the fire acting as projector and the cave wall as screen. Plato's point is that what is perceived to be true may not be what is true, and that representation may not be the same as reality. This, of course, has its basis in Plato's 'Theory of Forms', which will be discussed in Chapter 2 of this book, in relation to Lukács. Here it is, metaphorically, the 'Forms', the events taking place behind the prisoners, which are real (although, of course, these are not Forms in the true Platonist sense), whilst phenomenal experience is an illusion, or partial and incomplete expression of the real events. The allegory of the cave was – in part – intended to illustrate this disjuncture between 'real' and phenomenal experience. However, from a realist perspective, the allegory has its limitations.

Referring back to externalism, the moving shadows the prisoners see projected on the wall contain a substantial amount of information about the events occurring behind them, even if they do not tell the whole story; so, they are not entirely representational, or presentational. Additionally, taking a common-sense approach to the allegory, the prisoners, however much transfixed, should still be able to distinguish between the shadow-images and the cave wall, and the latter must, surely, appear more real than the former, because it will have a visual texture and substance that the shadow-images cannot have. The cave wall will also possess a degree of immutability that the shadow-images do not possess. Since the prisoners' condition of existence is that they are immobile, they should understand the immobile cave wall as more real than the moving shadows that flicker across it. The people moving behind the prisoners walk through the material environment that is the cave. Their movements are determined by information contained in the optical array which they experience. A light source (the fire) in that environment projects light rays that carry information to the wall of the cave, and those light rays are then reflected into the eyes of the prisoners. So, what the prisoners see is not entirely a representation, and is also an object as previously defined. It is, in part, opaque. The allegory can be reinterpreted from a realist perspective to mean that what is seen – the object – is not the same as material reality, nor what appears through the perspectives within the optic array adopted by those walking behind the prisoners: perspectives which produce different objects of perception. But neither is it fully a representation or an illusion. As it is perceived, it is a representation, a thing-in-itself, and contains substantial information about the external material reality that exists on both sides of the divide within the cave.

The fact that the shadow images projected on to the cave wall are not a succession of mobilised still images, as in a mechanically produced film, is not what is at issue here. The prisoners' 'cinematic experience' is of the movement-image, or 'proximal perceptual object', just as the film spectator's also is, and the origin (or part of the origin) of the film spectator's experience in a series of still images has been rendered extraneous (Ponech, cited in McGregor 2018: 233). As argued, that movement-image has representational properties, but it also has presentational properties as an object. That means that it should be considered as a present object with representational properties and not a present object without representational properties. Similarly, cinematic motion is 'perceptual' motion – that is, present motion – but nevertheless contains representational properties (Gunning, cited in McGregor 2018: 230). There is no need to repudiate representationalism entirely, nor endorse presentationalism entirely, and neither is it enough to talk about opacity/presentation and transparency/representation.

The notion of 'informational property' must also be brought in: informational property that carries information from real contexts. These notions of opacity, presentation, transparency and representation have also led to a certain redefinition of the Deleuzian movement-image. According to one writer, in both perception in general and the perception of film, what is perceived is a 'singleton'. A singleton is:

> A visible structure standing out from its background and other such structures in its vicinity. As such it is one perceptual target, perhaps among many, present in the display space . . . it is not an abstract entity but a tangible object of experience. Viewers are in sensory contact with it and have perceptual representations which are about it. (Ponech, cited in McGregor 2018: 233)

> Singletons are real and are not reducible to their constituent pixels or to any part of the visual display . . . The concept captures the intent of Currie's claims that: (a) the cinematic 'image is a particular thing and a thing that moves'; (b) 'cinematic images are real objects, reidentifiable across time and occupying different positions at different times during the viewing of the shot'; and (c) cinematic images are 'images of reidentifiable physical objects', or, more simply, a cinematic image is a 'particular reidentifiable thing'. (McGregor 2018: 233)[22]

There are, however, problems with the concepts of both the singleton and the pixel. The ideas of pixel and singleton refer to 'singular' things: the pixel as the smallest discrete unit, and the singleton as an 'identifiable visual structure' of these. If, however, we refer back to the notion of 'total relevance factor', which Casebier derived from Husserl, the film image is not a discrete thing containing discrete things, which, in turn, contain individual pixels; it is a filmic becoming that is a totality, and one that is experienced as a totality, within which the manifold relations pertaining will always be too complex and numerous to be identified as singletons in any orderly manner. The emphasis in the notions of pixel and singleton is on presentation rather than representation, and, as has been argued, representation must play a part. In addition, the account of input here remains weak.

CONCLUSIONS

The notion that the film is more than a representation, and is not secondary to what is represented, is behind much of what has been referred to as the recent 'ontological turn' in film theory. As one author has put it, when lamenting what may be called the previous 'representationalist turn':

> Film scholars and students are invariably drawn towards trying to determine what a film represents, that is, to looking at films as at best a secondary mode of being, so that any claim for the reality of films is most often met with either the blank stare of bafflement or outright repudiation. (Rushton 2011: 2–3)

Nevertheless, the critique of the 'representationalist turn' began some time ago, in the work of Cavell (1979), Lovell (1983), Deleuze (1983), Allen and Gomery (1985), Casebier (1991) and others. More recently, other theorists, including Rancière (2006), have focused upon the limitations of the idea of representation in film. Much of this work (including the author's own)[23] attempts to address questions of realism. For example, Allen and Gomery's *Film History: Theory and Practice* draws on the realist philosopher Roy Bhaskar's notion of deep-structured 'generative mechanisms', and Rom Harré's conceptions of the 'open system' and 'epistemological depth' (for the latter, see earlier in this Introduction). Allen and Gomery's work is realist-oriented in the sense that it presumes abstract, intermediary and empirical levels of causality, and, in terms of the abstract, this implies a conception of external reality. In general, a philosophical realist approach makes the link between representation, presentation and external reality. However, other work claims to be realist in a more phenomenalist sense and is more focused on the distinction between presentation and representation, as with Rancière's distinction between the 'aesthetic' and 'representative' regimes (Rancière 2006). Rancière's notion of the aesthetic regime is based on the idea that the film offers itself up as something to be meditated upon as a thing-in-itself, as a present phenomenon, whilst the representative regime refers to a more generic and conventionalised modality. Cavell offers a similar distinction between the 'absorptive' and the 'theatrical'. For Cavell, 'absorption' refers to complete identification with or surrender to the immediate object of contemplation. The term 'theatricality', on the other hand, refers to a work of art which is embedded in a context of external factors, such as institutional norms, expectations, requirements, codes and authority. The idea of absorption is another way of claiming for the reality and identity of the film image as movement-image. If the image is an entity, an object in the sense defined earlier, then the focus of the observer/viewer should be on grasping that reality and identity, rather than allowing that primal substance to become enveloped by the overall structure of the film, and the structures external to the film that are attendant upon it.

There is much more that could be said about Rancière and Cavell. However, neither of these figures is closely associated with the model of cinematic realism set out in this Introduction, and this is because, in different ways and to different extents, both are associated with a mainly presentationalist thesis. In terms of Cavell, that thesis is also related to a general Pragmatist position which is at odds with the approach adopted in this Introduction. As addressed earlier, in relation to Putnam and Peirce, the problem with Pragmatism is that it tends to bracket out notions of external reality in favour of reality as it is experienced. This means that Pragmatism does not adhere closely enough to the realist principle of 'epistemological depth', which also requires an understanding of external reality as structured in an ontological depth which includes strata which lie outside of experience. As this Introduction has argued, notions of presentation, and, for that matter, representation, are necessary, but not sufficient, and, although there is no need to deny either, there is a need to bring a third, crucial category, into the equation: ontic information – information about, and stemming from, material reality. This requires a robust account of 'input'. Gibson's and Rowlands's conception of information-bearing structures embedded in the optic array implies such a strong theory of input, one that links representation and presentation to reality; and that is something that Pragmatist, presentationalist and representationalist orientations cannot provide. The theory of cinematic realism, as set out here, draws on philosophical realism, 'externalism', the philosophy of science, the philosophy of perception, phenomenology, and underlying classical Marxist premises concerning realism. All of these 'make . . . a causal link between experience/appearances' and the world, and cede the presence of the world in those experiences and appearances (Lovell 1983: 23).

NOTES

1. The term 'skin' is often used within discussions such as this to demarcate what is internal and external, and that is how the term will be used here. The term does not refer to an actual epidermis.
2. The phrase 'veil of perception' has a long lineage within philosophy and is implied in the work of thinkers such as Aristotle and Locke. The phrase can be interpreted in various ways, relating to how absolute the 'veil' is.
3. A part of the brain concerned with the experience of emotion.
4. Brain structures that help control emotion.
5. An example here is John Locke's theory of 'primary' and 'secondary' qualities. A primary quality is an aspect of the object which influences perception, whilst a secondary quality is something that is produced by the sensory–cognate apparatus. We experience something as spherical because it is spherical in reality, whereas we experience something as red because our apparatus endows it with redness.
6. In using the term 'phenomenal' in this sense, Rowlands is not adopting a 'phenomenalist' approach, in which only sense data are said to exist, and neither am I (see Devitt 1997: 68–9, on phenomenalism).
7. The notion of the *Umwelt* will be covered in more depth later in this Introduction.

8. In *Post-Theory: Reconstructing Film Studies* (1996), Bordwell and Carroll note that Peirce later extended his first 'trichotomy' of signs to three such trichotomies, and, later, to ten (thirty signs). Most scholars in film studies, however, did not go beyond the first trichotomy (106).
9. Of course, some sorts of dwellings are not like this – igloos or circular mud huts, for example – but the general point made here should be clear enough.
10. I am retaining Gibson's nomenclature here, although I do not understand why 'moviemaker' should be one word and 'picture maker' two.
11. This notion of the 'pleasure' that is afforded by the God's-Eye-View of privileged spectatorship is also dealt with at length in psychoanalytic film theory, but that cannot be addressed in this Introduction.
12. Of course, the film stock may deteriorate over time, but this does not deflect from the general point made here.
13. Deleuze's distinction between the movement-image and time-image is not germane to the present discussion, so the time-image will not be discussed.
14. Ponech uses a term which is normally used in physiology, to mean the part of a – for example – limb that is closest to the centre of the body. Here, Ponech seems to mean that the 'proximal perceptual object' is immediately given 'close' to us as a foregrounded and substantial perceptual object.
15. In Bergson's terminology, the 'represented image': see Chapter 1 of this book.
16. This issue of the simplification of the flux will be considered in more depth in Chapter 1 of this book.
17. My translation.
18. My translation.
19. The definition of representation given here is in accord with the 'symbolic' definition of 'pure' representation given earlier in this Introduction.
20. An image from this scene is reproduced on page ii of this book.
21. It should be made clear at this point that the type of 'cinematic representation' to be discussed in this book is that associated with the mechanically produced and photographed film image. The implications of the digital film image, and of animation, will not be covered, as there is no space for that here.
22. The citations within this quotation are from Currie and Ponech, respectively.
23. For example: *European Film Theory and Cinema* (2001), *Realist Film Theory and Cinema* (2006), *Lukácsian Film Theory and Cinema* (2012) and (ed.) *The Major Realist Film Theorists* (2016).

CHAPTER I

Bergson, the Image and Time

Bergson's thought influenced the approach taken by Lukács in the writings by the latter to be considered in this book. This chapter will offer an account of relevant Bergsonian concepts as a prelude to the later exploration of Lukács.

THE BERGSONIAN IMAGE AND THE 'ENVELOPE' OF REPRESENTATION

In *Matter and Memory* (1896), Bergson seeks to steer a 'halfway' path between 'idealism' and 'realism' through his conception of the image. What Bergson means by the term 'image' is, however, not what is normally indicated by that term, and the Bergsonian image is a philosophical conception that possesses certain image-like properties. According to Bergson, the image has 'a certain existence which is more than that which the idealist calls a *representation*, but less than that which the realist calls a *thing* – an existence placed halfway between the "thing" and the "representation"' (Bergson 1991: 9). The image, existing in a domain halfway between thing and perceptual representation, is distinct from both thing and representation, but the latter is also connected to the thing through the image. The 'thing' exists outside of representation of it, the image exists apart from the thing but is influenced by the thing, the image influences representation, which cannot capture the fullness of the image, because the image is manifold in character, and human beings are unable to comprehend such a manifold reality. This is the, or, a, basis of Bergson's realism.

Our perceptual representations are essentially linear because we move through the world in a linear manner, one which repeatedly and unavoidably excludes alternative orientations. I cannot look in all directions at once. I turn to the right, and then to the left, and when I turn to the left what is on the right is 'unperceived/*inaperçues*' by me, even though it still exists: 'Here I am in the presence of images, in the vaguest sense of the word, images perceived when my senses are open to them, unperceived when they are closed' (17); '*Me voici donc en présence d'images, au sens le plus vague où l'on puisse prendre ce mot, images perçues quand j'ouvre mes sens, inaperçues quand je les ferme*' (Bergson 2015b: 4). Bergson's assertion that images can be 'perceived' is potentially confusing, given that he also implies that the image – at least in its fullness – cannot be perceived; but what he may mean is that he is in the presence of certain aspects of images, and that images per se are available to him in only the 'vaguest sense'. It is not the image, which Bergson also refers to as 'present image', but the perceptual representation of the image, which he refers to as the 'represented image', that is 'perceived'.

The present image persists outside of individual perception because, rather like an iceberg, the extent of its substance lies outside what is perceivable by the individual subject. This greater substance of the image is not so much 'submerged', as in the iceberg metaphor, but exists in a manifold, poly-relational sense. Any one image is ineluctably connected to the flow of time, to all other images, and to the images that came before it and will come after it. What we see in representation is the mere 'skin', or 'envelope', of the image, and, when the image is – necessarily for us – transformed into representation, this poly-dimensional multiplicity that moves within the flow of time is lost. Such a transformation suppresses:

> what follows it, what precedes it, and also all that fills it . . . it retain[s] only its external crust (*la croûte extérieure*), its superficial skin (*la pellicule superficielle*). That which distinguishes it as a *present* image (*image présente*), as an objective reality (*réalité objective*), from a *represented* image (*image représentée*), is the necessity which obliges it to act through every one of its points upon all the points of all other images, to transmit the whole of what it receives, to oppose to every action an equal and opposite reaction, to be, in short, merely a road by which pass, in every direction, the modifications propagated throughout the immensity of the universe. I should convert it into representation if I could isolate it, especially if I could isolate its shell (*l'enveloppe*). Representation is there, but always virtual – being neutralised at the very moment when it might become actual, by the obligation to continue itself and to lose itself in something else. (Bergson 1991: 36)
>
> (*neutralisée, au moment où elle passerait à l'acte, par l'obligation de se continuer et de se perdre en autre chose*) (All French text is from Bergson 2015b: 28)

The central distinction made here is between the image and its representation, between the 'present image' and the 'represented image'. The represented image is only the *enveloppe* of the image, and what is 'inside' the envelope is lost during the act of representation. The present image is an 'objective reality', but one which cannot be represented, because such representation cannot encompass the fullness of the present image; and, therefore, such representation remains only a 'virtual' reality. The reason why the represented image cannot embody the present image is that the represented image is what is given in perception and is what Bergson also refers to as the perceptual 'picture'. Perception has its own imperatives, imperatives that distance the act of perception from the real condition of the present image because of the need (*'l'obligation'*) to figure an act of representation (28). The perceptual system 'isolates' the envelope of the image, and is 'indifferent' to the rest; and it is through this act of isolation, required for the pragmatic self-interest of the individual, that perception occurs: 'the others [those aspects that are selected for representation], isolated, become "perceptions" by their very isolation' (Bergson 1991: 36) (*les autres, isolées, deviendront 'perceptions' par leur isolement même*') (Bergson 2015b: 29).

Bergson's theory of representation is based upon two central premises: first, that representation cannot fully represent the reality of image or thing, and, second, that representation is not entirely different from those realities: that is, is not wholly symbolic. In terms of the second premise, one of Bergson's *bêtes noires* is Berkeley. It was Berkeley's 'mistake' to 'place matter within the mind and make it into a pure idea' (Bergson 1991: 11). For Bergson, representation is not wholly symbolic because it is able to retain the envelope of the present image, and this means that the represented image partakes of an aspect of the present image: we can know part of the present image in the represented image, and, through that part of the present image, we can know part of the thing.[1] This also means that, because the image extends beyond representation, 'an image may be without being perceived – it may be present without being represented (35) (*une image peut être sans être perçue: elle peut être présente sans être représentée*) (Bergson 2015b: 27). If I look at an object, I see the representation of it: 'Now here is the image which I call a material object; I have the representation of it' (Bergson 1991: 35). If I look away from the object, the representation disappears, but the image continues to exist in its full and manifold state, a present image 'bound up with all other images', and open to different observers in different spatio-temporal situations. If I look back to the image, I can still capture only its 'superficial skin', and what is lost is the manifold character of the present image. If I look at a tree, I cannot perceive the manifold character of the tree (how the tree is perceived by others, from different spatial-temporal situations, now, and in the past), but I can perceive the tree shorn of that manifold character.

Underlying Bergson's conception of the image is a scientific conception of material reality as manifold at the most fundamental level: the universe is made up of elements that interact with each other to infinity, and Bergson was persuaded by the idea of the universe as a 'heap of matter which the imagination resolves into molecules and atoms' (Bergson 2015a: 143). Bergson lived through a period in which scientists were attempting to develop ever more unified conceptions of nature, and to view the universe as a connected whole. The influence of twentieth-century relativity theory and quantum theory on Bergson will be discussed later, but one nineteenth-century source for Bergson's vision of a unified universe was provided by the writings of the French physicist, philosopher and mathematician Pierre-Simon Laplace, who, in his *Essai philosophique sur les probabilités* (1814) and *Méchanique céleste* (1799–1825), imagined a hypothetical super-human intellect that could envision and grasp the unified relation that existed between all forces and positions of which nature is composed. This is very close to what Bergson, the philosopher and mathematician, imagines when he writes that:

> And the mathematician who knew the position of the molecules or atoms of a human organism at a given moment, as well as the position and motion of all the atoms in the universe capable of influencing it, could calculate with unfailing certainty the past, present and future actions of the person to whom this organism belongs, just as one predicts an astronomical phenomenon. (Bergson 2015a: 144)

It is this vision of material reality as an absolute totality that underscores the notion of the present image as manifold. The reality of matter consists in the totality of its elements and of their actions of every kind, and this is also the reality of the image world through which we access the reality of matter. We can try to imagine and even theorise that manifold reality, but we can only experience it intuitively, because it is 'structurally inaccessible' to thought (Guerlac 2006: 63). Bergson also points towards his conception of 'pure duration' (*durée pure*) in this respect when he imagines an unattainable form of 'pure perception' ('la perception *pure*'), in which it would be possible 'to obtain a vison of matter both immediate and instantaneous' (Bergson 1991: 34)/'*d'obtenir de la matière une vision à la fois immédiate et instantanée*' (Bergson 2015b: 26–7).

One final point that must be made in relation to Bergson's theory of the image is that the present image is not just a visual image, because it carries information about the material thing that relates to the composite physical nature of that thing: information that, consequently, is available to an amalgam of the senses, and not just the visual sense. The tree before me, as represented image, can be touched, smelled and heard, as well as seen, because its present image, available from a variety of spatial orientations, in the past, present and future, carries information about the material thing that we call 'tree' that relates to the composite physical nature of that thing: a thing from which the image also detaches as a 'picture'. The represented image is, plainly, available to all the senses: I can see, hear, smell and touch it. Nevertheless, Bergson refers to this sensuous phenomenal appearance as a represented *image* (*image représentée*), and this prioritises the visual, as, in normal parlance, an image is visual. Bergson also emphasises the visual through the use of the term and concept of 'picture', as when he talks about the present image detaching itself from the thing as a 'picture', and then offering itself in experience as the envelope of that picture: as *pictorial* (Bergson 1991: 36). Bergson also asserts that 'the object exists in itself, and, on the other hand, the object is, in itself, pictorial, as we perceive it' (10). For Bergson, therefore, perceptual experience is not just picture-like because it is mainly visual, but also because material reality is available to us via both the present and represented image in a picture-like form: in both cases, there is a predominantly visual capture of an object.

Bergson's notion of the image is not entirely based on sight and vision, however, because, and as suggested, the present image is a 'picture' open to all the senses, as is the represented image. By image, Bergson means something that embodies a range of characteristics and significations, as well as pictoriality. The present image is an assembly of information, some of which is pictorial, and some of this is captured by the represented image, which is also not entirely pictorial either. The term 'image', therefore, refers to something characterised by both the pictorial and aspects other than the pictorial. This composite nature also arises most evidently in the notion of the 'memory-image'. The memory-image has the same triadic structure as the present image. The triadic structure of the image is 'thing – present image – perception', whilst that of the memory-image is 'pure memory – memory-image – perception', where pure memory occupies the same place in the triad as the thing, or object, in material reality. As the memory-image appears as a pictorial mental image within consciousness, it is charged with the information emanating from pure memory, and is, consequently, not only pictorial. In *Matter and Memory*, Bergson also attempts to link the present image and the memory-image:

> Perception is never a mere contact of the mind (*de l'esprit*) with the object present; it is impregnated with memory-images (*des souvenirs-images*) which complete it as they interpret it. The memory-image, in its turn, partakes of the 'pure memory' (*souvenir pur*), which it begins to materialise, and of the perception in which it tends to embody itself: regarded from the latter point of view, it might be defined as a latent perception (*une perception naissante*) . . . Whenever we are trying to recover a recollection, to call up some period of our history, we become conscious of an act *sui generis* by which we detach ourselves from the present in order to place[2]

ourselves, first, in the past in general, then, in a certain region of the past – a work of adjustment, something like the focussing of a camera (*travail de tâtonnement, analogue à la mise au point d'un appareil photographique*). But our recollection still remains virtual . . . Little by little it comes into view like a condensing cloud (*comme une nébulosité qui se condenserait*); from the virtual state it passes into the actual; and as its outlines become more distinct and its surface takes on colour, it tends to imitate perception. But it remains attached to the past by its deepest roots. (Bergson 1991: 133–4) (text in French is from Bergson 2015b: 152–3)

The actual represented image captures the envelope of the virtual present image, and, as the present image is captured, the represented image is 'completed' and 'interpreted' by the memory-image in a 'work of adjustment' that also 'passes from the virtual to the actual'. The memory-image and the present image are both virtual, and both are actualised in an act of perception that is always impregnated with memory-images.

'THE IMAGE THAT I CALL MY BODY'

The present image is something that we can only have representation of, although, and as argued, that representation – the 'represented image' – is not entirely symbolic. However, according to Bergson, one form of present image can be experienced more fully, and this is because it is known 'from the inside through affect,[3] as well as from the outside', through perceptual representation (Guerlac 2006: 113). The present image in question here is the body. If I look at my hand, I see the represented image of my hand. I do not have the full, manifold present image. If I feel a sensation emanating from my hand, however, I have more than just the represented image. Bergson refers to this sensation as 'affection', or an 'affective state'. Affection adds an additional dimension. Perception takes place 'outside the skin', whilst affection takes place 'inside the skin', as interior, felt sensation. Inside and outside remain part of material reality, however, and, whilst Bergson claims that a 'fundamental difference' is marked by the fact that 'my perception is outside my body, my affection within it', he still insists that what is inside initially comes from outside: '*l'affection* doit, à un moment déterminé, surgir de l'*image*/affection must, at a certain moment, stem from the image' (Bergson 2015b: 53). Perception and affect also coincide when what is perceived comes close to the body: when 'the danger becomes urgent or the promise immediate'. Thus, the 'surface' of the body, the 'common limit of the external and the internal, is the only portion of space which is both perceived and felt' (Bergson 1991: 57). The surface of the body, and the body (Bergson often conjoins the two notions), constitute an 'ever-advancing boundary' between the external and internal, and, therefore:

> *une limite mouvante entre l'avenir et le passé comme d'une pointe mobile que notre passé pousserait incessamment dans notre avenir.*
> A moving limit between the future and the past, like a mobile point that our past continuously drives into our future. (Bergson 2015b: 83)

The body is a 'privileged image' not only because it is the *pointe mobile* at which affection and perception meet, but also because it necessarily occupies the centre of our system of representations as the carrier of consciousness and source of action. That system is what Bergson refers to as a singular 'system of images which I term my perception of the universe'. But, in addition to that, there is also a general system of images, which 'I term the *universe*' (Bergson 1991: 25). Material reality throws a manifold of present images into existence which project themselves towards us through rays of light, and which we, with our limited capacities, then attempt to represent. The images persist when we are not forming representations of them, but when we do form representations of them, we create a singular system of conjunctures out of this general system. This general system is 'relatively invariable in the universe' – the product of the interaction of matter and rays of light – whilst the singular system is 'infinitely variable in perception', and, consequently, in representation. This is Bergson's model of the 'two systems', sometimes referred to as the particular and general systems, or the 'first' (the universe) and 'second' (our perception of the universe) systems, making it clear that the second derives from the first (Lacey 1993: 117).

The particular, or second system, comes about because objects in the environment, objects such as and including the body, are given to us as representations of present images. The images act on us and we 'reflect' that action back on to the images to form representational images. That 'reflection' is perception: '*en cette réflexion consiste la perception extérieure/*in that reflection external perception consists' (Bergson 2015b: 54). The term 'reflection' is given in the 1991 English publication of *Matter and Memory*. However, Bergson does not employ its closest French equivalent, '*reflet*', in his book and instead prefers the terms *réfléchir* – as in '*le corps vivant . . . se réfléchit, sur les objets environnants, l'action que ces objets exercent sur lui/*the living body . . . which gives back after consideration, to objects within the environment, the actions that they had exerted upon it'[4] (Bergson 2015b: 54) – and '*réflexion*', as in '*en cette réflexion consiste la perception extérieure*'. There is a difference between the English term 'reflection' and these two French terms, as the latter imply something self-reflexive, considered and selective, rather than passive, involuntary 'reflection' (54). Accordingly, and to avoid confusion, the

French term *réflexion*, rather than the English term 'reflection', will be used from this point onwards.

The body 'struggles' (*il lutte*), or hesitates, because it is affected by exterior actions which may threaten its safety, and, even, its 'disintegration' (*menacent de le désagréger*), and, given this, a process of hesitancy, choice and selection is required before the body takes action. In line with the notion of *réflexion*, this also entails that not all the external actions exerted upon the body are reflected in an act of perception. Some remain outside of the second system. In addition, however, some of those actions are 'absorbed' into the body, to re-emerge as affection. This absorption is '*la source de l'affection*/the source of affection') (55). This absorption reinforces the point that affection arises from the image, from the outside; and, consequently, affection is said to be related to perception. In fact, affection is a form of '*perception toute spéciale*' (a very special form of perception) (55). Affection may well up inside the body, but its origins lie outside the body, and it is delivered to the body through an act of perception: '*la nécessité de l'affection découle de l'existence de la perception elle-même*/the necessity of affection follows from the existence of perception itself' (55). Bergson's position is, once again, a realist one.

Selective *réflexion* of external actions exerted upon the body (perception) takes place in order to assess how we act in relation to the things perceived. Perception is, hence, a field of 'virtual action'. The act of perception reacts back to the thing perceived, and that takes on a reality as appearance, but the body takes no actual action immediately, and only contemplates a range of likely possible actions concerning that appearance: '*Son action virtuelle concerne les autres objets et se dessine dans ces objets*/Its virtual action concerns other objects and becomes apparent [*se dessine*] in those objects' (55–6). Perception surveys a field of possibilities, and, so, in Bergson's terms, engenders a field of virtual actions. But affection is '*l'action réelle*/real action' (55). This is because affection is an actual condition of sensation felt within the body: something that *occurs*. A 'real' act of affection transpires within the body: '*Son action réelle le concerne lui-même et se dessine par conséquent en lui*/Its real action concerns itself and appears as a consequence in itself.' That act also remains within the body: '*et les actions réelles arrêtées par lui à l'intérieur de sa substance*/and its real actions are arrested by it [the body] inside itself/its substance' (56). Affection–sensation equates to real action, perception to possible action: '*celle-ci enveloppant une action réelle et celle-là une action simplement possible*/this one [affection] enveloping a real action, that one [perception] simply a possible action' (56). Bergson's argument that perception is virtual, and affection real, could lead to a prioritisation of the 'inside'. However, and as argued, Bergson claims that '*l'affection n'est pas la matière première dont la perception est faite*'/'affection is not the primary matter of which perception is made' (57). Perception begins in the world and is taken into the singular system of perception, and, although we are at the centre of that system, we are compelled to act in relation to the general system because of the existence of universal laws of nature.

The hesitancy involved in *réflexion* is central to Bergson's conception of free will because it establishes 'zones of indetermination', and it is these zones which are the source of free will (Bergson 1991: 39). The perceptual process enables the organism to understand and explore its environment. For a 'complex organism', this necessarily involves choice made during a period of reflection carried out within a zone of indetermination. Bergson also refers to this period of reflection, during which the organism 'hesitates' before acting, as the 'time of becoming'. When that period comes to an end, when a 'real' action occurs, 'the free action drops from it [the time of becoming] like an over-ripe fruit'. The emergence of the action following the time of becoming also contributes to a definite progression or 'expansion' of the self: 'I hesitate between two possible actions X and Y, and I go in turn from one to the other . . . the self grows, expands, and changes as it passes through the two contrary states' (Bergson 2015a: 175–6). The expansion of the self occurs because of the need to choose, so that what we have is 'a self which lives and develops by means of its very hesitations' (176). The hesitations which occur during the zone of indetermination and time of becoming also 'add nothing to what is there; they effect merely this: that the real action passes through, the virtual action remains' as un-acted upon (Bergson 1991: 39). The time of becoming/zone of indetermination, therefore, provides the facilitating framework within which free will and *réflexion* are able to emerge. What this also makes clear is that the free action is dependent upon the flow of time, without which, the 'time of becoming' could not occur. It is, therefore, and ultimately, the 'force of time that makes free will possible' (Guerlac 2006: 81).

Bergson also clarifies this time of becoming further, in relation to his rejection of the 'photographic' conception of perception. Here perception is conceived of as:

> taken from a fixed point by that special apparatus which is called an organ of perception – a photograph that would then be developed in the brain matter by some unknown chemical and psychical process of elaboration. But is it not obvious that the photograph, if photograph there be, is already taken, already developed in the very heart of things and at all the points of space? (Bergson 1991: 38)
>
> *la photographie, si photographie il y a, est déjà prise, déjà tirée dans l'intérieur même des choses et pour tous les points de l'espace?* (Bergson 2015b: 31)

The phrases 'already taken' and 'already developed in the very heart of things and at all the points of space' need to be dealt with separately, despite Bergson's elision of the two. In relation to perception, the only thing that can exist 'at all the points of space' is the present image. The present image is manifold, and it is this state that requires the perceptual system to make choices and create represented images from that manifold within a zone of indetermination. The represented image captures the 'envelope' of the present image only (although this is not the case with the body, because of affection), and, as previously argued, these represented images embody virtual possible actions, which may then lead to a 'real' act of free will, an act that is the outcome of a parade of hesitation as to choice that occurs within the time of becoming. The manifest world of the present image also carries on after the free action, and its associated represented images, emerge.

Whilst, however, a free action occurs, the represented images which appear are not 'snapshots' of the phenomenal horizon, as in the supposed 'photographic view of perception'. That perceptual outcome is part of an evolving process rather than anything fixed, and constantly changes within the flow of time. There is only constant change and movement, and the notion of the snapshot 'implies the absurd proposition that every movement is made of immobilities' (Bergson 1983: 308). In addition, when the represented image appears, it has already changed, so that what I perceive was what it was, because all perception is of the past: 'Every perception is already a memory' (Bergson, cited in Lacey 1993: 125).[5] Since, therefore, the present does not exist for us, a snapshot cannot be taken of it. The snapshot, therefore, is 'already taken' in that sense of Bergson's phrase, is not a snapshot of the present that has become the past but was always a snapshot of the past. It is impossible to take a snapshot of the present. A distinction can also be made here between the notions of 'snapshot' and 'envelope'. The notion of 'snapshot' implies a relatively full form of presentation, whereas that of the 'envelope' implies a far more schematic form.

The represented image is also not 'developed in the brain matter by some unknown chemical and psychical process of elaboration'. This would imply an 'internalist' account of perception which, given his realist stance on the nature of the image as possessing 'a certain existence', Bergson must reject (Bergson 1991: 9). Bergson maintains that perception captures something of the present image: its 'skin', or 'envelope'. The 'photographic view' of perception is based on the belief that the organism's perceptions are representations of what is external to the internal apparatus and that such a representation is categorically distinct from what is represented. However, and as argued in the Introduction to this book, if the representation is shaped to some degree by what is represented, then experience of material reality at the level of phenomenal experience will be the outcome of a combination of internal coding that is affected entirely by internal processes and internal coding that is also affected by external factors. In the latter case, the coding is not entirely representational. If we call that part of experience that is entirely coded by the brain 'representational' and that in which the coding is also shaped by material reality at the level of phenomenal reality 'phenomenal' (or 'ontic'), then 'phenomenal properties of experience [do not] reduce to the representational properties of that experience' (Rowlands 2003: 185). This is also Bergson's position.

Bergson also invokes a notion of the 'screen' in relation to zones of indetermination:

> /*il manque derrière le plaque, un écran noir sur lequel se détacherait l'image. Nos 'zones d'indétermination' joueraient en quelque sorte le rôle d'écran. Elles n'ajoutent rien à ce qui est; elles font seulement que l'action réelle passe et que l'action virtuelle demeure.*
> there lies unfulfilled behind the plate [the analogous photographic plate of the camera] the black screen on which the image can detach itself [in order to become final representation]. Our 'zones of indetermination' play in some sort the part of the screen. They add nothing to what is there; they effect only that the real action passes through, the virtual action remains. (Bergson 2015b: 32)

Bergson imagines the photograph – the 'plate' of representation, the outcome of a time of becoming – as 'translucent/*translucide*' (32), and as revealing the unfulfilled possibilities that appear on the 'black screen' beneath, which he then compares to a zone of indetermination and time of becoming. The black screen reveals the possibilities, until the image detaches itself/the free act takes place. The black screen is also analogous to the present image here, as a manifold from which the system of representation selects in order to act. Elsewhere, Bergson speaks critically and negatively about the 'cinematographic' view of perception, but his reference to the black screen here does not necessarily refer to the cinematographic screen. And yet, the notion of the screen as an ambiguous zone of indetermination and time of becoming, ripe with possibilities, and placed within duration, something that 'moves' and does not contain 'immobilities', could be taken to be a positive view of film.

CONSCIOUSNESS AND DURATION

According to Bergson, on the 'road of time', everything is 'undergoing change every moment', and 'the truth is that we change without ceasing' (Bergson, from *Creative Evolution*, cited in Larrabee 1949: 58). All of material reality, including consciousness, is bound up with the flow of time, or 'duration' (*durée*); and, in order to exist at all, material reality, including consciousness, must 'endure' through time (60). Indeed, it is impossible to conceive of a material reality, and consciousness, that does not change continuously; if it did not change, it could not exist, and, consequently, 'an object must indeed last through time if it is to be real' (Lacey 1993: 125). And time is also 'just the stuff that . . . [consciousness] is made of':

> For our duration is not merely one instant replacing another; if it were, there would never be anything but the present – no prolonging of the past into the actual, no evolution, no concrete duration. Duration is the continuous progress of the past which gnaws into the future and which swells as it advances . . . Our personality, which is being built up each instant with its accumulated experience, changes without ceasing . . . That is why our duration is irreversible. (Bergson, from *Creative Evolution*, cited in Larrabee 1949: 60–2)
> pure duration, of which the flow is continuous and in which we pass insensibly from one state to another . . . [is] . . . a continuity which is really lived. (Bergson 1991: 186)

Bergson's notion of duration refers to the flow of time and the general flow of 'becoming', which is the ultimate reality: 'reality itself', although the flow of time and this ultimate reality are inseparable (Bergson 1983: 343). Bergson also believes that, in order to contest the abstraction unleashed by science, we must become more aware of that ultimate reality: 'you must . . . install yourself within change' (308), the 'very flux of the real' (342) and 'becoming *in general*' (304). The notion of duration thus refers to an ultimate flow of becoming which encompasses the flow of temporality, and Bergson often refers to these two flows interchangeably, as when he claims that 'It is the flow of time, it is the very flux of the real, that we should be trying to follow' (342). If, however, temporality and becoming-in-general cannot be separated from each other, a distinction can be made between the two, in that, whereas becoming-in-general is material, temporality is not. Another way of putting this is to say that the former is *'substantive'*, the latter *'formal'*, 'abstract', or 'ideal' (Bunge 2006: 10).

When Bergson asserts that 'Here duration certainly seems to act like a cause,' he is referring to temporality, not general becoming; and 'it is temporality that causes the progression of the latter according to the arrow of time' (Bergson 2015a: 153). Temporality is – evidently – not a material thing, but 'a kind of force', which makes the 'universe unfold its successive states' (Bergson 1983: 339). Temporality is also a force which acts with a fixed 'velocity', one based on the invariable constant of the speed of light; and it is this consistent rate that governs the objective pace of the unfolding of general becoming (339).[6] Given this, the temporal process, as part of general becoming, is the force that governs the direction, manner and rate of unfolding of the latter. Bergson, however, wishes to make a distinction between the animate and inanimate, between 'life' and 'matter'; and, so, in relation to 'life', the temporal process, as *élan vital*, or 'vital impetus', is the force that governs the manner, direction and rate of unfolding of life within general becoming (Guerlac 2006: 7).[7] Temporality possesses a constant velocity that regulates general becoming, and, within that, the evolution of life; and, as with general becoming, 'the essence of life is in the [temporal] movement by which life is transmitted' (Bergson 1983: 128). However, temporality, as the superintendent of the direction and rate of evolutionary progress, also possesses an inner tendency to set the unfolding of life within general becoming along a path characterised by creative development:

> The universe *endures*. The more we study the nature of time, the more we shall comprehend that duration means invention, the creation of forms, the continual elaboration of the absolutely new . . . [which] . . . corresponds to an inner work of ripening or creating. (11)

This suggestion of the existence of an 'inner work', the 'vital impetus', or *élan vital* – an '*original impetus* of life' which passes on from generation to generation, within an imperative to create ever new forms – is the 'fundamental cause of variations' in species (Bergson 1983: 87), the source of Bergson's rejection of the Darwinist evolutionary theory of natural selection, and of his contention that evolution is chiefly characterised by creative development (63–4). Bergson's ontology of life is a positive one, based on the hegemony of creation. Life is not a bestial survival of the fittest and yielding of the unfit, but, rather, the unfolding of creative, affirmative energy within an overall process of division and rearticulation:

> Life . . . proceeds rather like a shell, which suddenly bursts into fragments, which fragments, being themselves shells, burst in their turn into fragments destined to burst again, and so on for a time incommensurably long . . . For life is tendency, and the essence of a tendency is to develop . . . [in the] . . . divergent directions among which its impetus is divided. (98–9)

Even so, the notion of *élan vital* makes Bergson's conception of duration and temporality even more complex, encompassing time as both duration and distinct from duration (when Bergson makes a distinction between time and general becoming), as well as force, energy and, now, life-centred *élan vital*. The uncertainty present here will benefit from further clarification, and, in order to bring that about, it will be helpful to address more recent critical writings on the nature of temporality. What follows, then, is a brief outline of certain formulations that bear on the course that Bergson takes, with the hope of further illuminating that course.

The first of these involves a distinction between time and what is in time. Music is often referred to when attempts are made to understand time because music has a tempo, or temporal measurement: 'We begin with the sound: a single piano note sounding, dying away – followed by another, sounding, dying away . . . what we are hearing is . . . something *in* time' (Bruzina 2000: 67–8). Here, the piano note, sounding, dying away, then sounding again, indicates a distinction between the temporalising process and what is temporalised by and within that process. This temporalising process also possesses a 'formal', abstract character that is distinct from and excludes phenomenal content – what is *in* time. In this sense, time 'belongs to a true metaphysical level of experience, where things are "experienced" . . . without being necessarily perceived' (Depraz 2000: 26–7). This is close to Bergson's position that time is both 'real' and 'metaphysical': a 'philosopher's time' (Murphy 2007: 70, 77).

The temporal process, as universal formal category, is the force that governs the rate of unfolding of general becoming, and, for general becoming to be perceived successfully, the observer must '*fall . . . in at one with*' that velocity and the phenomenal manifestation that is made available through that velocity (Bruzina 2000: 78). The phenomenal world, on the other hand, could not possibly 'fall in at one with' us (unless it was the product of mind); and, if our conscious epistemological experience did not fall in line with the ontological temporal process taking place in the world, we would not understand how to function in relation to that world. As beings in the world, and linked to an ever-changing world, our conscious experience of the world takes the form of an 'ongoing flow of consciousness's happenings . . . an individual's flow of experiencings (*Erlebnisse*)', that must also counterpart that taking place in the world (Larrabee 2000: 88–9). Our experience is always linked to what is happening in the world, and both are shaped by the temporal process, so that, at one level, we chiefly have consciousness of an 'ongoing flow' of phenomenal content moving according to the velocity of time, even though we may not be reflectively aware of that. There are two ongoing 'streams': the stream of general phenomenal becoming in the world, and the stream of individual conscious experience of that general stream; and these align so that consciousness is in accord with the world. This also corresponds with Bergson's previously discussed notion of the 'two systems' of represented images (Bergson 1991: 25). According to Husserl, these two streams together constitute 'the unitary form of all experiencings in the *one* stream of lived experience' where this one stream is both in the world and in our experience of the world (Husserl, cited by Bruzina 2000: 68).

Whilst, however, individual experience must fall in line with the velocity and direction of general becoming and the temporalising process, that experience also possesses its own volitional self-governance of variation. There is a temporal flow both in the world and in our experience of the world, and that flow leads to change and progression, both in the world and in our experience of it, and, here, a particular phenomenal content is, at one point, 'present' both in the world and in our perception, and then, at another, not present in our perception, though still persisting in the world, and changing at a rate compelled by the passage of time. Phenomenal content advances through time at a constant rate, and in accord with the arrow of time, because it is subject to a manner of unfolding determined by that rate and direction. Change to that unfolding, rate and progression can, nevertheless, be brought about within our experience by intentionally varying our spatial orientation: as we change our focus and gaze, phenomenal content, and unfolding, change within our experience, whilst still, at another level, progressing at a rate determined by the passage of time.

This notion of the world progressing in a fashion unrelated to us also has implications for our sense of existential connection to that world, a sense characterised by 'ambiguity' and insecurity (Bruzina 2000: 81). Radical change takes place in the world – a river suddenly overflows its banks – but that level of change is different in terms of probability from the relatively unpredictable and profuse changes of spatial orientation that we originate and experience. This also means that, as beings in the world, we are far less stable than a world which, none the less, provides a fundamental:

> framing of my experience. In other words, I do not possess temporality; temporality possesses me. My being is, therefore, essentially *ambiguous*: I am a being in time, that is, in the world, yet in my being I find the play [of presence and non-presence, see forthcoming paragraphs] originative of the world as such. (80–1)

As argued, Bergson conceives such ambiguity as the harbinger of free will and source of the free act (Bergson 2015a: 165). However, and in agreement with the above quotation, Bergson also argues that the individual's general position in relation to the world is indefinite compared to that world. For example, the relationship between material reality and the domain of present images is comparatively definite, whilst our representation of the image, and, therefore, of material reality, is only partial, and, comparatively, indefinite. As will be argued, this also has implications for our experience of the flow of time.

Bergson's central notion of duration consists of the process of general becoming and the temporalising process, and, in both, there is 'succession without distinction': a fluid continuity of rate and unfolding. There is, however, a difference (amongst others) between the temporalising process and general becoming, in that, whilst the former is only linear, the latter is both linear and non-linear. Succession without distinction in general becoming is characterised by both linearity and immediate and constant intecorrelation – by a situation in which everything is connected to everything else at some level:

> We can thus conceive of succession without distinction, and think of it as a mutual penetration, an interconnection and organisation of elements, each one of which represents the whole, and cannot be distinguished or isolated from it except by abstract thought. Such is the account of duration which would be given by a being who was ever the same and ever changing, and who had no idea of space. (101)

If such a being existed, that being would be able to look over the world and see that everything was interconnected. Such a being would, accordingly, experience 'pure duration', and 'pure duration might well be nothing but a succession of qualitative changes, which melt into and permeate one another, without precise outlines ... it would be pure heterogeneity' (104). Pure heterogeneity, which Bergson also calls 'confused multiplicity' (see later), is an organic-like conception, in which everything is characterised by an indescribable (to a human being) degree of instantaneous and persistent inter-correlation and inter-association. Every atom in the universe is connected to every other, and to the universe. It has been claimed that there is no 'ordinary-language' term, no 'linguistic tool' that is able to express this manifold reality, and that the sense must be intuited (Pullman, cited in Guerlac 2006: 40). Given that, however, it could be argued that Bergson's difficult concepts of confused multiplicity and succession without distinction serve well.

The problem is, as just indicated, that 'we find it extraordinarily difficult to think of duration in its original purity' (Bergson 2015a: 106), for three principal reasons. First, and as argued, in order to think about duration, we must represent it within ordinary-language terminology and concepts that are unable to encapsulate or express the manifold nature of duration. Second, we 'endure' alongside objects (*les choses extérieures*) that appear to be situated in space, and, therefore, in a condition of succession *with* distinction, and this fact that we 'do not endure alone' (*nous ne durons pas seuls*) prevents us from understanding the nature of duration as interminable, 'confused' becoming (text in French, Bergson 2013: 70) (text in English, Bergson 2015a: 106–7). Third, Bergson makes a distinction between experience and the way that the mind habitually works through representation, and, whilst representation will never be able to account for duration per se, it also, in addition, reworks experience, which is able to grasp duration intuitively, into a linear form, so that 'succession thus takes the form of a continuous line or a chain, the parts of which touch without penetrating one another' (Bergson 2015a: 101). Whilst, however, all this may explain why it is difficult to think of and 'represent duration in its original purity', an attempt can be made, by addressing that which is central to both temporality and Bergsonian duration: the issue of the transition from one state to another.

In terms of individual experience, the idea of a transition within phenomenal content suggests that, at a fundamental level, two primary categories are at work within the temporalising process: those of 'presence' and 'non-presence'. However, only one of these categories, presence, can exist within phenomenal reality and experience, whilst non-presence, evidently, cannot. And yet non-presence must still be part of the temporalising process, otherwise there could be no process. Non-presence must still be *'included* in the "right now" [of presence, but] . . . *not really* [be] *there*' (Bruzina 2000: 74). Temporality is, therefore, constituted by a process in which non-presence transitions into presence, then into non-presence, and then into presence again, and so on, within the onward flow of time; and this also means that the 'right-now' cannot by itself make the passage of time possible – there must be a passage from before to after the right-now in order to constitute change (73). And, as previously argued, the 'right-now' itself cannot exist in terms of *our* experience because 'we only perceive the past'; the right-now becomes part of the past before we can perceive it (Lacey 1993: 125). And yet, it cannot be argued that we perceive the past, because the past does not exist. What we perceive is not the past, but the 'tail' of the present, or the 'near-present' – the part of the present that still exists before it transitions fully into the no-longer – and, unlike in memory, where we have a mental representation of the distant past, here we have a perceptual representation of the near-present. Whilst, however, we perceive the near-present (or 'just-past') behind that perception, a play of transition from the not-yet to the right-now and then to the no-longer is constantly and simultaneously taking place, and we pass from one simultaneity to another.

This also means that the right-now must transition *within* non-presence, within a '*play of depresencing*' (Bruzina 2000: 79):

> Depresencing was the 'horizon' in which the 'not-yet' and the 'no-longer' were held within the 'right-now' while transforming into and out of it; or rather depresencing was the 'horizon' in which *something intended* was held within the 'right-now' precisely as passing from 'not-yet' and 'no-longer' into and out of the 'right-now' *as the only way it achieved presence, actuality and givenness*. The tones of music sound and are heard only because they *come* to sound and then pass away. (79–80)

The right-now, in the world, is pushed out of existence by the temporal drive to manifest an ever new right-now, and, within our experience, the right-now is driven out of existence by the temporal drive and our intentionality, which is embedded in change of a different order to that which exists in the world. The depresencing temporal horizon is constituted by the two categories of the not-yet and the no-longer, and, if the two fundamental universals of presence and non-presence are considered, we can say that the universal of presence is associated with the right-now, whilst the universal of non-presence is associated with two sub-universals: those of the not-yet and no-longer. Each of these plays a different role in relation to presence: one forces presence into existence, the other pulls presence out of existence. The present is drawn toward the no-longer, and the not-yet is drawn towards the present, in order to enable the passage of time. The present can be defined as the point in time when there is 'a maximum of actuality-in-presence in this same "right-now"' (78). However, such a concentration of actuality diminishes, the moment it is established: 'To-be-present-right-now, the moment of *maximal presence, is the very moment of the transition from en*presencing *to un*presencing' (75–6). The present moment can never be identified as such because 'there is no dividing line between the present and the past' (Gibson 1986: 253).

Nevertheless, although we cannot experience the present moment as a moment, we can still attend to its passing. It has been previously argued that temporal transitions occur both in the world and in our perception of the world. As I focus my attention on part of that world of being, I must also 'fall in line' with the process of temporal transitioning taking place within it. This is an everyday occurrence, but it can also be one experienced in a heightened state. Whereas it is impossible to hear or see the depresencing horizon of the temporal process, we can attempt to focus on the present moment, even as it slips into the past, and as a future implicit in it increasingly appears; and, in doing so, we can develop a heightened awareness of the 'radical force of the time of becoming' (Guerlac 2006: 63). Bergson attests that this is an 'extraordinarily difficult' endeavour, for reasons previously given, and, additionally, because we cannot observe the division-less passage of the not-yet into the right-now and then into the no-longer (Bergson 2015a: 106). As will be seen in following chapters of this book, however, this notion of 'tuning into' the 'radical force of the time of becoming' was to have a considerable impact on the ideas of Lukács and Kracauer.

One other point to make, in relation to temporality, is that, in addition to a temporal depresencing horizon of the not-yet and no-longer, the right-now also has a spatial horizon: 'the field of indefinitely continuing spatial expanse that lessens in determinacy in proportion to distance from the focal centre' (Bruzina 2000: 81). Any portion of this spatial field can be brought to maximal determinacy within experience with a shift of intentional aim, and, when that occurs, intentional aim also brings the ongoing temporal process to a point of maximal determinacy. As with time, however, the field of spatial expanse has its own presence, irrespective of the intentionality of any one observer. The 'right-now' is, therefore, the transitory intersection of two horizons: the spatial and the temporal. However, although all things exist in time, not all things exist in space. So, for example, physical and non-physical 'objects' all exist in time. Consciousness, however, as a category of 'non-physical object, whilst possessing temporal duration, does not exist in space. As has been argued, this distinction between consciousness, a domain of unmeasurable quality, and the spatial world, which consists of measurable quantity, is a key notion for Bergson, who wishes to distinguish consciousness from what he refers to as the 'extended' world, asking 'what can there be in common between the extensive and the intensive, the extended and the unextended' (Bergson 2015a: 3)?

Bergson's insistence on the distinction between space and time was to prove controversial after 1905, following the emergence of Einstein's influential theory of relativity, with its associated conception of 'spacetime'. The concept of spacetime combines the three dimensions of space and the one 'dimension' of time. Einstein also proved that time is affected by space, or, more specifically, a space that is subject to the force of gravity. This appears to imply that it is necessary to talk about spacetime, rather than space and time. Bergson, however, believed that to relegate time to only the 'fourth dimension' of spacetime was a mistake in human terms, because time, and not space, is the authentic domain of consciousness. Bergson insisted that the scientific conception of time was different from his own 'philosophical conception', claiming that Einstein's theory 'could not be appealed to either as supporting or confuting the metaphysics propounded in my various works, a metaphysics that has at its basis the experience of duration' (Bergson, from *The Creative Mind*, cited in Larrabee 1949: 132). Spacetime is a 'purely mathematical' concept, whilst duration is 'what is given in experience' (132); and the concept of spacetime is one formulated by 'science taken at its [abstract] limits' (131). Bergson accepted that spacetime may be a valid notion for matter, but not for mind, or for what is given in experience; and he argued that the proper province of science was matter, whilst that of mind was 'metaphysics' (130). Metaphysics also employs a 'different method' to that of science: whilst science mainly utilises mathematical logic, metaphysics draws mainly upon 'intuition' (122). Underlying all this is Bergson's insistence that scientific materialism is not enough to explain certain aspects of reality, and that metaphysical conceptions must also be engaged with.

In addition to his opposition to a conception of spacetime associated with Einstein, Bergson was also at odds with the latter's correlated theory of relativity. Bergson asserts that his conception of relativity must be distinguished from that of Einstein because the latter's formulation is 'independent of . . . the system of reference . . . and . . . consequently makes up a whole of *absolute relations'* (131–2). It is the replacement of the 'whole' with a 'whole of *absolute relations*', and the abandonment of the 'system of reference', that Bergson objects to, and, in his view, there *is* a whole: an 'absolute', or 'figure', within which there are things, relations between things, and forces that cause those relations. The 'system of reference' to which Bergson refers is the system of universal Newtonian Laws, and, in particular, the First Law of Motion, which states that, 'in an inertial frame of reference, an object either remains at rest or continues to move at a constant velocity unless acted upon by a force'. Bergson invokes the First Law of Motion because, in contrast to the theory of relativity, it implies a universal system within which the Law always applies. The physicist should 'inhabit' this system, within which the persisting 'figure' can be ascertained and relied upon (134). The problem with the theory of relativity, however, is that the 'concrete figure of the universe' will keep changing, as competing interpretations of the universe – different 'figures', none of which has a privileged system of reference – emerge (134). Because of this, Bergson believes, 'one is obliged to restore a shape to the world; but this will be to have chosen a point of view, to have adopted a system of reference'. The system chosen then becomes the 'central system' (135).

The influence of classical Newtonian physics, with its 'central systems', also led Bergson to put forward a model of 'absolute time' which contradicted the contemporaneous theory of relativity, and, in the debate which occurred between Bergson and Einstein over 1905–25, the latter claimed that Bergson's model was 'only a psychological time', without objective substance (Murphy 2007: 70).[8] However, it has been claimed that Bergson's model was later corroborated by developments in quantum theory (70). In their *The Undivided Universe: An Ontological Interpretation of Quantum Theory* (1993), David Bohm and Basil J. Hiley suggest an absolute model of time through their 'ontological' interpretation of the Second Law of Thermodynamics, and associated principle of entropy (cited in Murphy 2007: 77). This has since become accepted as a means – amongst others – of understanding why time moves in one direction, from the present into the future.

The Second Law of Thermodynamics has been variously interpreted but, in brief, and amongst other things, it asserts that natural processes run in one direction only and are not reversible. Thermodynamic energy always flows from hot to colder bodies, and this is not reversible under normal conditions. This flow, in one direction, is explained by the concept of entropy. Entropy is a measurement of the energy in a system that is lost as that system changes state, and, also, of the resulting increased degree of disorder in the new state. The two are related. The dissipation of energy that occurs during a change of state, as in heat flowing from a hot to a cold body, is lost forever, and cannot be recovered under natural circumstances. The dissipation means that the change is irreversible. Entropy is a measurement of that change and dissipation. But the change that takes place, as in the creation of a new state of a lukewarm body, also results in an equilibrium which is relatively more disordered in relation to the previous state. Entropy measures the change that takes place through the dissipation of energy, and the extended degree of disorder that occurs (Hawking 2016: 115–17). The new equilibrium does not persist, however, because all complex natural systems are non-uniform and unstable, and, because of that, are subject to change from one state to another. Entropy, therefore, marks an irreversible change, and that change, it is argued, is what drives the temporal process, at least at what has been referred to as the 'thermodynamic' level. From this perspective, what we call 'time', and the 'arrow of time', is the dissipation of energy that generates change, change that moves in one direction and becomes increasingly disordered, or, rather, constitutes new orders that are more disordered than the previous. In this sense, also, 'time' does not exist per se, and has 'no substance or reality' in itself (Murphy 2007: 70). What we have is a 'universal order of succession' which accounts for the irreversible movement from the past to the future (76).

Bergson's model of absolute temporality may not have been compatible with the notion of spacetime emerging from relativity theory, but it is compatible with the model just set out, derived from notions compatible with quantum theory. It is not necessarily the case that Bergson's conception of time was undermined by modern developments in physics.[9] Nevertheless, although the model just elaborated provides a scientific rationale for a universal model of time based on physical processes, Bergson did not view 'time itself' as a physical process, and his main concern was to develop a general, metaphysical category of time, and, in the process, provide science with 'the metaphysics it lacked' (77). Bergson's 'absolute' conception of time is a metaphysical 'virtual' one (69). Temporal change may exist in the world, in terms of the loss of energy and change of structure measured by entropy, but time itself is a general metaphysical category, or universal, with its own 'reality', and is not an illusion. All individual fluxes of time, past, present and future, are derived from this universal. In this sense, and as Gilles Deleuze puts it, individual fluxes are 'representative of Time' (Deleuze, cited by Murphy 2007: 69). Deleuze refers to this 'pure' and 'empty' form of time (which Newton also likened to an abstract, empty container) as *Aion*, the Hellenistic Greek term for the god of unbounded time. From *Aion* comes multiple empirical time, or *chronos*. *Aion* is, according to Deleuze, 'the transcendental virtual generator of multiple actual times' (76). This also corresponds to the earlier distinction given in this chapter, between 'time itself' and what is in time. The ideas of time as driven by the physical process of entropy, or by a 'transcendental virtual generator', are, evidently, quite different from each other, but they both have two key things in common: there is a singular, absolute factor involved, and what happens is irreversible.[10]

IMMEDIATE AND REFLECTIVE EXPERIENCE

Bergson's model of time is also related to a conception of the immediate experience of existence. Here, at this fundamental level, conscious experience comprises both sensations emanating from within the body – what Bergson refers to as 'affective sensations' – and sensations emanating from the world external to the body – referred to as 'representative sensations' (Bergson 2015a: 32). Both categories of sensation are intuitively 'felt', rather than thought, because this level of involvement exists outside of language and concept. This domain of immediate experience is also of the phenomenal horizon experienced by the subject, as the subject and that horizon move through time and space.

Bergson also makes a distinction between immediate and 'reflective' experience, the latter of which involves thought. Immediate experience concerns the way something feels to us and is experienced directly, whilst reflective consciousness 'objectifies experiences' through 'representative thought' (not to be confused with the representative *sensations* that occur in immediate experience) (Guerlac 2006: 62). Reflective consciousness, and representation, turn intensive qualitative sensations felt intuitively and existing in time into extended objects represented as existing in space. Although reflective consciousness objectifies through representation, it possesses an aptitude to grasp immediate experience and the reality of duration through a process of intentional meditation upon that experience and duration. Such comprehension is, nevertheless, circumscribed, because immediate experience can be fully accessed only through intuition; and intuition is not the native province of reflective consciousness. Even so, this does not mean that reflective consciousness should not *attempt* to understand and work in tandem with immediate consciousness, and such an endeavour is always necessary for practical purposes. In the modern world, however, reflective consciousness tends to dominate immediate consciousness and also compels us to employ representation in such a way that quantity and the extended are prioritised: representation – 'a sign, a symbol, absolutely distinct from true duration . . . we are compelled to borrow from space the images by which we describe what the reflective consciousness feels about time' (Bergson 2015a: 90–1). In this process, time is effectively turned into 'nothing but space' (91).

AESTHETIC EXPERIENCE AND FORM

One of Bergson's key notions is that of multiplicity, which he uses to characterise the nature of duration, quality, immediate experience, the image, temporality, and, also, space and quantity. Bergson defines multiplicity in two ways. First, there is quantitative multiplicity, which relates to discrete material objects and states of consciousness, and experience of those objects and states in which each is conceived of and perceived to exist alongside the other and separated from the other. Second, there is qualitative multiplicity, which relates to conjoined material objects and states of consciousness, and experience of those objects and states in which each is conceived of and perceived to exist as part of a manifold and not separable one from the other (Lacey 1993: 24). Bergson mainly uses the phrase qualitative multiplicity to refer to states of consciousness, arguing that 'inner multiplicity' and '*confused* perception' characterise 'the very depth of consciousness' (Bergson 2015a: 73). In terms of states of consciousness, the phrase 'confused perception' refers to information that reaches the sensory apparatus from the external world, whilst the phrase 'inner multiplicity' refers to sensations that arise within the body as affect, or 'affection'.

The notion of confused multiplicity also, however, reaches beyond states of consciousness to characterise the universe, and, as part of that, the image world as manifold. Bergson uses the term 'confused' here to mean 'conjoined', 'fused' or '*con-fused*' multiplicity; and, here, states, terms and things co-exist, and cannot be separated out into discrete elements in the way that factors pertaining to distinct multiplicity can (Guerlac 2006: 62). States of consciousness should be characterised by qualitative confused multiplicity, but, in the case of distinct multiplicity, are not, whilst the universe, and the image world, as manifold, should also be, but, in the case of distinct multiplicity, are not. They are not, because of the overbearing modern tendency to think 'spatially', rather than temporally: a tendency which leads to the 'confusion of quality with quantity' (Bergson 2015a: 74). Bergson's notion of the universe as a confused multiplicity is also in accord with the concept of 'non-localism', which is drawn from quantum theory, and which also contradicts the theory of relativity to which Bergson was so opposed. Here:

> connections exist not only between separated sub-atomic particles, but also between widely-separated parts of the universe. Indeed, if the Big Bang Theory of the origin of the universe is correct . . . then the universe as a whole can be treated as a single immense quantum system. (Murphy 2007: 74)

Bergson's conception of the universe as a single confused multiplicity is in accord with this non-localist quantum model of the universe and opposed to an Einsteinian conception of relativity, in which all physical interaction must take place through 'spatial contiguity' (74).[11]

In *Time and Free Will*, Bergson addresses the 'confusion between quality and quantity', and between qualitative and distinct multiplicity, by arguing that the verb 'to distinguish' has 'two meanings, the one qualitative, the other quantitative' (Bergson 2015a: 75–6). In a situation where many terms or objects can be 'distinguished' from each other, we have a case of 'distinct multiplicity', and, here, the terms 'are in juxtaposition, and we are dealing with *space* . . . Every number is one . . . but the unity which attaches to it is that of a sum, it covers a multiplicity of parts which can be considered separately' (75–6). To divide units from each other, or add units together, amounts to psychologically locating them in space, because time and duration are indivisible, and, therefore, not located, or locatable, in space. Bergson also argues that the notion of number implies a sum of presumed identical terms. These terms do not 'co-exist', as in an 'organic whole' (as organised together/*s'organisent ensemble*) (Bergson 2013: 51); they are separate; and if they did so co-exist, 'they will never lead us to the notion of number' (Bergson 2015a: 75). Number implies the counting of units that have a basic, or overriding, common denominator, and in counting (whether in addition or subtraction), all that the units do not have in common is 'eliminate[d]' (75).

There are 'two very different points of view' here: one in which a singular relation between two units is posited, the other in which a composite relation is posited. What is discounted in counting are the multiple similarities and differences – the *composite* reality – that persists between two units: a multiplicity which links the two units in multiple ways and occludes their separateness. What is *counted*, therefore, is only the basic, or 'simple', similarity between them – a basic denominator that also has the paradoxical effect of emphasising their separateness from each other because that denominator cancels out the composite reality: 'the idea of number implies the simple intuition of a multiplicity of parts or units, which are absolutely alike'. In counting and number, it must be assumed that the units are 'identical when they are counted', so that what we have is the identical units, and a series of such (76).

To illustrate this distinction, Bergson gives his example of a flock of sheep. There are fifty identical sheep-units in the flock if they are counted by number so as to arrive at a sum, but that neglects the individual differences that exist between the sheep: differences that mean that there are not fifty identical sheep-units, but countless different sheep characteristics which intermesh together, and ones of which a capable shepherd, or sheepdog, would be aware. In counting fifty sheep-units we erase the multiple relations that exist between the sheep, and the result is a reduction in and enervation of knowledge, as the 'particular features of objects or individuals', ones that are manifold within duration, disappear. (76). Bergson also gives the example of soldiers in a battalion: if the soldiers are counted, they are a collection of identical soldier-units; but if the roll is called, each soldier-unit is given a different and enhanced identity. Now, there is not one category of difference (the same, plus another of the same), but a relatively increased multiplicity of differences. If we focus on particularity that flows interactively and indeterminately through duration, rather than a basic generality that lies determinate in space, we cannot arrive at a definite 'total': 'we can of course make an enumeration . . . but not a total', because the enumeration will be potentially endless and incapable of leading to a total (76). Counting and distinct multiplicity limit this indeterminate process by turning that process into a determined state.

There is also a further distinction to be made here. If I count the roll and call out 'John Blake', then 'John Edwards', this is less of a discrete multiplicity than if I were to call out 'number one', then 'number two'; but it nevertheless remains only a relatively enhanced level of difference persisting within what still largely remains a discrete multiplicity. Moreover, when I say 'John Edwards', what has happened to John Blake? Bergson argues that, if we think spatially, Blake is waiting in space: 'it is necessary that each of these terms should remain when we pass to the following, and should wait, so to speak, to be added to the others' (Bergson 2015a: 79). But nothing can 'wait' in time, only in space, so that this amended example of discrete multiplicity still conforms to spatial thinking. So, how can we conceive the successive moments of time independently of space: 'what form does duration assume when the space in which it unfolds is disregarded/*quelle forme affecte la durée, quand on fait abstraction de l'espace où elle se développe*' (Bergson 2013: 50)?

The answer is that the experience of 'pure duration' must include experience of a confused multiplicity which includes both the present and the past. In a formulation that is in accord with what has earlier been described in this chapter as the 'passage-character' of time, Bergson asserts that duration, as confused multiplicity, must '*endure*' beyond the present moment, 'like the notes of a tune, melting, so to speak, into one another' (Bergson 2015a: 100). Because the notes are so closely connected, they permeate each other, like the parts of a living body, and are separated from each other only when written down, spatially, in notation. The experience of pure duration is the experience of this 'one-inside-the-other/*les unes dans les autres*', in a reciprocated diffusion, '*une pénétration mutuelle, une solidarité, une organisation intime d'éléments*' (Bergson 2013: 66), 'each one of which represents the whole, and cannot be distinguished or isolated from it except by abstract thought' (Bergson 2015a: 101). The form duration assumes when the space in which it unfolds is disregarded is a manifold one of experience of the 'confused mass/*la masse confuse*' of consciousness and the universe (Bergson 2013: 12).

The notion of confused multiplicity is, as Bergson argues, organic-like in character, particularly when associated with life, in relation to which Bergson talks about the 'movement of evolution/*mouvement évolutif*' (Bergson 2016: 47) as that aspect of general becoming that leads to the complexity and coexistence of life-forms. Confused multiplicity is the essence of duration, and flows onwards, impelled by the temporalising process, as the manifold of general becoming. And, at the core of this, is the notion of one change flowing into another, of one difference of kind changing into another in a succession without distinction, and this is also Bergson's model of aesthetic form. The one-inside-the-other form of the melody is a confused multiplicity in which the part, the single note, cannot be dissociated from the whole, and in which, in some sense, the past travels alongside the present along the trajectory of time. As confused multiplicity, aesthetic form also conforms to Bergson's notion of the 'two systems', in which the stream of general becoming and the stream of individual becoming come together. The melody progresses like an organic whole, and, as notes slip into the past, they are still 'inside' the present note. The melody is a circumscribed span of duration, as is our reflective experience, and our consciousness of the melody is thus 'situated at the junction of two streams', in which the confused multiplicity of affective consciousness meets the 'states of consciousness which represent an external cause' (Bergson 2015a: 72). A state of consciousness unfolds in pure duration like a melody does. In a melody, one note anticipates the next and refers to the preceding, and each note also remains connected to all the other notes. The melody is the formal representative expression of the form that duration assumes when we experience it truly:

> Pure duration is the form which the succession of our conscious states assumes when our ego lets itself *live*, when it refrains from separating its present state from its former states. (100)
> La durée toute pure est la forme que prend la succession de nos états de conscience quand notre moi se laisse vivre, quand il s'abstient d'établir une séparation entre l'état présent et les états antérieurs. (Bergson 2013: 66)

NOTES

1. It is worth pointing out the force of Bergson's opposition to classical representationalism, and also idealism, as in the following quotation, concerning the mindset of a hypothetical, prototypical representationalist: 'But here I am confronted by a transformation scene from fairyland. The material world, which surrounds the body; the body, which shelters the brain . . . he [the representationalist] abruptly dismisses, and, as by a magician's wand, he conjures up, as a thing entirely new the representation . . . This representation he drives out of space, so that it may have nothing in common with the matter from which he started. As for matter itself, he would fain go without it . . . Each attribute which you take away from matter widens the interval between the representation and its object . . . Above all, how are we to imagine a relation between a thing and its image, between matter and thought, since each of these terms possess, by definition, only that which is lacking to the other?' (Bergson 1991: 39–40). 'Let us no longer say, then, that our perceptions depend simply upon the molecular movements of the cerebral mass . . . but that these movements . . . remain inseparably bound up with the rest of the material world' (Bergson 1991: 24–5). The notion of representation is rejected by Bergson because of the radical separation between the world and the 'molecular movements of the cerebral mass' that the notion implies.
2. The verb in the French edition is '*replacer*', and this is also used in the 1991 English translation of *Matter and Memory*. But I think the English verb 'to place' is more appropriate.

3. The quotation is from Guerlac, although it should be noted that Bergson does not use the term 'affect'. Instead he uses the term 'affection'.
4. Unless otherwise stated, all translations are mine.
5. Lacey cites this as *Matter and Memory*, p. 194, but the phrase is not evident on that page.
6. It was not until the 1920s, when Bergson was in his sixties, that the notion emerged that certain particles could travel faster than the speed of light.
7. The term *élan vital* is sometimes translated as 'vital force', often in order to ridicule the notion of the existence of some mysterious new force within the universe.
8. In a sense, this is true. The theoretical physicist Stephen Hawking refers to three conceptions or models of time: the 'thermodynamic' (see later in this chapter on 'entropy), the 'psychological' and the 'cosmological', concerned with the expansion of the universe (Hawking 2016: 164). Bergson does not discuss either the thermodynamic or the cosmological conception of time directly (although a cosmological conception of time underlies his thought), and is mainly concerned with the psychological: the way that time is experienced within consciousness.
9. The Second Law of Thermodynamics and the notion of entropy can be associated with both classical and quantum statistics and mechanics, but some recent work has recurrently sought to link both Law and notion to the 'arrow of time' and quantum theory, including that of Hawking, Bohm and Hiley, and others, including the comprehensive Halliwell, Pérez-Mercader and Zurek (eds), *Physical Origins of Time Asymmetry* (1996).
10. Bergson's rejection of the concept of spacetime proved to be problematic, as the notion that time and space are related, and that both are affected by gravity, has become a standard assumption within modern physics. In fact, spacetime is even regarded as a fundamental constituent condition of the universe, initiated by the Big Bang, and which determines the structure and expansion (and possible collapse) of the universe. In this understanding, spacetime is the necessary 'medium', or 'entity', within which matter unfolds. However, Bergson was not concerned with the physical scientific justification for the idea of spacetime, and concomitant rejection of a separate or 'absolute' time, but with the experience of time within consciousness. Additionally, even given the venerable status of the idea of spacetime, different conceptions of that idea still hold, as do various outlying dismissals of the idea itself. Until the two fundamental physical theories of general relativity and quantum mechanics are unified, it may also not be possible to understand fully what spacetime 'is'. Eventually, the notion itself may be replaced by some other, in which case, Bergson's early rebuff may be revisited.
11. 'It could be argued that Bergson's conception of the universe as confused multiplicity implies – as earlier suggested – a cosmological conception of time that could be allied to his psychological conception of time. This, however, is a major subject of enquiry, that cannot be explored here.

CHAPTER 2

Introduction to Lukács: Essence, Phenomena and Temporality

This chapter will serve as an introduction to three subsequent chapters on Georg Lukács. It will not be possible to cover the general background and content of Lukács's thought in this chapter, and, instead, the chapter will focus on a central distinction that Lukács makes between the 'ideal' and the 'phenomenal'.[1] As will be argued, Lukács's shift from the first to the second of these terms in the writings explored in later chapters of this book evidences his shift from a Platonist to a more phenomenological position. Lukács's first major work, *Soul and Form/Die Seele und Die Formen* (1910), centres upon two concepts which have a long historical legacy within philosophy: those of 'soul' and 'form'. Both concepts will be discussed in greater depth later, but for now, and briefly, soul refers to human essence whilst form stands for that which enables essence to become manifest. One of the principal influences on Lukács when he was writing *Soul and Form* was classical Greek philosophy, particularly the thought of Plato and Aristotle, and this chapter will now explore that influence.

ESSENCE AND PHENOMENA: SOUL AND FORM

From 1000 BC to 700 BC, the Greek term for form, *eidos*, generally referred to visible form. This meaning of the term remained relatively constant until around 700 BC, after which, and over the period of pre-Socratic Greek philosophy (700–500 BC), it began to change. The transformation that took place related to an increased consideration of what there might be of more permanence that caused changeable visible form. So, the seventh-century BC philosopher Thales of Miletus argued that something called 'substance' underlay changing surface appearance, whilst another member of the same school, Anaximander, believed that an underlying 'principle of opposites' (warm to cold, dark to light and so on) arranged material reality (Guthrie 1967: 26). Later, the fifth-century BC philosopher and mathematician Pythagoras argued that an underlying order of 'intelligible structures', and not material elements, gives objects their outward form (36–7). The term *eidos* now referred more to the reality that caused what was increasingly thought of as mere appearance: a reality which 'persists through change . . . an underlying identity, a persistent stuff, a substance that is conserved' (24). This, more essentialist orientation, and, in particular, the Pythagorean concept of underlying intelligible structures, then provided the basis for the 'Theory of Forms' (or 'Theory of Ideas') of Plato (429–347 BC), in which *eidos* was now thought of primarily as 'Form', or underlying structure, rather than visual form (although, linguistically, the term retained its sense of visuality, seeing and so on), and referred to universal principles that lie beyond material reality, and of which material manifestations are – imperfect – copies. Plato was also influenced by the Pythagorean notions of the immortality of the soul and the transmigration of souls. It was, however, not this, but the Theory of Forms, which was to influence Lukács the most in *Soul and Form*, although, and as will be discussed, he was also influenced by Aristotelian conceptions of form which refuted that Theory.

In Plato's Theory of Forms, the 'Forms', or 'Ideas', are immutable, unlike the phenomenal world, which is characterised by changeableness; and this means that it is the Forms, and not phenomenal reality, that possess the greater value. There are, therefore, 'two worlds', the 'higher' world of the Forms, and the 'lower', phenomenal world. According to Platonist thought, each object and quality in the phenomenal world has its Form: there are, for example, many different tables in the world, but only one Form of 'table-ness', and all the tables experienced in the world are momentary and incomplete portrayals of that Form. The Forms relate not only to phenomenal experience, but also to conceptions of various kinds, such as, for example, the Form of 'Beauty Itself'. The question of exactly how many Forms there are has always been a matter of debate, but, in theory, there could be many. The Forms also set 'prescriptive standards'. At a mundane level this may amount to a principle of classification and separation: how many instances can be grouped together to come within the orbit of one Form, and which cannot? At another, level, however, as in the imperative Forms of 'Courage Itself', 'Friendship Itself' or 'Piety Itself', the Forms stand as pure and pre-eminent conceptual/ethical standards to be met, however inadequately, in the material world (Wiles 1999: 183–4). Some imperative Forms are also more important than others, and these, including 'Courage Itself', make up the 'Great Kinds of Forms', the most important of which are 'Good Itself' and 'Beauty Itself'.

Good Itself is the source of rational knowledge, and, therefore, 'the principle of intelligibility in virtue of which the Forms are knowable' (Melling 1987: 94). All instances of knowledge and truth in the world are but imperfect copies of, and made possible by, the existence of Good Itself, and it is also Good Itself, the source of knowledge, that makes the generality of Forms, and even the principle of Form itself, intelligible. Good Itself also has a regulative function in relation to other Forms in that it stands for things at their optimum, and Good Itself, therefore, directs things in the world into a condition where they are what they should be: 'if we know the good of something, we know its function, nature or essential structure' (Wiles 1999: 184). Good Itself is mainly comprehended through intellect, and Beauty Itself is chiefly known through intuition, and, in accord with the earlier correspondence between *eidos* and the visual that characterised much pre-Socratic thought, is also conceived of in primarily visual and imagistic terms. There are, therefore, 'two pathways' to an understanding of the Forms, and 'The aesthetic ascent of the soul to the intuition of Beauty is parallel to the intellectual ascent of the soul to the knowledge of the ideas' (Melling 1987: 100).

The notion of a *dyad* of great Forms, together with the Platonist dichotomy between the phenomenal world and the world of the Forms, influenced Georg Lukács greatly. However, Lukács does not use the term 'form' in the sense that Plato does, and, for Lukács, there are not many Forms, but one metaphysical principle of form – form as *the*, not *an* archetype; and, as a general metaphysical principle, a-temporal, immutable and 'non-genetic' (without beginning or end), the purpose of the principle of form is to enable the principle of soul to come into being (Goldmann 1972: 130). Form, for Lukács, is the general facilitating power that endows soul with the possibility of formation in the abstract, and it follows from this that, as individual manifestation within the phenomenal world, temporal, mutable and genetic (*with* beginning and end), the purpose of form is to enable individual, material manifestations of soul to come into being. Form is a metaphysical archetype of formation whose *raison d'être* is to make manifest soul; and soul is also a metaphysical archetype, but one of *thesis*, rather than formation, whose *raison d'être* is to become manifest within and through form. This also means that, at this metaphysical level, soul and form are, somehow, one: the two principles require each other. Without soul, there would be no need for form, because form is that which embodies soul – form is not merely that which embodies just any content; and, without form, soul can only be an abstraction. It is also at this point that the influence of Aristotle on Lukács becomes evident.

Plato's Theory of Forms was, to an extent, based on the previously mentioned concept of 'substance': the idea that, underlying the changes that took place within the phenomenal world, there was something that caused those changes. For Plato, that something was the Forms. Aristotle, however, dispensed with such abstraction, to argue that the primary material of experience, phenomenal 'matter', was physical, rather than metaphysical, and arranged by 'form': the instrument of shaping, or moulding of matter into substance – the compound of matter and form that is experienced and understood. An analogy sometimes used is the distinction between bricks and a house; the bricks are the matter, shaped by form into the house, the complex, or 'hylomorphic compound' that is substance (Shields 2007: 235).[2] The term 'hylomorphic' here stands for a fusion of matter and form that becomes substance. The notion also implies change because substance is the product of change and, as it takes shape, substance retains things, but also loses and gains other things: 'Thus, when a new house is built, after some process of building there exists something where earlier there had been nothing,' and, in this process, matter is both retained and dispensed with in the process of formation, as something new emerges (53).[3] Here, the hylomorphic substance is demarcated as a physical object, but Aristotle also argues that there can be pure substance as object, including, for example, mathematical substance, in which number is arranged via equation into the final mathematical 'substance', thereby adhering to the Aristotelian triadic model (57). *Both* matter and form are necessary for the compound substance – whether material or conceptual – to exist, and, once that substance does exist, matter and form cease to be two separate categories in a meaningful sense and become one thing; a *dyad* becomes a *monad*, a unit composed of two indistinguishable categories. Matter and form can be separated out via an intellectual, *a-posteriori* process, but only the 'object' they constitute exists, within either the sensible or conceptual realm (Guthrie 1967: 129).

One of the most innovative aspects of Lukács's *Soul and Form* is the new synthesis of Aristotelian and Platonist thought that is set out in the book, for it seems that Lukács has appropriated the empirical aspect of the Aristotelian distinction between matter and form and endowed it with a metaphysical dimension derived from Plato. In the metaphysical domain, Lukácsian soul and form, like the Platonist Great Kinds of Forms, are meta-archetypes, although, and as argued, in Lukács, there is only one archetype of form and one archetype of soul. These archetypes do not, however, generate a third factor in the metaphysical domain, as do Aristotle's categories in the material or conceptual domains: there is no third category that stems from their union (there is the relation of union itself, but that is a different matter). In Lukács, the third category, the equivalent of the Aristotelian 'compound substance', is given, as also in Aristotle, *in the material world*, and as what Lukács calls 'objectified' or 'non-objectified' form, and as the 'soul of form' (see later). Lukács's notions of soul and form are Platonist archetypes, or an archetypal *dyad*, which, when realised in instances in the material world, produce imperfect or abridged realisations of those archetypes, or that *dyad*. Metaphysical form can never be fully given in material form, just as metaphysical soul can never be fully given in such form. The overall model for Lukács's conceptions of soul and form is, therefore, derived from a combination of Aristotelian and Platonist premises, because Lukács conceived of form as a principle that enabled the principle of soul to become manifest in objectifications, in the same way that Aristotle argued that form enabled matter to become manifest as substance; and because Lukács then abandoned Aristotelian materialism to locate the principles of Aristotelian matter and form within a metaphysical, Platonist-like domain, where 'matter', in a non-Aristotelian manner, becomes the content of a transcendent soul, and form becomes the transcendent principle of manifestation of that content.

If Lukács's conception of form consists of a combination of ideas taken from Plato and Aristotle, his conception of soul is radically different from that advanced by the two philosophers. Influenced by Pythagorean ideas concerning the immortality and transmigration of the soul, Plato believed that, prior to birth in the material world, the soul existed in the metaphysical domain of the Forms because the soul, like the Forms, is 'eternal changeless and uniform' (Melling 1987: 71). In this existence, prior to material birth, the soul acquired knowledge of the Forms, and this also means that the soul, as disembodied spirit, possesses inherent intelligence, where that term is defined as an ability to acquire knowledge: knowledge that will eventually be applied in the material world. After death, the soul returns to the world of the Forms to await reincarnation. According to Plato's 'Theory of Recollection', after birth into the world, the soul is sometimes able to recall its previous existence within the domain of the Forms, and, through such recollection, an intimation of the Forms can be attained, one that is reached through the dual pathway of intuition and intellect referred to earlier (100). Such intimations are always incomplete, but, nevertheless, constitute a link between the Forms and physical existence.

Aristotle's conception of the soul is very different from this. For Aristotle, soul is more like a general condition of human consciousness, mind or psyche, which is essentially defined as the capacity of a conscious human being to possess awareness and acquire knowledge. This may then lead to action, but it is the condition of awareness and capacity to know, and the acquisition of knowledge that results from that, that constitutes the soul; and, given this, Aristotle characterises human beings as 'knowledge seekers' (Shields 2007: 16). This also means that the soul is mainly characterised by reason: reason is the essence of the soul, just as the soul is the essence of the body (290). As reasoning consciousness, the soul is not separate from the body, but is present within the body, and Aristotle rejects the idea that, after death, the soul could remove itself from the body as some sort of incorporeal identity. Soul is also of the same *kind*, although, of different *types*, for all beings, including human beings: a general a-temporal and a-historical condition of awareness and capacity to know, which also acquires and retains knowledge. Like Plato, Aristotle also believes that the soul was immortal, but Aristotle does not believe, as Plato did, that, after death, the soul separated from the body and migrated to a higher world, to await reincarnation. Aristotle's notion of the immortality of the soul is more complex, and equivocal, but none the less equally metaphysical. Aristotle invokes a conception of God, as the 'unmoved mover': the being that set the universe in motion. After death, the soul, as mind and reasoning consciousness, became absorbed into the 'one eternal incorporeal mind' of God, as if the reason that is of the essence of the soul joined with a universal power of reason (Guthrie 1967: 146).

Lukács's approach to the soul is quite different from that adopted by either Plato or Aristotle. Lukács is not interested in the notion of a heavenly existence that Plato's doctrine implies, and, for Lukács, there is no life after death. Soul, as metaphysical archetype, does not interact with souls and Forms in any instantiated or specified metaphysical domain. It is not *the* soul, but *soul*: not an entity, but an immutable field of value. Influenced by the Platonist notion of an assemblage, or unity, of the Great Kinds of Forms, Lukács also defines soul as an archetypal, a-historical and a-temporal regulatory standard and constituent of qualities. However, and to repeat, this archetype does not exist in any transcendental way, as Plato's Forms do, although, like Plato's Forms, it can also be conceived of in the abstract. The Lukácsian soul, unlike the 'Good Itself', is not something recollected in the present as a memory of the spirit world, but something imaginable in the present as a universal ideal. In *Soul and Form*, for example, 'soul' refers to 'ideal human essence', or 'authentic being' (Kadarkay 1991: 68). Such authentic essence is, by implication, defined 'a-temporally' by Lukács, who regards vital, though currently subjugated, authentic human nature as more or less immutable; and this a-temporal character is influenced by both Platonist and, as will be seen, Aristotelian thought again (Goldmann 1967: 167).

Aristotle's conception of the relation between the soul and God the 'unmoved-mover' is far removed from Lukács's conception of soul. Nevertheless, there is one respect in which it is similar: that respect in which Aristotle considers the soul to be a 'form'. To understand this difficult concept, it should first be recollected that, for Aristotle, form shapes matter, and that such shaping also evolves. If, as Aristotle does, the body is considered, analogously, to be the matter of the soul, then the soul, as life-principle that governs the body, can also be considered as the *form* of the body; and, in this case, the soul *is* the form, and it is the shaping action of this soul-form that leads to substance – to action, or praxis (Shields 2007: 291–2). The soul is the essence of the body and the essence of the soul is reason, and both essences shape matter (the body) into substance. This means that the soul, as reason, mind, psyche and life-principle, operates as shaping form, in the Aristotelian sense of that term, so that there is, in addition, no distinction between content and form: the soul is the form, and the soul is also the content.

There is a clear relationship here with Lukács's demand that form must be the vehicle for soul, or provide a 'shape' for soul, and that the only form that matters is the form that shapes and renders soul: the form that, as Lukács puts it, becomes 'the soul of form' (Lukács 1974: 164), *'die Seele der Form'* (Lukács 2018: 352). Lukács, however, does not intentionally employ a triadic model, as Aristotle does, and this means that, for Lukács, what form shapes *is* the final thing: form becomes soul, becomes substance in the Aristotelian sense. Nevertheless, a triadic model is implicit in Lukács's thought, because, for soul to become form and form to embody soul, a *process* of becoming and embodiment must take place, so that there are three elements: soul, a process of becoming, and form. In a piece to be explored in the next chapter of this book, entitled 'On the Phenomenology of the Creative Process', Lukács explicitly adopts an Aristotelian triadic model, as he explores the shaping process of artistic formation, and, here, soul is *progressively* shaped into form. 'On the Phenomenology of the Creative Process' is, however, atypical of Lukács's overall approach, and, in general, he does not explore process, only the content of the finished form.

The notion of a synergy between soul and form that Lukács also derives from Aristotle means that Lukács also makes no definitive distinction between soul and form: both are separate but are also, ultimately, one. At the metaphysical level, and, as argued, the two principles imply each other. At the material level, true form embodies soul, and soul appears through true form. Both are, consequently, concurrent. Of course, and as will be discussed shortly, Lukács prioritises soul-form over *mere* form, which, through 'technique', puts soul aside. In a work from his late period, a time which, it can be argued, returns to the concerns of the earlier period discussed so far in this chapter, Lukács argues that 'it is not the technique that should determine what should express the content, but it is rather the content that should regulate the application of technique' (Lukács, 'Technique, Content and Problems of Language' (1968), cited in Aitken 2012: 253). Here, 'content' stands for soul, and this also seems to equate with Aristotelian notions of the relationship between matter, form and the soul, where form, whose essence is soul, shapes matter into appropriate substance through 'technique'.[4]

In addition to the notion of the immutability of essence that he derived from Plato and Aristotle, Lukács also, and under the influence primarily of Platonism, defines soul in terms of a combination of aspects, rather than as a singular entity (Goldmann 1972: 129). However, Lukács also differs from Plato in the way that he differentiates the soul's constituent features. Plato, Aristotle – and Socrates[5] – all argued that the soul was divided into three parts, and, although they termed these parts differently, essentially, the tripartite distinction consists of reason, desire and 'spirit', where 'spirit' stands for a 'spirited, energetic, aspiring' and noble attribute of the soul, and 'desire' for a principled love of the beautiful (Melling 1987: 72). In the *Phaedrus*,[6] Plato defined these dimensions of the soul as 'reason', 'appetite' and 'spirit', where 'appetite' has a less noble and principled aspect, and stands for bodily desires, whilst spirit stands more for the spirit of *Eros* and the association with 'Beauty Itself' (73). Plato, therefore, makes a distinction between physical, bodily desire and the desire to experience the beautiful, an experience that may lead to the 'wondrous vision of Beauty Itself' (Guthrie 1967: 120–1). Socrates also maintained that one part of the soul, reason, should rule over the other parts, and that such regulation was the ideal 'natural condition of the soul' (Miller, in Ophuijsen 1999: 100–1). As has been argued, this was also the view of Aristotle, although Plato, given the mystical component of his thought, was more ambiguous on this issue.

Lukács discards the notion of the tripartite character of the soul espoused by Socrates, Plato and Aristotle, and, instead, posits a two-fold character, or two domains of the soul. This two-fold character may, nevertheless, still have its origins in Plato, for, if 'appetite' is removed from the scene, we have remaining the two noble forces of reason and spirit, and, as will be argued, this dichotomy does in fact constitute the basis of Lukács's conception of the soul. For Lukács, soul, as metaphysical principle, is made up of an amalgam of aspects. Some of these, such as 'intellect' and 'idealism', are intellectual or ethical in orientation, more 'serious' or lucid in tenor, and concerned with a categorical pursuit of essence both in general and in particular; and, in the latter case, within the material world, in an unavoidably pale imitation of essence. This will be referred to as the 'first' domain of the soul. Other aspects of the soul, such as, for example, *Eros*, or pleasure, are connected more to feeling, emotion and intuition, both in general and in particular; and, in the latter case, within the material world, in a similarly pallid facsimile of that essence. This will be referred to as the 'second' domain of the soul. The a-historical, a-temporal Lukácsian principle of soul, therefore, consists of an amalgam of aspects that fall into these two domains: domains which, as argued, can be referred to Plato's 'reason' and 'spirit'. In *The Theory of the Novel* Lukács also refers to soul and its two domains as constituting a metaphysical 'first nature' that is set against the 'second nature' of ordinary life: a second nature that can, to an extent, be associated with Platonist 'appetite', but which, for the young, idealist Nietzschean Lukács, is 'rigid and strange . . . a charnel house of long-dead interiorities' (Lukács 1971a: 64) – '*eine Schädelstätte vermoderter Innerlichkeiten*' (Lukács 2015: 55). Lukács's notions of soul, dating from 1910, and 'first nature', from 1915 (when the final draft of *The Theory of the Novel* was completed), do, however, essentially mean the same thing.

The fact that Lukács's conception of the soul exists as an ideal archetype that can be grasped to an extent in the phenomenal world also implies that this conception contains both metaphysical and existential aspects (Márkus 1983: 7). However, although, in the early aesthetic, both the abstract ideal of soul, and the possibility of the manifestation of soul within singularity, are emphasised, Lukács does not engage in any in-depth exploration of ideal-abstract categories at all, but, rather, gives prominence to the relationship between soul and singularity, so that, ultimately, his position amounts to a 'philosophy of individualism', rather than of essence (7). This emphasis on the relationship between the ideal and singularity, is, none the less, also partly responsible for the 'tragic vision' evident within *Soul and Form*, in that this emphasis leads Lukács to stress the extent of the chasm that exists between individual experience and the Ideal, and, consequently, the near impossibility of realising the Ideal within individual experience (Goldmann 1967: 169). Nevertheless, although Lukács did not explicitly or systematically define and describe the metaphysical archetypes of soul and form, these archetypes underwrite his thinking.

It has been argued earlier that soul and form imply each other and that, without soul, there would be no *raison d'être* for form, because form is that which embodies soul, and, without form, soul would always exist as a remote abstraction. At the metaphysical level, soul and form are, as argued, in a sense, one. Even so, whilst one, the two component parts must remain separable in the phenomenal world, because, in a world without form, the spirit would still remain as a possibility, whereas, in a world without soul, there would be meaningless form, and only 'a charnel house of long-dead interiorities' (Lukács 1971a: 64). Lukács, therefore, gives priority to soul. Soul, for Lukács, is what might be called an intrinsic universal, whilst form is an extrinsic universal. What is *centrally* important – that is, *intrinsic* – is soul; and form is, consequently, extrinsic to that. The elevation of soul above form in the phenomenal world is central to both *Soul and Form* and *The Theory of the Novel*, but it was also to remain an essential component of Lukács's thought throughout his career, where the division was frequently redefined in terms of the greater value of content over technique. The difference from Aristotle here is also worth pointing out. In Aristotle, form takes precedence over matter because it is the primary shaping force that governs the organisation of matter. But if the body is considered as the matter of the soul, then the soul is both the form and the soul of the body. Here, in Aristotle's materialist epistemology, there is no distinction between soul and form. In Lukács, however, there is a considerable difference between the two: soul is a metaphysical principle rather than the 'essence' of the body, and, as manifestation in the material world, it is far removed from Aristotle's more pragmatic account.

At the phenomenal, rather than metaphysical, level, the principle of form, that which realises soul, is also manifested through two distinct modalities, as 'objectified' or 'non-objectified'. The phrase 'non-objectified form' refers to a manifestation of soul within personal action in the material world and is non-objectified in the sense that such manifestation is essentially an act that does not result in the formation of an object. Non-objective form manifests itself in the material world but, relatively speaking, does not possess the persisting materiality that objectified form possesses. The non-objectified forms which Lukács explores in *Soul and Form* include, for example, the Danish philosopher Søren Kierkegaard's 'desire to see the absolute in life, without any petty compromise' (Kierkegaard's decision to abstain from marriage in order to devote himself to a study of Christian spirituality – an act that did persist, but not in the sense that a physical object persists) (Lukács 1974: 32). The phrase 'objectified form', in contrast, refers to the operation of form to manifest soul within the material work of art. Both objectified and non-objectified form are authentic – though still flawed – incarnations of soul, whilst, conversely, non-objectified acts and objectified works of art which are not incarnate in this manner are not classed as phenomenal 'forms' in the Lukácsian sense. The influence of both Platonist and Aristotelian principles are also evident here: the concept of soul is given in the Platonist sense of the Great Kinds; and the concept of form is given in the Aristotelian sense of something that shapes soul into substance.

In addition to the general distinction between objectified and non-objectified form, Lukács also makes an additional distinction between these which corresponds to one relating to the two domains of the soul, and to the Platonist dichotomy between reason and spirit. In Plato's conception of the soul, the forces of reason and spirit are two pathways towards an understanding of the Forms. Although reason and spirit may complement each other, the doctrine of the Theory of Forms still stresses their separate existence. Taking his cue from this, Lukács emphasises the autonomy of the two domains of the soul, as these are realised in the material world, in either objectified or non-objectified manner. In attempting to portray soul within the material world, objectified or non-objectified form must attempt to portray either the first or the second domain of the soul. There is no logical necessity to insist upon this separation, and the two could easily be conceived of as being portrayed or expressed together; non-objectified form, for example, could combine intellectual attempt and intuitive physical experience. Lukács does not discuss non-objectified form too much, however, because his principal concern, as a literary critic, is with objectified form, and, in terms of objectified form, and under the influence of the classical Greek doctrine of the parts of the soul, Lukács insists upon aesthetic specificity in the portrayal of the different domains of the soul: one type of form is aesthetically appropriate to portray the first domain of the soul, another, the second.

There are, however, grounds for misperception here, because Lukács's supposition of the two domains of the soul sometimes leads him to use language which appears, in a Socratic rather than Platonist manner, to prioritise the first domain of the soul. This arises when Lukács employs an idea and terminology of 'essence' to describe the first domain of the soul. Both domains of the soul constitute the essential soul. However, because he is often preoccupied with the classical drama during his early aesthetic, Lukács tends to use the term 'essence' to refer only to the lucid–intellectual–ethical domain; and this may lead to a misreading that the second domain is not somehow part of essence, and less important. It is, therefore, imperative to understand that, when Lukács uses the term 'essence', in relation to, say, the drama, this does not mean – within his framework – that this term, and its corresponding value, does not also apply to those mediums that are aesthetically appropriate to portray the second domain of the soul: those of the epic, novel and film; and what applies in these latter cases is a different sort of essence to that which applies in the drama.

These distinctions between the two domains of the soul and their related objectified forms in the material world are elaborated at length in the chapters in *Soul and Form* entitled 'On the Nature and Form of the Essay' and 'The Metaphysics of Tragedy'. In 'The Metaphysics of Tragedy' Lukács proposes a distinction between everyday experience in a fallen world and the experience of human essence which can be found within the classical Greek drama, particularly that of Sophocles, within whose forms the 'self' becomes 'soul', because the questions raised in them are always 'ultimate ones' (Lukács 1974: 155). Tragedy, therefore, is the form in which 'essential, true nature [becomes] more and more manifest' (Lukács refers to the first domain of the soul here, although, and as argued, what he calls 'essential true nature' also applies to the second domain). For Lukács, the key question for drama is, or ought to be, how essence related to the first domain of the soul can be given form in such a way that all detail is intimately linked to such essence, so that what we have is the 'soul of form' (164). When such constitution occurs in the drama, the detail, the 'sensuous immediate', also becomes greater than its mere existence as a sensuous instance because it becomes a vehicle for the expression of essence, and, in this process, all that is extrinsic to such expression is discarded. Lukács believes that this should always be the central concern of the great drama (156).

However, if the objectified form of the Sophoclean drama portrays, however imperfectly, the lucid essence of metaphysical soul, that essence associated with the relentless intellectual, rational and ethical affirmation of the Platonist 'Good Itself', the objectified form of the essay portrays, however imperfectly, that less-lucid essence associated with the intuitive, instinctive and emotional affirmation of the Platonist 'Beauty Itself'. Whilst the classical drama aims to arrive at a stripping down to fundamental inquiry, to the 'clear, harsh mountain air of ultimate questions and ultimate answers', the essay seeks to *suggest* expansively and impressionistically, and to address a range of intermediate and empirical matters (Goldmann 1967: 171). Whilst, therefore, the drama is related to the first domain of the soul, the essay form is related to the second, and 'One thing is certain – that if the drama stood at one end of the scale, the essay . . . would have to stand at the other. And this is not a scholastic classification; it has deep reasons within the soul' (Lukács 1974: 25) ('*Und dies ist keine Schulgliederung, sie hat tiefe seelische Gründe*', Lukács 2018: 56). What is at the other 'end of the scale' is, at a general level, freedom, or 'spirit', and what is associated with that; and, at a more particular level, the experience and portrayal of phenomenal reality, or, what Lukács would later, in *The Specificity of the Aesthetic*, call 'the forms of appearance', or *Erscheinung* (Aitken 2012: 88). Lukács's account of the essay form in *Soul and Form* is, however, only a prelude to his far more substantial exploration of the novel in *The Theory of the Novel*, where the novel is seen as satisfying the need to depict the forms of appearance. Lukács does not use the term *Erscheinung* in *The Theory of the Novel*, but he does employ similar formulations, including the notion that the novel is concerned with 'life', with the 'background' of things, and with 'pure feeling', all of which refers to the second domain of the soul (Lukács 1971a: 64). The novel is, therefore, related more to the second domain of the soul, and so, as will be seen, is film.

In both *Soul and Form* and *The Theory of the Novel*, however, an uncertainty can be detected as to whether, given both existential and modern conditions, form can achieve the manifestation of authentic soul in the phenomenal world. So, for example, on the one hand, and in positive vein, it becomes possible for the person, or artist, to manifest form, to circumscribed extent, in action or work of art, as a 'whole subject recreating, rediscovering and repossessing himself in a whole object', whether that object be work of art or action (Arato 1971: 130). On the other hand, however, and more negatively, the forms, whether non-objectified or objectified, are inescapably limited on existential grounds, and are, in addition, incapable of transcending a modern, fallen and ubiquitous 'ordinary reality' (Márkus 1983: 11). This latter perception is derived from the 'romantic anti-capitalist' critique of a 'culture-destructive' Western modernity which informs Lukács's early aesthetic (Löwy 1989: 190). A pervasive tension between pessimism and optimism over the possibility of the realisation of the soul within form is, however, detectable not only within *Soul and Form* and *The Theory of the Novel*, but also in the whole body of work produced by Lukács between 1908 and 1916, and which constitutes his early aesthetic.

TEMPORALITY

One of the central themes in that early aesthetic is that of temporality, and this also has ramifications for the two domains of the soul, and the forms appropriate to those domains. Lukács's understanding of temporality was, however, not a constant across 1910–16, and the formulations related to this in *Soul and Form* are not the same as those found in the later *The Theory of the Novel*. Furthermore, the change that took place here has implications for Lukács's approach to film, further increasing the importance of that change in relation to this chapter, and this book. It will, therefore, be necessary to outline the changing conceptions of temporality found in *Soul and Form* and *The Theory of the Novel*.

From the 1911 edition onwards, *Soul and Form* begins with the chapter on the essay form and concludes with the chapter on drama. It is, however, the latter, 'The Metaphysics of Tragedy' ('Metaphysics'), that best embodies Lukács's then conception of temporality, and, crucially, a-temporality, and which sets the overall tone for *Soul and Form* on these matters. In 'Metaphysics', Lukács writes that, in those moments of the Sophoclean drama when 'essential and true nature [becomes] more and more manifest' (Lukács 1974: 155), the normal involvement with temporality is suspended because such 'great moments' 'no longer lie within the plane [level] of temporal experience' (158) (*'es liegt nicht mehr in der Ebene der zeitlichen Erlebnisse'*, Lukács 2018: 340–1). The 'great moments' within the Sophoclean 'form', like 'essential and true nature', are associated with the first domain of the soul, and can, in the words of one Lukácsian interpreter, be characterised as *'significant a-temporal structures'* which render time motionless in order that the Absolute may be portrayed and experienced (Goldmann 1967: 169). In contrast to the a-temporal great moments generated by the great dramatic forms, 'ordinary life' is viewed as the cardinal opposite: as *flow*, a constantly – and meaninglessly – changing kaleidoscope of temporality which, as flow, inhibits the soul's ability to experience the ideal in the moment. If, therefore, the Sophoclean drama distils the absolute through transcending the remorseless flow of temporality, in ordinary life, temporality takes the form of a 'process of continuing decadence, as a screen which is interposed between man and the absolute' (176). But it is not just in 'ordinary life' that this continuing decadence persists. Time itself is of this manner: the 'eternal flow of time', the 'ceaseless flow of time' (Lukács 1974: 153), inhibits the 'unity of time' (*'Einheit der Zeit'*, Lukács 2018: 341) that is necessary for the appearance of the great moment, and, thus, the 'desire to come as close as possible to the timelessness of this moment which is yet the whole of life' (Lukács 1974: 158).

The distinction made here, between the a-temporal great moments and the 'continuing decadence' of temporal existence, has origins in the Platonist Theory of Forms, and implies that, for the most part, human beings are able to experience only decadence (the change and decay of all things within time), rather than 'essential and true nature'. The perception that temporality has been transcended is a false one, and, in addition, a fleeting one, because, after the great moment of the drama has passed, as it must, 'one has to fall back into numbness' [dullness] (153) (*'Man muss zurükfallen ins Dumpfe'*, Lukács 2018: 329). The tragic and pessimistic conception of temporality evident here also echoes Lukács's more general position in *Soul and Form* on the existential fate of individual consciousness within ordinary life. Nevertheless, whilst the great moment obtains, something remarkable happens. According to Lukács, the great moments do not possess temporal duration, and thus no longer lie 'within the plane of temporal experience' (Lukács 1974: 158), and this appears to mean that the formerly unattainable Ideal of soul *is* now obtainable within the material world, and within objectified form. This contradicts the assertion, earlier set out, that the perception that temporality had been transcended was a *false* perception, and, in order to explore this problematic further, it will be necessary to trace the path of Lukács's evolving conception of temporality over 1908–15. As will become clear, that path is an elaborate one.

Lukács's writings over 1910–20 appeared and reappeared in various combinations and publications. The first edition of *Soul and Form* was written in Hungarian and appeared in 1910 as *A lélék és a formák*. This edition, published in Budapest, contained eight chapters, six of which had previously appeared in the journal *Nyugat* in 1908, and two which were published for the first time in the 1910 book. In 1911 a German edition of the book, *Die Seele und die Formen: Essays*, appeared, with three new chapters. One of the chapters in the Hungarian version was removed, leaving ten chapters in total. These three new chapters were 'Über Form und Wesen des Essays: Leo Popper' (translated in the 1971 English edition, which appeared in the year of Lukács's death, as 'On the Nature and Form of the Essay: A Letter to Leo Popper'); 'Metaphysik der Tragödie: Paul Ernst' (translated as 'The Metaphysics of Tragedy: Paul Ernst' in the 1971 edition) and 'Über Sehnsucht und Form: Charles-Louis Philippe' ('Longing and Form: Charles-Louis Phillipe' in the 1971 edition). The first of these essays was written in 1910 and published for the first time in *Die Seele und die Formen* in 1911, whilst the latter two were first published in journals in 1911, and then republished the same year in *Die Seele und die Formen*.

This did not, however, add up to a complete conceptual continuity, and a distinction can be made between the 1908–10 Hungarian and additional 1910–11 German publications. The Hungarian writings were written under the oppositional spirit of 'romantic anti-capitalism' (Löwy 1989: 189), and an idealist rejection of bourgeois convention in which Lukács focused on the previously mentioned personal 'forms of . . . refusal or evasion' in the actions of figures such as Kierkegaard (Goldmann 1967: 171). It has been claimed that the predominant intellectual influence here was that of Nietzsche, and that the general Hungarian cultural and artistic context of a perceived contemporary 'crisis of the soul' under the onslaught of Western modernity played a role (Kadarkay 1991: 84). This orientation, with its Nietzschean sense of uncompromising personal idealism, is borne out most clearly in the chapters in *Soul and Form* on Novalis ('On the Romantic Philosophy of Life: Novalis'), first published in Hungarian in 1908, and Kierkegaard ('The Foundering of Form Against Life: Søren Kierkegaard and Regine Olsen'), first published in Hungarian in 1910.

However, the new writings in German of 1910–11 have an additional emphasis, and, in these, the influence of Plato, and an essentialist metaphysics, is considerable. Plato is also a presence elsewhere in *Soul and Form*: for example, in the chapter on the writer and literary critic Rudolph Kassner, entitled 'Platonism, Poetry and Form', first published in Hungarian in 1908, in which Lukács asserts that Kassner's reviews 'strip off the husk' of the plays he reviews, to focus on the 'kernel', and that the 'Platonist' is 'always close to things and yet distant from them in eternity . . . longing for certainty' (Lukács 1974: 20, 24). The Kassner essay illustrates an earlier influence of Plato on Lukács, but it is the two chapters that bookend *Soul and Form*, 'On the Nature and Form of the Essay: A Letter to Leo Popper' and 'The Metaphysics of Tragedy: Paul Ernst' – and particularly the latter, that evidence the influence of Platonist thought most clearly; and this influence also helps to explain the change that takes place in Lukács's writings over 1910–16, particularly in relation to notions of temporality, and, eventually, film. It appears that, around 1910, Lukács became more preoccupied with Platonist thought, and, also, with classical Greek tragic drama.[7] This is clear, for example, in *A History of Modern Drama*, which was published in Hungarian in 1911 but written over the few years prior to that (Kadarkay 1991: 57). It has been argued in this chapter that Lukács was influenced by a combination of Platonism and Aristotelianism. It was, however, the influence of Plato that was the greater, and that influence was also accompanied by, and/or influenced, an increasing general interest in metaphysics. In 1911, for example, Lukács co-founded the journal *A Szellen* (*The Spirit*), a periodical of philosophical–metaphysical stance, in which Lukács's 'Metaphysics' essay first appeared (Kadarkay 1991: 75).

The commentary on temporality and a-temporality that takes place in 'Metaphysics' is intimately bound to the Platonist 'two worlds' thesis, and, for Lukács, the ideal metaphysical world of the Forms is the domain of the a-temporal, the phenomenal world that of the temporal. This distinction between temporal and a-temporal worlds was also reinforced by the Neo-Kantian thought that Lukács engaged with when he was a student at Heidelberg university in 1913 (Parkinson 1970a: 3). Binary oppositions of the same type as the two worlds thesis abound in Kant and are often linked to a corresponding division between ideal and phenomenal categories. This includes Kant's distinction between the a priori and a posteriori judgement, in which the former is logically independent, and therefore independent of sense experience and judgements related to sense experience, whilst the latter is logically dependent on or entails other judgements, including those related to sense experience. The a priori judgement stands aloof from sense experience, whilst the a posteriori judgement is enmeshed in that experience (Körner 1955: 19–20).[8] The Kantian 'categories', the underlying fundamental principles and concepts of the Faculty of Understanding which order and synthesise the manifold of sense impressions, is also applicable here (Crowther 1991: 16), as, in terms of a 'two worlds' conception, is Kant's distinction between the 'noumenal' and 'phenomenal'.[9]

This binary opposition between ideal and phenomenal categories is also, and significantly, in relation to Lukács, related to temporality. Kant argued that the intuition possesses the power to comprehend the object of perception as a totality rather than in 'temporally successive apprehension', thus suspending that progression, so that the comprehension is 'a-temporal' (Crowther 1991: 169). Kant writes that

> the comprehension of the manifold in the unity, not of thought, but of intuition, and consequently the comprehension of the successively apprehended parts at one glance ... renders *co-existence* intuitable. Therefore, since the time-series is a condition of the internal sense and of an intuition, it is a subjective movement of the imagination by which it does violence to the internal sense. (Kant 1973: 107–8)

Our customary experience of perception is based on 'temporally successive apprehension'. This is the 'internal sense' that we have of the 'time-series'. However, 'by an act of "violence" to time we can suspend this progression and grasp all the parts in a single intuition of the whole ... without having successively to discriminate all its parts' (Crowther 1991: 169). The 'act of violence to time' consists, therefore, in an experience of a-temporal intuition, and, once more, we have 'two worlds': the first based in 'temporally successive apprehension', the second in a-temporal non-successive apprehension. However much Kantian conceptions of temporality may have influenced Lukács in the 1911 version of *Soul and Form*, however, and as argued, the greater influence was Platonism.

As indicated, in 'Metaphysics', Lukács draws a distinction between 'ordinary', or 'empirical', and 'real life'. In 'empirical life', 'nothing is ever fully and completely lived through' (Lukács 1974: 153). The opposite of empirical life is 'real life', in which the ideal is grasped: 'suddenly there is a gleam, lightning that illuminates the banal paths of empirical life' (153). In Platonist terms, this would amount to an intuitive comprehension of the Forms, whereas, in Lukács, it amounts to an intuitive comprehension of soul. But, as indicated previously, the 'great moment' 'cannot last' because human beings are part of the phenomenal, not 'real' world, and, so, 'real life' is unattainable in the end. We are trapped within the flux of temporality, just as Socrates, Plato and Aristotle argued that the soul was imprisoned within the mortifying body, which, according to Socrates, is 'forever breaking in on our search ... preventing our obtaining a clear sight of the truth' (Melling 1987: 66). The great moment must inevitably slip away. Lukács, however, argues that the tragic drama of Sophocles and others aims to slow down or halt this process, to come as close as possible to a condition of 'timelessness', so that a hypothetical 'unity of time' is achieved: a 'sudden standing still in the midst of the continual change of ordinary life . . . the becoming-timeless of time' (Lukács 1974: 158). This is what Lukács *actually* means when he says that the great moments do not possess temporal duration and no longer lie 'within the plane of temporal experience': he does not mean that there is an actual transcendence of temporality, but, rather, something that attempts to come close to that without ever reaching it (158).

There is a paradox at the heart of the tragic drama, and this is that essence, as Lukács characterises the great moments, cannot be experienced in-itself but only within material reality: in the 'sensual immediate', which is the contrary of essence (156). The paradox, therefore, is that, in the drama, an attempt is made to grasp the 'higher world' of ultimate essence through a sensual immediate that is fundamentally different from it, and, according to Lukács, also inferior to it. Lukács asks 'how can essence come alive? How can it become the sensual immediate, the only real, the only truly "being" thing?' (156). Lukács is not merely asking a rhetorical or predestinarian question here, and, on the contrary, his answer contains hoped-for grounds for sanguinity of sorts. The paradox of the drama in relation to temporality and phenomenal experience confronts Lukács with a dilemma, and he needs to find a route out of that in order to sustain his belief in the intrinsic value of the medium.

In effect, Lukács argues that 'real life' can be attained within the drama *to an extent*; the abstract Form of soul *can* enter the phenomenal world of dramatic forms in a substantive and authentic manner to a certain extent, and he argues this because he wishes to defend and honour the achievements of what, at that time, he still considered to be the most important artistic medium. If tragic drama has *raison d'être* it rests in this capacity to approximate to essence. Lukács's position here is ultimately founded upon what he calls 'faith', and a dogged determination to persevere in the face of the corruption provoked by the flow of temporality: one has to *believe* that a connection between the sensuous immediate and essence in the great moment is possible *to an extent*, and then seek to achieve that, or observe it, in the drama. There is a need to hope that the sensuous immediate is on the right path, and strive for that, because 'the more perfect a thing is, the more it is; the more a thing corresponds to its idea, the greater is its being'. Such correspondence can never be absolute, but it can still matter; and Lukács believes that this relative and circumscribed proximity and progress can occur in the tragic drama because 'Tragedy is the most real life that is'; because this art form is only concerned with essence and 'real life', however elusive that might be (156).

In this sense, real life can also become linked to lived life, and, when real life enters lived life, there is the 'immediately experienced reality of the great moments', and the 'essence of these great moments is the pure experience of self' (156). The ideal itself cannot be glimpsed, but the sensuous immediate of the great moment can – it is hoped – correspond to that ideal as closely as possible. As argued, belief, or 'faith', in this connection, is essential: it can only be believed that the great moment connects the sensuous immediate to essence in a meaningful manner. Anyway, according to Lukács, the resulting partial, or semi-essential, a-temporal stasis, is preferable to the temporal, empirical flux, which is characterised by 'deceptive veils, woven of gleaming moments and infinitely varied moods' (153), and, in which we are 'entangled by a thousand threads in a thousand accidental bonds and relationships . . . accidental and meaningless; everything that is could just as well be otherwise' (157).

This opposition between meaningful essence and meaningless empirical life is brought out even more starkly in another essay written by Lukács in 1910, entitled 'Aesthetic Culture'. According to Lukács, 'aesthetic culture' is the consequence of an attempt to distance culture from the depiction of essence and bring culture closer to the portrayal of life in all its transience. Lukács also argues that this outcome is largely achieved through the extensive deployment of 'transient' and 'accidental' 'mood':

> The essence of mood is its accidental . . . nature . . . life itself is seen as an endless sequence of transient moods . . . when all that was permanent disappeared from life, because the mood proved intolerant of what was permanent . . . It was born when life was stripped of all values . . . Aesthetic culture has a central tenet: the peripheral nature of all things . . . 'aesthetic culture', the 'art of life' glorifies the soul's debasement . . . aesthetic culture pulled art down to its own level, the petty ramshackle realm of perpetual indecision. (Lukács 1995a: 148–9)

Lukács repudiates culture which places transient superficiality above the artistic pursuit of essence, and this same tone of refutation also pervades the 'Metaphysics' essay. Nevertheless, Lukács is not targeting popular culture here, but what he sees as petit-bourgeois, pseudo-artistic culture. This is also made clear in 'Thoughts towards an Aesthetic of the Cinema', originally published in 1911, when he expresses the hope that the 'inconsequential literature of the stage' will be brought down, and the stage will 'once more . . . cultivate that which is its real vocation': a vocation which, as argued, is concerned with the establishment of the a-temporal 'great moment' (Aitken 2012: 186). The influence of Platonism is exposed here, but Lukács also reveals that he intends to take Platonist essentialism further than Plato did. In arguing that the drama can achieve, not just an imperfect copy of essence, but something approaching the perfection of essence, or that partakes of its substance, Lukács thinks that he, and through him, the drama, can 'transcend platonism':

> Tragedy is the becoming-real of the concrete, essential nature of man. Tragedy gives a firm and sure answer to the most delicate question of platonism: the question whether individual things can have idea or essence . . . only something whose individuality is carried to the uttermost limit, is adequate to its idea – i.e. is really existent . . . Thus tragedy's answer to Plato's verdict is to transcend platonism (162).
>
> *So beantwortet die Tragödie, mit einer Überwindung des Platonismus, das Urteil, das Platon über sie ausgesprochen hat.* (Lukács 2018: 348)[10]

Lukács final position, in the 1911 German edition of *Soul and Form*, is, therefore, a generally essentialist one, although he does not define essence in any categorical manner; the great moment, for example, is something that occurs within phenomenal reality, and not in an abstract domain of essence.

A distinction can, however, be drawn between *Soul and Form*, which is primarily concerned with drama, and the later *The Theory of the Novel*, which is primarily concerned with the novel. In *Soul and Form* the temporality of ordinary life is characterised as amounting to 'the most unreal and un-living of all conceivable existencies' (Lukács 1974: 153). However, in *The Theory of the Novel*, written in German between 1914 and 1915, first published in 1916, and then again in extended form in 1920, temporality is conceived of more positively, both as the imperative medium within which any act or portrayal of self-realisation must occur, and as capable of being shaped into a totality of sorts within the work of art (Goldmann 1967: 176). There is now no further point in adhering to an essentialist Platonist position, because the temporal flow is, in fact, what there *is*, and, therefore, that which must be encompassed. For example, Lukács now argues that phenomenally experienced time – 'real duration, real time' (Lukács 1971a: 151) ('*wirkliche Dauer, wirkliche Zeit*', Lukács 2015: 166) – is 'the life-element of the novel', a life-element through which the 'dissonance of life' (the far more negatively coloured 'anarchy of light and dark' cited in *Soul and Form*, Lukács 1974: 152) may be meaningfully portrayed, and in which a prevailing, not just momentary, totality of sorts, can be achieved.

This conception also leads Lukács to argue that the a-temporal 'great moments' of the drama, which he praised so much in *Soul and Form*, are now problematic, and for two principal reasons. First, the great moments are troublingly parasitic upon the stream of temporality because they depend for their 'existence' upon that flux-like vehicle whilst at the same time possessing a character alien to it. There is, in short, something ill-disposed and *disconsonant* about the situation. The stream of temporality, on the other hand, has no need of the great moment, and is good unto itself: it is 'entirely pure and unsullied' (Aitken 2012: 183).

Second, the great moments, by their very nature as ostensibly a-temporal Forms, cannot accommodate what was becoming increasingly important to Lukács: the temporality of the novel, and, also, of film. It, therefore, now becomes impossible for Lukács to talk about 'real time' (*wirkliche Zeit*) without meaning the temporality of phenomenal experience, because the great moment, like the Platonist Form, does not possess any 'time' at all, and, therefore, the notion of 'real time' is not applicable to it. By the same token, 'real life', or the 'living life', is no longer completely synonymous with an empirical life characterised by a 'surrender to transient moments . . . [and] . . . the random, chaotic, endless succession of moods' (Lukács 1995a: 148–9).

In *The Theory of the Novel*, therefore, under the increasing influence of phenomenology, and declining inspiration of Platonism, Lukács begins to consider the correspondence between temporality and 'form' (in the Lukácsian sense of manifestation of soul) to be of value per se. Now, the great moment, suffused with essence in the drama, is an anachronism which leaves the empirical world and real duration (*wirkliche Dauer*) too far behind, and Lukács turns to a form that can best embody that world and its temporality, one in which 'a clearly differentiated, concrete and existent world' is evident. This is the form of the 'renewed epic': a form in which man and the world can now constitute a 'totality' (Lukács 1971a: 152). But the 'great epic is a form bound to the historical moment', and now gone. Drama is now also largely irrelevant because the age of heroes and Socrates has gone,[11] whilst the novel, 'the form of the epoch of absolute sinfulness' (152) ('*die Form der Epoche der vollendeten Sündhaftigkeit*', Lukács 2015: 167), is now the dominant literary form, and 'must remain the dominant form so long as the world is ruled by the same stars' (Lukács 1971a: 152).

Lukács concludes *The Theory of the Novel* by suggesting that something approaching the renewed epic can be found in the novels of Tolstoy, in which a 'concrete and existent world' is displayed. That world does not, however, 'spread out into a totality . . . [that] . . . would be completely inaccessible to the categories of the novel', and which would characterise the renewed epic (152). 'In Tolstoy, intimations of a breakthrough into a new epoch are visible', but 'it is in the words of Dostoevsky that this new world . . . is drawn for the first time simply as a seen reality' (152) ('*geschaute Wirklichkeit*', Lukács 2015: 168). Dostoevsky 'did not write novels'; his works belong to the 'new world' of the renewed epic, and he may be the 'Homer or the Dante' of that new form (Lukács 1971a: 152). Essence is now redefined as residing within a 'new world' in which 'man exists as man' within a concrete environment, and the world has come into being as 'something natural and simply experienced' (152). This is the same world that Lukács, in *The Specificity of the Aesthetic*, and writing about film, would refer to as filled with the vibrant 'forms of appearance', and, whilst Lukács's conclusions in *The Theory of the Novel* may lead to Dostoevsky, they also lead to the concrete 'seen reality' of film. And, in fact, only a few years before Lukács wrote the above lines concerning the renewed literary epic, he argued in very similar terms that film was 'so strong, so exclusively empirically alive . . . everything is true and real . . . a new . . . unified and diverse world . . . [of] . . . maximum vivacity' emerges here (Aitken 2012: 183). During the remainder of his career Lukács changed his focus from drama to the novel. This would have almost certainly happened anyway. It does, however, raise the question as to whether his engagement with film over 1911–13, an engagement with a form in which 'essence is movement as such, perpetual flux', played a role in this transition (183).

A fundamental change appears to have taken place in Lukács's thought between *Soul and Form* and *The Theory of the Novel*, between 1910/11 and 1914–20. Various factors were involved in influencing this change, some personal, some historical; but these factors cannot be addressed here, given the space available.[12] Suffice it to say that Lukács shifted from an essentialist Platonist position in 1910–11, to one in which, by at least as early as 1914, he was prepared to embrace a transient, phenomenal flux which captured 'concrete and existent' reality and the flow of temporality. Essence, now, does not reside in the great moment, but in immediate experience. But, in fact, this transition is already apparent a few years earlier than that and can be found incubating within the inter-regnum between *Soul and Form* and *The Theory of the Novel*, in the two early essays to be considered in the following two chapters of this book: 'On the Phenomenology of the Creative Process', written in German over 1912–14, and 'Thoughts towards an Aesthetic of the Cinema', published in 1911 in Hungarian and republished in German in 1913. It is also from this point on, and until his conversion to Bolshevism in 1917–18, that the influence of Bergson comes to be felt.

NOTES

1. For more on that background see my *The Major Realist Film Theorists* (2016), *Lukácsian Film Theory and Cinema* (2012) and *Realist Film Theory and Cinema* (2006).
2. 'Hylomorphism' is a term developed in modern times from the Greek words 'hylē' (matter) and 'morphē' (matter).
3. There is, however, debate about the meaning of the term, as Aristotle changed his position on it over the years.
4. This notion that technique must be subordinate to content was also a central theme in Lukács's middle period (1917–58), in which, from a Marxist–Leninist perspective, he used the idea to denounce both modernism and naturalism, movements which, in his view, subordinated content to technique. Lukács took his cue here from, first, Engels, and then Lenin. However, the discussion of Aristotle that has just taken place in this chapter also indicates a much earlier source for this idea.

5. Socrates (469–399 BC), Plato's teacher in Athens. He wrote nothing himself, but is present, speaking through Plato, in Plato's various dialogues.
6. The *Phaedrus*, composed around 370 BC, a dialogue between Plato's character of Socrates and the character called Phaedrus. The dialogue covers a range of subjects, including that of love.
7. Lukács is mainly thinking of Sophocles (497/6–406/5 BC), and his dramas such as *Antigone*, *Oedipus Rex* and *Elektra*. In *Soul and Form*, Lukács refers to Sophocles' *Oedipus Rex* as 'the eternally great model for all drama that seeks the soul of form' (Lukács 1974: 164).
8. Examples would be, for a priori, the judgements that 'this flower is red' and 'the sun is shining' do not logically entail or contradict each other, and so are logically independent of each other; and, for the a posteriori, the judgements that 'this flower is red' and 'this flower is yellow' contradict each other, and are therefore logically dependent because each logically entails the negation of the other: the negation links them. All judgements which describe experience are also a posteriori because they are linked and reliant upon that which they describe (examples taken from Körner 1955: 19–20). The central point here is, as argued, the distinction between that which exists within a domain of logical independence, and that which is linked to the world of sense experience and description.
9. What is meant by 'noumenal' and 'phenomenal' is open to debate, with 'noumenal' being more open to interpretation. Generally, noumenal refers to the material reality that lies outside our sphere of representation, and from which the senses and cognitive processes constitute phenomenal experience for us. There can be no direct knowledge of the noumenal 'thing-in-itself', but the 'unknown and unknowable' is assumed to 'affect' our perception and understanding (Körner 1955: 91). Noumenal here is, of course, not the same as the ideal, non-phenomenal Platonist Form, but it does imply a similar distinction between experience and something outside of experience.
10. The phrase is difficult to translate into English. The English translation here is by no means literal, but does capture the essence of the phrase.
11. Lukács sets out his admiration for Plato's teacher, Socrates, in 'My Socratic Mask', a letter written to his friend Charlotte Ferenczi in January 1909, and in which he describes Socrates as a 'strong, self-assured man . . . [with] . . . a mind always on fire . . . In my view Socrates's life signifies a life without limits and restraints' (Lukács 1995b: 58–60).
12. Traumatic events for Lukács included, principally, the death of his friend Leo Popper, to whom the opening chapter of *Soul and Form* is dedicated, in 1911; the suicide of his erstwhile lover, Irma Seidlers, in the same year (*Soul and Form* is dedicated to the 'memory of Irma Seidlers'); and the outbreak of the First World War in 1914.

CHAPTER 3

'On the Phenomenology of the Creative Process' (Lukács 1914)

Lukács begins his mediation on phenomenology with recourse to a notion that he derived from his teacher at Heidelberg, Georg Simmel: that of 'objectification' (*Vergegenständlichung*), although Lukács does not use the actual term in 'On the Phenomenology of the Creative Process' ('Phenomenology'). 'Objectification' is not to be confused with Lukács's earlier formulation of 'objectified form' as that which stands for the work of art that embodies soul, and which constitutes the 'soul of form'. On the one hand, the concept refers to an innately human proclivity to shape material reality into the image and outward form of consciousness and make such 'objectifications' of consciousness concrete (Arato 1971: 130). Objectification is, therefore, a necessary aspect of the growth of human consciousness, and, at one level, leads to the formation of 'objectified culture', and, in this sense, 'the world of objectification is culture and culture is the development of the human essence beyond its natural state' (129). On the other hand, however, the creation of objects carries with it the risk that objectification, as a materiality distinct from consciousness, inevitably takes on forms of autonomy progressively more divergent from the authentic needs of consciousness, because such object-making constitutes a 'category of existence' which could not be entirely 'controlled or predicted' by consciousness (Márkus 1983: 8).

This latter conception of the opposition between consciousness and materiality influenced many of Lukács's writings over 1908–16, including 'Phenomenology', although, in the latter case, Lukács does not, as mentioned, employ the term objectification itself, but, rather, a range of synonyms, such as that the work of art is 'demarcated', is 'an independent substance' and possesses a 'self-enclosed existence', so that the work of art is 'so closed upon itself that its effect is dependent on nothing but the imminent relations of its elements' (Lukács 1972: 314). This creates a categorical gulf between the work of art and the 'lived experiences' of the artist, experiences which are unenclosed and uninterrupted. Indeed, the *sealed* work of art is 'inadequate for the transmission or mediation of lived experiences' precisely because it is sealed (314). In this notion of 'lived experience' as unbounded we also see the influence of Bergsonian phenomenology: of a notion of experience as characterised by an unending stream of subjective becoming. It is clear, that being the case, that, and as with *The Theory of the Novel*, Lukács has travelled far from the Platonism of *Soul and Form*; now, the 'great moments' of the tragic drama do not provide a 'pure experience of self' (Lukács 1974: 156), but are, rather, 'inadequate' to such provision, because the pure experience of self is now one of immersion within the flow of becoming.

In addition to this gulf between lived experience and the work of art, another related chasm also opens, this time between the artist and the work of art, because the artist is part of lived experience, and not the work of art as object. The creation of the work of art involves both an artist and a creative process, and the work of art is 'created in this process' (Lukács 1972: 314). However, once created, once the creative process has come to an end, the work of art, initially merely the 'vehicle' for the will of the artist, abandons the artist, and the artist's will, in order to become an autonomous entity: the 'vehicle of expression has itself become the goal, and has become an independent substance' (314). There is a certain *tragic* note in evidence here, one that, as argued in the previous chapter of this book, characterises much of Lukács's writing over 1910–16, in that the artist's 'will towards the work' (*Wille zum Werk*) must – unless the artist is impossibly naïve or intent upon denying the reality of the situation – inevitably be coloured from its inception by the realisation that the creative activities that take place will result in the dissociated 'substantiality and immanence' of the work of art (314). Creative intention is irrevocably linked to the fabrication of an object that then, as object, takes on its own substantiality and immanence apart from that intention; and Lukács also argues that, far from any naïve neglect or obstinate denial of acknowledgement, it is actually *through* this no doubt reluctantly acknowledged forfeiture, this accepted 'direction of the will', 'that creative intention may be defined' (314). At the heart of the making of art, therefore, is the realisation – and *will* – that what is made must be lost. The focus on process here, in addition to artist and work of art, also suggests a shift from the Platonist-inspired *dyad* of soul and form found in the earlier *Soul and Form*, to a more Aristotelean triadic structure, as well as to phenomenology.

In addition to the inevitable immanence and independence of the work of art as a consequence of its status as objectification, there is also an imperative aesthetic requirement for such: the immanence of the work of art must be sustained in order that the artist's 'will towards the work' should not be understood 'unambiguously', and ambiguity must persist as 'a structural fact of the aesthetic domain' (315). Here, Lukács disavows a romantic conception of art in which what is most important is the archaeology of the vision of the artist. The 'structural fact' of ambiguity resists such archaeology and thereby allows the work of art to be variously interpreted so that 'the most varied opinions . . . retain their relative validity' (315). This ambiguity and relativity regarding the source and identity of aesthetic intentionality and meaning, and the multiplicity of interpretation this ambiguity gives rise to, is an 'essential feature of art', and it is this feature that frees art from an unaesthetic fixity of meaning (315). The source of ambiguity is the fissure that transpires between consciousness and object. Once more, it seems, a shift has taken place, from the emphasis on essence in *Soul and Form*, in which matters 'have been stripped of everything that is not of their innermost essence . . . [and in which] . . . all the relationships of life have been suppressed', to the stress on indistinctness and multiplicity in 'Phenomenology': one that marks a transition between Platonist essentialism and phenomenological diversity (Lukács 1974: 155).

If, however, the ambiguity and relativity afforded by the mounting immanence of the work of art mediates the will-toward-the-work of and prospective will-towards fixity of meaning by the artist, that mediation, whilst furnishing ambiguity, also serves the growing animate immanence and autonomy of the work, which increasingly takes on a more integrated and unified 'life of its own, an existence [that eventually becomes] completely separated from the creator and his experience' (315). The initial challenge to a fixed designation of meaning may, consequently, gradually evolve into another, formal-immanent, imperative to do the same. For Lukács, in 'Phenomenology', the work of art is a sort of existent which, as it evolves into being, first enters into a dialectical exchange with the will-toward-the-work of the artist, but then increasingly exercises its own 'will' over its formation within the creative process. The internal relations of the work thus increasingly hold together and redirect the will of the artist as the will-toward-the-work is progressively absorbed *into* the work and altered in the process. This evolution of the work involves an 'autonomous willing and seeking' to arrive at a fruitful completion in terms of the interests of the work, and it is this escalating activity, in conjunction with the fact of separation between the work of art and the artist located in lived experience, that generates, first, the structural and intensely aesthetic indistinctness that is central to the work of art, and, second, the diminution and deflection of such indistinctness. In the end, the will-toward-the-work on the part of the artist can be perceived only indirectly and in part by the 'recipient or appreciator' who wishes to direct attention to that will, and, in fact, Lukács believes that such a requirement is anyway misdirected, indicating that his position is not based on romantic conceptions of authorship and creativity, but, rather, on modernist and phenomenological ones (315). None the less, Lukács does not, as might seem to be the case, adopt a fatalistic position here, one overly influenced by, for example, Simmel's negative conception of objectification, and, rather, sees the indistinctness which is central to the creative process as a potential outcome of a more auspicious fusion between the will-toward-the-work of the artist and the will-toward-the-work of the work of art. Under the influence of phenomenology, Lukács identifies the work of art not only as a final, discrete object, but also as one that is, in addition, inextricably related to the process of becoming which led to its appearance; and this relation means that aesthetic ambiguity is not, ultimately, at grave risk.

In his account of the relationship that persists between the artist and the work of art Lukács takes a 'phenomenological' approach, one in which the work of art is primarily regarded as an evolving entity-in-itself rather than a representation or copy of something, and one that, accordingly, 'exists' within the phenomenal flux of lived experience alongside human consciousness and other objects. Lukács's 'Phenomenology' essay, as with phenomenology in general, can, consequently, be associated with the critique of representationalism explored in the Introduction to this book, and, also, concomitantly, moves away from the Platonist notion of phenomenal appearance as an – albeit flawed – representation of the Forms. There is, however, an important distinction to be made here in relation to the critique of representationalism that Lukács mounts. Lukács's overall stance is influenced by two factors. The first is the existential distinction between consciousness and objectification which he derived from Simmel, and in which objectification is a 'category of existence': a materiality categorically dissimilar to consciousness that cannot be 'controlled or predicted' by consciousness, but which, none the less, exists within the phenomenal flux alongside consciousness (Márkus 1983: 8). Here, the emphasis is on being and stasis, rather than on becoming and progression within the phenomenal flux: the art object as comparatively persisting 'presence', with its own reality, and as a relative *compression* of the flux. The second factor in this critique of representationalism is the general phenomenological insistence on the reality of phenomenal experience *as* flux, and, here, the emphasis is placed on becoming and progression, rather than on (relative) being and stasis within the phenomenal flux: experience as constitutive of its own evolving reality (although a reality that is also inter-subjective); and, additionally, experience of the process of art-making, as constitutive of its own evolving *uncompressed* reality within the flux.

The distinction within Lukács's critique of representationalism now becomes clearer: the first approach and influence against representation emphasises the *relatively bounded* aspect of the existence and reality of the work of art as an identifiable 'object' embedded within the phenomenal flux, whilst the second emphasises the *objectively unbounded* aspect of the existence and reality of the work of art as an identifiable *process* embedded within the phenomenal flux. Whether bounded or unbounded, art object, experience and art process possess their own phenomenal realities, and so are not considered to be representations, but, rather, objects of experience. By the terms 'object', and 'objectification', then, Lukács means something that is relatively bounded and closed (and, of course, he does not mean a *physical* object, like a DVD of, for example, *Citizen Kane*; he means the relatively bounded presentation that we encounter within the viewing experience of that film; *Citizen Kane* does not change *fundamentally*, from viewing experience to viewing experience).[1] By the term 'work', on the other hand, Lukács means something that is both bounded and unbounded. The bounded aspect of the work, the relatively finished state as presentation within experience that has just been mentioned, is something akin to the phenomenological 'purposive project'; whilst the unbounded aspect, the process of becoming that state, a process open to change at most if not all points, is more akin to the general flow of experience within the *Lebenswelt*, or life-world.[2] Jean Renoir's 1939 film *La Règle du jeu* did not just 'appear'; it evolved through a process of work-making that was open to change at most points. The *work*, therefore, contains both a relatively bounded and relatively unbounded aspect. However, both these also emanate signification that becomes incorporated within the ongoing stream of becoming within the *Lebenswelt*. Lukács's conception of the work, therefore, consists of three aspects: first, the relatively bounded presentation which is experienced; second, the relatively unbounded process of bringing the work of art to fruition; and, third, the interaction of both of these with the field of experiential connotation. The concept of 'work' overrides that of 'object', and what is involved in that concept ensures the indeterminacy of the aesthetic.

In 'Phenomenology', Lukács does not discuss the relationship of phenomenal experience to either perception or 'external reality' (the 'thing-in-itself', discussed in the Introduction and Chapter 1 of this book) because he is primarily interested in the evident reality and existence of phenomenal experience, and this leads him to insist that the work of art should be regarded as an entity rather than a representation, and, as argued, an entity that is both bounded and unbounded. The notion that an entity is unbounded may appear contradictory, but the unbounded dimension of the entity consists, as argued, of both the process of making, and an immaterial field of connotation that Lukács feels is connected to the ambiguity that is central to the aesthetic domain. The bounded and unbounded aspects of the work form an existent phenomenal totality. Roberto Rossellini's 1954 film *Voyage to Italy/Viaggio in Italia* is both bounded and unbounded. Conceived of as bounded, *Voyage to Italy* has a 'self-enclosed existence' and a 'life of its own' in terms of its relatively purposive and tabulated aspects (Lukács 1972: 315); but, conceived of as unbounded, it is part of a process of making that was embedded within the life-world, and concomitant assemblage of signification that extends into the phenomenal flux of lived experience during the act of spectatorship, past, present and future. What this also makes clear is that the idea of the work is conceived of in terms of the notion of totality, a notion that is central to Lukács's thought. In *Soul and Form* Lukács argued that a sense of totality had disappeared from modern human experience, and that, nevertheless, 'faith' in such totality remained 'the a priori basis for the whole of [human] existence' (Lukács 1974: 156). This emphasis on totality also underlines the later 'Phenomenology' essay, in which totality is conceived of in the phenomenological terms just set out.

The relatively bounded and unbounded aspect of the work, and situation of the work within the *Lebenswelt*, also imply that the work is constantly changing, and this involves two aspects. First, the work evolves according to its own immanent imperatives and the will of the artist. Second, the work evolves in relation to the phenomenal flux of lived experience, which, as argued, can be characterised as an emanation of signification from the work that incorporates with the ongoing stream of becoming within the *Lebenswelt*, part of which involves acts of spectatorship. Lukács's position here appears close to Bergson's conception of 'duration'. It will be recalled from Chapter 1 of this book that, according to Bergson, everything is 'undergoing change every moment' (Bergson, cited in Larrabee 1949: 58). All of material reality, including consciousness, is bound up with the flow of duration; and, in order to exist at all, material reality, including consciousness, must 'endure', or change (60). Duration is the 'continuous progress of the past which gnaws into the future and which swells as it advances (60) ... pure duration, of which the flow is continuous and in which we pass insensibly from one state to another ... [is] ... a continuity which is really lived' (Bergson 1991: 186). This is a continuity which 'is really lived', and which also characterises objects within phenomenal experience, including objects that are works of art. The work of art is an existent 'undergoing change every moment' within the flow of duration whilst it is being made. After it is made, as a *work*, in the Lukácsian sense of that term, it retains a relative constancy that is different *in kind* (to use Bergson's terminology) from whatever relative constancy can be attributed to lived experience; and, as will be argued later, that constancy – on the part of both work and consciousness – may, or may not, contribute towards the authentic requirements of consciousness.

Whilst, as argued, Lukács's stance largely dispenses with a romantic fixation on the psychological authorial aspect of the creative process in order to focus on the phenomenology of the work of art as autonomous (bounded) and non-autonomous (unbounded) existent, he, nevertheless, still wants to insist on a role for the artist because the artist is an uncommon individual, potentially able to 'transcend the inadequacy, fragility and transience of actual experience', not in a romantic sense of voicing personal subjective 'vision', but in the more *constructive* sense of bringing transient and exiguous experience into an ordered unity of meaning, and then aligning that unity with the developing forms of the work, so that a 'harmony' of the two is established, albeit one in which (and as will be discussed later) the final form of the work ultimately transcends the activity of the artist and leaves the artist behind (Lukács 1972: 317). Other individuals, including artisans of various sorts, may make 'works' of a sort, but those individuals are not required to have and may not possess the latent 'transcendent' ability that the artist is capable of possessing, and the works they make are not required to have and may not possess, or evoke, such transcendence. Although they do possess the emanation of signification that spreads from the work into the ongoing stream of becoming within the *Lebenswelt*, such emanation will not be as meaningful as that emerging from the genuine work of art, and, in fact, in Lukácsian terms, such efforts do not amount to genuine 'works' at all. As in *Soul and Form*, in which the term 'form' is deployed, in the 'Phenomenology' essay, the term 'work' stands for authentic and meaningful praxis.

As suggested, Lukács conceives of the artist in a phenomenological sense, as an individual who brings disordered experience into favourable arrangement, and then orients that with the incorporations generated by the evolving forms of the work. Totality does not reside within the Platonist Great Kinds of Forms, but arrives in the world as the result of a process of shaping that takes place within phenomenal experience; and this also means that there is no *soul* to be embodied in the work of art, in the sense of the immutable a-temporal essence conjured in *Soul and Form*, only a certain superior understanding or interpretation of reality. One can, none the less, see the origins of this conception of the artist as someone who puts disorder into order developing in certain sections of *Soul and Form*. When, for example, Lukács discusses Goethe, in an essay on Novalis, originally written in 1908, he argues that 'Goethe alone achieved it' [order] [although faced with] 'an anarchy of instincts, a triviality that lost itself in a welter of moods and details . . . His conquests were of such a kind that newly discovered deserts turned into gardens' (Lukács 1974: 43–4). This is, essentially, the non-psychological, 'constructivist' concept of authorship that appears in the 'Phenomenology' essay of 1914. However, this does not equate to the notion of soul, and, in fact, the term 'soul' does not appear in 'Phenomenology'. That term *did* have a romantic aspect, linked to the 'romantic anti-capitalism' that influenced Lukács when he was putting together the various editions of *Soul and Form*. It seems, therefore, that the move into phenomenology has led Lukács to adopt a less potent, more pragmatic and lower-key position over authorship, and one in which, as will be seen, the work, eventually, even becomes entirely separate from the source of authorship.

In addition to such fashioning of experience, the artist is also charged with the realisation of a 'hidden goal', one which underlies both that fashioning, and other aspects of authorial intentionality. Lukács argues that the artist must attempt to find an adequate aesthetic form for the ordering of 'lived experience', an experience that is, after all, 'independent of [the work of] art and has its own existence'. Lived experience is categorically different from aesthetic form, and it is this difference that is the source of the problematic of finding the right form to fit the existential order fashioned – at this point immaterially – by the artist. What is 'hidden' here is that latent form, which lies undesignated and unestablished before it is brought into being (Lukács 1972: 315).[3] There is a genus of reference to the Platonist Great Forms here, in the sense that aesthetic form is conceived of as existing in some latent non-material state, waiting to materialise in order to make experience manifest itself appropriately; and this is, essentially, also the same way of thinking as that which appears in *Soul and Form*, in which the purpose of form is to express soul in an adequate manner. In both cases, aesthetic form is determined by the need to depict existential content. As claimed, however, Lukács makes no recourse to metaphysical or meta-phenomenal notions of soul and form in 'Phenomenology' and does not define significant 'lived experience' in any essentialist fashion.

It is also no easy matter to find this hidden form, because the existential order fashioned by the artist's imagination is, as argued, categorically different from the assemblage of forms that might encapsulate it and eventually appear in the work; the lived experience of the artist, which occurs within the ever-continuing phenomenal world, and partakes of the interactive and indeterminate character of that world, cannot be encapsulated easily within a bounded work that is necessarily 'inadequate to the transmission and mediation' of its changeful nature (314). It is, then, the bounded aspect of the work which acts as a barrier to the transmission of unbounded lived experience into the work, and which makes the realisation of the 'hidden goal' a difficult one. The hidden goal of appropriate form is elusive because it must bind together in some fashion that which is innately unbound, and because it is also impinged upon by the developing forms of the work, which organise form in relation to the formal requirements of the work, rather than in relation to any obligation to embody existential content. Lukács's turn to phenomenology has, to an extent, created a greater barrier to the substantive realisation of soul than was apparent in *Soul and Form*. In that work, this barrier was erected by virtue of 'objectivations' and 'empirical life', but the 'great objectivations' were still able to overcome that impediment to a significant extent. Nevertheless, whilst, in 'Phenomenology', even the great objectivations are now strongly impinged upon by the objectification that constitutes the final work of art, Lukács's conception of the 'work', as opposed to aesthetic *object*, encompasses the relatively unbounded process of bringing the work of art to fruition, and, also, the insertion of that within the field of ongoing connotation; and this ensures both the ongoing indeterminacy of the aesthetic, and the enduring possibility of the realisation of soul. The change, here, is from the difficulty involved in realising an a-temporal metaphysical archetype within objectification, to the difficulty involved in realising existential experience within objectification: a change which implies a move from Platonist essentialism to the phenomenological quotidian.

There is also another sense in which Lukács's concerns here differ from those expressed in *Soul and Form*. It was argued in the previous chapter of this book that a synthesis of Aristotelian and Platonist thought can be found in the pages of *Soul and Form*, and that Lukács has taken the empirical Aristotelian distinction between matter and form, where matter means basic content, and form means shaping principle, and endowed that distinction with a metaphysical dimension derived from the Platonist Theory of Forms, in which essential form and essential content co-exist within an a-temporal metaphysical domain. For Lukács, and as argued in the previous chapter of this book, as a general metaphysical principle, the purpose of the principle of form is to enable the metaphysical principle of soul to come into being (Goldmann 1972: 130). In *Soul and Form*, Lukács's conception of form as a principle that enables the correlated principle of soul to become manifest is analogous to Aristotle's materialist conception of form as that which enables matter to become manifest within material substance. However, Lukács sets aside Aristotelian materialism in order to trace the principles of Aristotelian matter and form within a metaphysical, Platonist domain, where matter, in a non-Aristotelian manner, becomes the content of transcendent soul, and form becomes the principle of potential manifestation of that content, and where, in the phenomenal world, instances of soul are then given particular material form. Because of this, there is no strong sense within *Soul and Form* of soul requiring the *right*, or the *one* form, no sense of a need to realise the *particularised* 'hidden goal' referred to in the previous paragraph; but, rather, there is a sense that there is transcendent soul and form and phenomenally realised soul and form, and that phenomenal renderings of soul can be realised in a range of forms. In 'Phenomenology', however, Lukács turns back to an Aristotelian modality of form and content, where content, as lived experience, *must* be shaped into the right form; this is the 'hidden goal'. As with Aristotle, form is now a shaping principle that figures content into what Aristotle calls 'substance', but which Lukács (analogously) calls the 'work'; and, also as with Aristotle, the two require each other in order to come into being as the work/substance (Guthrie 1967: 129). In 'Phenomenology', and in line with phenomenological methodology, therefore, Lukács adopts a more particularised perspective.

In 'Phenomenology', Lukács uses the phrases 'lived experience' and 'adequate aesthetic form' in what he takes to be a 'phenomenological' sense: 'we are dealing with phenomenological, and not psychological characteristics of the creative process' (Lukács 1972: 315). The artist fashions transient lived experience into an imaginative order that possesses existential meaning: into what, in *Soul and Form*, Lukács referred to as 'non-objectified form', and which, in 'Phenomenology', refers to an internalised pre-configuration of content, one which has yet to be given form. The artist then attempts to find an appropriate 'objectified form' for that (although the phrases non-objectified and objectified form do not appear in 'Phenomenology', they will be used here occasionally, as they are instructive). Returning, also, to another notion that appears in *Soul and Form*, that of the two domains of the soul, discussed in the previous chapter of this book, and which, in the later *The Specificity of the Aesthetic*, are redesignated as 'being' (*Wesen*) and 'appearance' (*Erscheinung*) (and, although these terms do not appear in 'Phenomenology' either, they will sometimes be used here because they are also instructive) (Aitken 2012: 88); we can imagine (because this follows from Lukács's general stance during the period) that the artist's 'experience', when organised into non-objectified form, consists of both a sense of human meaningfulness (being) and more empirical awareness of material reality, including the phenomenal world (appearance). This is then shaped into objectified form within the work. Such shaping must also adhere to the 'hidden goal' previously referred to, of finding the right form for that experience. In this scenario, therefore, it is the organised lived experience of the artist that initiates the work and determines the form of the work; and such determination is, therefore, based on a fusion of experience, and form that is directed by experience.

As indicated, however, Lukács's new phenomenological orientation none the less also points to an alternate scenario, one in which aesthetic form is not primarily developed within the work in order to embody the experience of the artist, but in order to endow the work progressively with its own 'self-enclosed existence' (Lukács 1972: 315). Here, within this phenomenological perspective, the work of art, as entity, seeks to realise its own amalgam of being and appearance, rather than perform as a vehicle for that of the artist, whose will-toward-the-work, must, as argued, always be made ambiguous anyway by the striving into existence of the work towards its own immanence. In this scenario the work creates a potential chasm at the phenomenological heart of the creative process and contributes to the continuing subjugation of mankind by and within the world of objects. Influenced, perhaps, by his newly consummated detachment from Platonist essentialist dichotomies, and, as mentioned previously in this chapter, Lukács, none the less, prefers to view this opposition between consciousness and the work more as an associated opposition rather than unbridgeable chasm, and even in terms of a productive fusion between the will-toward-the-work of the artist and the will-toward-the-work of the work of art, in which both play a required role within the overall process of rendering soul into form, as follows (315).

At the beginning of the process there is the involvement of the artist, charged with portraying the experience of *Wesen* and *Erscheinung*. To do so, the artist must possess 'experience-evoking powers'. First, the artist must possess the power to fashion the experience of *Wesen* and *Erscheinung* into a significant non-objectified disposition: an *order*, as previously argued, one distilled from the 'anarchy of instincts', 'moods and details' that make up lived experience

(Lukács 1974: 43–4). Second, the artist must possess the power, inherent in the will-toward-the-work, to embody that experience within aesthetic form. As the process of creative activity evolves, the artist applies their experience-evoking powers based on their experience, their will and organisation of artistic technique, in order to find an aesthetic form (the 'hidden goal') adequate to that experience. As this process continues, however, the work of art increasingly develops its own autonomy and immanence. There is also the issue, referred to earlier, that the progressively 'bounded' character of the work is incapable of containing the unbounded character of lived experience, leading to the further 'self-enclosed existence' of the work (Lukács 1972: 315). Lukács, therefore, imagines a struggle taking place between the experience-evoking powers of the artist, powers that are intent upon realising the work as that which is dependent upon that experience, and the innate 'abstractly formal' experience-evoking powers of the work, powers that are intent on realising the work as that which is 'dependent on nothing but the immanent relations of its elements' (314). Nevertheless, the dialectic that Lukács imagines taking place here between artist and work does not remain in equilibrium as the creative process continues, and as the work of art progressively takes on what will become its terminal form.

Lukács makes a distinction between three scenarios in this respect, one inevitable, the other two conflicting, and possible. The unavoidable scenario is that the work will ultimately become autonomous of the artist. The possible scenarios are that the autonomous work of art *will*, or *will not*, emerge as an ensouled aesthetic unity of experience-evoking and abstract-formal powers, one in which *Wesen* and *Erscheinung* are realised within a significant objectification. The 'abstractly formal', experience-evoking powers of the work always hold an innate ability to render existential experience; otherwise there would be no reason to bring the work of art into the world of being in the first place. And, although those powers are mainly directed at the realisation of the principal objectives of the work – to achieve a coherence and autonomy as a phenomenological thing-in-itself – what Lukács refers to as the 'great objectivations' are able to transcend such systemic formalism and become the soul of form. Accordingly, in 'Phenomenology', the 'tragic vision' (Goldmann 1967: 169) that characterises Lukács's thought in *Soul and Form* is qualified to an extent by this posited possibility of achieving an effective portrayal of *Wesen* and *Erscheinung* in the object; and this qualification is also then taken further through recourse to a rather Bergsonian phenomenological term, that of 'intensity'.

As the first chapter of this book outlined, for Bergson, states of consciousness are qualitative and temporal, rather than quantitative and spatial. As such, they are 'intensive', rather than 'extensive'. An intensity is a qualitative state of consciousness existing in time which is caused by something quantitative existing in space, and, that being so, the intensity is a 'sign of the quantity' that caused it; 'we suspect the presence of the latter behind the former' (Bergson 2015b: 224). Following Bergson, Lukács interprets the notion of intensity in the sense of a state of consciousness caused by something in the extended world, but he diverges from Bergson in interpreting the notion mainly in terms of conscious reaction to experience in general, and, in particular, a reaction that can vary in intensity. Unlike Bergson, he also interprets the term in its sense of indicating an *intense* reaction. Bergson talked about a range of conscious states growing in intensity. For example, the sense of 'joy' begins with a hopeful turning to a future 'pregnant with an infinity of possibilities', whilst, with 'extreme joy, our perceptions and memories become tinged with an indefinable quality, as with a kind of heat or light', and we experience an overall impression of joyful accomplishment (10). By intensity, however, Lukács mainly means a powerful intensity, as in Bergson's formulation of the experience of extreme joy, and this is linked to the distinction he makes between 'ordinary' and 'real' life in *Soul and Form*, and which is restated in 'Phenomenology': a distinction in which real life is lived intensely. By intensity, Lukács also refers to the artist possessing an intense impression about the experience of the world, and not about the artist, as in a romantic disposition. Lukács's phenomenological realism is projected outwards to the world, rather than inwards to the psyche. It is also this intensity, drawn from the lived experience of the artist, which finds a place in the work, thereby achieving a relatively effectual portrayal of *Wesen* and *Erscheinung*, albeit one that is still mediated by the abstractly formal orientation of the work.

Nevertheless, that effectuality is also mediated by another, additional factor, one related to representation, and, here, Lukács also takes another notion from Bergson: the idea that, when intensity is transferred from consciousness to a representational form, an attenuation of intensity necessarily occurs. According to Bergson, 'a deep-seated feeling is nothing else than the feeling itself', but when an *account* of that feeling is given, as in a work of art, the primal feeling is both transformed and diminished: 'if I try to give you an account of this psychic state, I shall be unable to make you realise its intensity except by some definite sign', a sign that, moreover, necessarily moderates the original (185). A state of consciousness is a primal exclusive entity and cannot be transferred to something else as it is. It is also in this same sense of felt feeling caused by a context that then becomes diminished through the act of transference and representation that Lukács employs the notion of intensity. Lukács says that the experience-evoking will of the artist is directed at the work in the hope that there will be 'the strongest intensive and extensive effect' made upon the work: in other words, that the work will come to realise both the initial intense emotion, and the 'extensive' forms appropriate to such realisation (Lukács 1972: 315). But he then goes on to argue that the forms mediate this intensity, and, in this process, the intensity is lessened, and, accordingly, becomes 'less adequate in content' (316).[4] It is, consequently, not only the powers inherent to the work that attenuates the will-toward-the-work, or what, in *Soul and Form*, Lukács calls 'real life' and 'soul', but also representation itself, and, here, Lukács returns to the idea of general 'objectification' (*Vergegenständlichung*) that he inherited from Simmel; the dialectic which Lukács posits in 'Phenomenology', between the ability of the work both to advance and to restrain the will-toward-the-work, is similar to Simmel's contention that 'the world of objectification is culture and culture is the development of the human essence', and also his conflictual view that objectification, as a materiality distinct from consciousness, may take on an autonomy that may eventually diverge from the authentic needs of consciousness (Arato 1971: 129).

As we have seen, Lukács, argues that, for experience-evoking power to have a powerful effect, to affect the work intensely, it must presuppose an initial vibrant intensity within the consciousness of experience of the artist. However, and in a difficult formulation, he also posits the existence of 'such an intensity in the – immanent – emotional essence of the forms themselves' (Lukács 1972: 316). The forms of the work, it seems, possess, within themselves, an emotional essence which generates intensity, or is intensity, so that, as the work develops, its inner evolving logic, partly driven by that emotional essence, as well as by the will-to-the-work of the artist, expresses such intensity. It is important to remember that Lukács is primarily concerned with the relationship between the world, the artist and the work of art. Nevertheless, a theory of spectatorship is also apparent here, partly related to the notion of aesthetic ambiguity as that which enables *different* spectatorships, but mainly, and although never explicitly articulated, based around an inter-subjective model of spectatorship that may be derived from and is fully compatible with phenomenology, and in which, for both Bergson and Husserl, there is a necessary common widespread agreement on what many things mean and are. This, for example, is the basis of Husserl's notion of the 'natural attitude': what is given in experience is generally assumed to be true and real, and we have various beliefs about aspects of experience that we ordinarily take to be true or untrue, so that 'to live' 'is always to live-in-certainty-of-the-world' (Husserl 1970: 142). At a basic level, without such certainty, the world would not make sense. This is also the basis of Bergson's contention that 'For common sense, then, the object exists in itself' (Bergson 1991: 10). Spectatorship may be a matter of individual consciousness, therefore, but such individual consciousness is, in general, in agreement with that of other individual consciousnesses. If that were not the case, then, amongst other matters, cinematic spectatorship, one based on projection in front of an audience, would not be possible.

This approach to spectatorship allows Lukács to assume that the meaning of the work, though containing ambiguity, will nevertheless be widely understood. As a 'work', for example, a performance of *Oedipus Rex* has its own coherence, and cannot just be interpreted in any way whatever. Understood in this way, the 'immanent emotional essence' of *Oedipus Rex*, the essence that stems from the interior of the work, that which is immanent within the work, as the work is experienced, is an intense emotionality that is derived from the perceived central coherences of the work, coherences that are actively looked for by an audience seeking accustomed knowledge; and, as a consequence, the relation of that to the will-toward-the-work of Sophocles becomes largely irrelevant. Sophocles may well have sought to express his consciousness of experience of life in ancient Athenian society, or Theban society, or of the mythical story of Oedipus; but that no longer matters. In the same way, in a film such as *The Rules of the Game*, Jean Renoir may have sought to express his consciousness of experience of France's descent into war in 1939, but that also no longer matters, and what does matter are the immanent emotional essences that stem from the central coherences of the work, and the way that those are perceived by an audience actively looking for those. Lukács presumes that, in aesthetic experience, the engagement with accustomed coherence is more important than the experience of novelty. Lukács's phenomenological stance rules out a romantic conception of authorship, and, indeed, marginalises the notion of authorship itself: it is the work that matters. However, that stance also relegates conceptions of the aesthetic based on notions of originality and innovation: conceptions often thought of as central to the aesthetic. In everyday existence, and engagement with art, it is familiarity, and present *knowledge*, rather than the new, that is the more important.

There are, therefore, at least ten core parts to Lukács's phenomenology of the aesthetic process, which take place in a chronological order: (1) world, (2) artist, (3) lived experience of the world by the artist, (4) interior ordering of that by the artist, (5) will-toward-the-work of the artist, (6) evolution of abstract-formal forms of the work, (7) will-toward-the-work of the forms, (8) role of the innate emotional essence of the forms, (9) an inter-subjective conception of meaning and spectatorship, and, (10) final work of art. There is also a division here between 1–5 and 6–10, indicating a progressive separation of work from artist. Given all this, and if intensity is conceived of as a qualitative state of consciousness, then the relation between world and artist becomes clearer: experience of the world is the source of the qualitative state of intensity that appears within the overall consciousness of the artist, and, although, as it appears, that is mediated through the biography, psyche and body of the artist, it is, nevertheless, the primal relation of intensity to source that is of the greater consequence. The objective is then to express that mediated intensity within the forms of the work. This will, in turn, be further mediated by the abstract-formal imperatives of those forms, some of which take the shape of immanent emotional essence. This also suggests two possible scenarios. One is that, as the work evolves, the intrinsic emotional essence of the work becomes 'ensouled' to a substantial extent, because it is pervaded by the intensity reaching it from the artist. The other is that it becomes less ensouled because it resists and transforms the intensity reaching it from the artist. In either case, however, in the process of objectification, the process of transfer of personally experienced intensity *into* the work, a diminution of initial intensity takes place. What is lost, therefore, is the primal relation between consciousness and experience of the *Lebenswelt* – a *Lebenswelt* characterised by indeterminacy – and this means that any determinate non-objectified or objectified shaping of that which takes place already constitutes a departure from the primal reality.

Even given the diminution of the primal relation that takes place when that relation appears within the consciousness of the artist, Lukács, nevertheless, wishes, as previously argued, and under the influence of Simmel's concept of objectification, to retain an important role for the artist vis-à-vis the work; and this leads him to argue that, within the work, the formal-evoking powers of the work cannot take over completely from the experience-evoking powers of the artist. Although, in terms of the formal-evoking powers, intensity arises from the internal relations of the work, the representation of experience-evoking intensities is initiated by the artist, not the work; and the artist also remains an active participant in the creation of the work until it is complete. This leads Lukács to draw a distinction between the 'fulfilled or realised formal', and 'abstractly formal' (Lukács 1972: 316). The fulfilled or realised formal refers to the presupposition of an initial intensity related to the experience of the artist which is then represented (fulfilled–realised) as intensity in the formal substance of the work, and, here, the forms mediate that intensity whilst still preserving much of the initial identity. The intensity originating from the artist is fulfilled formally: its beginning finds completion, albeit a mediated one, within the forms of the work. The phrase 'abstractly formal', on the other hand, refers to the previously mentioned innate capacity for the portrayal of intensity that is present within the forms of the work. The intention of the fulfilled–realised formal, an intention external to the work, is to represent intensities in relation to the experience-evoking powers of the artist. The abstract–formal can facilitate this but may also frustrate it by acting in accordance with the needs of the work, although, and as mentioned, this cannot entirely be the case.

Lukács also argues that the powers of the abstract–formal are offset by something in the very nature of aesthetic form: the fact that its principal function is neither to portray the experience-evoking powers of the artist, nor to manifest its own immanence, but, and in a more general realist sense, to convey a content that must initially come from outside the work, and from the primal relation. Lukács views this as a general, realist and phenomenological aesthetic principle, and one which both mediates the tendency of the forms of the work to develop in line with their own interior imperatives, and plays a role in limiting a will-toward-the-work of the artist that is psychologically impelled, and imperfect as consequence. Given this realist phenomenological orientation, a conjectured 'part II' of the 'hidden goal' referred to earlier can be considered. Part I of the hidden goal, it will be recalled, was for the artist to find the appropriate formal representation for the artist's experience. Part II of the hidden goal might be for the artist to achieve a rapprochement, a '*harmonia praestablita*', as Lukács puts it, between the appropriate formal representation of that experience, and the evolving forms of the work, in such a way that the work develops in accord with the general phenomenological principle of constantly attempting to convey what is outside, including that which is outside the direct experience of the artist (317). An artist who can achieve *that*, who can intuit what lies beyond their own experience, and somehow place that alongside their will and the forms, would probably produce a great work of art. In *The Rules of the Game*, for example, there is a sense that the film captures a variety, complexity, density and indistinctness that have their origins in the experienced world of the time, and which extend beyond Renoir's intentionality and the determining structures of the work. The value of this film lies, ultimately, in the quality of its depiction of the manifold. The 'immanent emotional essence' of the film, that which is derived from the central coherences of the work, has its roots in that depiction. A similar point is also made by Siegfried Kracauer, in a piece which will be considered in Chapter 10 of this book. Kracauer compares a historian's rectilinear account of life in Weimar Germany with his own experience of the period as one full of 'fluctuating opinions, agonising doubts and spontaneous decisions' which should not be turned into a 'rigid historical account' because experiences 'slip through the net of the concepts and labels' (Kracauer 1995b: 86–7). Lukács's 'general aesthetic phenomenological principle would seek to recover such fluctuating, spontaneous experiences.

Related to this, and, like Bergson, Lukács also wishes to make a clear distinction between the 'psychological' and 'phenomenological'. For Bergson, psychology, in focusing on what consciousness does for practical purposes, divides consciousness into 'clearly characterised states' (Bergson 2015a: 139). Consciousness, is, however, always of phenomenal experience, and is fluid and undividable: 'the deep-seated conscious states . . . are pure quality; they intermingle in such a way that we cannot tell whether they are one or several' (137). As cited in Chapter 1 of this book, Bergson uses the term 'multiplicity' to describe this condition, and Lukács's conception of the way that aesthetic form *should* function resonates with this. For Lukács, the external content that aesthetic form must convey may arrive through the conduit of the artist, but the artist is, as argued, embedded within a multiplicity of content-generating contexts that spread beyond her or him.

And yet, despite the phenomenological orientation just set out, at least near the beginning of the 'Phenomenology' essay, there is also a residue of Platonism: a rearticulation of the foundational terms of soul and form found in Lukács's earlier writings, but one that is also, at the end of 'Phenomenology', eventually given a distinctly non-Platonist and rather Aristotelian orientation. At a general level, the relation between external content and aesthetic form set out in 'Phenomenology' is analogically comparable to the relation between the metaphysical principles of soul and form in *Soul and Form*; one in which the overarching purpose of form is to convey soul. In 'Phenomenology', Lukács dispenses with the metaphysical but retains the general principle, and then, finally, gives it a phenomenological bearing: the purpose of aesthetic form is not to convey 'soul', but, instead, a significant field of content within the phenomenal world which flows towards the artist and is channelled by that artist into the work, where it is met by the forms. The metaphysical Platonist aspects of *Soul and Form* have been exchanged for a less abstruse Aristotelian model of phenomenal appearance in the world; matter and form produce an outcome, substance, just as significant external content and aesthetic form produce an outcome, the work.

Lukács closes his account of aesthetic phenomenology with a consideration of distinctions between ethics, logic and aesthetics; and a related distinction between universalism and empiricism, which he also associates with one between Platonism and Aristotelianism/phenomenology. As previously argued, Lukács's phenomenological approach to art in this essay conceives of the work of art as a thing-in-itself, eventually separated from the artist who made it, so that the work eventually even stands 'at an unreachable height above its creator' (Lukács 1972: 322). The work of art, as inter-subjectively understood 'work', with its own central coherences and immanent emotional essences and configurations, is experienced, within a state of consciousness, as an entity. Lukács, nevertheless, views this separation of artist from work in terms of a 'productive subject' (the artist) beneath a 'value', the value being the work. The value here, however, also has a material dimension, and so is a phenomenological 'fact' (321), and this marks a distinction between the work of art as value, and value within the fields of logic and ethics. In other words, the work of art is an objectification (although, and as will be argued shortly, it is not only an objectivation and has an immaterial dimension). Lukács, for example, and in a clear reference towards Platonist metaphysical essentialism, argues that 'in logic or ethics . . . the subject submits himself to eternal norms . . . seeking to come close to them' (322–3). In ethics and logic, the 'value', the 'eternal norm', is a universal 'which stands above the subject [and] can never be totally achieved' (323).

Such lack of attainment is, notwithstanding, unimportant in the end, because what matters – Lukács adopts a more phenomenological or Aristotelian posture now – is the will to realisation and the consequence of that in the material world: 'man has the duty to realise that which is above him, but with this willing, the duty is fulfilled'. Such 'willing' cannot take place without attendant consequence, and so the *true* 'ethical sphere' does not really include 'that which is above', but the act of will and its materialisations which occur in the phenomenal world 'below' (323). In both logic and ethics, therefore, 'it can only be a matter of an unending process of approach' towards the value, which exists in a noumenal Platonist sense, and cannot be fully realised. In fact, when the latter is, mistakenly, sought, 'the subject does not [attempt to] attain it as a [human] subject any more', but as some illusory superhuman entity. Instead of such 'beholding of archetypes', the 'logic of spontaneous thinking' should acknowledge concepts such as 'new' and 'development', which 'occur in the sphere of approach' to the subject-matter in the world, and, when this occurs, the subject does not merely 'behold' but also 'realise[s] . . . value' (323).

Lukács then goes on to argue that 'value realisation' in aesthetics is 'the diametrical opposite' to such realisation in ethics and logic (324). In aesthetics, the 'value' does not hover above the work of art in an unreachable Platonist sense. The value *is* the work, and exists only when the work of art is realised: 'the aesthetic value, the work of art, originates only in, through, and with the process of its realisation' (324). In this phenomenological stance, there is nothing to behold beyond the work of art, and, that being the case, any 'eternal laws' that can be imagined only exist as they are made material in the work of art: 'the eternal laws, whose fulfilment makes the work a work, have no possibility of existence separable from their fulfilment' (324). Seeking for such laws would also be misplaced, because that would depart from the immediacy of the encounter with the work. Works of art also appear as *individual* fulfilments, each different from the other, each an autonomous realised 'value', and there is a similarity here with Bergson's account of states of consciousness, each of which is qualitatively different from the other (see Chapter 1).

Because works of art are different from each other, the transcendent 'ought' that exists in ethics does not apply, and, in aesthetics, this 'ought' 'is not fixed and unattainable but something necessarily fulfilled. It is also *because* each work of art is different from all other works of art that it possesses aesthetic value. Aesthetic value consists of difference, singularity and heterogeneity in objectification: in the *is*, and not in the transcendental normative 'ought' of ethics. Lukács concludes his essay by arguing not only that each work of art is 'new', but that it is a 'new form of being' which 'transcends' the creative process that brought it into being, although that process remains inside the '*Problematik*' of the work (324). In other words, the work of art not only is the fulfilment of the creative process but also contains the genesis of that process and its unique problematic (this, again, can be related to Bergsonian notions of the past persisting within the present).

Lukács's conception of the 'work' is, accordingly, a composite one. As a new form of being, the work is an objectification that exists in the world, and this means that it is a particularity, and that aesthetic value is based in its singularity and 'immediacy' of experience (324). On the other hand, the work of art as unique objectification also has its own unique 'problematic', conceived of in somewhat Bergsonian terms as an aura of 'multiplicity' in which, to use Bergson's terminology, a *'confused* . . . multiplicity' of meanings is generated (Bergson 2015a: 73). The work of art can, consequently, be regarded as a concrete multiplicity and union of concrete and abstract. As a *concrete* multiplicity, the work of art is also responsible for the 'super-personal tragedy of the artist', who becomes separated from the work that the artist creates: 'My works are nearer heaven, but I sit here' (Lukács 1972: 235). Notwithstanding such loss, however, Lukács remains more sanguine than he was in *Soul and Form*. The work of art may be the product of a struggle between objectification and human meaning, but it is a product in which human meaning remains, as the 'experience' and 'will' of the artist secures a place within the work. Lukács may conclude the essay with a note concerning the 'tragedy' of the artist, but the notion that the work of art not only is the fulfilment of the creative process but also contains the genesis of that process carries greater weight in relation to the idea that the will of the artist remains in the work. Lukács does not give up Plato and Kant entirely (as he does after 1917), but the influence of phenomenology now directs him towards issues related to temporality, and the forms of appearance that he will explore in relation to film in 'Thoughts towards an Aesthetic of the Cinema'.

NOTES

1. For a fuller definition of the notion of 'object' see the Introduction to this book, in which object is defined as 'entity', rather than physical object.
2. See Chapter 6 of this book, on Husserl's conception of the *Lebenswelt*.
3. The notion of finding the form adequate to the experience, or what Lukács would later call 'content', was to become a key notion for Lukács from 1917 onwards, and would shape his understanding of realism, naturalism and modernism, an understanding in which all form that was not appropriate to express content would be ruled out as largely irrelevant.
4. I have been unable to acquire 'Phenomenology' in the original German. The translation I have before me, by Glenn Odenbrett, reads 'the mediation of intensities, which, because of this mediation, become inadequate in content and are gradually falsified'. However, terms such as 'inadequate' and 'falsified' appear to be too strong when related to what Lukács says elsewhere in 'Phenomenology'. As a consequence, I have amended this quotation as it appears.

CHAPTER 4

'Thoughts towards an Aesthetic of the Cinema' (Lukács 1913)

'Thoughts towards an Aesthetic of the Cinema' ('Thoughts') was originally published in Hungary in a German-language newspaper in 1911, and was then republished on 10 September 1913, on the front page of the *Frankfurter Zeitung und Handelsblatt* newspaper. It is the 1913 publication that is discussed here.[1] It is almost certain that Lukács began writing 'Thoughts' after he had completed the essays which eventually appeared in *Soul and Form*, and it is clear that temporality has now become an increasing concern, as, in 'Thoughts', many of the themes found in *Soul and Form* are fixed more plainly on the experience and representation of temporality. Although primarily concerned with film, 'Thoughts' also carries on Lukács's preoccupation with classical Greek theatre, and the discussion of film in the piece is framed by that preoccupation. This chapter will, consequently, begin with Lukács's consideration of the theatre.

THEATRE

Lukács speaks about art in a broad-spectrum manner in 'On the Phenomenology of the Creative Process' ('Phenomenology'), and without referring to any specific artistic medium, because he is concerned with the common phenomenology of the creative process. In 'Thoughts', however, he is preoccupied with two artistic mediums: theatre and film, and the relationship between the two. Lukács begins 'Thoughts' with an opening section on the theatre, and by returning to one of the themes explored in 'Phenomenology': the notion of the 'will-toward-the-work'.[2] So, for example, when describing what he feels is fundamental about the theatre in 'Thoughts', he asserts that 'the basis of theatric effect rests . . . in the power of a human being, in the living will of a living human being' (Lukács, in Aitken 2012: 181). In 'Phenomenology' Lukács argues that this living will towards the work eventually meets a tragic fate, as the completed work divorces itself from the artist and their will (Lukács 1972: 325). Although there is a degree of inconsistency here, in that Lukács also attests that the work of art is not only the fulfilment of the creative process but also contains the genesis of that process, implying that the will of the artist remains within the work to an extent, it is in general the case that, in 'Phenomenology', Lukács tends to emphasise a dichotomy between will and work (324). This is true of all the arts: *Oedipus Rex* of Sophocles is profoundly detached from its author, just as the *Mona Lisa* of Leonardo da Vinci, possibly the best-known work of art in history, is disconnected from its author. In both cases, however, the 'living will' of the artist persists as part of the embedded genesis of the creative process: a persistence informed by knowledge and experience brought to bear in the act of viewing. In this sense, also, the living will is somehow *in* the painting.

In the classical tragedy, however, there are at least two principal living wills. First, in *Oedipus Rex*, there is the living will of Sophocles, and, second, there is the living will of the actor playing Oedipus, and it is the latter that is important for Lukács. That living will is directly present and does not become divorced from the work because the performance is the work. Of course, any encounter with a work of art is a presentational, phenomenal experience, whether that be reading a book, or watching a film. Lukács's point is that, in the theatre, that presentational experience involves encounter with a 'living human being'. This may also apply to arts such as, for example, dance; but Lukács does not bring this issue up. Instead, he focuses on the presentational experience of the drama, in which the living will of the actor is accentuated and engaged with by an animate audience: 'the living will of a living human being, which radiates out unmediated and without impediment, onto a correspondingly living assemblage' (Lukács, in Aitken 2012: 181). For Lukács, therefore, drama is realistic, because, as in everyday experience, an existent encounters another existent; but drama must also rise above this realist foundation to distil the essence of such an encounter. In 'Phenomenology', Lukács sets out a composite model of the work of art, one in which an art object was associated with an immaterial aura of signification which encompassed the central coherences and 'immanent emotional essence' of the work as experienced within a presentational experience (Lukács 1972: 316). In 'Thoughts', written around the same time as 'Phenomenology', Lukács retains this broader notion of the work in relation to the theatrical performance, but adds the more specific aesthetic dimension of the presentational experience as involving the relation between living human beings. In the classical theatre, therefore, the central coherences of the work are experienced as a relation between existents. In 'Thoughts', as in 'Phenomenology', the work manifests itself as ongoing process during the act of aesthetic experience long after the act of creation has come to an end;

and, in both pieces, Lukács is also concerned with the work, and its experience, rather than the artist who made the work. Lukács's notion of experience here is, none the less, essentially ubiquitous in character, and he does not focus on the make-up of the audience, perhaps involuntarily imagining himself to be the vessel of the 'living will' invoked.

Although the concern with process in the 'Phenomenology' essay implies something that takes place over the course of time, Lukács does not discuss time per se in the piece. In 'Thoughts', however, and under the influence of Bergson, temporality is at the forefront of his thinking, and this leads him to stress the fact that the theatrical enactment and act of spectatorship are processes that take place within time. The greater focus on temporality during that enactment and act also becomes more apparent when Lukács attests that the living will of the actor is linked to another attribute of the theatre: the 'absolute *present*'. Once more, the emphasis here is upon time, and the problems caused by the temporal flow, as the living will of the actor, whilst confined within the flow of time, nevertheless attempts to decelerate that flow in order to enlarge a sense of existence within the present moment (Lukács, in Aitken 2012: 181). The objective is to render the immaterial aura of signification which encompasses the central coherences and immanent emotional essence of the work as articulate as possible. Lukács's formulation of the absolute present is a gesture towards the 'great moments' which, in *Soul and Form*, were, seemingly, able to stand outside the flow of temporality, so that there was a 'sudden standing still in the midst of the continual change of ordinary life' (Lukács 1974: 158). As reasoned in Chapter 2 of this book, Lukács does not argue that an actual transcendence of temporality takes place, but that there is an attempt to come close to that without ever reaching it. In the drama, therefore, and following the general tenor of his thought in both 'Phenomenology' and 'Thoughts', the metaphysical domain cannot be reached, but proximity to it can be attempted as an imperative, to be achieved through the intensification of the experience of the moment (156–7) in order 'to come as close as possible to the timelessness of this moment' (158). Lukács adopts this perspective because he wants to endorse what he then considered to be the most important aesthetic medium: the classical drama. As he proceeds to develop his position in 'Thoughts' in relation to film, however, he progressively distances himself from that perspective.

This is made clear when Lukács insists, in 'Thoughts', that the 'absolute present' is a necessarily transient moment because it occurs – as it must – within the interminable flow of time. The union of will and work within the great moment has a 'transitory nature' (Lukács, in Aitken 2012: 181). The classical Greek drama strives to overcome this transient reality because such drama is ineluctably driven towards the prescient moment of destiny and the turning point of fate, and, in such drama, whilst the psychological perception that the absolute present persists (it cannot persist in a phenomenal sense), it remains the 'sensuous expression' and embodiment in time of tragic 'destiny'. That being so, the great moment in the drama can be said to possess this imperative psychological aspect, an aspect that also means that it is only the seeming-perception of the present that matters, whilst 'the past is merely a framework, in the metaphysical sense, something entirely without purpose . . . And in terms of destiny, the future is entirely unreal and meaningless' (181–2). In the great moment, the past is already a faded 'framework' that no longer matters, whilst the future is 'meaningless' because that future is marked by expiration: by 'death, which brings all tragedies to a close' (182). Nevertheless, because the absolute present is ultimately transitory, the psychological questions and answers evoked within that present must also constantly slip away, as time flows on. Lukács accepts this, but still insists upon the psychological imperative of the attempt to enact and experience the absolute present in the drama as much as possible: to present and experience the central coherences and immanent emotional essence of the work as articulately as possible. In the account of the tragic drama that opens 'Thoughts', therefore, and before turning to film, Lukács meditates upon the contradictory reality of temporality as consisting of both the absolute present and the flow of time, and, in doing so, he also seeks to endorse the drama as an aesthetically specific – although, as will be seen, also paradoxical – art form of the absolute present.

Lukács accepts that the absolute present can neither be attained in an absolute sense, nor held on to in a relative sense, and that the flow of temporality is, consequently, interminable. However, he also attempts to amend the consequence of this truth for the theatre by turning to the reality of phenomenal experience, and the 'fact' that existence takes place only within the phenomenal present moment; and, that being so, also within the psychological absolute present. Consequently, in his opening deliberations on the theatre Lukács attempts to elaborate a 'metaphysics' of the present moment that will act as a support for the notion of the moment of the absolute present, asserting that 'Through the becoming-present of the drama this metaphysical feeling becomes immensely augmented in immediacy and sensuousness: man's deepest truth and position in the universe appears as a self-evident reality' (182).

Here, Lukács combines the present moment and the absolute present of the great moment: it is, for him, a 'self-evident reality' that we can live to the maximum only in the instance of the present moment, and, as Lukács would have it, this also entails that the same is true of the 'becoming-present of the drama' in the absolute present. However, Lukács's attempt to elaborate a metaphysics of *both* the present moment and the absolute present is not a genuine one at this point, because he is still mainly interested in the latter, and with the psychological sense of time seeming to stop within the great moment, rather than the phenomenal experience of time passing through the present moment.

None the less, despite such adherence to the quasi-a-temporal and quasi-Platonist notion of the absolute present, Lukács's writing in 'Thoughts' increasingly engages with the idea of phenomenal experience, particularly the experience of temporality, as the influence of Bergson, and, especially, the key Bergsonian notion of the value of attendance to the present moment within the flow of time, becomes more evident. As described in Chapter 1 of this book, there is no 'present moment' as such, only a ceaseless transition from the 'not-yet' to the 'right-now' to the 'no-longer', with the 'right-now' being the 'moment' of utmost but yet still itinerant concreteness: 'To-be-present-right-now, the moment of *maximal presence*', is also '*the very moment of the transition*' from the present, and this 'constitute[s] the "passage" character that is the very essence of the "right-now"' (Bruzina 2000: 75–6). Lukács is fully aware of this passage character and accepts that the absolute present of the theatre cannot exist as any kind of present moment and cannot last. Nevertheless, he goes on to argue that this inevitable transitory aspect both endows the drama with a phenomenological integrity in relation to temporality and does not require an abandonment of the notion of the psychological great moment: 'The stage is the absolute present. The transitory nature of its achievements is not a regrettable weakness . . . it is the necessary correlate and sensuous expression of destiny in the drama' (Lukács, in Aitken 2012: 181).

The psychological absolute present is part of the phenomenal world and depends upon a sensuous expression that, whilst appearing to halt the flow of time, is also inevitably marked by a transitory temporality, and the 'necessary correlation' here is between apparent presence and inescapable transience. For Lukács, the specific aesthetic character and mission of tragedy are founded upon this dialectic of a resonant present which is destined to collapse. Destiny *is* transient, as all things are; and such transience is as much a part of tragedy – or at least a substantial part – as are the psychological great moments in which it appears that the temporal flow is decelerated. Tragic classical drama may possess 'great moments' of the seeming absolute present, but 'destiny' in the drama appears at the finale of a *process*, and process implies change. The story of the drama is transitory in the sense that, in this art form, a process takes place that will inevitably lead to death, and the experience of the drama is also marked by this knowledge that, however great the moments enacted by the characters are, the doom of those characters is predestined. There is, therefore, a basis for theorising the co-existence of both the phenomenal present moment as involved in the passage character of time, and the psychological great moment as similarly involved, although, at this point in his essay, Lukács is still concerned more with the psychological great moment than the phenomenal present moment. Lukács, therefore, argues that this dialectic between the present moment that becomes the great moment, and the pull of the flow of time that brings an end to that great moment, is aesthetically specific to the drama (as argued, he does not mention other likely arts, such as dance). Already, however, we see a shift from an emphasis on stasis to one on process, and one which characterises the discussion of film in 'Thoughts'.

Given what has just been said, any coherent 'metaphysics' of the absolute present of tragedy imagined in 'Thoughts' would be required to account for both the psychological union of concrete and abstract that occurs within the experience of the absolute present and great moment, and the transitory phenomenal character of that union. Such a requirement is, as has been argued, implicit in Lukács's conception of 'destiny' in the drama as concentrated process. In general, Lukács does attempt to fulfil such a requirement in 'Thoughts', although, in the opening sections of the piece, he continues to give priority to the absolute present in order to define the aesthetic specificity of drama in relation to that of film, drama being more related to stasis, film to transience. Nevertheless, an example of the attempt to fulfil this two-fold imperative can be seen in the following quotation: 'The "present", the being-here of the actors, becomes fatefully evident, and, therefore, appears as the deepest expression of a human being in the drama who is at the mercy of fate' (182). There are two distinct parts to this quotation. First, and, once again, Lukács combines the notions of the absolute present and present moment. As in both *Soul and Form* and *The Theory of the Novel*, so in 'Thoughts', Lukács argues that the experience of the absolute present in the great moment is one related to human authenticity and vitality whilst – this is not implied directly in the above quotation, but characterises much of Lukács's writing of the time – the experience of change is more associated with inauthenticity and lack of liveliness. However, and second, the quotation also implies change of a more resonant timbre: the character – for example, Oedipus – is 'at the mercy of fate', and such mercy, or, more likely, lack of such, must occur at the end of a process of animated, not inconsequential change. Furthermore, if the great moment is at the *mercy* of a fatalistic temporality, then it is that temporal process, and not the great moment, which becomes the crucial determining factor. Whilst defending the drama, therefore, Lukács prepares the ground for an understanding of the importance of film.

FILM

Lukács begins his account of film by asserting that awareness of any present moment, and not just a great moment, is important. Authenticity is now defined phenomenologically, and is related to experience of the present, which is encountered within mindful attention to the unfolding moment: a moment that, Lukács now contends, lies at the core of our phenomenal existence. Lukács, therefore, now comes to value mindful existence within the present moment as an end-in-itself and related to a kind of reality; and this is different from the experience of the much rarer great moments that he lauds in *Soul and Form*, and at the beginning of 'Thoughts'. If any moment can now be phenomenologically significant, then the multiplicity of moments inevitably become more manifest and foregrounded than is the case with the much rarer number of great moments in the drama. The invocation of the authentic quotidian moment in its diversity also implies attention to the transitions between moments, because the quotidian, as experienced, is not only numerous, but also constantly changeable; and this phenomenal–temporal perspective of change impels the previously Neo-Platonist Lukács further in the direction of a concern with the transitory, and with a medium that is fully caught up in such transience, as he continues to explore key respects in which film is likely to be noticeably at odds with the drama.

In the experience of film, both the ubiquitous present moment and any imagined great moment are embedded within the special temporal flow that film presents: a flow that, as generally uninterrupted succession, may be more disposed to the portrayal of the present, rather than great moment, whilst, and in contrast, the drama, in which the present and great moments are embedded within the general quotidian temporal flow of phenomenal being, presents a flow which, as psychologically interruptible succession, may be more disposed to the portrayal of the great, rather than present moment. The temporal flow that film captures is fundamentally continuous, although bounded by the frame of the image. That flow can be interrupted by editing, but, at a basic level, film, and particularly some of the early films that Lukács was familiar with, such as the Lumière brothers' 1895 film *L'Arrivée d'un train en gare de La Ciotat/Arrival of a Train at the Station of Ciotat*, 'record' the continuity of the temporal flow.[3] On the other hand, the dramatic performance takes place within the flow of overall phenomenal experience, and, consequently, the continuous temporal flow can be interrupted in various ways, just as it is in everyday experience.[4] This leads Lukács to argue that the presence of the psychological great moment may be less aesthetically germane to film than that of the present moment in flux, and that 'the essence of cinema is movement as such, perpetual flux, the never-resting change of things' (183). Lukács does not, in addition, regard the resultant attenuation of the great moments that this intimates as a weakness of the medium, but, rather, as an aesthetically specific condition: 'This is not a shortcoming of cinema, it is its line of demarcation: its *principium stilisationis* [central principle of style/form]' (182).

The suggestion that film presents a 'special' temporal flow also implies that film presents a different 'world' to that of everyday phenomenal experience. When we watch a drama, the actors are part of our everyday phenomenal world, or horizon, whereas, when we watch a film, there is an additional self-contained and different phenomenal field active within, but also distinct from, our general phenomenal horizon. We exist within our phenomenal horizon, which spreads out around us, but we do not exist within the phenomenal world of the film, which exists as a sub-division within our phenomenal horizon that possesses its own rules; and we are also aware of our phenomenal horizon, and of the place that film occupies within that horizon (if I watch a film on a screen, I am still aware of the phenomenal horizon spreading around the screen). The special temporal flow that film presents, together with the empirical content of what is presented, can, therefore, be said to constitute a different kind of world from the phenomenal world we inhabit, even though it remains part of that environment. Based on this, Lukács emphasises the difference between phenomenal world and film world by stressing the contrast between the special temporal flow of film and its empirical content, and the general flow of temporal experience and its content. However, Lukács also goes further in asserting that difference and contrast by claiming that the film world does not need to conform to the physical laws that govern our experience: film 'is . . . not bound to our reality', in the sense that the technical means of the medium, such as 'reverse-motion', can overturn the regulations that order that reality (184–5). Film does share certain things with what Lukács calls the 'living life', or phenomenal experience, and is, consequently, 'not [entirely] the opposite of the living life . . . only a new aspect of it' (182); and what film adds to the already persisting living life, what is 'new' about film, is the sense of 'unlimited possibility' that the medium raises up by virtue of its ability to capture the disordered multiplicity of the content of the temporal flow (a real content that we otherwise habitually ignore), and by its ability to overturn the normalising constraints of physical existence (183). What Lukács invokes here is film as a realm of freedom and dimension of the soul. Film draws our attention to an empirical reality that is often obscured by the exigencies of 'ordinary life', and, in doing so, frees us from those exigencies, and film also stands in opposition to a 'causality' that often works in the service of institutionalised ordinary life: 'There is no causality involved . . . *Everything is possible*: that is the world view of the cinema . . . "possibility" as a category opposed to "reality" . . . the two categories are put on an equal level' (183). Related to this is also that, whilst the 'being-here' and 'becoming-present' of the drama tend to emphasise human being, the *being there* of film, with its overwhelming visuality, tends to emphasise 'nature', so that, in Lukács's vision, the terms 'nature', 'possibility' 'freedom' and soul become conjoined (182)

Another respect in which film differs from Lukács's understandings of both drama and phenomenal experience is that, even when the evolving world of the film conforms to the passage-character of temporality (the evolution of the 'not-yet' into the 'right-now' and then into the 'no-longer' along the 'arrow of time'), and to customary phenomenal spatial relationships, and although we may also follow the evolution of that filmic world in a way that is comparable to how we follow the evolution of the phenomenal horizon, that filmic world was constituted *in the past*: it was *recorded*. In drama, everything unfolds within the normal, present temporal passage-character of the phenomenal horizon, whereas, in film, that unfolding took place in the past, and the only thing taking place in the present (or near present), *now*, is the replaying of the recording, and the act of viewing it. In film, we view, in the present moment, something that occurred in the past, when that past was itself a present, whereas, in the drama, and in phenomenal experience, what we see is present as our present. In film, there 'are only the movements and actions of people, but *not people*' (182). The people who participated in the making of the film are no longer *there*, in our present, although they have left some, but not all, aspects or traces of themselves in the film, and, for Lukács, 'The absence of this [past] "present" is the essential characteristic of the cinema' (182).

In this sense, the film provides an incidental account of the past, even though the original intention was to film the present, with no thought of providing an account of the past, and so the film only became a record inadvertently, in terms of intentionality, though necessarily, in terms of the passage of time. Of course, this will be true of any account of the present, which will eventually become an account of the past because of the action of the arrow of time. What concerns Lukács, however, is, on the one hand, the closeness between the filmic recording of the present that has become an account of the past, and the phenomenal experience of the present; and, on the other hand, the distance between the two, because, in film, we have *both* a closeness – a '*truth-to-nature*' (*Naturwahrheit*) (184) – *and* a distance, because film displays a 'life without presence, a life without fate . . . a life without background or perspective' (182). In film, consequently, we have an account of the past that is like our experience of the present, whereas, in drama, we have an account of the present which is comparable to our experience of the present: life *with* presence. As mentioned in Chapter 1 of this book, however, we do not actually live in the phenomenal present, but in the phenomenal recent past. Given that, it might be more appropriate to rephrase the above as follows: in drama we have an account of the recent past which is similar to our phenomenal experience of the recent past, and which contains a life with presence; whilst, in film, we have an account of the less recent, or distant past, which is comparable to our phenomenal experience of the recent past, and displays 'a life without presence'.

All aesthetic mediums are experienced in the recent past, but, because film is, at one level, a record, the experience of what is presented in film is one that occurs in the recent past but is also about something that occurred in the distant past (and the same is true of photographs). For example, the events and array of significations that are presented in Sergei Eisenstein's *Battleship*

Potemkin during a viewing taking place in the recent past (for example, *about now*) were originally recorded in 1925. Film is, consequently, by virtue of its capacity to record, and to varying extents, always a medium of the distant past experienced in the near past, and this raises the analogous issue of memory. Although Lukács does not discuss memory per se in 'Thoughts', he does bring up the issue of film as record, and, therefore, as a presentation of the distant past. For example, film shows the '"how" of events', how things *happened*, and Lukács, also, seems to refer to – his – 1913 experience of watching the Lumière brothers' film *L'Arroseur arrosé/The Waterer Watered*, which was originally recorded in 1895, and which presents an event that occurred then (184).[5] Bergson was a major influence upon Lukács at this time, and the idea of film as a kind of presentation of the distant past, and, significantly, a preservation of that, experienced at the point of spectatorship, is similar to Bergson's conception of memory, in the sense that, in both film and memory, there is an engagement with an image from the past-present in the present (or near present, or recent past) which preserves that past-present.

There are, of course, several crucial differences between film and memory, and also, more pertinently, between what Lukács says about film and what Bergson says about memory: differences which, whilst indicating the influence of Bergson on Lukács, also reveal why Lukács was not particularly interested in memory in 'Thoughts'. First, and obviously, what Bergson calls the 'memory image' is an interior manifestation, whilst the engagement with film is part of external phenomenal experience.[6] Second, and perhaps less obviously, according to Bergson, when we recollect, 'we detach ourselves from the present in order to place ourselves, first, in the past in general, then, in a certain region of the past – a work of adjustment, something like the focussing of a camera' (Bergson 1991: 133–4). Watching a film does not, however, constitute an intentional act of recollection in the same sense, although recollection may emerge from the experience as a secondary category, if, for example, we, as viewers, associate what we see with aspects of our own past. In memory, intentional recollection and preservation are associated primary categories, whereas, in film, recollection and preservation are associated secondary categories; and what they are secondary *to* is the category of *presentation*. When watching a film, in general, we are not trying to experience a sense of recollection and preservation primarily, but presentation. For a general viewer, for example (as opposed to an academic), the fact that the past-present – the present that became a past – no longer exists is not significant per se, or at least that viewer does not generally seek to revive it in any substantive manner: we – as general viewers – do not *primarily* 'place ourselves in the past' in any major intentional attempt at recovery, as with memory. On the contrary, whilst noting the presentation of the past-present, the prevailing tendency is to experience the world of the film as one occurring in the present (near-present), as a presentation. On the face of it, therefore, there seems to be an incongruity between film as record and film as presentation, with the latter taking priority. In 'Thoughts', however, Lukács seeks to unite the two terms.

In 'Thoughts', Lukács is chiefly concerned with the role film has in preserving the past-present as presentation, and, here, the presentation, whilst experienced as a presentation, still has its source in the record that is preserved; and so the presentation is dependent upon the record and could not appear within experience without that. So, for example, Lukács asserts that 'The livingness of nature (*Lebendigkeit*) here acquires artistic form for the first time: the rushing of water, the wind in the trees, the stillness of the sunset and the roar of the storm, as natural processes, are here transformed into art' (184).

Leaving aside the issue of film art, an issue which arises only briefly towards the end of 'Thoughts' (although the topic of theatrical art permeates most of the essay), this quotation can be rephrased to say that, 'for the first time', the preservation of *Lebendigkeit*, of the 'wind in the trees', is transformed into presentation, but that the presentation would not be possible without the initial preservation. What is new in film is this capacity to record and preserve a past-present section of the phenomenal temporal flux experienced as a presentation of the flux in the near-present. Photography, in contrast, is able to record and preserve only a past-present *instance* of the phenomenal flux experienced as a presentation of that instance in the near-present.

This is also different from memory, in two respects. First, the focus on the past-present in memory does not seek to preserve, and, indeed, is unable to preserve, the entirety of that past-present, and focuses instead on the more meaningful features of what is recollected.[7] Film, on the other hand, by virtue of its empirical capacity, can preserve and present, if not the entirety, at least a great deal of what was evident within the temporal phenomenal flux at that past-present moment; for example, in the Lumière brothers' *The Waterer Watered*, film is able to present a rich empirical tapestry encompassing people, objects and gestural movements evident within the flux. Of course, prioritisation takes place here, as with memory, say, between foreground and background events, but the greater empirical content remains the case, and, in his later *The Specificity of the Aesthetic*, Lukács would go on to insist on the capacity of film to render that empirical content in an equivalent manner, as a 'concrete totality' (Lukács, in Aitken 2012: 85). Second, memory is, in essence, subjective, whereas the film presentation is, in essence, inter-subjective: the central coherences encountered through engagement with the bounded film presentation, whilst spectated subjectively, do not stem from subjective memory, but from sources external to that. For example, when I watch *Battleship Potemkin*, I experience a presentation with a bounded set of central coherences, and that experience of bounded coherences arises from my inter-subjectively gained knowledge: knowledge about Marxism, the founding of the USSR, the aims of

Eisenstein and the Soviet montage cinema of the 1920s and so on. Similarly, when I watch *The Waterer Watered*, the bounded central coherences that are presented involve knowledge relating to culture and society in France 1895, the nature of work and workers, childhood, and, if I am an academic, of then practices of narrative, editing and so on. External knowledge is not brought to bear in the same way in memory. One final distinction between film and memory which also follows on from this, and which is relevant to Lukács, is that the act of memory seems to require a greater degree of intentionality than the act of watching a film. When watching a film, for example, the initial focus is on the world of the film in order to enter that world, and, after that entrance, the world of the film cannot be refocused in the way that the memory image can be, because the world of the film is sustained by its own internal laws and imperatives: it is a bounded presentation. More personal control is involved in memory than in film. However, in 'Thoughts', Lukács is not so interested in the scope of human personal intentionality; and this is also why he has relatively little interest in memory. Instead, he is interested in the relation between the film world and the material world, and particularly nature, because, with film, 'Man has lost his *soul*, but gained his *body*' (184).

As argued, in 'Thoughts', Lukács is chiefly concerned with film's capacity to record and preserve a past–present section of the phenomenal temporal flux experienced as a presentation in the near-present, and, here, the presentation, whilst experienced as presentation, has its source in the record that is preserved. Lukács's position can, therefore, be described as a form of phenomenological realism. However, because it has its own world, Lukács also argues that film does not always have to conform to that position, and the general laws governing phenomenal appearing and experiencing; and that, when it does not, what then appears is a 'life of a completely different kind [a] . . . fantastic life' (182). In other words, Lukács sees film as operating in two ways, and, correspondingly, fulfilling a dual purpose. On the one hand, there is the *constructive* preservation and presentation of the phenomenal-temporal flux, and its content, the flux in which human beings actually exist; and there is no doubt that Lukács sees this rendering of the phenomenal real as related to the aesthetic specificity of film. On the other hand, however, Lukács also discusses film in relation to the 'forms of refusal' that he discussed in *Soul and Form*: refusal, that is, to accept the compromises and limitations instituted by the 'iron cage of modernity', and, here, film is able to undercut the otherwise immovable logic that underscores that cage.

In this alternative 'cinema of the fantastic', there remains a presentation of the phenomenal–temporal flux encountered in the near-present, and, indeed, also, and within that, a presentation of a past-present section of the flux, although this will, obviously, not be as coherent as in a cinema of phenomenological realism. What is different, however, is that, in the cinema of the fantastic, the emphasis will be on the orchestrated ordering and arrangement of the flux, rather than on an attempt to capture the flux in its quotidian integrity. Editing is, therefore, related to the anarchistic, deconstructive and vibrant forms of refusal, whilst the image is related to the constructive presentation of the persisting world. Lukács's evocation of a cinema of the fantastic in 'Thoughts' has been interpreted by some scholars as an endorsement of an anti-realist cinema (for example, Levin 1987). However, this is a misreading of the situation, and, in fact, the cinema of the fantastic appears in only a small section of 'Thoughts', whilst the bulk of the text is concerned with issues of phenomenological realism, or distinctions between film and drama. Lukács also follows the path set out in *Soul and Form* here: whilst acts of deconstructive personal refusal, or 'non-objectified form', carried out by such as Kierkegaard and Novalis, are important, the pro-active 'objectified form', which faces reality directly and presents reality in a permanent work of art, is by far the more important. Similarly, whilst the cinema of the fantastic as a form of refusal remains valid, it is, as argued, the idea of film as a form of phenomenological realism that dominates 'Thoughts'; and, here, also, the notions of the 'work', and objectified form, are associated with phenomenological realism, whilst the cinema of the fantastic is seen as more akin to the anarchic rebellious spirit which impels deconstructive non-objectified form, a 'form' without a form. The cinema of the fantastic is a valid form, but is, nevertheless, compromised by its deconstructive, rather than constructive, relation to the flux. Additionally, whilst, in his early phase, Lukacs does not address the term 'realism' as much as he does in his mature phase, in *The Theory of the Novel*, in particular, he frequently discusses both the epic and the novel in relation to how the two mediums render or invoke the world of their times.

It is also important to understand that Lukács uses the term 'fantastic' in two different ways in 'Thoughts'. First, there is the usage just referred to, in which editing is used to undercut normal causality: 'when a cigar gets bigger whilst being smoked' and so on (Lukács, in Aitken 2012: 185). Second, however, is the more important notion that film presents a fantastic life shorn of context, or 'soul':

> The cinema merely presents actions, but not their cause and meaning: its characters merely have movements, but no souls, and what happens to them is just an event, and not destiny . . . a world of premeditated and inevitable soullessness arises; a world of pure externality. (184–5)

The fantastic life of film is, however, not to be confused with the 'ordinary life', or 'lived life': phrases which stand for a diminished existence drained of meaning. In *Soul and Form*, Lukács described ordinary life as a condition in which we are 'entangled by a thousand threads in a thousand accidental bonds and relationships . . . accidental and meaningless; everything that is could just as well be otherwise' (Lukács 1974: 157). The fantastic life of film does have some shared characteristics with ordinary life, such as a lack of context and soul, and, in 'Thoughts', Lukács begins by addressing this aspect of the fantastic life negatively, because 'Thoughts' begins with a discussion of the medium which most embodies soul: the theatre. According to Lukács, what we find in film is:

> A life without presence, a life without fate, without reasons, without motives . . . without background or perspectives . . . It is a life without measure or order, without essence or value; a life without soul, made up of pure surface . . . a life the innermost of our soul never wants to become nor can become identical with. (Lukács, in Aitken 2012: 182)

However, when he turns more fully to film, Lukács argues that this life without soul can also become a life which avoids becoming 'crushed by the abstract monumental weight of destiny' that permeates the drama (184). The 'world of pure externality' exhibited in film, whilst lacking soul, avoids that crushing weight, and, correspondingly, outside of the drama, the repressive instrumentality that clandestinely governs the 'accidental bonds and relationships' of ordinary life, and which is, moreover, intimately bound to language. In contrast to the lack of weighty destiny, and an array of meaning, rendered through language, that, ultimately, serves the interests of the rulers of capitalist modernity, the visual world of pure externality brought forth by film can be associated with a consequential sense and form of freedom:

> The *revocation of the word*, and along with it, of memory, of duty, and of the obligation to oneself and the idea of one's own selfhood, does, when the wordless is remoulded into a totality, render everything light, exhilarating and soaring, frivolous and dancing. (184)

Externality may exclude soul, but it also helps to counteract the 'iron cage of modernity' through a revocation of the word and focus on the visual. Lukács speaks of a sense of existential *release* here, of becoming *unshackled*: one that is afforded by the emancipatory 'light[ness]' intrinsic to the film medium. This was also a common theme in the discourse on film known as the 'Kino Debate', which took place in Germany at the time, and to which 'Thoughts' was a contribution (Aitken 2012: 29–31). For example, Béla Balázs, whom Lukács's knew well at the time, argued that 'it is film that will once again bring out the unmediated visibility of the individual who has been buried under meanings and words', and enable that individual 'to experience concrete, immediate reality' (Balázs, cited in Kaes 1987a: 24). What Lukács adds to this here, however, is the more specific notion that, when the visual 'wordless' is 'remoulded into a totality', that totality differs fundamentally from the totalities of ordinary life. The remoulding takes place through the shaping actions of the film, and the totality which emerges is one that encompasses a consequential sense of 'exhilarating' freedom that is closely linked to the idea of totality. Reconsidered in terms expressed earlier, we can say that the totality of film that is experienced as bounded presentation exhibits this form of cathartic freedom related to the intimation of a meaningful totality; one that is at odds with everyday experience within 'ordinary life'. Writing about Lukács's later *The Specificity of the Aesthetic* (1963), one writer has maintained that 'the term [and concept of] totality is of crucial importance' to Lukács, as both a 'criterion of evaluation' and a 'criterion of life, of reality'; and we can also see such a measure of criterial importance emerging in 'Thoughts' (Pascal 1970: 147).

In addition to the sense of liberation from overbearing destiny and corrupted logic brought about by the fantastic life of film, there is also another aspect to that life, and one that is, once more, related to phenomenological realism. In *Soul and Form*, Lukács decried the empiricism that permeated ordinary life, preferring, instead, and under the influence of Platonism, the heroic idealism of the tragic drama. In 'Thoughts', however, the fantastic life of film is seen as comparable to one type of experience of the living life: empirical, immediate experience of that life. When we experience phenomenal reality within our everyday phenomenal horizon, at one level, what we experience occurs before us as an empirical manifold without any kind of circumstantial framework of explanation. This is fundamental to the nature of immediate experience, and, Lukács argues, to film. In Chapter 2 of this book it was argued that Lukács spoke positively about immediate experience as being related to one of the two domains of the soul. The first domain of the soul is made up of aspects such as 'intellect' and 'idealism', and is 'serious' and lucid in tenor; the second domain is made up of aspects such as feeling, emotion and intuition, and is also focused upon immediate experience of the material world. The fantastic life of film, therefore, presents us with the second domain of the soul, and one which is experienced as a bounded presentation of the material temporal flux.

Lukács's engagement with materialism in 'Thoughts' is, consequently, and as previously argued, also directed at temporality, and at the way in which theatre and film appear to approximate to different types of temporality. At the beginning of 'Thoughts' he returns to the notion of the 'absolute present', a notion that appears in 'The Metaphysics of Tragedy' chapter of *Soul and Form*. However, later in 'Thoughts', he finds such a notion paradoxical. The 'paradox' here is entailed by the fact that the absolute present is situated within the temporal flow, and, consequently, cannot be a discrete 'moment':

> The temporality of the stage, the flow of events taking place upon it, is always something of a paradox: it is the temporality and flow of great moments, something which has a deep inner quality of rest, as of something almost brought to a halt, become eternal; and this is a direct consequence of the influence of the excruciatingly strong 'present'. (Lukács, in Aitken: 182–3)

Lukács then proceeds to argue that this paradox can be interpreted propitiously in order to distinguish stage from film in terms of best mode of temporal development to be employed in each medium. Lukács proposes two different 'temporal categories': in the drama, there is or should be an attempt to bring things 'almost [but of course not completely] . . . to a halt', and, thereby, preserve the absolute present for a while, so that its 'strong presence' can be felt as a decelerated 'flow of great moments'; in film, on the other hand, the attempt should be to depict the reality and character of the temporal flow as flow, a flow that is both 'empirical' and indeterminate. These two 'different temporal categories':

> correspond to the different fundamental principles of composition of stage and cinema. One is purely metaphysical, keeping everything empirically alive at bay; while the other is so strong, so exclusively empirically alive, un-metaphysical; that through this extreme disposition another completely different metaphysics comes into being. In a word: the fundamental law of linkage for the stage is that of inexorable necessity, whereas, for cinema, it is that of unlimited possibility. (183)

There are, of course, *not* two 'temporal categories' at play phenomenologically, and this means that it is film, rather than the drama, that adheres the closest to the *one* temporal category: that of the undivided temporal flow. In portraying the temporal flow, film can present 'unlimited possibility' because the flow is characterised by such multiplicity, and this notion of the flow as a multiplicity of prospect has affinities with, and was doubtless influenced by, Bergson's conception of the impressionistic experience of duration within immediate consciousness. In *Time and Free Will*, for example, Bergson describes such consciousness as possessing a qualitative intuitive 'multiplicity' and freedom from the logical representational modality of 'reflective consciousness' (Bergson 2015a: 75); and, in 'Thoughts', Lukács similarly claims that film can bring about a 'revocation' of that which is central to logic – 'the word' (Lukács, in Aitken 2012: 184). Lukács's 'completely different metaphysics' of film is, therefore, premised upon a vibrant empirical multiplicity, unregulated by established protocols of 'necessity'. It should, however, be remembered, and, as previously argued, that this 'unlimited possibility' that is related to the aesthetic specificity of film is also one that is premised upon phenomenological realism; the unlimited possibility and empirical aliveness referred to relate to the multiplicity that characterises the experience of what Bergson calls duration, and should not be associated with later forms of formalist, anti-realist or reflexive post-structuralist/post-modernist cinema.

In *Time and Free Will*, Bergson also relates immediate consciousness of duration to the 'dream state'. In the dream state, our 'ordinary conception of duration' is overcome. In the dream state 'we shall witness the joining together or rather the blending of many ideas' (Bergson 2015a: 136). Similarly, in 'Thoughts', Lukács refers to 'seamless succession' as the essence of film (Lukács, in Aitken 2012: 183). In the dream state, which does not necessarily require dreaming, but rather a certain attitude of openness towards phenomenal reality, everyday reality also becomes illuminated and vibrant: 'All your sensations and all your ideas seem to brighten up: It is like childhood back again' (Bergson 2015a: 8). In 'Thoughts', Lukács relates film to both childhood and the dream. For example, he writes that, in a film (that may or may not be based on the cinematic essence of seamless succession), 'the child that is alive in each human being is set free' (Lukács, in Aitken 2012: 184). In addition, and in part because of this child-like affinity, film 'finds its correspondence in the . . . dream' (183). As in a dream, the content of film can be characterised by a:

> maximum vivacity (*Lebendigkeit*) . . . suggestive linkage through mere sequence; strictly nature-bound reality and extreme fantasy; the becoming-decorative of the non-pathetic ordinary life [ability to make ordinary things appear more meaningful or magical] . . . a liveliness that is not bound to the content and limitations of ordinary life. (183)

The German word *Lebendigkeit* means liveliness, or 'living-ness', or 'filled-with-life'; and Lukács relates this to both the dream state and the essential 'film state'. Once more, however, it should be emphasised that, in relating film to the illogical, free world of the dream, Lukács is emphasising the relation which film has to the multiplicity and flow of phenomenal experience. Whilst he notes the ability of film to replicate a dream-like world, and in a manner that serves favourably to deflect governing rationalities, he does not endorse a cinema of the dream, but one in which the focus is upon a dream-like form of phenomenological realism. The 'dream-state' of film is necessarily linked to the presentation of an empirical reality.

In 'Thoughts', Lukács does not invoke the idea of time per se, as Bergson does, but he does repeatedly summon up the world of appearance as something that moves through time. So, for example, film can depict 'the rushing of water'

(184). Set against this are those elements that inhibit the perception of the flow of time: the 'spoken word, the sounding concept' (184). Just as Bergson links the notion of 'succession without distinction' to duration and intuition, and 'succession with distinction' to science and logic, Lukács links the notion of filmic *Lebendigkeit* to duration and intuition, and the 'word' and 'concept' to the aesthetically 'paradoxical' form of the drama. Yet, the word dominates modern life, and this is where film becomes important, because, at least within its ambit, film can affect a 'revocation of the word', and, in doing so, become an alternative and radical 'place of *amusement*' (185). Lukács ends his essay by focusing upon the category of amusement in film as a form of enchantment, or liberation, rescuing that category from its 'crude and primitive' use within ordinary life, and establishing it as a new form of the epic, as 'rich and innerly adequate' in its depiction of 'externality', as was the depiction of interiority in 'the Greek stage . . . for a Sophocles' (185), so that:

> while amusement was condemned to be portrayed in a rather crude manner on the stage, because its content contradicted the forms of the drama-stage, it can, nevertheless, in the cinema, find an adequate form that is internally appropriate, and thus truly artistic, even if that is still rare in the cinema of today. (186)

In 'Thoughts', therefore, film is related to *Lebendigkeit*, externality, movement and fluid succession, and to notions of alternative amusement, freedom, liberation and the portrayal of externality; whilst drama, by virtue of reliance on the word, is related to interiority, stasis and the division of time, and to notions of – at least potential – domination and subjugation (central features, after all, of the classical Greek drama). And the way forward, for both mediums, is to explore what is aesthetically central to each: in the case of drama, an interiority bound ineluctably to the problem of language, and, in the case of film, an exteriority that is largely free of such a problem.

CONCLUSIONS

As argued in Chapter 2 of this book, in the 'Metaphysics of Tragedy' essay in *Soul and Form*, Lukács is chiefly concerned with the Platonist 'Idea' or 'Form', and the way that the great moment in the drama can embody this. However, in 'Thoughts', written one or two years after 'Metaphysics', Lukács – to some extent tentatively – questions the ability of the great moments to stand outside of or apart from the flow of time, in either a literal or a symbolic sense. In 'Thoughts', the great moment is now something *almost* but still *not* 'brought to a halt' (183). Now, the 'paradox' of the drama is more fundamental: the 'temporality and flow of great moments' (182) encompasses two antithetical categories: those of 'flow' and static 'moment'. But it is flow that must predominate, because everything is in a state of becoming and nothing *is*.

In 'Thoughts', therefore, Lukács refers to the 'transient' character of the absolute present and great moment, and such transience entails that such moments can only be, and as argued in Chapter 2 of this book, moments in a metaphorical and psychological, but not phenomenological, sense. Nevertheless, whilst he now accepts this irrefutable fact, Lukács also continues his attempt to conceive of these as existing as moments in a certain manner – as 'almost halted', and he also links these to the phenomenal present moment in order to justify this. If there is a 'present moment', then the great moments can also (somehow) persist in the present for a longer period, before inevitably slipping away into the flow; and, here, the flow can be decelerated. But, and as previously attested, this argument is an entirely metaphorical one and not demonstrable in any phenomenological sense in relation to temporality, because the transition from the 'right-now' to the 'no-longer' is instantaneous, and beyond any human capacity to perceive. The despairing elision made between the great moment and the present moment here is fallacious, as the two are categorically distinct, the former being simply a misapprehension, the latter a reality, albeit, one that cannot be grasped through human capability. At one level this untenable stance is a residue of the Platonism that influenced 'The Metaphysics of Tragedy' essay, and one that Lukács would soon discard. At another level, all Lukács is really saying here is what common sense would prescribe: that some segments of temporality can be experienced psychologically as lasting longer than others; and, here, there is, in fact, no need for recourse to such an imaginary notion as the 'great moment'.

At certain points in 'Thoughts' Lukács still, nevertheless, wants to distinguish the great moment from the present moment in the above sense because he is still concerned with the aesthetic specificity of the drama, and this, in turn, means that he continues to value the great moment over the present moment. In contradistinction, however, and as he turns to film, and refers to what he now calls the genuine 'living life', rather than ordinary life, he begins to argue that awareness of the present moment – of 'man's actual position in the universe' – can also be related to human authenticity; and that, because film is structured like the temporal flow, the psychological great moment that he perceives to exist in the drama has less impact than the persistent pull towards change exercised by that flow. Now, towards the finale of 'Thoughts', it is the phenomenal present moment that is the more meaningful. And, at least in this sense, film, unlike drama, is *not* a paradoxical aesthetic medium in relation to the reality of the temporal flow. The mission of film is to depict the living life, in all its empirical, indeterminate detail, and, sometimes, also in accordance with the logic of the 'dream-state'. The final accent in 'Thoughts' is, therefore, very different to that in the earlier 'The Metaphysics of Tragedy' essay, and, in 'Thoughts', Lukács celebrates film for being a medium akin to the temporal flow; and, as an aesthetic medium characteristic of the temporal flow, the mission of film is to portray that phenomenal reality (184).

It seems, therefore, that the encounter with film may have altered Lukács's general position, reinforcing some of the points he had made earlier in the 'On the Nature and Form of the Essay' chapter in *Soul and Form*; and, as argued in Chapter 2 of this book, that alteration also seems to make its presence felt later in *The Theory of the Novel*, the first draft of which was written in 1914, and in which Lukács views the novel as carrying out the same sort of depiction of the forms of appearance and duration that he celebrates in film in the 1911–13 'Thoughts'. Lukács begins *The Theory of the Novel* by setting out a division between the drama and the epic, and then by proceeding from epic to novel, leaving the drama behind in the process. What is happening in 'Thoughts', therefore, is that Lukács finds himself at the beginning of this transitional process, not yet abandoning the drama, but none the less moving away from a Platonism that he had coupled with the drama, and towards a phenomenology of film that would eventually lead on to his life-long engagement with the novel. As we will see, these positions also eventually influenced his understanding of film in *The Specificity of the Aesthetic* (1963).

NOTES

1. There have been several translations of the article, all, therefore, having different page numberings, according to the source. The translation to be used here is my own, as it appeared in my *Lukácsian Film Theory and Cinema* (2012), and the page numbers used in this chapter relate to that.
2. 'Will-toward-the-work', *Wille zum Werke* (Lukács 1972: 314).
3. The concept of 'recording' is a complex and multilayered one, and will be explored in depth in this book in the chapters which focus on the work of Siegfried Kracauer.
4. For more on this subject, see the Introduction and Chapter 1 of this book, on the nature of the temporal flow.
5. It is not entirely clear that Lukács is referring to this film. However, what he says indicates that he might be, and, if that is not the case, he is almost certainly talking about a similarly early film, made long before 1913.
6. For an account of 'externalism' and 'internalism' see the Introduction to this book.
7. This is also a point made by Siegfried Kracauer in his 'Photography' essay, which will be considered in Chapter 8 of this book.

CHAPTER 5

The Specificity of the Aesthetic (Lukács 1963)

Lukács's middle period covers the time from his conversion to communism in 1917 to the late 1950s. From the late 1950s onwards, Lukács attempted to promote a model of democratic socialism, including for his native Hungary, and adopted a more favourable disposition towards modernism in the arts, a modernism that he had previously criticised. During this late period, which lasted from the late 1950s until his death in 1971, Lukács also returned to some of the key themes of his early period, and some of these found expression in relation to film in *The Specificity of the Aesthetic/Die Eigenart des Ästhetischen* (*Aesthetic*) (1963).[1] Between 1954 and 1956 Lukács wrote a number of journal articles on philosophical aesthetics, which were then republished as a collection in 1957 as *On Besonderheit as a Category of the Aesthetic/Über die Besonderheit als Kategorie der Ästhetik* (*Besonderheit*). In this work Lukács is concerned with both identifying the specificity of the aesthetic and prioritising the need to engage in more concrete, rather than abstract, philosophical inquiry. Lukács was, however, not entirely concerned with aesthetic matters in *Besonderheit*, a relatively minor and arcane work which, none the less, succeeded in arousing the ire of the communist establishment, because its focus on what Lukács called the 'dialectics of the particular' was interpreted – correctly – as a metaphor for a need to cast off official communist models of polis and replace those with a more liberal 'Hungarian road to socialism' (Kadarkay 1991: 445). *Besonderheit* provided a foundation for the *Aesthetic*, which, as mentioned, marked a return to some of the issues which Lukács had explored in his early work. In particular, the *Aesthetic* returned to a model of human essence, or *Wesen* (being), now also referred to as 'species essence/being', or *Gattungswesen*, which had its source in the various conceptions of authentic being found in *Soul and Form*, *The Theory of the Novel*, 'On the Phenomenology of the Creative Process' and 'Thoughts towards an Aesthetic of the Cinema'.

In the *Aesthetic*, the term *Gattungswesen* is also used in relation to the notion of 'reflection', because Lukács feels obliged to pay attention to the Leninist conception of reflection (*Widerspiegelung*). Lenin's *Materialism and Empirio-Criticism* (1912) was still a standard text within the Soviet Bloc whilst Lukács was writing the *Aesthetic*, and dealt with, amongst other matters, how perception could be considered as a 'reflection' of things in the world, and, as, consequently, possessing a 'realist' relation to those things:

> Anybody who reads *Anti-Dühring* and *Ludwig Feuerbach* [works by Friedrich Engels] with the slightest care will find scores of instances in which Engels speaks of things and their reflection in the human brain, in our consciousness, thought, etc. . . . not symbols of things [but] 'image', picture or reflection. (Lenin 1972: 34)

Our knowledge of reality is not just symbolic, and, therefore, not entirely representational, but converges with reality to a degree, as an 'image', 'picture' or 'reflection' does. When, for example, Lukács discusses the relationship of perception to external reality, he argues that 'the colour green appears in consciousness as a physiologically necessary reaction to a determinate frequency of vibrations' reaching the sensory apparatus from the external world, and this 'reaction' is more than just a symbolic representation because it is conditioned by that 'frequency of vibrations' (Parkinson 1970a: 117).

Although Lukács covers this area of perceptual experience to some extent in the *Aesthetic*, as in the above quotation, he is far more concerned with how reflection works at a general, rather than perceptual level: as a broad-spectrum 'formulation within consciousness of the relationships in which men stand to the experienced world' (Pascal 1970: 148). This is not just an existential given but also a means of realising authentic species essence, and human beings *should* strive to arrive at an adequate understanding of how they stand in relation to the world. The use of the term 'reflection' here is, therefore, a gesture to the authority of Lenin, and, in the *Aesthetic*, is applied in the broad sense just referred to, rather than the more specific way that Lenin addresses the term. That application also indicates a continuity between Lukács's early and late aesthetic positions, as, it will be recalled that, in 'On the Phenomenology of the Creative Process', for example, Lukács points to the artist's need to find the 'experience-evoking' formulation that embodies that artist's own relation to and understanding of reality (Lukács 1972: 315). Of course, such a formulation within consciousness must then be given form, either 'non-objectified', as in personal action, or 'objectified', as in a work of art; and, in the latter case, reflection is an objectified formulation of 'the relationships in which men stand to the experienced world'.

In the *Aesthetic*, Lukács also gives this conception of objectified reflection an additional sense, and one that, yet again, refers to his earlier work, by insisting that it be reconceived as 'double reflection' (*doppelter Widerspiegelung*) (Lukács 1981, II: 467/187). The term 'double reflection' refers to an objectified reflection of *Wesen* (being) – or what Lukács, now, increasingly refers to as *Gattungswesen* – and *Erscheinung*: the world of phenomenal forms (*Aesthetic II*: 477/188). As in the early work, so in the *Aesthetic*, *Wesen* and *Erscheinung* stand for the two domains of authentic being (or, the 'soul', in the early aesthetic): *Wesen*, standing for an engagement with the 'ultimate questions and answers' which, in *Soul and Form* and *The Theory of the Novel*, Lukács argues can be found in the Sophoclean drama; *Erscheinung*, for the free and visceral experience and representation of the phenomenal forms of reality which, he argues at some length in *The Theory of the Novel*, can be found in the classical Greek epics of Homer.[2] As has been argued in Chapter 4 of this book, in 'Thoughts towards an Aesthetic of the Cinema ('Thoughts'), Lukács makes much of the ability of film to render the latter, and this trope is continued in the *Aesthetic*, where film is said to be able to portray the:

> unlimited diversity of everyday life . . . The whole environment of man, nature, flora and fauna (*Aesthetics II*: 477/196) . . . [a] universality of represented objects . . . It is this foundation which makes film's inherent homogenisation [complete picture] of everyday life absolutely sufficient for its purposes . . . makes possible the depiction of a world . . . in the inexhaustible diversity of its appearances. (*Aesthetics II*: 200)

In fact, in the *Aesthetic*, Lukács argues that the initial representational mission of the epic has now passed to film, a medium better able to capture this vibrant world of existence (Aitken 2016: 210); and, in analogous vein, just as, in *Soul and Form*, Lukács argues that the uneven, non-totalising essay form is suited to the representation of an indeterminate world of appearances, in contrast to the depiction of an eventually determined soul in the drama, so also, in the *Aesthetic*, he argues that film 'has the highest affinity' to another type of abridged, fractional work – 'the novella, the short story' (*Aesthetic II*: 205).

Lukács's argument that film retains a special ability to represent the forms of appearance, together with the phenomenological focus implied by his account of the 'unlimited' and 'diverse' 'world' made available by film, also leads him into an engagement with the temporality of film. According to Lukács, film's 'closeness to life' (*Die Lebensnähe des Films*, *Aesthetic II*: 475/189) means that a new relationship between artistic form and perceptual experience has become constituted because perceptual experience set within the course of temporal duration is, for the first time, brought into correspondence with an artistic form that is similarly set within such a course: 'film is the only art in which visibility and the real course of time are categorically linked' (*Aesthetic II*: 474/193). This reiterates the argument set out in relation to film in 'Thoughts'. There are, nevertheless, also differences between the two works in relation to the treatment of temporality. For example, in 'Thoughts', Lukács discusses the 'fantastic' manner through which film is able to alter the depiction of temporality, so that the latter is no longer 'bound to our reality' ('Thoughts': 184). Here, filmic visibility and the 'real course of time' are *not* 'categorically linked'. As argued in Chapter 4 of this book, however, this 'anti-realist' theme is not the central one to be found in 'Thoughts', and, in contrast, that theme is preoccupied with phenomenological realism. Lukács also continues in an anti-realist vein to some extent in the *Aesthetic*, however, and as in 'Thoughts', he does so by prioritising the realist proclivity of the medium when presenting such a 'fantastic' temporality. So, for example, Lukács argues that the photographic realism of film is able 'to lend a manifest and evident reality to the most extreme phantasm'. It is, none the less, the capacity to render 'evident reality' that is more important than the facility to render 'phantasm' (*Aesthetic II*: 202), and this implies that the phantasm takes on a phenomenological form that connects it to the typical or normal forms of phenomenological appearance, and, therefore, to human essence within the double reflection. Phantasm it may be at the level of concept, but its imaginary conceptual aspect is pulled back into concrete *Erscheinung*. A depiction that is partly based on a fantasy-concept is given in such tangible material form that the concept is overwhelmed by that detail.

In 'Thoughts', Lukács also addresses the equivalent of *Erscheinung* – the perceptual forms of phenomenal appearance[3] – but he does not equate those forms with the fantastic and makes a clear distinction between the real concrete forms and the concocted, imaginary phantasmal. As argued, it is the 'evident reality' referred to in the *Aesthetic* that is more important than the 'phantasm'; and the fantastic is, consequently, invoked in relation to an irregular and arbitrary amendment of the forms of appearance from their normal phenomenal condition. For example, Lukács describes hypothetical film scenes in which objects and events move differently through time and space: 'when a cigar butt becomes bigger while being smoked, until the moment arrives when the complete cigar is placed back into the box' ('Thoughts': 185). Here, the fantastic, based upon a fanciful reverse of time, is related to a conceptual understanding that is inherently variant and indeterminate, and this is different from phenomenal encounter, because non-variant and determinate phenomenal reality cannot go backwards in time. The depiction of a fantastic reality is, therefore, related to the *idea* of overturning the laws of nature, and not the actual possibility of doing so within phenomenal experience; and this also echoes the distinction that Lukács draws in 'Thoughts' between the psychological 'great moment' and the phenomenal present moment, where the former is imaginary, the latter real.[4] It should also be noted that, in the example of the time-reversed cigar-smoking just given, at the end of the fantastic sequence, the scene returns to normal reality, as the cigar 'is placed back into the box'. Even in 'Thoughts', therefore, with its ostensible endorsement of a 'cinema of the possible' and 'fantastic', the underlying phenomenal realism of film is more important than the ability of the medium to alter that.

In the *Aesthetic* Lukács has no time for implausible scenarios related to toppling the laws of nature: scenarios that, even in 'Thoughts', were not proposed as presenting anything other than a whimsical possibility of transcending the constraints of phenomenal experience. It has been claimed that, in the *Aesthetic*, a certain 'normative' attitude towards filmic realism can be discerned that is at odds with the more 'dialectical' approach (that is, acceptance of the fantastic, as well as realist potential of film) found in 'Thoughts'.[5] However, this is a misreading of 'Thoughts', and, in both the latter and the *Aesthetic*, a principled belief in the reality, fidelity and crucial standing of phenomenal experience, phenomenological insistence upon the necessity of what Husserl called the 'natural attitude' to the world, and what Bergson called the experience of 'duration', is discernible.[6] Accordingly, in the *Aesthetic*, Lukács places limits upon the cinema of the possible, because such possibilities hover superstructurally over what is real: our actual existence in a phenomenal horizon, and in a material present moment that is part of the onward flow of time. The *Aesthetic* is, therefore, preoccupied with film's ability to depict a realistic phenomenal flow of temporality existing within a realistic phenomenal 'life-world', or *Lebenswelt*;[7] and this also echoes a theme found in 'Thoughts', in which it is argued that 'The livingness (*Lebendigkeit*) of nature here acquires artistic form for the first time: the rushing of water, the wind in the trees' ('Thoughts': 184). Such *Lebendigkeit*, when linked to the notion of *Lebensnähe* (closeness to life), implies a realistic depiction of the forms of appearance, and one that is, necessarily, embedded in an onward flow of real-time duration: 'in film real-time prevails' (*Aesthetic II*: 474/193).

It has been argued earlier in this chapter that a key notion in the *Aesthetic* is that of the 'double reflection' of *Wesen* and *Erscheinung*. Yet, it seems that it is the latter that plays the major role in film whilst the former plays only a minor one. The model of film that thus emerges here is impressionistic and empirically based, and could even be described as 'naturalist' in that sense.[8] In 1963, however, Lukács has a problem. Since 1917, and following the line laid down by Engels and Lenin, and then inscribed into socialist realist dogma by Andrei Zhdanov in 1934,[9] Lukács had consistently denounced naturalism. Naturalism was associated with Western culture and society, rather than the 'socialist' culture that had emerged within the Soviet Bloc, and elsewhere. Yet, and as just posited, the model of film form that Lukács develops in the *Aesthetic* appears to be fully compatible with naturalism. This concerned Lukács so much that he felt compelled to assert that the approach he advocated 'must not in any way be referred to as naturalism' (*Aesthetic II*: 481/200), and, in the *Aesthetic*, he states that, whilst 'a naturalism, which elsewhere appears the converse of art, might be artistically possible in film', this is, in fact, not the case (*Aesthetic II*: 479/198).

Prior to the publication of the *Aesthetic* in 1963, Lukács had been forced to engage with an important and controversial work of literature: Alexander Solzhenitsyn's *One Day in the Life of Ivan Denisovich* (*Ivan*) (1962). This novel presented Lukács with the same problem he was facing at the time with film: that is, Solzhenitsyn's work appeared to be a work of naturalism.[10] Committed as he was to the development of an autonomous socialist cultural sphere, and as the leading literary theorist within the Soviet Bloc, Lukács felt that his task was to draw *Ivan* back into that sphere and Bloc, and avoid appropriation of the work within a framework of Western naturalism. The solution he arrived at was to reintroduce *Wesen* back into the scenario in a more imperative manner, and, thus, in his 'Solzhenitsyn: *One Day in the Life of Ivan Denisovich*', published in 1964, one year after the appearance of the *Aesthetic*, Lukács argues that *Ivan* 'stands in marked contrast to all the trends of naturalism' (Lukács 1971b: 19) because the novel 'exert[s] a strong symbolic effect' through 'description', whilst what is symbolised is 'Stalinism', and the horrors meted out to human beings by a Stalinist penal system that was linked to the larger Stalinist dictatorship (Lukács 1971b: 14).[11] Here, *Wesen* is brought back into the equation. However, Lukács had already arrived at this formulation in relation to film in the *Aesthetic* when he asserted that 'the philosophical artistic meaning of naturalism consists in that, in naturalism, the being that appears wanes, or even completely vanishes, behind . . . appearance' (*Aesthetic II*: 479/198); and that, in contrast to this, film should portray relations of being and appearance as they 'persist side by side' (*Aesthetic II*: 481/200). Where the latter is achieved, the film in question would not be 'naturalist', but would, none the less, still be highly descriptive. Lukács's formulation of being and appearance persisting 'side by side' also must be understood in the sense of one being capable of becoming more prominent than the other, rather than the two being of equal standing, and, as his writing elsewhere in the *Aesthetic* makes clear, in film, it is appearance that should play the leading role. This also becomes clear when Lukács addresses the issue of '*das fruchtbare Moment*'.

In the *Aesthetic*, Lukács does not allude to the notion of the 'great moment' that was discussed in depth in *Soul and Form* and 'Thoughts', but he does have recourse to what is much the same thing: 'what Lessing called the fruitful moment' (*das fruchtbare Moment*), and one that is now 'necessarily absent from film' (*Film . . . das fruchtbare Moment gennant hat*) (*Aesthetic II*: 474/193–4). If, however, the fruitful moment is necessarily absent from film, then so, to a large extent, must be *Wesen*, or, at least, one crucial aspect of *Wesen*. In dealing with film in the *Aesthetic*, Lukács makes a distinction between two categories of *Wesen*. The first is the trenchant 'great' or 'fruitful' moment that Lukács discusses in *Soul and Form* and 'Thoughts', whilst the second conforms more closely to what Lukács, later discussing *Ivan*, calls 'a strong symbolic effect [attained] through description'. Here, being is more like a general and underlying effect which pulsates beneath the descriptive body of the work, and it is this, rather than the great moment, that, according to Lukács, is germane to film. In the *Aesthetic*, for example, Lukács expands on this conception of *Wesen* when discussing the films of Charlie Chaplin, arguing that Chaplin is a symbol for 'the masses within the context of contemporary capitalism', and that his films 'express the socio-economic conditions at a high level of typicality' (*Aesthetic II*: 489–90/208). Here, a 'high level of typicality' parallels the 'strong symbolic effect' that Lukács discerns in *Ivan*, and, in the case of both *Ivan* and of film, such typicality is, according to Lukács, at odds with a naturalist approach.

Lukács's repudiation of naturalism in both *Ivan* and film was to be expected, given the political context within which he was writing, and given his own history of aversion towards naturalism. Nevertheless, the new model of *Wesen* that he developed in order to effect such a refutation is not particularly convincing, both in itself, because the notion is set out in imprecise and inconclusive manner, and given the overwhelming emphasis on description that pervades the account of film given in the *Aesthetic*. This new model of *Wesen* is, essentially, referenced in order to designate both *Ivan* and film as politically acceptable. Allowing for this, however, it could also be argued that what Lukács is pointing to is something like a mode of expression which functions like the underlying harmonies in a piece of music. If foregrounded melody can be said to be analogous to the events taking place at the level of plot and narrative in a film, then background harmony can be said to be analogous to the role of audiovisuality in generating mood and broad symbolism. If that is the case, then this notion of *Wesen* comes close to another Lukácsian concept related to film, that of *Stimmung*, or 'atmosphere', which Lukács also called 'the central motivating principle of film effects' (*Aesthetic II*: 490/100). Nevertheless, and, as argued, in the treatment of film in the *Aesthetic*, the overwhelming emphasis is on description, and on the forms of appearance, or *Erscheinung*.[12]

That stress is also reinforced by the importance placed on another key notion within the *Aesthetic*: that of the 'just-being so' (*Geradesosein*) of things. It will be recalled that, in *The Theory of the Novel*, and, to an extent, in 'Thoughts', Lukács invoked the idea of the 'absolute present' in the drama not as something that stood outside the flow of time but as something that lay within that flow, so that the absolute present must inevitably slip away into the flow of time. The absolute present was not, after all, a 'moment', but a process. The same also applies to the notion of *Geradesosein* that appears within the pages of the *Aesthetic*. The notion of the 'just-being-so' of things has various sources, including Hegel's concept of the 'concrete universal' (see following paragraph), a reading of Hegel by Engels, and the Marxist–Leninist repudiation of empiricism and 'neo-positivism'. As the notion developed within the Marxist tradition it was used in order to emphasise the movement of the dialectic between thesis and antithesis, whilst also pointing to the point of synthesis (*Geradesosein*) as part of that process; and this model of continuous stasis and change was then deployed to counter an ideology of empiricism and neo-positivism which was deemed to function as an instrument of bourgeois capitalist modernity. Lukács adopted this model of process and stasis, and this meant that he did not, and could not, regard either the encounter with *Geradesosein* within perceptual experience, or its portrayal in the film image, in terms of the grasping of a 'moment'. The Hegelian–Marxist notion of *Geradesosein* must also be distinguished from the Kantian concept of the 'thing-in-itself' (*Ding an sich*). The notion of *Ding an sich* implies that what we experience is mere 'appearance', and not the thing-in-itself that gives rise to that appearance. Such an 'idealist' approach is in contradiction with the previously discussed, realist, Leninist concept of 'reflection', a concept which exercised a strong influence on Lukács whilst he was writing the *Aesthetic*. *Geradesosein* is, therefore, neither moment nor mere appearance, but the product of a process that is linked to external reality.

Given this, Lukács wants to argue that 'just-being-so' is not an absolute singularity, but a complex in the process of evolving. Lukács derives this composite idea of *Geradesosein*, in part, from Hegel's *Phenomenology of Spirit*, where empirical particularity is defined in terms of the 'this' (*Dieser*) – the immediate object of sense perception, or what Hegel calls 'sense-certainty' – but in which the 'this' is also regarded as a mediated 'concrete universal', rather than unmediated concrete singularity (Desmond 1986: 21). According to the idea of the concrete universal, every particularity may be concrete in one sense but is also inextricably associated with, and cannot be distinguished from, a range of universals and aspects in another sense. So, for example, a tree may be experienced as if it were a concrete entity but is also inextricably linked to a range of universals such as 'wooden-ness', 'green-ness', 'tree-ness' and so on. In addition, the tree is also a composite entity in that it consists of various properties, including shape, size, weight, texture and colour, so that no specific 'tree' can be directly pointed to; we cannot encounter the tree as a bare 'this', even though the presumed experience of such encounter is necessary to our experience (Desmond 1986: 21). The bare 'this' is, in fact, a combination, and, for Lukács, therefore, and under the influence of Hegel and dialectical materialism, to all intents and purposes, there are no empirical things but only empirical complexes and processes.

In addition to the Hegelian concept of the concrete universal, Lukács also derives this composite concept of *Geradesosein* from Engels's reading of Hegel in the former's seminal 1885 'Letter to Minna Kautsky': a short text which, none the less, had a major impact on the classical Marxist aesthetic tradition. In the *Aesthetic*, Lukács cites the 'Letter', in which Engels argues that, in true realist literature, 'everyone is a type, but also simultaneously a single individual (*bestimmter Einzelmensch*), a *Dieser*, as old Hegel would have expressed himself': a singularity, with an array and aspects (*Aesthetic II*: 232). Like the Leninist notion of 'reflection', Engels's definition of type, and associated reference to the Hegelian notion of *Dieser*, had also passed into communist aesthetic orthodoxy by the 1930s, and Lukács felt duty-bound to resort to those definitions. In the *Aesthetic*, for example, he argues that singularity (*Einzelheit*) is a 'micro-totality', or 'micro-complex', possessing its own spheres of meaning: its own mini-grouping of properties and relations. Lukács also refers to these spheres of meaning as spheres of 'speciality' (*Besonderheit*), a term he uses in the *Aesthetic* to indicate an intermediate, inter-connected field of meaning, and he argues that 'the *Einzelheit* [singularity] has its own *Besonderheit* inherent to itself' (*die Einzelheit ihrer eigenen Besonderheit inharant ist*) (*Aesthetic II*: 232). In terms of temporality, consequently, the notion of 'just-being-so', taken from Hegel via Engels and Lenin, refers to a multiplicity within singularity existing within the flow of time. It does not stand outside the flow of time, and, on the contrary, Lukács argues that, for *Geradesosein* to be represented properly, it must be as a 'transition between past and future' (*Aesthetic II:* 474/194).

In addition to Hegel and the Marxist tradition, Lukács's conception of *Geradesosein* is also derived from phenomenology, and, particularly, from something similar to the phenomenological model of time which was discussed in Chapter 1 of this book, although precisely where Lukács derived his ideas on temporality as set out in the *Aesthetic* remains unclear. According to Lukács:

> in film, as in any real-time sequence, the moment of the present (*Moment der Gegenwart*) is a real moment of transition between past and future. Normally we have experienced the past as moments of the present, moments that vanish into the past in front of our eyes. Only a second before its passing that present moment also had the potential to become part of a threatening or alluring future. (*Aesthetic II*: 475/194)

Geradesosein may stand here for an intense drawn-out experience of the phenomenal forms of appearance (*Erscheinung*) within what amounts to a perception of the present moment (*Moment der Gegenwart*), and Lukács insists that such experience, which possesses an 'authenticity' because of its focused attention to phenomenal 'reality itself' ('the source of such authenticity is reality itself/*Die Quelle dieser Authentizität ist aber die Wirklichkeit selbst*'), must be retained as 'an essential element of . . . film art', because the encounter with the just-being-so of things is an authentic aspect of human perceptual experience (*Aesthetic II*: 473/193). The *Geradesosein*-like image, or sequence, therefore, possesses an authenticity that is derived from the reality of human experience that takes place within the 'present moment', an experience which is of a singular complex undergoing transmutation during the passage of time, and must also be retained so that film plays a 'decisive role . . . in establishing the visual affectiveness and authenticity of the thing-like existence (*gegenständlichen Existenz*) of all objects' (*Aesthetic II:* 484/203). Lukács makes an imperative claim for film here: that film can play a 'decisive role' in enabling us to experience the material content of phenomenal reality within the deaccelerated flow of time. The 'thing-like existence' of that content is important because, in terms of a realist phenomenology, and, also, in keeping with Husserl's notion of the 'natural attitude towards the world' (see the following chapter of this book), it infers a certain refuge from relativism. Whilst the concept of *Geradesosein* implies a movement and complexity as counter to any naïve empiricist objectivism, therefore, the 'still-point' that it implies also stands against the sort of relativism that Lukács contests.

Lukács, therefore, makes two related claims for film. First, film can embody and present an encounter with a just-being-so of things that is an authentic aspect of human perceptual experience. Second, film can play a key role in making apparent 'the thing-like existence of all objects'. The just-being-so of things and thing-like existence of objects appear to mean the same or similar thing, and both point to Lukács's commitment to phenomenological realism, and to his related belief that film should facilitate meditation upon phenomenal reality. There is, nevertheless, a potential difference between the two concepts that becomes apparent when Lukács deploys another central concept of the *Aesthetic*: that of the 'field of objects/objectivity' (*Felde der Gegenständlichkeit*). The experience of the just-being-so of things can, at the level of *logos*, stand for common inter-subjective understanding of various matters, as well as for a direct and intimate encounter with that which is given within the phenomenal field: in other words, for the significant relations of different sorts which human beings are capable of experiencing within the field of representations. The notion of *gegenständlichen Existenz* of objects, however, relates only to the significant encounter with phenomenal objects and directs attention at that materiality. Both notions, as suggested, are encompassed within the meta-concept of *Felde der Gegenständlichkeit*, which encompasses the totality of possible representations (*Totalitäts der Gegenständlichkeit*), including those related to phenomenal, ethical, aesthetic, intellectual and other domains. There is, therefore, and as previously suggested, a potential difference between the notions of the just-being-so-of things and the thing-like-existence of things, with the former notion being the more expansive in terms of its additional reference to *logos*. However, in discussing film, Lukács does not really use the notion of just-being-so in relation to *logos* because he is so taken with the idea of film as an 'art of visibleness' (*Kunst der Sichtbarkeit*) and 'visual definiteness' which presents externality, rather than interiority. It is true that he does say, at one point, that film's 'closeness to life' embodies a 'tendency to portray life as immediately transparent and graspable', something that is 'also true for the everyday person in relation to his/her own environment', and this could include *logos* (*Aesthetic II*: 475–6/195–6). In general, however, in relation to film, the domain of *Wesen* and *logos* is restricted, and that of *Erscheinung* and phenomenalism expanded, and, consequently, the notions of just-being-so and thing-like-existence will be treated as similar here, despite the differences between the two concepts just expounded.

As suggested, the idea of the 'totality of objects' can also mean the 'totality of representations': the universal 'field' of that which 'relates to man' and which is possible to portray within the aesthetic sphere. However, Lukács believes that the '"world" of film' cannot accommodate the totality of representations because it cannot encompass the intellectual sphere as fully as literature can:

> As an art of visibleness film cannot escape this categorical inevitability (*Aesthetic II*: 475/194) . . . The representation of the totality of objects, the highest and most poignant form of synthesis that great epic literature is able to arrive at on this field of objectivity is closed off to film. This also points to the practical significance of those limits to the 'world' of film . . . that is to say, the great diversity of objects can only reach such a totality through the exercise of intellectual acts. The objects themselves, in their immediate real-being, merely reveal the concrete possibilities for the formation of a genuinely epic totality of objects; and such a totality itself only emerges as a result of the process of men in action becoming conscious of their relations to the world of objects within the intellectual orientation of the great epics. (*Aesthetic II*: 205)

Lukács is writing in the early 1960s here, in the *Aesthetic*, but his train of thought on these matters had already developed before that, since at least 1954, when he wrote the first chapters of what would eventually become the 1957 *On Besonderheit as a Category of the Aesthetic*. It is not surprising, therefore, that, in a 1958 response to his student, István Mészáros, published in the Italian Marxist film journal *Cinema Nuovo*, Lukács makes much the same point:

> And this issue of the totality of objects requires much reflection. I am very doubtful if it can be compared to film. In my opinion, if a film is related to a literary genre, it is more likely to be so with a short story

rather than a novel, and even a short story is unacquainted with the requirements of the totality of objects. The fact that in the novella and in the film much importance is also given to the world of objects of a particular period of life that is represented, does not yet signify the totality of those. (Lukács, in Aitken 2012: 127–8)

The 'world of objects' of film is, primarily, the 'outside world', or *Aussenwelt* (*Aesthetic II*: 478/95), and does not constitute the totality of objects because such totality includes interiority. Furthermore, the 'requirements of the totality of objects' imply, precisely, totality: a wide-ranging and comprehensive exploration. The notion of the totality of objects, therefore, refers to the representation of a combination of phenomenal encounter and interior consciousness over a broad canvas. The empirical focus of film means that, as with the novella, film cannot reconstitute the totality of objects, only a more limited 'world of objects', and, accordingly, the ability of film to capture the just-being-so of the thing-like existence of objects within the phenomenal field, and within the flow of temporality, is of primary importance, although other 'objects', of a more intellectual or conceptual nature, can be accommodated to an extent. It is, additionally, important to appreciate that the notion of the 'field of objectivity', the field from which totalities of objects can be constructed, does not just refer to that which is visually phenomenal, although it can include that. This becomes clear when it is considered that the aesthetic form in which such totalities can best be constructed, that of the novel (or, in earlier days, the epic), has no meaningful visible physical form. It is, also, essential to appreciate that one of Lukács's key categories, that of totality, one that is 'of crucial importance to Lukács's literary criticism', does not seem to apply to film (Pascal 1970: 147), and it also follows from this that literature is superior to film, because the totality of objects can, finally, be achieved only 'through the exercise of intellectual acts'. Lukács makes the same point, but in relation to painting, in another article published in *Cinema Nuovo* in January–February 1969, when he asserts that a painting cannot 'express intellectual problems intellectually' (Lukács, in Aitken 2012: 258).

Lukács attempts to avoid, at least to an extent, the presumed aesthetic hierarchy involved in this position over film and literature, through his concept of 'indefinite objectivity' (*unbestimmten Gegenständlichkeit*), which refers to the characteristic tendency of a film or painting to express meaning indirectly, through intuitively grasped evocation, rather than directly, through linguistic conceptual explication (*Aesthetic II*: 475/194). Such expression, however, necessarily consists of an intangible and nebulous array of possible meanings which the film (or painting) must seek to channel, or 'minimise' (*Minimierung*), in part, also, because the 'visual definiteness' and 'sense of factuality/truthfulness' of film (*tatsachengemäßen Sinn des Films*) promote, by virtue of that very indefiniteness and empirical indeterminacy, an extensive array of indefinite objectivity which only adds to the indeterminacy inherent in evoked, intuitively grasped meaning. The idea of indefinite objectivity is, however, not particularly set out in relation to film in the *Aesthetic*, and Lukács's insistence that the totality of objects can, finally, be achieved only through intellectual means reveals his overriding commitment to literature and drama (*Aesthetic II*: 475/194). This commitment is also reflected in the fact that Lukács sees no problem with the fact that, whilst the plastic arts can both express interiority and show the external phenomenal world, literature is entirely abstract, and cannot show the material world. In fact, ultimately, Lukács develops the idea of indefinite objectivity in order to emphasise the superiority of literature over the other arts, and to place those other arts within a category different to that within which literature is to be placed. If all the arts were placed in the same category, and intuitive evocation given the same status as linguistic conceptual exposition, there would be no need for a delimited secondary notion of indefinite objectivity. It should also be noted that, whilst, in the *Aesthetic*, Lukács adopts the stance that film cannot represent the totality of objects, in the earlier 'Thoughts towards an Aesthetic of the Cinema', he takes a different position, and refers to the 'homogenous, harmonious, unified . . . world' which appears in film (Lukács, in Aitken 2012: 183). In 'Thoughts', Lukács also asserts that the fact that film cannot present the 'great moments' and 'absolute present' of the classical tragic drama (see previous chapter of this book), is not a 'shortcoming' of the medium (182). In 1963, however, he seems to imply that it is so in relation to the novel.

As argued, the notions of the field of objects and totality of objects refer to the relations between human beings and the world, and the way in which those relations may be represented. As such, the notions could apply to the scientific as well as aesthetic domains. Lukács, however, makes a distinction between the two domains, and one that also has implications for film. The 'double reflection' that takes place within the partial or complete totalities that emerge upon the field of objectivity concerns human 'being in the world', and, in Lukács's general scheme of thought, it is 'human being, rather than the world, that has priority'. Whilst, therefore, 'reality is man's dialectical being in nature', the dialectic is not an equivalent one, and the double reflection amounts to a primarily 'anthropological process' (Pascal 1970: 148). Within that process, and according to Lukács, the double reflection that takes place within science produces totalities of representation in which the search for general laws takes precedence over the attempt to understand the dissimilitude inherent within individual experience. The method of science is, consequently, one of 'de-anthropomorphisation' (148). On the other hand, the double reflection that takes place in art produces totalities of representation in which the attempt is made to portray the variability and distinctness intrinsic to the 'personal immediacy of experience' (148).

The method of art is, as a result, one of 'anthropomorphisation'. It should also be remembered that Lukács's elevation of the particular encompassed a political, as well as aesthetic dimension. For example, and as mentioned earlier in this chapter, the 1957 *On Besonderheit as a Category of the Aesthetic* enshrined a 'dialectics of the particular' designed to challenge the authoritarian political system in Hungary (Kadarkay 1991: 445).

Whilst film, like painting, is an 'art of visibleness' and indefinite objectivity, Lukács, nevertheless, thinks that there is a problem with the mechanically produced photographic basis of film, and a problem that does not pertain to painting. A painting, such as one by Rembrandt (whom Lukács mentions), is anthropomorphic because it was produced by an artist and expresses an array of intrinsic human meaning (*Ansichsein*) (*Aesthetic II*: 477/88). As argued in this and previous chapters of this book, Lukács characteristically makes a distinction between consciousness and objectivation, a distinction which he first derived from Georg Simmel's conception of 'objectification' (*Vergegenständlichung*). Whilst the fashioning of objects is an intrinsic characteristic of human praxis, Lukács, following Simmel, argues that, within modernity, such object-making also constitutes a 'category of existence' which could not be entirely 'controlled or predicted' by consciousness (Márkus 1983: 8). Nevertheless, great art, or the 'great objectivations', transcend this, because it and they are fashioned for, and achieve, the purpose of authentic human 'self-cultivation' and the 'cultivation of ourselves', and because they retain the traces of authentic human consciousness (Arato 1971: 129–30).

In Rembrandt's 1633 *Portrait of Saskia*, one of many paintings which Rembrandt made of his companion, a ruffled Saskia engages the viewer directly through her gaze, inviting the viewer to contemplate her somewhat depleted condition. There is also a degree of reflexive, generic reference apparent here, as Saskia is theatrically posed and dressed to play a role. Other generic features are also at play. Whilst showing us aspects of Saskia's ageing physicality, the painting, partly through that, expresses an interiority of signification which we can imagine; and viewing the painting undoubtedly has the potential to add to 'the cultivation of ourselves'. Lukács would also not identify this painting only as a final entity, but as one that is related to the process of becoming which led to its appearance. To return to the terminology of 'On the Phenomenology of the Creative Process', this painting is both 'bounded' and 'unbounded' (Lukács 1972: 9). The bounded aspect of *Portrait of Saskia* is related to the relatively constant horizon of presentation and interpretation within experience that occurs whilst viewing the work, a constant horizon that is also linked to comparatively fixed presuppositions concerning what a painting by Rembrandt is most likely to signify; whilst the unbounded aspect is related to the process of becoming of that state and the inconstant horizon of presentation and interpretation which results from the subjective and inter-subjective positioning of the viewing subject within the life-world.

According to Lukács, however, the still image of the film shot is largely devoid of the *ánthrōpos* associated with the aura of a Rembrandt painting because it is generated by a machine, not a human being. The image is also a snapshot, and, as such, involves very little process of coming into being, a process which is characteristic of the arts (a novel is not written in a day). The film shot also shows only, or mainly, externality, and not interiority. It also cannot be experienced as a field of connotation that interacts with the viewer's subjective and inter-subjective experience, because it is not even meant to be viewed as it is. The film shot is 'de-anthropomorphic' because it cannot embody or evoke the unbounded aspect of aesthetic experience that reaches out to a viewer who wishes to understand the process of becoming of the work, and the way in which the work relates to his or her own subjective and inter-subjective understanding of things. The film still is a 'not yet aesthetic . . . simple reflection' (*Aesthetic II*: 472/192). What lies at the basis of the film medium, therefore, is this minuscule, not-yet aesthetic image, and, because the aesthetic is so central to human experience, this image is de-anthropomorphic as well as non-aesthetic. What the image makes available is a schematic rendition of the forms of appearance, and weak sense of interiority. In 'Thoughts towards an Aesthetic of the Cinema' Lukács does not address the photographic basis of film, but he does describe the film medium itself as presenting such a 'life without soul': what is presented in film is externality – a world without 'essence and value; a life without soul, made up of pure surface' (Lukács, in Aitken 2012: 182). Nevertheless, in 'Thoughts', Lukács argues that this was not so important, because such absence meant that film was better able to render the 'forms of appearance' (*Erscheinungsformen*), and also a modality of soul linked to such forms: one which takes authentic pleasure in phenomenal encounter with the 'livingness (*Lebendigkeit*) of nature' (184). This is obviously a far more affirmative account than the one given of the inhuman 'not-yet aesthetic film shot' in the *Aesthetic*. Whilst, however, Lukács is talking about film in 'Thoughts', and not, explicitly, the film still, when he refers to film as presenting a world of 'pure surface', he clearly refers to the photographic aspect of film, and not, for example, aspects related to editing, such as the ability of film to present a world characterised by 'unlimited possibility' (183). It is also this consideration of the photographic aspect of film, one not considered in 'Thoughts', that Lukács sets out in the *Aesthetic*. In the *Aesthetic*, the phrase 'world of pure surface', as just rendered, does not – in general – refer to the *moving* film, but to the film still, a shot that cannot embody or evoke the unbounded aspect of aesthetic experience.

In the *Aesthetic*, Lukács asserts that the moving film 'anthropomorphises' the de-anthropomorphic 'photographic basis' of the medium:

> Photography, as a starting point, is, as such, de-anthropomorphising; it is the film technique, which is itself a reflection of reality, which is able to suspend such de-anthropomorphism, and render what is depicted similar to the normal visibleness of everyday life (*Aesthetic II*: 468/188) . . . [and] closer to the forms of appearance of everyday life/*Erscheinungsformen des Alltags*. (*Aesthetic II*: 470/190)

When Lukács uses the term 'photography' here, he does not refer to photography in general but to the photographic still image of the film, or 'photographic recording' (*photographische Aufnahme*), generated by the filmic apparatus (*Aesthetic II*: 473/192).[13] That 'photographic recording' is also not entirely de-anthropomorphic because it is a *recording*, or 'reflection' (*Widerspiegelung*). Lukács employs the term reflection in its Leninist sense here, to mean perceptual reflection, and in the broader sense of an attempt to understand reality. Thus, he refers to *both* the photographic film still image, and the use of technology and technique to make that image move, as 'reflections'. The film shot may be de-anthropomorphic in the sense given earlier, of being unable to embody or evoke the unbounded aspect of aesthetic experience that a viewer engages with when that viewer wishes to understand the process of becoming of the work, and the way in which the work relates to his or her own subjective and inter-subjective understanding of things. This is because the shot lacks process and context: is a snapshot of 'pure surface'. The shot is, however, also anthropomorphic to an extent because it is, precisely, a reflection, albeit a 'simple reflection':

> each and every photographic image . . . generated by the filmic apparatus possesses a very concise authenticity . . . [the film image is a] . . . simple reflection (*einfachen Widerspiegelung*) . . . each photograph has to suggest the following: at the moment of the shoot the represented object looked indeed like it appears on the photograph; the lens is impersonal. (*Aesthetic II*: 472–3/192)

This is a rearticulation of the Leninist conception of reflection as more than just representation: 'of things and their reflection in the human brain, in our consciousness, thought, etc. . . . not symbols of things [but] "image", picture or reflection' (Lenin 1972: 34).

The moving image anthropomorphises, not just because it moves per se, but because it is now, as a moving image, able to embody or evoke the unbounded aspect of aesthetic experience that a viewer participates with when that viewer wishes to comprehend the genesis of the work, and the way in which the work relates to experience. The 'not-yet aesthetic' potential of the still image has been released because the shot has now become part of a process, and one which inevitably involves context, because context is necessarily built up over the span of temporal duration during which the process lasts, in terms of both the evolution of the film presentation, and the evolving experience of the observer. This is also a process which is meant to be *seen*; it is the medium of film as experienced phenomenon that is perceived, whereas the still image is, as Lukács puts it, merely the 'not-yet aesthetic' 'starting point'. When the still images, as 'simple reflections' which have limited anthropomorphic status, begin to move, they form complex reflections which take on a greater anthropomorphic status, and which reflect both perceptual experience, and broader aspects of experience, including what Lukács calls the 'double reflection' (*doppelten Widerspiegelung*) of *Wesen* and *Erscheinung* (*Aesthetic II*: 472/192). Because the film still now becomes part of a process, the process of the becoming of the work becomes apparent, and, as that occurs, the viewer mobilises his or her own subjective and inter-subjective understandings as part of the interpretative experience.

In arguing that film anthropomorphises the photographic film still, Lukács also appears to draw on something like the Aristotelian triad of 'matter', 'form' and 'substance' which influenced him in his youth, and in which matter is 'formed' into substance (see Chapter 2 of this book). Here, the 'matter' of photography is 'formed', through the application of 'film technique' (*Filmtechnik*), into the phenomenal substance that is the film, and such formation is also able to bring the film image 'closer in appearance to the normal visibleness of everyday life/*auf und nähert das Abgebildete der normalen Sichtbarkeit des Alltags*' (*Aesthetic II* 468/188). Despite the notion of the 'double reflection', therefore, the main anthropomorphising outcome to occur in film is the achievement of an appearance of being close to the visuality of everyday experience, and it follows from this that film technique must be deployed to reinforce that. Lukács argues that film form must be determined by film content, where that content is, primarily, the forms of appearance as they are close to life. When films depart from that, as in, say, the 1920 film *The Cabinet of Doctor Caligari*, which Lukács discusses in the *Aesthetic*, it is because another kind of content, one determined by the requirements of plot, narrative and theme, takes priority. As is well known, Lukács's contention that content must determine form was sometimes used by him to criticise a modernism in which, according to him, the reverse was the case. Here, however, it is film's closeness to the phenomenal appearance of daily life that matters most, and it is that content that film form must present. Lukács is not concerned with a content of plot or narrative-based subject-matter, but with a content of phenomenal visuality. Film may not be able to present a totality of objects, or representations, as a novel can, and this means that there are limits upon the extent to which film can be anthropomorphising, but, through a focus on phenomenal visuality, the medium can still play an important role in the process of aesthetic anthropomorphism.

All of the above points to a filmic phenomenological realism, and this is further reinforced by the contention that the presentation of *Geradesosein* and the thing-like existence of objects (see earlier in this chapter) is conceived of as a kind of 'moving point'; and that film must respect both the psychological slow-moving point of *Geradesosein* and the phenomenal arrow of time, in a way that conforms to our general experience of phenomenal reality. This also means that the account given in the world of film, in terms of both being-so and flux, must be 'transparent and graspable': 'Film's closeness to life (*Die Lebensnähe des Films*) means . . . the tendency to portray life as immediately transparent and graspable, a demand that is also true for the everyday person in relation to his/her own environment' (*Aesthetic II*: 476/195–6). Lukács relates film to the phenomenological notions of the 'pre-givenness' of experience and the 'natural attitude towards the world' here: notions based on the conviction of a fundamental unity of consciousness and the world (Moran and Mooney 2002: 167). Consequently, Lukács argues that the attempt to bring film closer to perceptual experience, to the 'forms of experience of everyday life (*Erscheinungsformen des Alltags*)', is essential (*Aesthetic II*: 470/190).

As argued, Lukács contends that film should be considered as a medium of the phenomenal, temporal flow and horizon. However, in the *Aesthetic*, he is also, paradoxically, troubled by the idea of the work of art as constituted by flux, not only because that idea bears a similarity to the Western existentialist notion of the individual as haphazardly 'thrown' into the flux of existence, but also because the idea of flux bears a similarity to the characteristic style of a naturalism inadmissible within classical Marxist aesthetics.[14] As a consequence of this discomfort Lukács introduces both a new and an old idea into his account of film in the *Aesthetic*, both of which are meant to counter the idea of the work as flux. The new idea is the empirical notion of *Geradesosein*, which has already been discussed at length in this chapter, and which can be conceived of at this point as something that will slow down the temporal flux so that the phenomenal present moment can be better and longer observed. The old idea, similar to, but also different from, that of *Geradesosein*, is the notion of *Wesen*. The impressionistic and naturalist aspect of the model of film that Lukács lays down in the *Aesthetic* led him to resurrect the notion of *Wesen* as a corrective to that aspect, and, with that, the idea of the great moment resurfaces. The idea of empirical *Geradesosein* is related to the notion of *Erscheinung*, or 'appearance', and is fully compatible with the naturalist and impressionistic model of film that Lukács sets out in the *Aesthetic*, because, whilst the notion does figure the psychological slowing down of time, it is also concerned with the everyday concrete and empirical. *Wesen*, however, is another matter, and, whilst similarly aiming to slow down the temporal flux, is idealist and abstract in temper.

As suggested, *Wesen* sometimes appears in the pages of the *Aesthetic*, including the chapter on film, in order to continue the doctrinaire classical Marxist repudiation of naturalism. Lukács's final and unconvincing position on this aspect of film in the *Aesthetic*, therefore, is that film, although a medium of the temporal flow, cannot be so entirely, and must accommodate *Wesen*. Amongst other matters, this also means that the division that Lukács first drew in 'Thoughts', between drama as a medium of *Wesen* and film as a medium of *Erscheinung*, is no longer acceptable to him, but not for any rationally valid reason. As a consequence, the two categories of *Wesen* referred to earlier are drawn upon: the trenchant 'great' or 'fruitful' moment that Lukács discusses in *Soul and Form* and 'Thoughts'; and the background-permeating symbolic effect attained through description, which Lukács conjures up when discussing Alexander Solzhenitsyn's *One Day in the Life of Ivan Denisovich*, and, also, in the *Aesthetic*, the films of Chaplin. As suggested, however, Lukács's position on this is unpersuasive.

CONCLUSIONS: THE INFLUENCE OF BERGSON; *ERSCHEINUNG AND WIDERSPIEGELUNG*

There is little doubt that Lukács was influenced by Bergson. These influences are, however, neither direct nor explicit, but tend to intermingle with other influences. Whilst the connection is strongest in the early period, it can also be found in the *Aesthetic*. For example, one key Bergsonian idea is the distinction between the 'present image' and 'represented image' (see Chapter 1 of this book), in which the represented image is not just a representation but partakes of some of the substance of the present image. This fits well with the notion of 'reflection' which Lukács inherited from the Marxist tradition, in which the image is more than just a representation: Bergson's represented image includes the 'skin' or 'envelope' of the present image, whilst Lenin's 'reflected images' are, similarly, more than just 'symbols of things' (Lenin 1972: 34). In the *Aesthetic*, Lukács is mainly concerned with the idea of reflection as operating at a general level, as a formulation within consciousness of human relation to the world. However, he also considers reflection at the more concrete level of perceptual activity, and in ways which adhere to a realist Leninist or Bergsonian account of representation and presentation. For example:

> The technical level of film takes from its very outset, and for granted, the reflection of a given reality, even though the end-product will always be a representation of reality and never reality itself . . . the primary,

purely technological form of film [photography] . . . is already nothing other than a visual reflection of reality . . . of course, photography is a reflection of reality, not reality itself. (*Aesthetic II*: 188–92)

In the above quotation Lukács does claim that 'the end-product will always be a representation of reality and never reality itself', but there is no way of understanding this statement other than by surmising that what he means is that the end-product will be a reflection, not 'representation', of reality. The reflection cannot be reality itself, of course, but it can still be more than just a representation. Lukács, unsurprisingly, makes no reference to the existence of an unreachable 'image world', as Bergson does, as his Marxist–realist position in the *Aesthetic* will not allow him to suggest such an idealist notion. Neither, also, does he presume that what we see in either perception or the photograph is an inferior account, as is the case with Bergson's theory of the image. Nevertheless, and despite these differences, there is a shared emphasis on the notion of presentation, as opposed to representation.

There is also a relationship, but at the same time a difference, between Bergson's dismissal of the 'photographic' and 'cinematographic' conceptions of perception, and Lukács's argument that the photographic basis of film is 'de-anthropomorphising' (although, and as previously argued, not entirely so). It will be recalled that Bergson dismissed the photographic conception of perception because that conception considered perception to be a snapshot 'taken from a fixed point by that special apparatus which is called an organ of perception'. Bergson also relates this misconception to the 'cinematographic view of things', in which perception is understood in terms of a linear partitioned series of such snapshots (Bergson 1991: 38). In the cinematographic view we have succession, rather than a photographic snapshot, but still one that is distinguished in terms of quantity and division, rather than quality and continuity. What links this to Lukács is the notion that what is lost in the photograph is the fluid continuity that characterises experience. For Lukács, the photograph, as reflection, is more than a representation, is, in part, 'anthropomorphic', but still, nevertheless, renders static what is continuity. What film then does to the photograph, and as previously argued, is to 'anthropomorphise' this reflection further through 'the unwinding of film [that] brings the medium closer to the visual apperceptions of everyday life' (*Aesthetic II*: 473/192). The photograph is not only a representation but also a reflection, and film is even more of a reflection than photography, because of its ability to illustrate the animated 'apperceptions of everyday life'.

One final connection between Bergson and Lukács that can be considered here relates to Bergson's model of 'confused multiplicity' as 'organic' in character. I have argued elsewhere that an underlying formative 'episteme', with organic-like characteristics, underlies much of Lukács's thought, from the early period to the late, and that this episteme also becomes more pronounced in the late period (Aitken 2013a). In the posthumously published *The Ontology of Social Being* (1971–3), for example, that episteme is embodied in the idea of the 'complex', which, Lukács argues, is the 'primary form of [social] existence' (Lukács, in Pinkus 1975: 17). The model of the complex set out in the *Ontology* indicates a fluid and interactive phenomenon, consisting of elements and relationships which come together to form a relatively coherent, though also contradictory and mutable, clustering within social experience. Experienced everyday life consists of encounter with a matrix of such 'complexes', and social being consists of this 'dynamically contradictory . . . [set of] . . . totalities' or 'complexes' (Lukács 1982: 72). This same episteme can also be found within the *Aesthetic*, in the concept of *Besonderheit*, or 'speciality', which, Lukács argued, is also the 'central aesthetic category' (Parkinson 1970a: 115). *Besonderheit*, which has been discussed in the previous chapter of this book, is constituted similarly to the complexes found within social being, and embodies the same degree of evolving, transient, interactive coherence that is characteristic of the Lukácsian episteme.

Bergson's model of confused multiplicity is, as argued, organic-like. However, it also has a poly-dimensional and manifold quality that goes well beyond the boundaries of any supposable organism, and the Lukácsian episteme is, in contrast, more linear and enclosing. Confused multiplicity, in Bergson, is also primarily concerned with internal affective states and individual consciousness, whilst the Lukácsian episteme is more concerned with relations between individual agents. The Lukácsian episteme also has more in common with the 'linear' version of confused multiplicity that Bergson characteristically applies to art. Here, instead of a manifold model of confused multiplicity, Bergson employs a 'one-inside-the-other' model (see Chapter 1 of this book) (Bergson 2015a: 13). In addition to the more organic notion of confused multiplicity, therefore, in which there is a 'mutual penetration, an interconnection and organization of elements, each one of which represents the whole, and cannot be distinguished or isolated from it except by abstract thought' (101), there is also this 'one-inside-the-other' model, and this is closer to the Lukácsian episteme.

The central influence on the Lukácsian episteme is, however, not Bergson, but the key notion of *Erscheinung*, a notion that determines that representation should analogically replicate the impressionistic phenomenal horizon of appearance as that horizon moves forward through time. Lukács did not derive the idea of *Erscheinung* from Bergson, but from Kant and the Marxist critique of Kant. In the *Critique of Judgement* Kant uses the term *Erscheinung* to refer to the phenomenal figuration of the primary datum of sense perception (*Erscheinungsdatum*): a datum which is organised into representations of the material world – that unknowable world of the 'thing-in-itself' (Zamitto 1992: 49–50). The process of *Erscheinung*, of the appearance of the world, is also related to will, because Kant makes a distinction between the passive reception of sense data (*Empfindung*), and the active figuration of those data into a field – *Erscheinung* – that refers back to external reality (50). The German term *Erscheinung* is normally translated as 'appearance', but is also linked to vision, and, therefore, to visual appearance (*Erscheinungsbild*); this combination of visuality and quotidian phenomenal appearance is also what Lukács means when he uses the term *Erscheinung* to refer to an 'unlimited [visual] variety of the world of film/*die unbeschränkten Mannigfaltigkeit der Filmwelt*' (*Aesthetic II*: 478/197) that embodies the 'unlimited diversity of everyday life/*die unbeschränkten Mannigfaltigkeit des Alltagsleben*' and the 'whole environment of man/*die gesamte Umwelt des Menschen*' (*Aesthetic II*: 477/196).

As has been argued, in Marxist dialectical materialism the absolute Kantian dichotomy between representation and the material world is rejected, and a more linked dialectical relation is held to obtain. This is summed up in Lukács's adoption of the notion of 'reflection', and Lukács's conception of *Erscheinung* also refers to appearances which are linked in some way to external reality. In this sense, as a phenomenological realist and Marxist, Lukács is also an 'externalist', as that term is defined in the Introduction to this book. In addition to the connection between representation and world implied by the notion of reflection, Lukács also gives *Erscheinung* a more vibrant resonance, so that *Erscheinung* now stands for a viscerally vivid reflection of phenomenal reality, echoing both Lukács's treatment of film in 'Thoughts towards an Aesthetic of the Cinema', and his treatment of the Greek epic in *The Theory of the Novel*, in which he describes the epic as the first artistic form to celebrate the 'luminous meaning to be found in life' (Lukács 1971a: 50). It is also worth pointing out that Lukács's conception of 'reflection' also embodies the same kind of dialectical relation and connection to the visual as does *Erscheinung*. *Widerspiegelung* can just mean simple 'reflection', but so too can '*Spiegelung*', and, accordingly, *Widerspiegelung* can mean something more than simple reflection: more like 'reflection back', or 'reflection against'. The German term *Wider* generally means 'against', or 'back', but it can also mean 'reflect' as well. As with *Erscheinung*, all of this implies a certain degree of transformation of what is reflected. *Widerspiegelung* can, in addition, also mean 'mirroring', and, is, therefore, associated with the visual image. Lukács uses these two terms throughout the *Aesthetic*, and not just in relation to film, but their relation to the visual makes them appropriate for his consideration of film.

NOTES

1. There are difficulties in referencing this work. First, the original German work is inaccessible to most readers, and the only translation available is in my *Lukácsian Film Theory and Cinema* (2012), making it necessary to cite that, rather than the original.

Second, and in contrast, the 2012 work translates only one chapter from the two-volume *Aesthetic*, which means that reference to other parts of the *Aesthetic* must be given in their original pagination. Third, the translation of Lukács's 'Thoughts towards an Aesthetic of the Cinema' that is cited in this chapter is also from this 2012 book, and this means that, for example, the normal reference figure of '(Aitken 2012: 184)' does not indicate whether the refence is from the *Aesthetic* or 'Thoughts'. In order to minimise confusion, I have, therefore, used the following procedure. Where this chapter, on the *Aesthetic*, refers to 'Thoughts', I have used the abbreviation of the essay's title alongside page numbers from the 2012 book: '('Thoughts': 182)'. This makes it clear that the citation refers to 'Thoughts' rather than the *Aesthetic*. Where the reference is from the *Aesthetic*, but is *not* translated in the 2012 book, I have given the reference, for the first time, as, for example, '(Lukács 1981 II: 202)', or '(Lukács 1981 I: 202)' (for the second and first volumes of the *Aesthetic*, respectively), and, thereafter, as '(*Aesthetic II*: 202)' or '(*Aesthetic I*: 202)'. This is also in order to bring the reference in line with the references from the *Aesthetic* which *are* translated in the 2012 book (all in *Volume II* of the original German work). In the latter case the pagination is given of both the German original and the 2012 book together, with the pagination of the German original coming first. The first such reference will read, for example, '(Lukács 1981 II: 470/184)', and, thereafter, '(*Aesthetic II*: 470/184)'.
2. It is possible to imagine the concepts of *Wesen* and *Erscheinung* applied to non-objectified form, as in an act suffused with both moral concern and physical engagement. However, and as argued in previous chapters of this book, Lukács rarely considers non-objectified form.
3. Lukács does not use the term *Erscheinung* in 'Thoughts'.
4. As argued in Chapter 4, it has a *reality*, but is not a 'moment' as such.
5. Tom Levin (1987), 'From Dialectical to Normative Specificity: Reading Lukács on Film', *New German Critique*, 40 (Winter): 35–64.
6. See Chapter 1 of this book on Bergson and Chapter 6 on Husserl.
7. See the following chapter of this book for more on the concept of the *Lebenswelt*.
8. Lukács's engagement with naturalism is widely covered. For more on this issue, see my *Realist Film Theory and Cinema: The Nineteenth-Century Lukácsian and Intuitionist-Realist Traditions*, Manchester: Manchester University Press, 2006; and Linda Nochlin's *Realism: Style and Civilisation*, Harmondsworth: Penguin (1979).
9. Andrei Zhdanov, Soviet Communist Party leader and cultural ideologue, closely associated with Stalin. Died in 1948.
10. The novel, set in a Soviet penal labour camp, or 'Gulag', is descriptive, has little overarching context, and focuses on the minutiae of everyday life in the camp.
11. During this period Lukács developed his theory of 'Stalinism', the notion that the problems of oppression and persecution prevalent in the Soviet Bloc were the product not just of an individual, Joseph Stalin, but also of an institutionalised system, which he called 'Stalinist'. Lukács's theory of Stalinism brought him into conflict with official communist forces that were attempting to differentiate themselves from the Stalin epoch, and blame the problems of that epoch on the historical figure of Stalin. Lukács, however, felt that the Stalinist system still pervaded the Soviet Bloc after the death of Stalin in 1953.
12. The concept of *Stimmung* will not be addressed here, as space will not allow. For a discussion of the concept see my *Lukácsian Film Theory and Cinema* (2012) and the 'Introduction' to my *The Major Realist Film Theorists* (2016).
13. Whilst Lukács does not, as mentioned, talk about photography in general, his position, none the less, implies a general distinction between photography and film, with the latter being the more anthropomorphic. It is interesting, but perhaps coincidental, that this

stance was also adopted by the philosopher and psychologist of perception James J. Gibson (see the Introduction to this book).
14. During the late 1940s Lukács travelled to Western Europe in an attempt to promote both his theory of 'critical realism' and the official Soviet model of 'socialist realism'. During these trips he entered into heated debate with Jean-Paul Sartre, and was strongly critical of some of the existentialist notions advocated by Sartre.

CHAPTER 6

Husserl, *Epochē* and *Lebenswelt*

The notion of the 'life-world', or *Lebenswelt*,[1] relates to 'our status as beings in daily life' (Natanson 1973: 20). That status is a generally unanalysed life of everydayness and quotidian routine: what is typically experienced as normal and familiar, and, also, strange (for what is strange should also be considered 'normally strange'). Husserl also refers to the typical attitude towards this life and the world as the 'natural attitude', one in which life is generally lived with certainty concerning everyday expectation. The concepts of the lifeworld and the natural attitude will be explored in greater detail later in this chapter. First, it will be necessary to explore the stepping back from the lifeworld and natural attitude that is implied by the phenomenological reduction, and *epochē*.

EPOCHĒ

The Greek term *epochē* means something like 'suspend', and, in Husserl, generally refers to a deferral of the natural attitude, and, accordingly, a 'withholding [of] assent' to the expected reality of the world (57). Husserl argues that *epochē* should bring about a temporary 'inhibiting' or 'putting out of play' of all 'positions taken toward the already-given Objective world . . . all existential positions'. This, however, 'does not leave us confronting nothing. On the contrary we gain possession of something by it' (Husserl, from *Cartesian Meditations*, cited in Natanson 1973: 59). That 'something' is what follows the *epochē*, and what the *epochē* makes possible. The *epochē* provides the grounding for phenomenological analysis and description of experience to take place, and that analysis and description occurs through the exercise of the phenomenological reduction. *Epochē* makes possible the disclosure of a new configuration of experience, and the practice of reduction then analyses and describes that. In the process, new knowledge is generated, and insight is gained into the operations of the natural attitude. The notion of the phenomenal reduction can be variably interpreted, and different 'reductions' have also been posited by various scholars. However, for present purposes, two forms of reduction will be posited here: the 'eidetic', and 'phenomenological'.

Eidos is the Greek word for 'essence', and, in eidetic reduction via the *epochē*, an attempt is made to understand what is essential to what appears within the phenomenal field in terms of phenomenal or conceptual configuration, and not in terms of what that means in relation to context, connotation or phenomenal surface detail (surface and essence are antithetical notions) (Natanson 1973: 65). So, for example, and in terms of phenomenal appearance: I look out from the window of my office and – at this moment in time, and from this perspective in space – I see a line of washing that includes a black dress. I also see a brick wall, and, behind that, a group of trees whose leaves reflect the sun. All of this is replete with knowledge that I have about it. I know, for example, that the black dress belongs to my wife and that it was washed this morning; and I also know that the trees form part of a country park and were planted to counter a historical deforestation in Hong Kong, where I currently live. I know that this country park is also one of several nearby. The view that I have of these trees is itself possible only because the estate where I live was built near to the country park, but not in the country park: something that I know to be prohibited. I also believe, naïvely, that everything in the view before me has a 'fixed and abiding reality' (Bell 1990: 172). Finally, I see all of this in immediate, phenomenal detail.

Although the account just given attempts to describe literal content as perceived from one point in space and time, it also contains a significant amount of a priori held knowledge that is not phenomenally present in the view but in my head. Now, if the *epochē* is performed, I would bracket out that knowledge, so that, as Husserl puts it, 'doxic commitment' is adjourned, and 'all [our] natural interests [related to the natural attitude] are put out of play' (Husserl 1970: 152). Then, eidetic reduction would attempt to describe phenomenal appearance from which as much knowledge as possible about what appears has been bracketed out, and, within which, underlying structures also begin to be detected. Now, the trees, denuded of any knowledge about them, and stripped of surface detail, have become a block of dark, variegated green, interspersed with white patches of reflected light. The washing has become a tapered and asymmetrical patch of black, moving erratically (the movement is caused by the wind, but I do not need to know that in order to make the reduction). The view also contains the sounds of insects and birds, and these have now become a series of sound frequencies coming and going through the flow of time. As that time flows by, I also see movement occurring across some of the parts of the phenomenal field before me. I could then go into further descriptive detail in this eidetic account, closely observing and describing, for example, the precise shapes and sounds of everything within the field, because, in the performance of eidetic reduction, 'the decisive factor lies, above all, in the absolutely faithful description of what is actually present . . . and in keeping at a distance all interpretations that transcend the given' (Husserl, from *Ideas*, cited in Bell 1990: 197). And, what is 'given' is also a more structural reality that underlies particularity: a certain reality that lies beyond and is obscured by the immediately concrete, and which is now brought to awareness.

The account of the reduction just given can be taken a step further by comparing that reduction with another, and what would then emerge through this comparison would be a greater understanding of the essential characteristics of each of the two phenomena under consideration. Husserl called this relative manœuvre of the reduction 'free variation in imagination', one in which 'an example is freely and yet methodically varied until the essential structure of the phenomenon . . . is made apparent' (Casey 1977: 75). Of course, the eidetic reduction, and free variation in imagination, not only are confined to the experience of phenomenal visuality, but can also involve interior psychological experiences: what, for example, is essential to the experience of, say, 'isolation', and how does that differ from what is essential to the experience of, say, loneliness, or loss? Teasing these differences out would target essence, but an essence that would, none the less, remain indefinite, because the eidetic reduction takes place within the parameters of experience, and experience is always indefinite in character: always surrounded by a fringe of meaning.

The supposed value of the eidetic reduction lies in the undertaking of an inquiry into the meanings and aspects of phenomena that are concealed by immediate appearance, and in the bringing of these to awareness, and, also, in enabling a greater mindfulness of how and to what the natural attitude ascribes meaning, and, correspondingly, what that attitude also conceals. Matching this latter is that the reduction also enables an enhanced understanding that the phenomenological world does not need to be, and indeed is not, inevitably suffused with the knowledge attributed to it by the natural attitude. As a result, eidetic reduction enables a heightened consciousness to emerge concerning the phenomenal world, the natural attitude, the 'I' of the observer, the activities of the 'I', the history of the 'I' and world, activities of remembering and anticipating, awareness of the phenomenal flow, and the activities of seeing, hearing and the contemplation of objects, as these are transformed by becoming separated off from taken-for-granted meaning. All of these and their interaction can enter awareness during eidetic reduction, but largely through description; and it has been argued elsewhere that such description is not sufficient, and should be followed by more substantive analysis, and that, without such analysis, phenomenological methodology is 'intrinsically not only one of the most timidly conservative, but also one of the most dogmatic of all philosophical standpoints' (Bell 1990: 197). On the other hand, and as argued, a detailed account of the given can provide insights into the nature of perceptual encounter, and, additionally, can act as a basis for aesthetic treatment. For example, if the person performing the eidetic reduction was a film-maker, providing a detailed description of a scene in which the underlying aspects of that scene are represented, that might be an appropriate end in itself, even though relatively little conceptual analysis may be involved. This issue will be addressed further in the following chapters of this book, when Siegfried Kracauer's theory of film is discussed.

The eidetic reduction is only the first stage of reduction, and a prerequisite for the second: the 'phenomenological reduction', and its attendant 'transcendental subjectivity'. Phenomenological reduction (also referred to as 'transcendental reduction' by Husserl) is premised upon the movement from 'believingness', or embedded subjectivity (characteristic of the natural attitude, and, also, to an extent, of the eidetic posture), to 'transcendental subjectivity'. I look at the same scene described earlier, but, in phenomenological reduction, 'I' am now a supposedly 'pure observer', not an individual with a history and context. This pure 'I' must now take up where the eidetic reduction left off and go further. Eidetic reduction, the first stage of reduction, brings the various factors under scrutiny into greater clarity, but remains unavoidably connected to the natural attitude to an extent, and this means that what Husserl calls 'pure description' is, consequently, limited by such connection. In phenomenological reduction, that connection, as well as the knowledge-factors accruing to it, must be bracketed out, and 'transcended'. Part of this also involves the separation of the 'I' from the 'we'. In the connection between 'I' and 'we', the 'I' remains necessarily connected to history and context, and, therefore, to the natural attitude. The bracketing out of the history of and relation between the 'I' and 'we', and also of the shared world and its history, constitutes a movement 'from the "I" as a communally-grounded reality' connected to the natural attitude and eidetic reduction to a 'pure subjectivity that is ultimately the individual's *own*, his "ownness", in Husserl's language' (Natanson 1973: 71).

What Husserl calls the 'sphere of ownness' refers to 'the total nexus of that actual and potential intentionality in which the ego constitutes within himself a peculiar ownness' (Husserl, from *Cartesian Meditations*, cited in Bell 1990: 216). However, the sphere of own-ness is not entirely 'pure' in relation to the first reduction and is so only in relation to the second. In the first reduction the psyche appears 'inside' the ego to a greater extent than is the case with the natural attitude, rather than completely 'outside' and connected to the world; but it is still, nevertheless, connected to 'outside' through the natural attitude and its attendant knowledge and beliefs, and the two are also mutually confirming because the inherent belief in the given reality that pervades the natural attitude seeps into the first reduction and entails that this sphere of own-ness cannot analyse consciousness independently of context (Russell 2007: 68). Husserl characterised the eidetic reduction as 'transcendentally naïve' because it is unable to grasp the need to surpass the natural attitude fully in order to achieve a transcendental subjectivity, and, thus, the eidetic remains within the realm of the 'psychological': 'The I which occurs in the world with other I's and other entities is a psychological I. That means it is looked on as the soul of a body which belongs thus to the corporeal world' (Biemel 1977: 295). Here, the eidetic reduction is sometimes referred to as the 'psychological reduction' (Russell 2007: 68). Husserl is not, however, saying that the eidetic reduction lacks value as a consequence of this, and its value lies, to a large extent, in that the connection to the natural attitude means that the *world* is 'posited': 'To look at something as posited means to consider it as standing there . . . as occurring independently of the observer' (Biemel 1977: 296). In *The Crisis of European Sciences* (*Crisis*) (1936), Husserl discussed such independently assumed or ascribed 'posited-ness' of the world at length, but, in that work, he also emphasised the type of self-dependent 'positing' of what is 'posited' that phenomenology accomplishes within the transcendental reduction:

> To understand something as positing means to grasp it in its proper relations to the observer and thus not as detached from him and independent but, on the contrary, as – so to say – brought forth by him . . . phenomenology . . . puts into question the existence of an entity with regard to its relation to actually functioning subjectivity. [In science and psychology] '"the world" . . . is the foundation; for us, it is just this foundation that has been taken away by the epochē' . . . the objective world becomes a particular kind of subjective one. (Husserl, from *Crisis*, cited by Biemel 1977: 296)

In the second reduction, this is, as suggested, more the case than with the first, as a 'transcendental subjectivity', one which surpasses the connection between inside and outside, focuses on the stream of consciousness; and what is also transcended here is not just the outside but also the interior psychological psyche, which, like the 'outside' world, is disregarded. Husserl speaks of this second domain of own-ness as the 'sphere of pure evidence', or 'sphere of pure given-ness'. Given-ness, or evidence, denotes that which is given to us in a confirming manner within the natural attitude and first reduction, whilst pure given-ness, or pure evidence, denotes that which we experience when we transcend the natural attitude and first reduction. In the second reduction, both the psyche and the world are 'left behind' and this leaves only the phenomenal 'stream of conscious experience itself': an 'independent sphere of given being' (Russell 2007: 68). In this sense, within the second reduction, 'a consciousness which is not personal, is imaginable' (Husserl, from *Ideas I*, cited in Russell 2007: 68); and the psyche gives way to '"transcendental subjectivity": a stream of consciousness . . . which is no part of the world at all' (68). And yet, at another level, the stream of consciousness, although 'not personal' in a psychological sense, is also concomitant with the pure ego, and this is the source of Husserl's conception of the transcendental:

> It is the motif of enquiring back into the ultimate source of all the formations of knowledge, the motif of the knower's reflecting upon himself and his knowing life . . . grounded purely in this source . . . this source bears the source *I-myself*. . . The whole set of transcendental problems around the relation of this, my 'I' – the 'ego' . . . and again, around the relation of this ego and my conscious life to the *world* of which I am conscious and whose true being I know through my own cognitive structures. (Husserl 1970: 97–8)

What the second reduction aspires to, then, is engagement with the stream of consciousness, and such engagement may even lead to the 'annihilation of the world' by the stream of consciousness: '*Consequently no real being*, no being which is presented and legitimated in consciousness by appearances, *is necessary to the being of consciousness itself*' (Husserl, from *Ideas I*, cited in Russell 2007: 69). Experience can be considered as apart from the positing of any factual being, so that transcendental consciousness and 'real world' 'exhibit a radical separability', thus leading to the 'essential detachableness of the whole natural world from the domain of consciousness' (69). This means that a '*new region of being never before delimited in its own peculiarity* . . . a region of *individual* being' is opened (70). 'Transcendental phenomenology', and the concomitant intellectual position of 'transcendental idealism', are, accordingly, associated with the study, or experience, of this 'new region of being'. On the face of it, Husserl's conclusions appear solipsistic. Consciousness is conceived of as 'non-natural', the 'phenomenological residuum' that is separate from the world. The 'real world has *appeared* to us all along *as* the real world', and transcendental phenomenology studies this appearing (70). The 'ultimate horizon is subjectivity of consciousness' and this means that a 'veritable abyss' now 'yawns between consciousness and reality' (71). 'All objectivity, therefore, has its "origin" in transcendental subjectivity' (71), and consciousness 'needs nothing in order to be' (72).

Husserl asserts that 'the total phenomenological attitude and the *epochē* belonging to it are destined to effect . . . a complete personal transformation, comparable in the beginning to a religious conversion' (Husserl 1970: 137).

Understood this way, the reduction appears close to practices of meditation, or mindfulness. Like such practices, the phenomenological reduction is an activity undertaken in order to achieve existential benefit. Husserl, for example, claims that the reduction 'bears within itself the significance of the greatest existential transformation which is assigned as a task to mankind as such' (137). This 'task' is to become more aware of the 'new region of being', the 'subjectivity of consciousness', and this awareness will be transformative because it will disclose the existence of this fundamental region of being, which is not so much 'new' as newly discoverable and discovered. Seen in terms of mindfulness, the benefit brought by the reduction might consist of enhanced awareness of the present moment and the evolution of that moment through time, something that, as has been argued in previous chapters of this book, was important to both Bergson and Lukács. One philosopher has dismissed the reduction as an 'esoteric experience' that 'cannot be communicated': 'I have tried to follow Husserl's instructions for the performance of the phenomenological reduction . . . and certainly there was not opened up to me "a new region of being never before delimited in its peculiarity"' (Bell 1990: 162). However, if the reduction is seen as a form of esoteric meditation, then what is meditated upon is the 'subjectivity of consciousness'. I stare out of my window and experience all that I previously experienced in eidetic reduction. But now, I take another step, and focus on what I experience as a stream of phenomenal content, moving through the flow of time, from the present into the future. A picture has appeared, accompanied by sounds of various sorts, the thoughts going through my mind, the sensations emanating from my body, and physical forces acting on my body (sunlight, wind, rain and so on), 'whose true being I know through my own cognitive structures' (Husserl 1970: 98).

What is significant, within the context of this book, is that the type of meditation on being within the present moment during the second reduction could find expression in a film. If I placed a camera before my eye, and the outcome was a film, I would lose something of the experience just set out above. I would, for example, lose bodily affect and the thoughts traversing my mind. What would be retained would be the audiovisual aspect of my stream of consciousness, observed, when I watch the film later, from the perspective of the second stream of consciousness I experience at that later moment of spectatorship: a second stream of consciousness which would now include that film within it, as well *as* bodily affect and the thoughts traversing my mind. The latter experience of spectatorship would also enable me to employ memory to recollect elements of the first stream of consciousness. For another spectator, watching this *ciné vérité* film for the first time, what would appear would be the same audiovisual depiction, this time observed without any primary memory, as part of the stream of consciousness of that spectator. Husserl's 'thought experiment' regarding the 'annihilation of the world' could thus be performed during the act of filmic spectatorship. Spectatorship – for the spectator/cameraperson – would now consist of a meditation upon the interaction between two streams of consciousness, and the experience of thought and affect, as a flow of experience persisting through the present moment; whilst for a second spectator, it would comprise a meditation upon the film as part of one steam of consciousness, and the experience of thought and affect as part of such a flow of experience. It also becomes possible to imagine a film so constructed as to facilitate such meditation.

It has been questioned as to why the attention to consciousness just referred to should require a radical bracketing out of the natural attitude, with all the knowledge of the world that the attitude contains: why 'post-reduction consciousness must also be innocent of any reference to the world or to anything in it' (Bell 1990: 166). Similarly, it has been argued that it is impossible to bracket out the natural attitude entirely, and 'annihilate the world'. For example, the account of conscious subjectivity given earlier inevitably contains aspects of the natural attitude because the mind is unavoidably full of reference to that attitude. It is also difficult to imagine how the aesthetic could be related to the 'transcendental realm' supposedly made available through the reduction because aesthetic experience would be unable to bracket out the natural attitude. In fact, both the stream of consciousness, and any aesthetic portrayal of that, must always remain related to what Husserl himself calls 'doxic modalities': commonly shared modes of belief which are inevitably related to the natural attitude (cited in Bell 1990: 166). Amongst other matters, this would seem to indicate that the second reduction, as Husserl conceives it, might not be able to exist in any meaningfully pure form as far as film is concerned. Given this, the phenomenological account of film spectatorship just given could be amended, as follows: spectatorship – for the first spectator/camera – could be understood as now consisting of a meditation upon the interaction between two streams of consciousness, and the experience of thought and affect, as a flow of experience persisting through the present moment, but one in which the natural attitude, with its concomitant knowledge, constantly intervenes. What was said earlier regarding a second spectator would still apply, but also with the qualification just given. As in the previous case, it is also possible to imagine a film so constructed as to facilitate this.

The same problem of the difficulty in bracketing out doxic modalities also applies to Husserl's conception of the 'split ego'. The transcendental reduction is 'an exclusion which is destined to reveal consciousness again as "residuum" . . . that is, as an ontological "region"' (Ricœur 1996: 91). In the transcendental residuum, what is left is *only* 'this ego, with its ego-life' (Husserl, from *Cartesian Meditations*, cited in Bell 1990: 167): a realm of 'transcendental being' (Bell 1990: 168). This position leads Husserl to posit a 'splitting of the ego'. The 'naïve' ego is not part of the transcendental world because it remains connected to the natural attitude, and, therefore, this means that 'the phenomenological reduction splits the ego into two': the empirical ego remains within the framework of the natural attitude, whilst the phenomenological ego becomes a 'disinterested onlooker' existing beyond the naïve ego in an 'absolute sphere of egological being' (Husserl, from *Cartesian Meditations*, cited in Bell 1990: 169). As previously stated, however, it has been questioned whether the transcendental phenomenological ego, and 'absolute sphere of egological being', could be cut off entirely from the empirical ego and natural attitude. Given this, it might be better to conceive of the phenomenological reduction as a procedure which enables consciousness to be engaged with through a new and different perspective as a stream of consciousness that is necessarily linked to doxic modalities, and one that can also be portrayed in aesthetic form, including that of the film. This would make it unnecessary to think in terms of experiencing, or portraying, a new realm of transcendental being.

Husserl was aware that his approach, including his notion of the 'annihilation of the world', could be interpreted as excessively idealist, and attempted to deflect that charge by posing a rhetorical question, in order to then refute it:

> When I, the meditating I, reduce myself to my absolute transcendental ego by phenomenological *epochē*, do I not become *solus ipse* [a sole/isolated self]; and do I not remain that, as long as I carry on a consistent self-explication under the name of phenomenology? (215)

Husserl's refutation is to argue that the reduction, as a procedure and act, first, is only temporary, and, second, also 'adds something' to the natural attitude towards the world and the naïve ego; and that something is the residuum of transcendental consciousness (this notion of the reduction as 'adding' something will be returned to later, when the idea of the life-world is addressed). In this sense, 'The world presented in the natural attitude is neither denied nor abandoned; it is, instead, reconstructed' through an augmentation (Natanson 1973: 42). It has also been argued by one advocate that Husserl does not advance a solipsistic position in his writings because 'absolute consciousness' (transcendental consciousness) still includes the appearance of the world as it is experienced in the stream of consciousness: we see the appearance of objects as they come into view so that 'I have the world of objects and a relation to them' (Russell 2007: 72). In this interpretation, what is included in transcendental subjectivity is 'people, things, ideas, etc.'; the entities are not contained in consciousness but the experience of them is, and these existents are considered solely in terms of how they are experienced. This perfectly reasonable argument, nevertheless, does not deal with the issue of how this 'experience' is able to bracket out the natural attitude: how the 'appearance of the world' can be void of knowledge of the world.

A similar criticism to that of the inherent solipsism of the phenomenological attitude towards the world (once more, set up here in order to be refuted by an advocate of Husserl) is that this attitude retreats from the empirical livingness of the world into essence: 'the individual is ordered to abandon ordinary life and enter a conceptual monastery . . . While the real world goes on, the phenomenologist resides in timeless, historyless, seclusion' (Natanson 1973: 42). The refutation of this is that the *epochē*, and forfeiture of the natural attitude towards the world, are, and as previously contended, only temporary, and done in order to interpret the world of the natural attitude from another perspective. Accordingly, and as argued, the natural attitude is 'neither denied nor abandoned' (42). Neither, it is argued, is this a 'subjectivist' discipline', as is sometimes claimed, because the attention of phenomenology is always 'directed towards what is presented in experience', and not to what is hidden in the depths of the psyche; the phenomenological reduction is 'extrospective', rather than introspective (43). One possible defence of the reduction is, as suggested, that it is merely a procedure for arriving at a different perspective on things. But this implies that, as a procedure, it should be capable of being clearly delineated. And yet, exponents of Husserl argue that it 'would be incorrect to treat the reduction . . . as an easily summarized mental technique, the various forms of which can be easily given' (Fink 1970, cited in Natanson 1973: 76)! According to this view, the reduction is inherently marked by 'obscurity and opaqueness' because it represents something that transcends normal human matters; and, therefore, 'to understand the reduction, one must perform it', and, in doing so, hope to achieve a 'good' analysis of it (Natanson 1973: 77). Consequently, 'The paradox of explaining the reduction would seem to be analogous to the problem of trying to understand Freudian psychoanalysis without undergoing analysis oneself . . . to understand the reduction one must perform it' (76–7).

In *Crisis*, Husserl attempts to link the phenomenological reduction to the world, and so deny that his approach is solipsistic. It was argued earlier that the stream of conscious experience and the pure ego are one, and, in *Crisis*, Husserl also links both to the 'world'. Husserl argues that there is a 'correlation' between the world and the stream of conscious experience encountered in the phenomenological reduction: between 'the world itself and world-consciousness' (Husserl 1970: 151). The 'correlation' is taken for granted within everyday experience. World-consciousness refers to the conscious life of subjectivity, a subjectivity that must be 'of . . . ', where the ellipsis necessarily stands for the world. And, when subjectivity is experienced during the reduction, the world does not disappear, 'it is just that . . . it is under our gaze purely as the correlate of the subjectivity which gives it ontic meaning, through whose validities the world "is" at all' (152). The world 'is', but, during the reduction, it is viewed, and, therefore, 'is', only as the basis for what appears during the reduction, giving what appears 'ontic' significance. In the reduction, the world is 'reduced' to the world experienced as phenomena within world-consciousness, and the 'mundane ego' of the natural attitude is further 'reduced' to a pure ego that experiences that consciousness; and, as argued, these two reductions are necessarily 'correlated' (Kockelmans 1977: 280). What the reduction does, therefore, is disclose this

> universal, absolutely self-enclosed and absolutely self-sufficient correlation between the world itself and world-consciousness ... And there results, finally, taken in the broadest sense, the absolute correlation between all meaning and beings of every sort and every meaning, on the one hand, and absolute subjectivity, as constituting meaning and ontic validity in this broadest manner, on the other hand. (Husserl 1970: 151–2)

The world is, therefore, not lost within the reduction, and, consequently, there is no imperative to 'abandon ordinary life and enter a conceptual monastery' (Natanson 1973: 42). What is explored in the phenomenological reduction is the correlation between the world and world-consciousness; and this is also only a temporary reduction, made in order to explore – for a conditional period – how conscious experience is taking place. The world 'has not disappeared', but, 'through the *epochē*, I stand *above* the world, which has now become for me, in a quite peculiar sense, a *phenomenon*' (Husserl 1970: 152).

As such, this phenomenon must also be considered as a-thing-in-itself, rather than a representation of something else, and Husserl argues that his stance is not a 'representationalist' one. Husserl argues against representationalist positions in which it is posited that the mind constructs a representation of the outside world, because the implication of such positions is that we merely 'live in a world of "copies" or "imitations" without ever seeing the "originals"' (Russell 2007: 81). In contrast to this, Husserl contends that a perception is an original: a *consciousness* that is correlated to something in the world, and 'not merely of a representation of something in the world ... consciousness reaches to the things themselves and not just to poor shadows of reality' (81):

> Experience is the performance in which for me, the experiencer, experienced being 'is there', and is there *as what* it is, with the whole content and the mode of being that experience itself, by the performance going on in its intentionality, attributes to it. (Husserl, from *Formal and Transcendental Logic*, cited in Russell 2007: 81)

Representationalism cannot apply to perceptual experience in any literal or unadulterated sense because that which is ostensibly represented cannot be pointed to, as we cannot step outside of our conceptual schemes in order to prove such a relation; and it also follows that, if that which is represented could be pointed to, that, itself, must also be a representation of something else; and, so on, ad infinitum. In terms of perception, therefore, 'the representationalist theory leads to an infinite regress' (81). The phenomenal manifestation of the material world is, consequently, both 'our' reality, and *a* reality, not a representation of a reality. Whatever processing procedure our perceptual apparatus undergoes, as internal material structures encounter external ones, that procedure does not produce a copy of those external ones. Instead, the procedure grasps material reality at a certain level as a thing-in-itself within consciousness. The internal process tries to counterpart, at a certain level of human capacity, things happening in the rest of the material world, and, when the internal process achieves such consonance, the phenomenal world 'appears' as it does, and as it always has, probably since the emergence of homo sapiens. This is the 'correlation between world and world-consciousness' that Husserl discusses in *Crisis* (Husserl 1970: 151).

For Husserl, there are two things which make the correlation possible, one given to consciousness, the other made available to consciousness. What is made available to consciousness but not given to consciousness is what he calls the '*hyletic* content'. Husserl mainly derives the ancient notion of *hyle* from Aristotle, where that notion refers to the underlying or 'first matter' of the cosmos: 'something underlying and persisting' through immediate appearance (Shields 2007: 55) In Aristotle, this underlying matter becomes 'form' when it is altered, when what persists is changed in some way. 'Form', therefore, is what occurs to 'first matter' in an 'episode of change', and the existence of change is, consequently, also a precondition for the existence of form, which is the result of an intentional alteration of matter (55–6). First matter, therefore, is 'inert material waiting for the imprint of *nous*, or reason' (Herman 2013: 36). In Husserl, this 'matter' is a mass of detail available to but *not given to* consciousness, which consciousness passively receives and 'registers', and which does not itself possess meaning. *Hyletic* data are in 'perpetual flux and movement' and are, in Husserl's words, '*really* immanent': that is, the data exist per se as a basis for sensory experience and are not 'intentionally immanent', shaped into perception through the imprint of *nous* (Husserl, from *Ideas I/Ideas*, cited in Bell 1990: 173). The *hyletic* data also have a determinate character, and, as such, and as what is available to consciousness, act as a relation between consciousness and the external world. *Hyletic* data, therefore, like sensory data in Kant or Hume, are not graspable in-themselves, and only enter perception when they are transformed by the intervention of *nous*. They are, in other words, not 'phenomenal' in character, and this has led some phenomenologists, most notably Maurice

Merleau-Ponty, to dispute their existence on the basis that 'experience simply does not contain anything corresponding to the notion of a pure hyletic datum' (Merleau-Ponty, from *The Phenomenology of Perception*, referenced in Bell 1990: 174). According to Husserl, the *hyletic* data are transformed by consciousness, and appear in consciousness as a '*noetic* act' (an act of understanding, or activation of the *nous*), and this transformation also corresponds to Aristotle's notion of 'form'. The *noetic* act, also referred to as the '*noesis*', seeks to order the flux into unified and meaningful unities, and each of these unities is the *noema*, the '*noematic* core', 'object core' or *noemata* of experience (what the *noesis* is about, or directed at).[2] It is important to understand, however, that the way that Husserl's model is understood in this chapter is that the 'registration' of *hyletic* data, and the organisation of those data via the *noesis* into the *noema*, takes place in relation to material reality, so that there is no radical separation between consciousness and material reality, a separation that would amount to solipsism, as has sometimes been taken to be the case with regard to Husserl.[3] If they exist, *hyletic* data, as meant here, must form a relation between consciousness and external reality, and this also corresponds to Husserl's principle of the unavoidable correlation between world and world-consciousness.

There are, however, two problems with Husserl's model that emerge when anticipating the analysis of Kracauer and film that will take place in the following chapters of this book. First, and following Merleau-Ponty's critique, *hyletic* content is 'sub-phenomenal', and, consequently, not experienceable. Husserl's notion of *hyletic* data, therefore, seems to remove a whole realm of existence from conscious experience and representation (174). The second problem with the notion of *hyletic* data is that they seem to exist as 'raw material' outside of signification, and therefore conform to what has been described as a 'myth of the given' (197). This notion has also been criticised by Merleau-Ponty, who argues that whatever we experience is always shrouded in a fringe of meaning from the start, and this means that there is no 'neutral' material which is then interpreted. According to Merleau-Ponty, there is no stage of perception that is 'passive', and all stages of perception are 'intentional' and related to interest (referenced in Matthews 2007: 35). In fact, most theories of perception also reject this notion of a 'raw material' that 'corresponds to nothing in our experience' (Merleau-Ponty 1962: 3). When turning to Kracauer, in the following chapter of this book, it also makes little sense to talk about invisible *hyletic* data, as it would mean thinking about 'material' aspects of the film image as existing at a sub-perceptual level. When we watch a film, what we see is the *noema*: our interpretation of the sense data projecting from the film. Any sub-phenomenal data are of no concern, just as they are not in daily life within the life-world.

THE LIFE-WORLD

> CONSCIOUSLY WE ALWAYS live in the life-world . . . Conscious of the world as a horizon, we live for our particular ends . . . a self-enclosed 'world'-horizon is constituted . . . and we have an eye only for this horizon as our world and for its own actualities and possibilities – those that exist in this 'world' . . . That this whole effective life and this whole work-world is held within the always obviously existing world in the most universal and full sense of the life-world . . . we have our particular world . . . our horizon of interest. (Husserl 1970: 379)[4]
>
> Calling to mind what has repeatedly been said: the life-world, for us who wakingly live in it, is always already there, existing in advance for us, the 'ground' of all praxis whether theoretical or extratheoretical. The world is pregiven to us, the waking, always somehow practically interested subjects, not occasionally but always and necessarily as the universal field of all actual and possible praxis, as horizon. To live is always to live-in-certainty-of-the-world. (142)
>
> The material plena – the 'specific' sense-qualities – which concretely fill out the spatio-temporal shape-aspects of the world . . . these qualities, and everything that makes up the concreteness of the sensibly intuited world . . . the certainty, binding us all, of one and the same world, the actuality which exists in itself, runs uninterrupted through all changes of subjective interpretation. (33–4)

In the above quotations from *Crisis*, Husserl refers to both the 'life-world' and the '*plena*'. As the above usage suggests, the term *plena* designates the material data perceived by and given to the senses, and Husserl also refers to this world of the *plena* as the *Plenum*. *Plenum* implies the entirety of something: in this case, the manifold of conscious experience. Sometimes, Husserl appears to equate the life-world with the *plenum*, as, for example, when he describes the life-world as 'the world constantly given to us . . . the sphere of what is actually experienced and experienceable' (51–2). These words can be understood as referring to either what is *given* to us, or what *is*: to part (given) or whole (is). In this chapter, however, they will be interpreted as meaning that the life-world constitutes what is given, not what is. What *is*, the manifold, is the whole, whilst the life-world is to be considered a component of the whole. This distinction between part and whole must also be extended into one between parts of the part, because the life-world itself is divisible into two main areas, one of which, moreover, is also further – and interminably – divisible. The two provinces of the life-world are the 'perceptual' and the 'cultural'. The first of these encompasses perceptual experience alone, whilst the second encompasses perceptual experience and what Husserl calls 'cultural' experience within a community, where the term 'cultural' is meant in a broad sense of encompassing the generality of everyday norms, beliefs and expectations pertaining to a community: 'all sciences and arts, together with all personal and social configurations and institutions, insofar as it is just the world actual for me' (187), 'all traditional norms, those of right, of beauty, of usefulness, dominant personal values, values connected with personal characteristics, etc.' (287).

Whether the life-world is understood as perceptual or cultural, however, it is always concerned with everyday practical consciousness and activity: the so-called 'mundane' or 'naïve' world of habitual, lived and generally non-reflective experience (Natanson 1973: 128). In this sense, the life-world constitutes the source of all experience, and is the 'sole absolute foundation' of all experiential practices, including those pertaining to higher-level theoretical reflection (Bell 1990: 228).

This conception of the life-world is based on the premise that what is given in the life-world is assumed to be true and real. In the life-world we are confident about the reality and veridical character of our perceptual understandings, and we also have various beliefs about aspects of the life-world that we ordinarily take to be true or untrue, and which, ordinarily, turn out to be so, so that 'to live' 'is always to live-in-certainty-of-the-world' (Husserl 1970: 142). This is what Husserl calls the 'natural attitude' to the life-world, and, consequently, it seems that the notion of 'the life-world does not . . . differ from a daily natural attitude' (Mickunus 1997: 190). The natural attitude towards the world is, therefore, based on the belief that the world has a being outside of mind, and generally makes sense (Natanson 1973: 65). This natural attitude to the life-world is not particularly based upon self-reflection, although it can include 'reflection on its own activity' to some extent (21). We can, for example, become more conscious of things that normally occur without being noticed. This 'noticing' is unplanned, an act of fluctuating 'happenstance', and this always-present possibility of 'becoming aware' is an intrinsic aspect of the natural attitude (21). Nevertheless, the natural attitude is, generally, based in an unreflective, taken-for-granted 'faith in the givenness of the world as real' (23). That faith in the reality and meaning of the world is also experienced immediately and intuitively through directly perceived encounter because that is how we experience the world at a fundamental level (23); and, yet, the life-world, as 'one reality for all of us', also means that all 'normal' human beings adopt the same natural attitude, and that, consequently, 'Men simply accept the givenness of an intersubjective reality in which essentially the same world exists for us all' (24). This focus on a shared inter-subjective reality of the life-world is also central to *Crisis*.

Nevertheless, this assured given-ness of the life-world through the natural attitude also includes a degree of ambiguity over the meaning of things and relationships, and the given-ness of experience is, accordingly, necessarily accompanied by a 'fringe' of indeterminate meaning and 'undefined possibilities' (25). As we move through the life-world, a range of likelihoods exist pertaining to what to do, what to become aware of and so on, and, consequently, nebulosity is ever-present against the backdrop of the self-possessed belief in the given-ness of the world: something *in* the field may be put into question, but not the field itself. There is, thus, a mutual trust amongst human beings over what Husserl calls the 'General Thesis' of the natural attitude, 'according to which the real world about me is at all times known . . . as a fact-world *that has its being out there*' (Husserl, from *Ideas I*, cited in Natanson 1973: 28). The natural attitude, 'naïve believing-in-the-world', also has two central interpretative modalities: those of continuity and repetition, which are, in addition, deployed in a 'story-like' fashion. As we experience the world through the natural attitude, we do so in this diegetic manner; we engage in an ongoing interpretation of a scene, as if following the unwinding of a narrative. This tale is always open to amendment, but is also, none the less, driven by perceptions and expectations of continuity and repetition, and will also have a beginning, middle and end, as befits the assured character of the natural attitude. Continuity, the perception that one thing will successfully follow on from another, and repetition, the belief that what worked before will work again, constitute what Husserl calls the 'one can always again' and 'so forth' stance that informs the general thesis of the natural attitude and the story-like orientation of the individual within the life-world. (Natanson 1973: 35). And all of this adds up, further, to the 'central impulse of the general thesis of the natural attitude': the 'fixed and abiding being' of the life-world and the 'ascription of reality to the parade of consciousness'. As argued, ambiguity may be present, but the core of our lives is lived within a state of imperative common certitude (36). As also argued, however, a cultural life-world is not the *plenum*, which contains many such worlds, and the self-possessed self-affirming natural attitude of a cultural life-world may also stumble against another within the unpredictable plenitude of the world.

The concept of the life-world does not generally encompass theoretical practices, of one sort or another. Such practices exist in any community, and, therefore, any cultural life-world, but they are built upon the foundation of the life-world. So, for example, the life-world can be considered as a 'complex whole that possesses physical, mythical, social, political, aesthetic, mathematical, sexual, historical, and ethical properties and dimensions . . . along with the complex relations in which they stand to one another', and where all this exists at the level of given-ness (Bell 1990: 227). This given-ness of these 'properties and dimensions' is the 'sub-soil' upon which theoretical practice, and theoretical reflection, is established (230). But such reflection is always an abstraction from, and idealisation of, the indeterminate, concrete life-world, and, for Husserl, this is particularly the case with the key target of *Crisis*, science, which 'mathematicises' the life-world:

> In geometrical and natural-scientific mathematization, in the open infinity of possible experiences, we measure the life-world – the world constantly given to us as actual in our concrete world-life – for a well-fitting *garb of ideas*, that of the so-called objectively scientific truths... It is through the garb of ideas that we take for *true being* what is actually a *method*. (Husserl 1970: 51)

Although arising from within the life-world, science is secondary to its essential foundation, and, in order to return to that foundation, we must set aside the immaterial modus operandi of science: one which fixes a 'garb of ideas' over the indeterminate 'sensible plena' of the 'concretely intuited' life-world (51). This notion of returning to the basis of the life-world also became, to an extent, more important in the late work of Husserl than the notion of the phenomenological reduction, which implies a 'stepping back' from the life-world and bracketing of the natural attitude. This notion of return to the life-world also influenced the reappraisal of the idea of the life-world undertaken in the work of Merleau-Ponty, where the emphasis is now on the deployment of phenomenology to 'get back to that underlying foundation of ordinary human experience which is the source of science and all other theoretical activities' (referenced in Matthews 2007: 13). For Merleau-Ponty, as, indeed, for Husserl, science is a 'second-order expression' of the life-world, and it is the latter which is the 'homeland of our thought' (Schmidt 1985: 37). In a similar vein, although, in *Crisis*, Husserl still speaks of *epoché*, with its concomitant suspension of 'natural' knowledge of the life-world, the principal objective is none the less to restrict the remit of abstract theoretical preconceptions (Matthews 2007: 13). In *Crisis*, consequently, Husserl asserts that the first task of *epoché* in phenomenological methodology is to rule out 'all participation in the cognition of the objective sciences... even any position on their guiding idea of an objective knowledge of the world' (Husserl 1970: 135).

The cultural and perceived aspects of the life-world are, in practice, inseparable from each other within the natural attitude. At the perceptual level, there is, of course, a necessary identity between all cultural life-worlds in the world, or *plenum*, because perception and the perceptual apparatus are constant factors within that world. Although perception is always of a segment of the material world, and never of the *plenum* in its totality, as manifold, the rules that govern that segment are constant, predictable and (in terms of modern humankind) a-historical, because perceptual structures have not changed for a long time; our perception of the life-world today may, consequently, be as it was 200,000 years ago, when *Homo sapiens* first appeared. The life-world, at the perceptual level, has, therefore, more or less always been there for consciousness in the same manner (Carr 1987: 215). Beyond that fundament, however, and at the cultural level, there is relativity. The cultural life-world is historical and relative because understandings of what are familiar and typical change through history, and are, additionally, relative to different communities of agents existing, and co-existing, during the same time-frame. Sometimes, this relativity may also become apparent, when something occurs that is outside of our typical expectations, and what is 'outside' of the cultural life-world in this sense is the cultural 'world' which encompasses the overarching *plenum* of cultural possibilities. When something unexpected and unfamiliar occurs within our cultural life-world, something that enters our life-world from the world, we may, in addition, also become aware of a distinction between our life-world and the broader cultural world, and one that may, accordingly, make the insular limits and limitations of our life-world – and of certain aspects of the natural attitude – more apparent (Natanson 1973: 133–4). As modern people, however, and subject to a barrage of information from the media, we are always aware, to an extent, that there are other cultural life-worlds, and, so, are less likely thrown into disarray when we encounter something 'strange' to our life-world. In this sense, twenty-first-century people are relativists in a way that earlier peoples were not, or at least not to the same extent.

In addition to the relativity of different cultural life-worlds, such worlds may also vary in terms of the extent to which they are perceived from the inside to be historical and relative: a cultural life-world dominated by immutable ideas or doctrinal edict may exhibit a greater sense of permanence than one based on (for example) secular–liberal values more capable of grasping and endorsing the relativity and changeability of things and meanings. Some such comparatively 'permanent' cultural life-worlds (such as may be found, for instance, in primitive, isolated indigenous tribes) may not even possess any conception of historical change or relativity (or, if they do, it may be very different from a modern conception of these). A cultural life-world may also possess a combination of all these, and such a life-world may be in 'constant tension', where 'each mode of awareness strives to establish its own supremacy over others' (Mickunus, in Hopkins 1997: 207–8). At the level of the natural attitude, the fundamental characteristic of the life-world, this could also be debilitating, and result in incompatible manifestations of one sort or another. This could be of an extreme nature, as with oppositions between, say, sets of fundamentalist and non-fundamentalist values, or less extreme, as in an opposition between, say, conservative and liberal values.

The cultural and historically relative aspect of Husserl's late conception of the life-world has led to attempts to link that conception, and Husserl himself, to various schools of conceptual relativism, including the language-based paradigms of discourse and 'apparatus theory' which developed during the 1970s and after. The notion of the life-world was philosophically fashionable in the 1950s and 1960s, prior to the emergence of such theory, and against the contemporaneous context of a widespread interest in existentialist phenomenology, as practised by philosophers such as Jean-Paul Sartre and Merleau-Ponty (Carr 1987: 227). After the emergence of the 'linguistic paradigm', however, the a-historical dimension of the concept of life-world was marginalised and the historical notion of the cultural life-world recuperated within the framework of various conceptual relativisms. Nevertheless, the conception of the life-world found in *Crisis* is also directed *against* forms of relativist theory, because the a-historical aspects of the life-world are, precisely, taken to underlie and enable the historical–cultural ones. The life-world', at the perceptual level, and, also, at the cultural level of categorical 'given-ness' that stems from the perceptual level, has always been there for consciousness, in the same manner, and in a way that transcends cultural relativism at other levels (215). The life-world, therefore, 'does have, in all its relative features, a *general structure*. This general structure, to which everything that exists relatively is bound, is not itself relative' (Husserl 1970: 139). It is, additionally, and as argued, a characteristic of the natural attitude that, although we live in our own subjectivities of 'appearances', we do not think that 'because of this, there are many worlds. Necessarily, we believe in *the* world'; and we do so because it is both rational and pragmatic to believe in a common world that lies outside our individual subjectivities (23). The 'basis' of the life-world is perceptual experience and a given-ness attendant upon that which is also the basis of the natural attitude, and Husserl refers to this as the 'a priori' of the life-world: the a-historical factor that all life-worlds, despite their many differences, have in common (Carr 1977: 208).

All of this is at odds with a relativist disposition that impends rationality, as is made clear in *Crisis* when Husserl asserts that 'skepticism . . . actually represents a collapse of the belief in "reason"', and that a 'normative relatedness to what, since the beginning of philosophy, is meant by the word "truth"', and 'what is', is essential to a rational and progressive 'humanity' (Husserl 1970: 12–13). Husserl's search for essential and a-historical factors, for the 'what is', is, therefore, underpinned by a belief that this is what philosophy ought to do, and so, he talks about a philosophical 'naïve faith in reason' as essential to 'secure rational meaning for . . . individual and common human existence' (13). If this faith in essence – in the 'what is' – is not kept, and relativism promoted, 'we find ourselves in the greatest danger of drowning in the skeptical deluge and thereby losing our hold on our own truth' (14). Husserl links reason with realism here: 'It is reason which ultimately gives meaning to everything that is thought to be' (12). However, reason is also predicated on what has elsewhere been called a 'realism of intent': although objective truth is unobtainable, the intent to pursue such truth is a rational and necessary thing to do (Trigg 1989: 201–2). As Husserl puts it in *Crisis*:

> If man loses this faith [in reason and truth], it means nothing less than the loss of faith 'in himself', in his own true being . . . [this is] . . . something he only has and can have in the form of the struggle for this truth . . . True being is *everywhere* an ideal goal, a task of epistēmē or 'reason'. (Husserl 1970: 13)

Husserl's rejection of 'skepticism', and pursuit of the 'what is', are also grounded in his conception of intesubjectivity. For Husserl, particularly in late works such as *Crisis*, a sense of inter-subjectivity is an intrinsic component of the ego, of the 'sphere of ownness', because my consciousness of being stems from both the cultural life-world that I am placed within and that surrounds me, and from the knowledge that the 'I' is surrounded by the 'They' – the many; and because this sum gives the 'They' an incidence that the 'I' cannot disregard. I know, for example, that I must interact with the others to prosper. Although I have my own consciousness and am primarily concerned with what is of use and interest to me, I am also aware that I exist in a life-world alongside others who are also concerned with what is of use and interest to them; and I understand that dialogues and concessions must take place within this manifest. My sense of existence as an ego is, consequently, defined by a sense of existence shared with other egos. I know that there is a 'thereness' for everyone, as well as 'I', and, thus, when I experience the world, I experience it not as a private world, but as an inter-subjective one that is there for all. I am aware of my own being and I suppose the existence of being in others existing within my life-world:

> all of us together belong to the world as living with one another in the world; and the world is our world, valid for our consciousness as existing precisely through this 'living together' . . . we, in living together, have the world pregiven in this 'together' . . . the world as world for all, pre-given with this ontic meaning. Constantly functioning in wakeful life, we also function together, in the manifold ways of considering, together, objects pregiven to us in common. (108–9)

Husserl calls the process through which an intimation of inter-subjectivity takes place 'apperception', or 'appresentation':

> It is implicit in the sense of my successful apperception of others that their world, the world belonging to their appearance-systems, must be

experienced forthwith as the same as the world belonging to my appearance-systems; and this involves an identity of our appearance systems. (Husserl, from *Crisis*, cited in Vandevelde 1996: 13)

I perceive my own ego directly, within the 'sphere of ownness', and 'apperceive' other egos indirectly, as my ego expands its perspective out from itself to encounter 'the other' (13). At the basis of this process is the experience of the presence of another person as proximate 'animate body'. This is the 'point of departure' for then appresenting, or apperceiving, the other as possessing 'constitutive and intentional achievements'. I experience inter-subjectivity by first 'pairing' my ego with another body, then with a 'psychophysical ego, and, finally, by expanding such a combining-outwards to accommodate the 'They' (13). In this process I come to appresent them as other egos existing within an appearance-system that is identical with my own and, therefore, 'valid for everyone', and I can also, as a consequence, 'appresent what they see from their perspective, thus appresenting a second stratum of what I then perceive as objective' (13–14). As Husserl puts it: 'The experiential phenomenon, Objective Nature, has, besides the primordially constituted stratum [in my sphere of ownness], a superimposed second, merely appresented stratum originating from my experiencing of someone else' (13). Inter-subjectivity, ultimately, comes down to 'the presence of two Egos', one of which occupies the sphere of ownness, and such occupation means that an 'other' can be apperceived as constituted outside the sphere of ownness, but as sharing the same 'appearance system' (14).

Unison of the 'what is', therefore, lies at the heart of inter-subjectivity, the natural attitude and the 'meaning fundament' of the perceptual and given life-world; and, in terms of the latter, such unity is also inferred at the primary level of the perceptual process itself, as we construct unity from fragments of perceptual readings (Carr 1977: 209). Our perception can only ever be fragmentary, and we cannot grasp the totality of things within perception. However, although, in ordinary perceptual activity, I see something only in part, in order to make it meaningful in a practical sense I 'mean it' as a whole – with all the parts that are not given to me when I perceive it from a particular angle. In visual perception we see only the surface of things, but we intend the whole thing: the object as a whole, 'itself-there' (Natanson 1973: 131). In addition, I also perceive the object, and mean it as a whole, across the passage of time. As I perceive the object, I perceive it in the present, but the present is linked to the past and future: there is continuity with what is no longer perceived and what will be perceived – what Husserl refers to as 'retentions' and 'protensions' (Husserl 1970: 168). When I 'intend' something as whole through a variety of glances, I bring that thing into unity, drawing upon the typicality that is characteristic of the natural attitude. This is an ongoing procedure of intending as whole and marks the essential continuity-establishing of consciousness within the life-world and flow of time in relation to retention and protension (Natanson 1973: 132). And this intending as whole – as a unified thing – also means 'intending it as a unity for my fellow men as well as for me' (132–3). So, what we do in consciousness within the life-world is, from a variety of perceptual acts, of fragments, construct a unity that accommodates the inter-subjective, and it is this that guarantees the 'sameness in the experience of objects' in the life-world, and guarantees the familiarity that is characteristic of the personal and inter-personal life-world.

One final point to make is that Husserl was not inflexibly anti-science. *Crisis* may have had as its target the abstractive activities of science, but this does not mean that science is conceived of as separate from or alien to the life-world. Such a position would be untenable, because science makes constant practical incursions into the life-world, and a considerable amount of the contemporary life-world is constituted by science in this practical sense (cars, smartphones, central heating, X-ray machines). This is also even more the case today than it was in Husserl's time. In this sense, the 'useful articles' created by science have become part of the '"ground" of the modern life-world', to the extent that it has been argued that science cannot now be disentangled from the life-world (Mickunus, in Hopkins 1997: 192) and that, consequently, no 'pre-scientific' life-world is now graspable (197). Although the pre-scientific life-world did exist in the past, before the rise of science, that is out of sight now. Science also stems from the life-world, even if it cannot be distinguished from the life-world. All scientific procedures are, for example, carried out within the life-world, the 'sub-soil' of all theorisation. All scientists exist in the life-world, as well as the laboratory (191).

Husserl's main point about science in *Crisis* was that it was responsible for the development of an account of reality that was increasingly at odds with our everyday experience, and that there was now a need to refocus our attention back on to that experience. The concept of the life-world was important for Husserl when he wrote *Crisis* because, during the late nineteenth century, and early decades of the twentieth century, science, particularly physics, was increasingly unfolding an account of reality that seemed very different from that encountered in personal and inter-personal experiential encounter with the world.[5] In addition, that world was increasingly defined as a realm of mere 'appearances', and reality itself as something inaccessible to the senses, and, therefore, to ordinary persons in their everyday lives (Carr 1987: 229). 'Appearance' was by no means inferior to 'reality' as far as Husserl was concerned. The term 'phenomenology' is derived from the Greek word meaning 'appearance', and Husserl wished to focus on how things 'appear' to us, not as an inferior realm, but as the 'things themselves' as they appear. For Husserl, the 'crisis' of European science was brought about because the hegemony of science had 'contributed to our estrangement from our world and ourselves' (Carr 1987: 229); it was this which impelled him to advance the notion of the life-world, and the imperative need to return to that world. As the following chapters of this book will show, this notion of return to the life-world was also central to the thought of Siegfried Kracauer.

NOTES

1. In this chapter, the phrase 'life-world' will generally be used in place of the term *Lebenswelt*.
2. This is the admittedly simple definition of *noema* attempted here. It should, however, be understood that the meaning of Husserl's notion of *noema* is contested, and that other, more extensive, definitions exist.
3. For example, Bell (1990: 52) argues that this was the case with Husserl's early work, as in *Ideas*, but less so with later works such as *Crisis*, although Bell also embeds this distinction within the general idealism that he ascribes to Husserl.
4. Capitalisation is Husserl's.
5. This was also a central factor in Bergson's critique of science (see Chapter 1 of this book).

CHAPTER 7

Introduction to Kracauer: Abstraction, Redemption and Modernity[1]

Siegfried Kracauer's late conception of cinematic realism was influenced by ideas taken mainly from Immanuel Kant and Edmund Husserl, and, to a lesser extent, from American philosophers such as John Dewey, William James and Alfred North Whitehead. In terms of Kant, Kracauer was chiefly influenced by two related Kantian concepts: the 'harmony of the faculties', and *Naturschöne*. The phrase harmony of the faculties refers to a harmony between the 'faculties' of the 'Understanding' and 'Imagination'. For Kant, the creative faculty of Imagination unites the sense impressions which human beings experience into evolving assemblies and designs, whilst the faculty of Understanding then applies regulative concepts and classifications to these. The 'harmony' of these faculties occurs when the Understanding seeks order and entireness, and interacts with the Imagination in such a way that the latter is caused to seek meaningful formations and a sense of wholeness in the object of contemplation (Crowther 1991: 49). The harmony of the faculties is additionally important for two reasons: first, the aesthetic pleasure experienced during such harmony is conducive to the generation of authentic or apposite moral feeling (the harmony of the faculties 'disposes us to moral feeling'); and, second, such an activity of seeking harmony is related to freedom, as it is a free intentional act (50). The harmony of the faculties, accordingly, links the object of scrutiny – something in nature – to 'the concept of freedom . . . [and] . . . at the same time promotes the sensibility of the mind for moral feeling' (Kant, cited in Crowther 1991: 49). As will be argued later, and in subsequent chapters of this book, these actions and consequences of the harmony of the faculties were an important influence on Kracauer, who believed that film could provide the foundation for an experience analogous to that engendered by that harmony, one able to address authentic aspects of human nature; and, here, 'moral feeling' is reinterpreted as a type of authentic and free scrutiny and experience of the world's 'thisness' (Jay 2012: 229).

At a fundamental level, the object of scrutiny that involves the harmony of the faculties is nature, and all things in nature, where the term 'nature' stands for both the ground of all our experience and all that exists in a physical sense. Nature, in the latter case, as the noumenal 'thing-in-itself', presents itself to us through our representations as an empirical multiplicity that must be made sense of, and Kant argues that, when such sense is successfully made, the reflective judgement then engenders a feeling of pleasure that, as argued, is also related to freedom and moral imperatives. Kant also contends that 'reflective judgement' proceeds by assuming that what is encountered in the engagement with nature 'has been designed by some artificer with the express end of facilitating human cognition', so that a quest for such design takes place (45). A special form of reflective judgement– the aesthetic – could, evidently, be applied to the scrutiny of works of art, but could also be applied to that of nature, where the term nature now stands: not for nature in the sense of the entire physical world of 'things-in-themselves', but the experienced phenomenal world of things in nature, and, in particular, the greater and imposing constituent features of the natural world, rather than the more restricted and confined world of human habitation and project.

Kant refers to such judgement and contemplation of nature as the experience of *Naturschöne*. *Naturschöne*, 'natural beauty', refers to the satisfying meaningful formations and sense of totality found when the Kantian categories of the Imagination and Understanding are brought to bear during the contemplation of nature; and, here, the harmony of the faculties, and the pleasure arising from the successful implementation of the reflective aesthetic judgement, is achieved through the encounter with the natural environment. In *Naturschöne* the witnessed abundance of the natural milieu enables the Imagination to explore diverse possible structures, formations and movements freely, seeking the traces of the hidden hand of the artificer, and this also enables the Understanding to shape and regulate, but also be affected by, such unhindered exploration. This also occurs when encountering a work of art, but, in the confrontation with nature, the empirical richness of the natural environment offers the basis for more complex autonomous interaction between the Understanding and Imagination than can be afforded by art. As with the harmony of the faculties, *Naturschöne* is related to the concept of freedom, and to a 'moral law' whose essence is the consciousness of freedom (49). The Kantian idea of natural beauty resonates through Kracauer's *Theory of Film*, but his understanding of the concept was also influenced by his friend Theodor Adorno's historical assessment of the concept, in which Adorno argues that the demise of the concept in recent times, and more general lack of meaningful experience of nature that was concomitant with that, were the result of an ongoing capitalist degradation and exploitation of nature. There was, consequently, an urgent need to reverse that through a return to a contemplation of natural beauty that could be facilitated by film

(Bratu Hansen 2012: 230).² A general opposition between nature and human society can also be found in Kracauer's writings, one based on the characterisation of an 'immutable', 'unchanging' nature, and a human history that is always subject to change, and, in modern times, also likely to subjugate nature to its will (Gerhardt 2015: 237). Nature is also relatable to science, in that the first is subject to and the second driven by a search for immutable, universal laws. The crucial difference between the two, however, for Kracauer, is that the experience of the immutability of nature is something that should be incorporated as a necessary common grounding within experience for an otherwise disparate human history, whilst the abstractions and generalisations associated with the scientific method engender abstract certainties inimical to the 'irregularities' that characterise that history. The application of such method to human history would, consequently, 'prevent freedom' (237).

In *Theory of Film*, Kracauer conceives of the world presented by film as analogous to the natural world that is explored through the prism of *Naturschöne*. The world that appears in film, and which he wishes to identify, is made up of richly empirical and dense 'unshaped matter' (Robnik 2015: 265): a finely textured canvas to be explored in order to find the patterns left by the artificer (although Kracauer does not posit an artificer), and one which, in analogy with the Kantian concept of aesthetic, reflective judgement, encourages forms of exploration that will also bring the explorer into more authentic contact with their relation to their experience of being. In order to achieve this, the Kracauerian observer moves into 'the world of reality' (Mülder-Bach 1998: 9), and the world of the film, in order to return to 'the things themselves' as much as possible – although that can never be absolutely possible (Jay 2012: 229); and the rediscovery of the 'world of objects and man's place in its changing constellation' is the objective that is sought (Jay, citing Sabine Hake, in von Moltke and Rawson 2015: 229). Films following such a template would be rich in tangible visual detail and contain variable configurations and figures which tempt the spectator to search for such. These films would not be governed by plot, narrative or characterisation, but by a current of concrete, empirically rich imagery. This passage, and the images within it, would also be largely indeterminate rather than established, whilst leaving opportunity for ordering activity to occur, just as, in the harmony of the faculties, the reflective judgement assumes a hidden artificer, and, thus, a hidden order to be sought out against an indeterminate context. As with the harmony of the faculties, such a quest would also link the concepts of freedom and moral calibre to the activity which the film induces. That activity is based on close observation of the fabric of the film: in the 'evocation of self-consciousness and self-knowledge in the things observed. To observe a thing means only to arouse it to self-recognition' (Jay 2012: 231). Underlying Kracauer's approach, therefore, is this observational 'surrender' to 'concrete reality' (Rudolf Arnheim, cited by Robnik 2015:

265), a surrender which also presents a decisive possibility: that of 'attaining once more the world before man, before our own dawn' (Gilles Deleuze, cited by Robnik 2015: 266).

It also follows from the concept of *Naturschöne* that such films would be, or could be, generally concerned with the representation of nature and landscape, or be so formed that nature and landscape repeatedly encroach into any human-centred narrative that may be present, introducing areas of indistinctness in the process. Such films 'reveal' the landscape, and the objects within it, in a process of what Walter Benjamin called 'profane illumination' (illumination of the ordinary); such films are 'engaged in terms of substances', and have an 'ontological compunction' (Jay 2012: 232). But such an ontological compunction also involves the *presentation* of movement, and temporality, so that what we have is the 'event of a moving image': an engagement with substances progressing within the temporal flux through a movement which is experienced as a 'being-there' for us (Jay 2011: 84). Such films do not so much present themselves for viewing as a 'having been there', as, it has been claimed, is the case with photography (Seel 2008: 175), but as a 'realism of particulars' and a 'being-there' that is given to our contemplation, and which, in the process, leads to a 're-enchantment' of such (Jay 2011: 85).[3] Films following such a course might include those of Michelangelo Antonioni, whom Kracauer mentions, particularly *L'Avventura/The Adventure* (1960), with its juxtaposition of character and landscape; or, for a later example, those of Werner Herzog, who comes after Kracauer's time, and particularly documentary films such as *Encounters at the End of the World* (2007), with its numinous evocation of the lunar-like Antarctic terrain, and utopian gauge and potency of the natural world, both of which, with the assistance of an evocative musical score, interpose between the spectator and the more 'project-oriented' interviews which make up the bulk of the film. Such sequences of images break out from the generic conventions that surround them to be considered '*on . . . [their] . . . own merits*' (Adorno 1997: 199), as audiovisual presentations of a 'realism of particulars' (Jay 2011: 73). But, in addition to that, such sequences of images build on what they are, essentially, anyway: 'Images are not reflections, shadows or artifices, they are living beings, that is to say organisms endowed with desires' (Rancière 2011: 30). Other film-makers who fit this mould might include Robert Bresson, Theo Angelopoulos, Andrei Tarkovsky, and more recent film-makers associated with the movement of 'slow cinema'. Many of these films are relatively 'realistic'; elsewhere, however, Kracauer remarks on how 'insertions' of 'physical reality', to be considered 'on their own merits', interrupt the progress of the narrative in a modernist film such as Luis Buñuel and Salvador Dalí's *Un Chien andalou/ An Andalusian Dog* (1929).

Un Chien andalou is a surrealist film, and, as such, one that Kracauer is prepared to consider of value to an extent, because he believes that the surrealists were committed to the ideal of an indeterminate, empirical cinema which would be capable of engendering self-determined associative, meditative and revelatory activity in the mind of the spectator that was focused on the interior world. It is because of this that he considered films such as *La Coquille et le clergyman/ The Seashell and the Clergyman* (Germaine Dulac, 1928) and *L'étoile de mer/ The Starfish* (Man Ray, 1928) to mark an important shift from the exploration of artistic form as an end in itself, to the investigation of subject-matter associated with the interior *Lebenswelt* (Aitken 2001: 177). Kracauer also approved of surrealist films because of their appropriation of psychoanalytical theories derived from Sigmund Freud, Carl Jung and others: theories which Kracauer drew upon directly in his *From Caligari to Hitler* (1947), and other writings. These theories are of value to Kracauer because they are concerned with 'inner life', a substantive aspect of being; but they are also problematic as they are appropriated within surrealism, because, in the latter case, inner life becomes the greater focus than 'outer reality'. Additionally, however much Kracauer may have been indebted to Freudian and Jungian theory in *From Caligari to Hitler*, in *Theory of Film*, conceptions of the psychological unconscious are far less important than the Husserlian concept of the *Lebenswelt*, and an associated 'realism of [external] particulars' (Jay 2011: 85): whilst films that portray the *Lebenswelt* were 'cinematic', those which portrayed the unconscious were 'merely surrealist' (Kracauer 1997: 191). For Kracauer, therefore, and despite his appreciation of surrealist films, such films none the less turned their backs on the *Lebenswelt* too much:

> It is not as if the surrealists denied that the 'outer skin of things, the epidermis of reality . . . are the raw material of the cinema,'[4] but they unanimously hold that this shadowy and ephemeral material gains significance only if it is made to convey man's inward drives and concerns down to their unconscious roots . . . To the surrealistic film-makers, then, camera-reality is a sort of limbo; and they seize on external phenomena for the sole purpose of representing the inner world in its continuity. It is the only reality that matters to them. (189)

Kracauer argues that the surrealist attempt to 'render visible' inner life adds an important extra element to the portrayal of the physical 'epidermis of reality' found in more realistic films and may thus come to constitute a completer picture of reality (189). However, he adopts this position only to an extent, and, in contrast, believes more insistently that surrealist films take the portrayal of inner life so far as to undermine the rendition of physical reality. For Kracauer, physical objects should not be 'swallowed up by the relational contexts in which they are embedded', including that of interiority (Jay 2012: 232).

The other problem that Kracauer identifies with surrealism is an overabundance of conceptual tropes, which he feels is associated with a focus on interiority that subjects the latter to logical scrutiny and inference. In *Theory of Film*, following the German philosophical critique of modernity which stretches from Kant to himself and beyond, Kracauer argues that 'conceptual reasoning' has come to overly dominate modern life (Kracauer 1997: 264). One of the key concepts that Kracauer developed in his Weimar writings, and which also permeates the pages of *Theory of Film*, was that of 'abstraction'. The idea of 'abstraction' is premised upon the belief that modernity is so subjugated by systems of technical and conceptional rationality that immediate experience of the material environment as an imaginable and actual object of observation has become sharply attenuated, and, consequently, more 'abstract': 'abstractness – a term denoting the abstract manner in which people of all walks of life perceive the world and themselves' (291). The notion of abstraction is also related to Kracauer's conception of ideology as a fixed and determined structure of conceptual reason that imposes itself upon the individual subject. Here, in the opposite modality of the free and moral quest that takes place within *Naturschöne* and the aesthetic reflective judgement, the array of meaning is closed down and determined. In *Theory of Film*, Kracauer also sees such closure as particularly embodied in the 'tragic' drama, or literary equivalent: 'The tragic conflict materialises only in a closed universe . . . Tragedy presupposes a finite, ordered cosmos' (266). What Kracauer is opposed to, therefore, is the configuration that locks meaning down, rather than, as with *Naturschöne*, one that opens meaning out. As argued earlier, this is also his position on history and historiography: history is full of 'discontinuities and contingencies', and historiography should acknowledge that, and avoid the elaboration of systematic, overgeneralised explanation (Kracauer 1995b: 37).

Like the tragic, systematic history, and ideology, 'symbolism' in surrealism also works to close down the array of 'potentialities', and, accordingly, Kracauer argues that the 'symbolic function assigned to surrealistic images' in surrealist films 'automatically prevents them from unfolding their inherent potentialities' (Kracauer 1997: 190), and thus brings surrealism into association by implication with the general injurious hegemony of conceptual reasoning within modern life. It is not, therefore, only the prevalence of concepts in surrealist films that Kracauer objects to, but also the use of the symbol which has a direct and fixed meaning. In addition, Kracauer asserts that surrealist films are not even able to depict 'inner life' as well as 'realistic' films are:

> Films devoted to physical reality – cinematic films, that is – represent inner-life configurations. They are no less capable than surrealistic films of doing so, but they leave it to the spectator to apprehend their possible references to inward reality. (190–1)

Kracauer, on that account, prefers 'inner life', with its non-perceptual content, to be inferred by the spectator, rather than directly foregrounded in the work; and, in adopting this position on inferred interiority, and as will be apparent from earlier chapters of this book, he is close to Lukács's notion of 'indefinite objectivity', one which also implies the indirect expression and reception of interiority, rather than any contrived manufacture of such. In fact, Kracauer sometimes seeks to bracket out interiority, in a return to the *Lebenswelt*, or at least to seek a state of 'lowered consciousness', in order to 'release . . . [the spectator] . . . from the grip of consciousness', including self-consciousness of the workings of the mind, and in order that the spectator 'absorb . . . the images as they happen to follow each other on the screen' (159–60). Consciousness is inherently related to abstraction, whilst perception is inherently related to the concrete, and, within the modern world, the hegemony and 'grip of consciousness' over human existence as a physical reality can be counteracted by 'the images [of the world] as they happen to follow each other'.

In many ways, the notions that Kracauer derives from Husserl underpin those that he derives from Kant, and, so, Kracauer's use of Husserl's model of the *Lebenswelt*, a model discussed in depth in the previous chapter of this book, reinforces the idea of *Naturschöne* in that, in both cases, and amongst other similarities, concrete empirical indeterminacy is emphasised. The difference between the two concepts lies in the junction of the human and natural implied by *Lebenswelt*, as opposed to the primary focus on nature in *Naturschöne*; and this difference, and reliance on both concepts, afford Kracauer's thinking a degree of hybridity, and also indecision, when he comes to explore particular films, sometimes focusing on human interactions, as in Vittorio De Sica's *Umberto D* (1953), sometimes on the visual landscape, as in Joris Ivens's *Regen/Rain* (1929), and sometimes more on the confluence of landscape, nature and human predicament, as in Michelangelo Antonioni's *L'Avventura/The Adventure* (1960). In general, however, if the idea of *Lebenswelt* appears to prevail over that of *Naturschöne* in Kracauer's thought because of the human dimension implied by the former, it is an idea of *Lebenswelt* that nevertheless still prefers to emphasise the non-human within that overall context; and, so, Kracauer commends films in which narrative and human dilemma are present, but prefers those in which such narrative and dilemma are more often interrupted by projections of 'physical reality', as in *La Strada/The Street* (Federico Fellini, 1954), a film that, according to Kracauer, is 'soaked in the street world' of quotidian, material indeterminacy (255). As one writer has put it, for Kracauer, film is, or should be, 'a medium en route to "existence"', where existence means the experience of physical existence within the world (Koch 2000: 103).

If the notions of *Lebenswelt* and *Naturschöne*, when applied to film, suggest that film should have a fluid, organic-like structure, these Kantian and Husserlian concepts also imply that a Kracauerian film would be perceptually realistic in terms of the overall structure of the image and sequence because these concepts appear to entail a considerable degree of similitude with phenomenal experience. This would also direct the activity of the spectator into one disposed to 'discover and articulate materiality', and, consequently, to enact the 'process of materialisation' during the film-viewing experience itself (Bratu Hansen 2012: 261). Here, what the film sequence also affords is a distinction between our structured modes of seeing, which are determined pre-existing discourses, and 'that which momentarily eludes and confounds such structures' (268). Such a sequence can lead to the observer performing something like the Husserlian *epochē* during the act of watching the film, during the enactment of the process of materialisation, in which the typical pragmatic approach to the world is bracketed out, and a 'nonanthropocentric world' becomes evident (270). This kind of film would be compatible with certain kinds of modernist, as well as realist, film-making. One of Kracauer's favoured films, *Regen*, provides a good example of modernist Kracauerian cinematic realism. *Regen* is characterised by symphonic form, cutting on movement, an indeterminate, flowing interaction between rain and the city that the film portrays (Amsterdam), the use of special effects techniques, montage editing, and an abundance of close-ups which create graphic, yet ambiguous, effects. When writing *Theory of Film*, Kracauer was influenced not only by post-war Italian neo-realism, but also by pre-war modernist films associated with the 'city symphony' cycle of the 1920s, including *Regen, Rien que les heures/The Book of Hours* (Alberto Cavalcanti, 1926), *A propos de Nice/On the Subject of Nice/* (Jean Vigo, 1930), *Berlin: die Symphonie der Grossstadt/ Berlin: Symphony of a Great City* (Walter Ruttmann, 1929) and *The Man with the Movie Camera* (Dziga Vertov, 1929), as well as Dadaist films such as *Entr'acte/Intermission* (René Clair, 1924).

One of the aspects of these films that Kracauer appreciated was that, in them, story did not outweigh visuality, and he endorsed the attempt to 'shake off the fetters of the intrigue [the story film] in favour of a purified cinema' of phenomenal visuality, citing Jean Epstein calling the story a 'lie', and asserting that 'There are no stories. There have never been stories. There are only situations without tail or head; without beginning, centre and end', and Germaine Dulac, insisting that 'those who imprison cinematic action in a narrative [are guilty of] a "criminal error"' (178–9). It was, therefore, the quest for a more purified form of cinematic specificity shorn of the supremacy of story which Kracauer valued most in these films: a quest that was similar in essence to his own mission to formulate a predominantly visual–aural, rather than narrative-based, model of cinematic realism. It is also apparent that Kracauer's antipathy towards story is related to his more general conception of ideology as a conceptual structure that imposes itself upon the spectator and deters the free and moral quest that takes place within *Naturschöne* and the aesthetic reflective judgement, and which is also implied by the notion of *Lebenswelt*: Kracauer, for example, praised *Entr'acte* because the film did not contain any 'recognisable principle or message' (182–3). Those films which purvey 'ideology' merely add to the general sense of 'ideological homelessness and existential despair', which is an inevitable outcome of the imposition of enclosed systems, of one sort or another (Mülder-Bach 1998: 13). On the other hand, when accounting for history and historiography, Kracauer insists upon the need for stories: the historian 'must tell a story', because human history is always changing, and the historian must, therefore, put it into some kind of order (Gerhardt 2015: 237). But Kracauer's advocacy of story here is misleading, because, in terms of both film and historiography, and as will be set out in the remaining chapters of this book, there is, in Kracauer's method, a two-stage approach, in which the first is one of observation, and the second, formation. The story-telling of the historian is, like the story-telling of the film-maker, predicated upon an initial – and crucial – stage of observation. In addition, the stories that the historian and film-maker tell would be indeterminate in character, and not 'enclosed'.

Notwithstanding his endorsement of films such as *Entr'acte*, which he refers to as 'avant-garde' in *Theory of Film*, Kracauer is critical of films which overimpose formal editing structures upon the presentation of physical reality, and complains, for example, that some of the editing in *Berlin: die Symphonie der Grossstadt* and *The Man with a Movie Camera* is 'purely decorative': that is, weighs down upon the revelation or redemption of physical reality (Kracauer 1997: 65). Films such as these 'cover' reality as much as conventional films do, whilst, and in contrast, a film such as *Regen* 'captur[es] material phenomena for . . . [their] . . . own sake' (39). Films which cover reality also function like 'art in the traditional sense', in that, like ideological structures, they transform the world through the deployment of aesthetic conventions that, in covering reality, also, and even if inadvertently, 'sustain . . . the prevailing abstractness' (301) and 'shut out nature in the raw' (185). This was, for example, the basis of his criticism of the impressionist cinema of Dulac, Abel Gance, Marcel L'Herbier and others, which, Kracauer felt, was responsible for films that transformed reality excessively for aesthetic ends. However much he endorses some of the city symphony films, however, it still appears that, in general, Kracauer is more comfortable with – or at least less doubtful of – 'realistic' films such as *La Strada* than he is with modernist films such as *Regen*; and, there is also something of a paradox here, because few films fit the overall Kracauerian model better than *Regen*, and it could even be argued that, in fact, that model is better suited to these forms of lyrical, impressionistic modernism than to a talk- and plot-laden film such as *La Strada*.

This paradox is best approached through the difficulty that Kracauer has dealing with the issue of language in film. The evocation of the flow of the

Lebenswelt that can be seen in a film such as *Regen*, and, to a lesser extent, *La Strada*, does not, for Kracauer, rule out the existence of areas of conceptuality within films, and, in accord with the notion of *Lebenswelt*, he discusses the rationale for the presence of conceptual 'purposive projects' in films. This is set out in *Theory of Film* in a short passage entitled 'Conceptual Reasoning', in which Kracauer argues that purposive projects can have a role to play in film, but that role should not be a leading one. Conceptual thought is related to 'purpose', and purpose – like ideology – engenders a 'closed universe . . . a finite, ordered cosmos' that is the opposite of the open universe and unordered cosmos of the *Lebenswelt* and *Naturschöne* (266). Kracauer, for example, criticises the presence of such 'closed universes' of rhetoric in the moral homilies which Charlie Chaplin resorts to in films such as *Limelight* (1952) (264): a film that is also filled with the sort of 'Exclusive concern with human interaction' that delimits depiction of the *Lebenswelt* and is closely related to conceptual reasoning, and which Kracauer disapproves of as a consequence (265).

Conceptual reason and structured verbalisation should, consequently, have only a minor role to play in film, and their 'adequate representation [must] involve . . . inanimate objects . . . as equal partners' (265). Without such 'equality', film cannot portray the *Lebenswelt* adequately. But, once more, a paradox emerges, because Kracauer also goes on to say that 'conceptual reasoning is an alien element on the screen', and, if that is the case, if it is indeed 'alien', how can it also be an 'equal partner' to the cinematic inanimate (264)? As argued, the general model which Kracauer builds in *Theory of Film* seems closer to a film such as *Regen* than to one such as *La Strada*, and, yet, throughout the pages of his book, he continues to reference wordy films such as *La Strada*, *The Nights of Cabiria* (Federico Fellini, 1957), *Paisà* (Roberto Rossellini, 1946) and *Pygmalion* (George Bernard Shaw, 1938), as though he is unable to face or think through fully the consequences of his logic and position. Kracauer does, it should be said, propose something of a resolution to this in *Theory of Film* – namely, the 'episodic' film, which alternates between the human-animate and the inanimate; and, to this, he also adds the notion of 'permeability'. A film such as *La Strada* is episodic and permeable because the film's narrative and plot are regularly interrupted by images of physical reality. It could be argued, none the less, that such interruption and permeability, and also the films referred to above, are still not fully compatible with the foundational concepts of *Naturschöne* and *Lebenswelt*; and the three chapters of this book which follow will now, amongst other matters, explore how Kracauer seeks to work through such apparent incompatibility, and the paradoxes just referred to, whilst continuing to draw on these foundational concepts, or their equivalent.

NOTES

1. This short chapter provides a context and starting point for the closer analysis of Kracauer's thought carried out in the following chapters of this book. It does not attempt a detailed overall appraisal, in the way that the introductory chapter on Lukács did. That is partly because there has been considerable coverage of Kracauer elsewhere, whereas that is not the case with Lukács and film.
2. Bratu Hansen cites Adorno's *Aesthetic Theory* (1970) in this respect, which appeared after Kracauer's death. Nevertheless, Kracauer had been familiar with the concept of natural beauty through earlier discussions with Adorno, as well as through his own reading of Kant.
3. This issue of the 'presentness' of film is considered in greater depth in the Introduction to this book, whilst the concerns with a re-enchantment of the world and a realism of particulars are returned to in Chapters 8–10.
4. This is a quotation from André Artaud, which Kracauer gives as 'The Shell and the Clergyman: Film Scenario', *Transition* 19–25 (June 1930): 65.

CHAPTER 8

'Photography' (Kracauer 1927)

Kracauer's 'Photography' essay was one of a number that he wrote and published between 1921 and 1931 on a range of social, political, cultural and intellectual issues. These works were mainly published in the newspaper *Frankfurter Zeitung*, the 'Photography' essay appearing as 'Die Photographie' on 28 October 1927. The essay was also one of twenty-four published together in *Das Ornament der Masse: Essays* (1963). Following the publication of *Theory of Film* in 1960, Kracauer 'rediscovered' his early Weimar essays, although this occurred whilst he was developing his thoughts on historiography, thoughts which would eventually find expression in his 1968 book, *History: The Last Things Before the Last* (Kracauer 1995b: 4) (henceforward '*History*'). Kracauer oversaw compilation of the Weimar essays into the 1963 volume, which was then followed by a posthumously published second German edition in 1977, and, then, by an English translation: *The Mass Ornament: Weimar Essays*, much later, in 1995, the publication of which initiated a resurgence of academic interest in Kracauer within English-language film studies. Against the context of the ascendency of post-modernist tendencies and anti-realist 'apparatus theory' from the 1970s onwards, Kracauer had sometimes been viewed as a 'normative' theorist of cinematic realism, and his *Theory of Film* (1960) as a work which displayed a 'tendency to generalise, to subsume particulars within conceptual constructs' in a manner that was anathema to post-modernist sensibilities (Schlüpmann 1987: 98). Following the appearance of *The Mass Ornament*, however, Kracauer became increasingly regarded as a more politically acceptable 'phenomenological' observer of 'individual manifestations of daily life . . . dwelling upon them reflectively', and without the normative bias allegedly apparent in *Theory of Film* (98).

The *Frankfurter Zeitung* was a crucial channel for the so-called 'Kino Debate' that took place in Germany during the 1910s to 1920s, in which intellectuals such as Georg Lukács, Rudolf Arnheim, Béla Balázs, Walter Benjamin,

Bertolt Brecht, Ernst Bloch, Kracauer and others addressed the significance of the still relatively new medium of film in a series of short essays (Kaes 1987b: 24); and most of Kracauer's essays in *The Mass Ornament* can be related to this context. The medium of photography itself, of course, emerged long before (almost 100 years before) Kracauer's 'Photography' essay appeared in 1927, and so was hardly a new phenomenon. One reason why Kracauer chose to write about it in 1927, however, was that, by the 1920s, a whole new group of photographic mediums had appeared, including the illustrated magazines that Kracauer mentions in 'Photography', as well as film newsreels, leading to what Kracauer called an overwhelming 'assault' of photographic images (Kracauer 1995a: 58). Whilst, in addition, by 1927, the era of the early 'scenic' documentary film had passed,[1] and had been replaced by the age of the feature film, Kracauer still alludes to those early films in the 'Photography' essay, when he associates the photograph, as 'optical sign', with the moving optical signs found in the photographic sequences of such films (54). Also an influence was the documentary style of the New Objectivity art movement, prevalent in Germany from the mid-1920s until the rise of Nazism in the early 1930s, including the photomontages of John Heartfield and others that Kracauer also refers to in 'Photography', works which 'stir up the elements of nature': that is, rearrange the normal visual aspects of the image (63). It has also been argued that the 'mood of sobriety and moderation' that marked some New Objectivity works of art continued to influence Kracauer in the writing of *Theory of Film* and *History* (Jay 2012: 229). Kracauer, like his friend Walter Benjamin, was also fascinated by the technology of photography, and Kracauer's 1927 essay influenced Benjamin's 'A Short History of Photography', written in 1931, in which Benjamin states:

> After all, is it not so that all great conquests in the realm of forms come about as technical discoveries? The forms that will be decisive for our epoch lie hidden in machines, and we are only just beginning to suspect them. (Benjamin, cited in Leslie 2000: 46)

This was also the attitude that Benjamin took forward in his well-known essay, 'The Work of Art in the Age of Mechanical Reproduction' (1936), in which he argued that mechanical reproduction had weakened the power of the 'aura' of the traditional, individual work of art; and this is also the stance that Kracauer had adopted towards photography a few years before, when he wrote both that photography is 'at its most elevated when it finds the object appropriate to its technology', and, also, that the technological mass reproduction of images endangered the subsistence of more authentic non-technological accounts of human subjectivity (Kracauer 1995a: 53). This approach did, however, render itself susceptible at the time to the Marxist-inspired charge of 'technological determinism', one levied against Benjamin over the 'A Short History of Photography' essay by his colleague, Theodor Adorno (Leslie 2000: 47). Nevertheless, and despite such censure, Benjamin and Kracauer remained convinced that the technical aptitude that photography possessed to render material reality was important, and that, as one commentator on Benjamin has put it, 'Mechanically made and reproduced art will catch its secrets in a scientific process that is magical' (47).

Kracauer's 'Photography' essay is founded upon his conception of the nature of the modern condition as constituted by a sense of alienation. Into this disordered state enters photography: for Kracauer, a key player in the struggle for and against alienation, and a struggle which Kracauer refers to as the '*go-for-broke game* of history' (Kracauer 1995a: 61), 'das *Vabanque-Spiel der Geschichte*' (Kracauer 2017: 37). During the 1920s and 1930s Kracauer believed that a 'crisis' of modernity was looming, in which the negative forces of modernity, those of disenchantment, fragmentation and alienation, would either become more hegemonic, or be overturned in a move backwards towards earlier forms of human meaningfulness, and more authentic experience of reality (Frisby 1986: 121). Kracauer's position on modernity, and, through that, photography, stemmed directly from the German philosophical critique of modernity in which he was immersed. At the time of writing the 'Photography' essay, Kracauer was influenced by a range of contemporary thinkers, including Max Weber, Wilhelm Dilthey, Georg Simmel and Edmund Husserl. In addition, he also continued to be motivated by the writings of Kant and Marx. These thinkers drew attention to the problems that modernity, and, in most cases, capitalist modernity, posed for true human being and society; and the same was true of thinkers connected to the Frankfurt School Institute of Social Research, such as Theodor Adorno and Max Horkheimer, to whom Kracauer was initially related through his friendship with Walter Benjamin.

Amongst the group of more contemporary thinkers here, a distinction of sorts can be drawn between the Frankfurt School and schools of phenomenology, including those directly associated with Husserl. For example, Frankfurt School theorists such as Max Horkheimer rejected what Kracauer, in *Theory of Film*, would also later characterise as the 'narrow descriptive' aspect of phenomenology (Kracauer 1997: 3). In another respect, in his Weimar essay 'Catholicism and Relativism' (1921), Kracauer also treated an attempt to use 'phenomenological' method to justify a belief in religion with some disdain. Essentially, the advocate of this approach, the philosopher Max Scheler, referred to Husserl's notion of the 'natural attitude' (see chapter six of this book) to justify a 'naïve knowledge of God that every person endowed with reason can obtain at any time by means of a religious act'; and Scheler also contended that the natural attitude provided the 'underlying foundations for the systematic construction of a natural theology'. Kracauer, however, regarded this attempt to relate religious 'faith' to the Husserlian notion of the quotidian natural attitude as misplaced, and, ultimately, an intellectual 'failure' (Kracauer 1995a: 203–4). In doing so, he was also defending what he took to be proper 'phenomenological philosophy' against such appropriation, just as he rejected narrow and overly descriptive applications of phenomenology (Kracauer 1995a: 205).

These criticisms of certain types of approaches to or characteristics of phenomenological methodology were not, however, particularly relevant to Kracauer when he came to write the 'Photography' essay, and what was of more pertinence to him was that phenomenologists such as Husserl held to the same view as did members of the Frankfurt School, and contemporary thinkers such as Simmel: that capitalist modernity had inculcated a general dehumanisation of human experience. Kracauer was familiar with Husserl's thought from the 1920s onwards, and, in his essay in *The Mass Ornament* entitled 'The Crisis of Science/*Die Wissenschaftskrisis*' (1923), argues, in a way that is indistinguishable from Husserl's general position, that 'Eliminating relativistic [or free] thought, cutting off the perspective on to boundless infinities – all these are tied to *a real* [and for Kracauer, negative] *transformation of our entire essence*' (223). Kracauer also says much the same over forty years later in *Theory of Film*, when he describes the 'reign of science and technology' as destined to 'eliminate the qualities of things' (Kracauer 1997: 300). Kracauer became familiar with Husserl's seminal *The Crisis of European Sciences*, with its elicitation of the importance of the quotidian 'life-world' (*Lebenswelt*), and the threat posed to everyday experience in the life-world by scientific and capitalist modernity, when the book appeared in 1936. The impact of the book was increased in 1938, upon the death of Husserl. All this affected Kracauer when he was preparing the first draft of *Theory of Film* around 1940, and Husserl also influenced the 1968 *History*, a book in which the concept of *Lebenswelt* is frequently drawn upon. As suggested, however, long before that, in the 1920s, Kracauer was able to address a considerable body of ideas which engaged with phenomenology and the problems of modernity, and this general intellectual climate provided the basis for the 1927 essay on photography. As will also be argued later, this philosophical discourse went on to shape the conceptions of modernity and photography to be found in Kracauer's *Theory of Film* and *History*, and it will be claimed that, in contrast to what others have asserted (Schlüpmann 1987, Bratu Hansen 1997), no distinction of substance can be drawn in respect to this between Kracauer's English-language post-war writings and his German writings of the Weimar period.

In 'Photography' Kracauer explicitly refers to the problem of modernity as one closely related to capitalism, and he also goes as far as to describe photography as a 'secretion of the capitalist mode of production', and, accordingly, also associated with the problem of modernity (Kracauer 1995a: 61). Kracauer sees capitalist modernity as driven by a desire, one related to the interests of the ruling classes, to evacuate meaning from the world and replace such meaning with dull mechanical routine. In a world 'emptied of meaning' (Kracauer, cited in Frisby 1986: 183), what is mostly left out is context and history, and Kracauer argues that a corresponding voiding of this also takes place within photographic representation. As with the experience of a capitalist modernity devoid of meaning, there is only exteriority to be found within the photographic image: a 'barren self-presentation of spatial and temporal elements [which] belongs to a social order which regulates itself according to economic laws of nature', or nature seen only through the prism of brute and inequitable economic imperatives (Kracauer 1995a: 61). Kracauer's characterisation of capitalist modernity as a force which had emptied history of meaning was partly drawn from his reading of Marx during the 1920s. From this reading, Kracauer, and others at the time, developed an understanding of history as an evolving process of 'disenchantment' under capitalism, in which dehumanisation continued unchecked, and in which the system also sought to deny historical change in order to present itself as inevitable and hide alternatives to itself (Mülder-Bach, in Kracauer 1998: 12). 'History', therefore, had to be rescued from the anti-historical and regressive tendencies of the capitalist system, so that the human-oriented values the system sought to obscure could be revealed in their diminished but nevertheless persisting scope and passage through the course of time. As suggested, Kracauer also believed that photography was associated with the attempt to obscure such values, and that the medium had to be engaged with and challenged. Kracauer's interest in photography was, therefore, not only an aesthetic, but also a historical–political one.

It follows from the characterisation just given that, by a positive sense of the term 'history', Kracauer means something like the engagement with an authentic and value-laden story about persons in the world and their meaningful relations with that world, and not any sort of 'neutral' account of things. Here, 'history' is a certain type of 'experience' of being (Robnik 2015: 258). As will be seen in later chapters of this book, this notion of history as the experience of a history of quotidian significance and interaction is crucial not only to the 'Photography' essay but also to *Theory of Film* and *History*. In 'Photography', however, this idea of history is also associated with a phrase that Kracauer does not employ in these two later books: that of the 'memory image'.[2] The memory image is, as the phrase suggests, the immaterial vision that 'appears' during the act of memory, and such a vision and image is authentic because it always and necessarily attempts to encapsulate human-oriented significance; memory, or at least emotionally laden memory, only appears out of a well of felt significance. Kracauer begins 'Photography' by referring to the image of a 'film diva' seen in an illustrated magazine. She is twenty-four years old. This image of the diva is a contemporary one. Kracauer does not name the year, but it is probably 1927, and 'September' of that year: 'The date is September . . . Time: the present'

(Kracauer 1995a: 47). The image of the diva that Kracauer views is, consequently, taken relatively recently. As such, the photograph remains interpretable through the perspective of the contemporary viewer's intimate knowledge of the diva: 'Everyone recognises her with delight, since everyone has recently seen the original on the screen'/*Jeder erkennt sie entzückt, denn jeder hat das Original schon auf der Leinwand gesehen* (Kracauer 2017: 21).[3] The image is interpreted through that remaining, and still resonant, knowledge and memory. Here, the photographic image of the diva is close to what Kracauer calls the 'ur-image' (*das Urbild*), in that it corresponds closely to the history and essence of the diva, as that history and essence is perceived to be the case, and, consequently, the photograph is able-to-be seen through the perspective of the ur-image. Kracauer sometimes conflates the phrases 'ur-image' and 'memory image', but what he really means is that the memory image can be close to the ur-image, or further away from it, and, as time passes, the distance between the ur-image and the memory image increases, a development that Kracauer illustrates by turning to another photograph: that of the 'grandmother'.

'Is this what grandmother looked like?' (Kracauer 1995a: 48). The photograph was taken in 1864, when the grandmother was only twenty-four, and, by 1927, the grandmother is no longer alive, and the photograph shows an image taken over sixty years earlier. Those who view the photograph in 1927, her supposed 'grandchildren', are now far removed from the memory image as ur-image, and their memory image of the grandmother is only a schematic one, and perhaps derived entirely from second-hand sources, such as this photograph. The 'ur-image has long since decayed', and, consequently, the photographic image alone is unable to 'reconstruct the grandmother' (48). What is seen is not really the grandmother, but 'any young girl in 1864', and 'the 'traditional costumes' of 1864; and the image merely 'serves to illustrate the costumes of the period ... the grandmother dissolves into fashionably old-fashioned details ... an external decoration that has become autonomous' (48–9). All the photograph can do is show an externality that has become devoid of interiority. Unlike the memory image, which always seeks what is authentic, even though that quest becomes more difficult as time goes by, the photographic image simply records the superficial detail of things: 'the smile has been arrested yet no longer refers to the life from which it has been taken', and, instead of the grandmother, the photograph shows 'cinched waists, crinolines, and Zouave jackets' (48). Initially, therefore, as in the case of the photograph of the diva, the photographic image functions something like the memory image as ur-image. Eventually, however, as in the case of the photograph of the grandmother, it turns into something inhuman, and, for Kracauer, this means that photography possesses an inherent danger, and one that is exacerbated by the society from which it emerges: one that is embedded in a capitalist modernity that similarly seeks to remove value from experience. For

Kracauer, therefore, the memory image as ur-image, and the photographic image, are 'antithetical' (Bratu Hansen 2015: 99). (From this point on, the phrase 'memory image' will be mainly used to refer to memory image as ur-image, although the phrase 'ur-image' will still be used occasionally.)

Kracauer writes that 'the meaning of memory images is linked to their truth content' (51). The memory images 'enlarge themselves into monograms of remembered life' and are full of the life of the original (55). What is remembered is what is taken to be true about the person, otherwise it would not be remembered. But what is also important here is that, from the outset, the memory image does not attempt a complete record of the person remembered. Memory is partial and selective. Memory's records are 'full of gaps'. Memory 'does not pay much attention to dates', and may appear to be, in a sense, 'arbitrary' (50). In the chapter – also entitled 'Photography' – in *Theory of Film*, to be discussed in the next chapter of this book, and in which Kracauer again evokes the image and memory of the grandmother, this time in relation to a passage taken from Marcel Proust's *Remembrance of Things Past*, Kracauer quotes Proust's narrator claiming that memory is part of the 'animated system', and cannot be disentangled from subjectivity:

> We never see the people who are dear to us save in the animated system, the perpetual motion of our incessant love for them, which before allowing the images that their faces present to reach us catches them in its vortex, flings them back upon the idea that we have always had of them, makes them adhere to it, coincide with it. (Kracauer 1997: 14)

Here, the 'animated system', and 'idea', refer to a still living person, one who is not yet one who can be encountered only in a photograph. But the principle remains the same as in the 1927 essay: whilst the animated system deals with present encounter, the memory image as ur-image deals with remembered encounter, and both are selective. In experiencing the photograph of the diva, and, before the image can present its 'face' to the viewer, it is caught up in the 'vortex' of animated memory and, also, in the case of Proust's narrator, 'love'. As, however, the ur-image fades, it is the 'face' of the photograph that predominates, whilst the vortex of the animated system subsides; and the face of the image does not select at all, but, rather, seeks to show everything that appears on its surface, what Kracauer calls the 'natural image'.

The memory image as ur-image, or close to ur-image, can also be associated with forms of representation, and Kracauer talks about how painting, like the ur-image, can portray the authentic or substantive history and being of a person. The portrait, in the hands of the right sort of painter (say, Rembrandt), does not try to portray the 'natural image', but the image that somehow evokes the history and being of that person. In this way, the painting is able to replicate analogously the 'transparency' of the memory image: a transparency that allows the history and everyday truth of the person portrayed to be expressed and intuited through the image (hence the 'transparency' of the image) (52).[4] The memory image, and what might be referred to as the 'painting image', are experiences, and, although the painting is a material entity, it is the experience of its viewing which is meant by the phrase painting image, and which is, consequently, also related to the experience of the memory image, as Kracauer defines that. The experience induced by the memory and painting images is a 'layered', or diaphanous, one, whose transparent stratum and inner compass pull the engaged spectator ever deeper into its depth. Kracauer also relates this effort to portray the memory image and painting image as ur-image, and the enduring failure to do so, with the 'prevailing social order' (53). The memory image is a memory not only of the truth and history of a person, but also of that person's relationship to the world, and, in a sense, one can say that memory always links the person to other things: to a necessarily immaterial (immaterial because it is a mental image) environment of sorts. In addition, the memory image can also be a memory of a place or thing, and not only a person, and a place or thing in which what Kracauer calls the 'valid organisation of things', and the 'right order of the inventory of nature', is also encompassed (62–3).

The notions of 'validity' and 'right order' here relate to the way that the memory image creates or intuits a history and truth about the person, place or thing in which consciousness and the world are related to each other through the prism of authentic history and being. 'Validity' and 'right order', therefore, are related to the 'ur-image', and this also means that representation can act in the same way; a self-portrait by Rembrandt displays the 'valid organisation of things' and the 'right order of the inventory of nature' in relation to the ur-image. In the portrait, for example, objects in the painting, and the painted background to these, are formed in order to capture this valid organisation. In this sense, the experience of the self-portrait by Rembrandt, or the ur-image in the recently taken photograph, convey the transparency of the situation, and so act like a 'magic mirror', rather than an empirical–photographic 'mirror of nature' (52). Nevertheless, although the material configuration of the painting, and whatever composition has gone into the photograph, may facilitate an experience of the transparency of the situation, the 'magic mirror' is the experience of transparency and authenticity itself. Kracauer also proposes a history of the development of representation in relation to the ur-image. In the beginning, or, at least, in a period prior to the hegemony of capitalist modernity, there was a closer connection between consciousness and the world: a time when persons, places and things were viewed more commonly through the perspective of authentic human history and being; a time when the ur-image was more actively sought for through representation. Whether there was ever such a time, the fact is that, according to Kracauer, experience of the ur-image remains a continuing possibility, and Kracauer refers to such experience as the 'natural constituency' of 'consciousness'. As such, as an ever-present constituent feature of consciousness, the ur-image can also be subject to representation and experienced through representation (60).

This theme of an original and or authentic union between human beings and the world, and representations of the world, and then loss of that union, is common to the 'romantic anti-capitalist' tradition in general, and can be found, for example, in the early writings of Georg Lukács. In *Soul and Form*, for instance, Lukács refers to an original 'transcendental' human condition in which an effective identity existed between the soul and social and natural formations within the world. In this situation, human being was at one with the world and, consequently, able to experience, and represent, a sense of totality. Following this primal state, however (which, in terms of Western society, Lukács situates in time as existing prior to the rise of classical Greek civilisation), there arose a need to develop society further, and this required the increasing independence and autonomy of consciousness from the world. But consciousness then created more and more objects, and a parallel 'object world' was formed which was increasingly alien to consciousness (Márkus 1983: 8). In *The Theory of the Novel*, Lukács relates this developing existential situation to various 'historical–philosophical' contexts, and associates a literary form with each of these, until he arrives at the nineteenth-century novel. As history progresses, and society becomes increasingly fractured and object-oriented, a general belief in the meaningfulness of life wanes, and this also causes works of art to become increasingly abstract, until, by the nineteenth-century novel, a general sense of the futility of life prevails, one which reflects the diminished character of the human condition within modernity (Lukács 1971a: 108). Against this context, according to Lukács, the artist must strive to reconstitute the 'positive meaning – the totality' (34).

The similarities between what Lukács says here and what Kracauer argues in 'Photography' are many and are engendered by a shared influence stemming from the writings of Simmel, Dilthey and others. Kracauer was familiar with Lukács's *The Theory of the Novel* and wrote an 'enthusiastic review' of the book (Mülder-Bach 1998: 8). In Lukács's notion of the 'transcendental homelessness' which has emerged in a fallen world, a notion that is set out in that book, we can also see one of the influences upon Kracauer's notions of the loss of the ur-image, and of the 'valid organisation of things' and 'right order of the inventory of nature'. Like Lukács, Kracauer also argues, in 'Photography', that, as consciousness became more independent of nature in order to rise above a brute liaison with the latter, it became more removed from a sense of the totality of identity of man and the world. As with Lukács, who argues that, as the grasp of totality dissipated, the Greek classical tragedy and epic gave way to a more decentred and nebulous form of literary representation in the novel, Kracauer also argues that loss of union with nature affected forms of pictorial representation. Initially, for example, the 'symbol' partook of a sense of the totality of that initial relationship between nature and consciousness, but, as 'the meaning of the image becomes increasingly abstract and immaterial', 'consciousness . . . departed from its natural "self-consciousness" (*Naturbefangenheit*) of the world (Kracauer 1995a: 59).[5] And, just as Lukács regarded the novel as correlative of a modernity increasingly shorn of value, so Kracauer regarded photography as the imagistic reflex of a radical separation between consciousness and nature within modernity. As he put it, 'The foundation of nature devoid of meaning arises with modern photography'; and such a foundation also corresponds to and propels capitalist modernity, as the latter seeks to win the 'go-for-broke game of history'/the dangerously risky final confrontation with history/'*das Vabanque-Spiel der Geschichte*' (60).[6] In *The Theory of the Novel*, Lukács argues that Miguel de Cervantes's *Don Quixote de la Mancha* (1605) constituted 'the first great battle of interiority against the prosaic vulgarity of outward life' (Lukács 1971a: 104); and, in 'Photography', Kracauer argued, similarly, that photography, albeit involuntarily, now possibly marked the last such aesthetic battle in a perilous concluding confrontation.

At one point in 'Photography' Kracauer introduces a distinction between the 'image-idea' and the 'idea' (Kracauer 1995a: 58). The term 'idea' refers to the human significance of something and can, accordingly, be related to Kracauer's notion of the memory image as or close to ur-image, whilst the phrase 'image-idea' refers, at one level, to the embodiment of the idea in a representational image: an embodiment that, unlike the idea, may or may not remain close to the ur-image. Image-ideas can, consequently, embody the idea to a greater or lesser extent. In the 'symbol', for example, there is a full and resonant 'incorporation of the idea', a synthesis of image and idea, and of consciousness and nature, whereas, in other forms of pictorialism, the idea is modified and made more intangible by its assimilation within an image whose degree of abstraction also reflects the character of the social formation from which it has emerged. In photography, what, above all, turns the idea into the image-idea is the emptying of context and replacement of that with an endless 'contiguity' of images: 'The *contiguity* (juxtaposition/*Nebeneinander*) of these images systematically excludes their contextual framework available to consciousness. The "image-idea" drives away the idea' (58). Here, the juxtaposition is not linked to sense, and is, simply, juxtaposition per se, so that the images cannot be related to each other, and such an absence of relation denies context, and, the idea. Kracauer also introduces the additional notion of the 'monogram' here. Like 'ur-image' and 'idea', 'monogram' means something like the totality and identity of significant human-oriented meaning, including being and history, accruing to a person, place or object; as representation becomes more abstract, the 'monogram' is left further behind and replaced with mere superficial detail – the 'residuum that history has discharged' (55). This also leads Kracauer to argue that, in an age of mass-produced photography, the 'blizzard of photographs betrays an indifference towards what the thing means' (58). Such images 'are constructed not out of the monogram of the object but from a natural perspective [surface-empirical *Natürlichen*] which the monogram does not capture', and which is not capable of embodying the deep meanings contained within the monogram (61). The 'capitalist mode of production' is based on mass production of commodities meant to be consumed at a superficial level only, and, as part of this, an eternal present is signified; the success of capitalism is based on a denial of 'death' – 'That the world devours them is a sign of the *fear of death* (*Todesfurcht*). What the photographs by their sheer accumulation attempt to banish is the recollection of death, which is part and parcel of every memory image' (59). What Kracauer is principally alluding to here are 'American illustrated magazines' which 'equate the world with the quintessence of . . . photographs' and which, consequently, give the world a 'photographic face' (59). Photography, in this modality, and, more generally, is a 'secretion of the capitalist mode of production' (61) (a product of – comes out from – the capitalist mode of production/*Der kapitalistische Produktionsprozeß hat sie aus sich herausgesetzt*) (Kracauer 2017: 37).

The photographs in the illustrated magazines may deflect the engagement with time and death that is present in every memory image, but Kracauer also points to another kind of presentation of time in the photograph, and one in which the 'fear of death' *is* engaged with. Photography is a 'snapshot' of time. Photographs enable the observer to 'glimpse a moment of time past', in a manner that disturbs, because what is caught sight of in an old photograph of a person or place is always a life that has come to an end or a place that has changed irredeemably. The places seen have all now disappeared, or changed, and the person discerned is no longer the same, and is, perhaps, no longer alive (48–9). So, in terms of time, what we see, in the photographed person, is a life with a masked and unknown future at the moment that the photograph was taken, but also a life that, in our present moment of viewing the photograph, no longer has an ongoing future, but does have a future that has become known, to one extent or another, because that future has been subsumed within, and turned into, a past. When we look at the photograph of the person in his or her prime, we already know their fate, so that what we perceive is a kind of innocence, or naïvety, because that person is unaware of the fate that will befall them. Photographs represent what is 'utterly past, and yet this detritus was once the present' (56). This is why the image of the person in the photograph is like that of a 'ghost', because that person really was once alive, and this also implies that something 'terrible' has happened: in fact, a death:

> Grandmother was once a person . . . Now the image wanders ghost-like through the present, like the lady of the haunted castle. Spooky apparitions occur only in places where a terrible deed has been committed. The photograph becomes a ghost because the costumed mannequin was once alive. (56)

This aspect of the ghost-like persona can be related to the animated sphere; we may experience disturbance at the sight or consciousness of any person's demise, and we may experience it more acutely in terms of the ur-image of the person we once knew. However, Kracauer is clearly not talking about the contiguous 'blizzard of images' found in illustrated magazines here, and the sense of loss and vulnerable impermanence that is felt comes from a closer scrutiny of the individual photograph. Individual photographs are better able to preserve that aspect of the memory image as ur-image which relates to a meditation on such loss, whilst combinations of photographs submerge that aspect beneath an unending a-temporal present. As has been argued, when the photograph is viewed close to the time of its taking, the ur-image can be experienced. However, it also seems that, when the photograph is an 'old' photograph, that aspect of the ur-image that is concerned with loss and vulnerable mortality is still apparent: 'A shudder runs through the viewer of old photographs' (56). Kracauer, however, does not think that this partial experience of the ur-image is by any means the chief aspect of photography, and, as argued, that aspect lies in the ability of photography to describe externality in detail, revealing the – mainly trivial and incidental – empirical details of past time, 'details which eventually annihilate the person':

> So that's how women dressed back then: chignons, cinched waists, crinolines and Zouave jackets. The grandmother dissolves into fashionably old-fashioned details before the eyes of the grandchildren' (48)
> What appears in the photograph is not the person but the sum of what can be subtracted from him or her. The photograph annihilates the person by portraying him or her . . . the photograph gathers fragments around a nothing. (56–7)

And, as argued, that which is most at odds with the ur-image, idea and monogram, the ability of photography to record data rather than indicate value, means that photography is an appropriate aesthetic medium for a capitalist modernity that has become shorn of authentic meaning and which seeks to perpetuate that. Capitalist modernity seeks to project the 'surface' of things only, and, as part of that, the photographic mediums are the 'natural ally' of capitalist modernity (Mülder-Bach 2015: 284).

It has been argued elsewhere that, in writing *Theory of Film*, Kracauer was influenced by Bergsonian notions such as '*durée*/duration', and that this had its source in 'early French theorists' he had read from the 1920s onwards (Bratu Hansen 2012: 272). In Chapter 1 of this book, on Bergson, it will be recalled that Bergson had argued that the experience of time in the modern world was one in which a temporal continuum that is indeterminate is transformed into a spatial continuum that is fixed, and this is also more or less what Kracauer means when he states that, in photography, temporal continuity is altered, so that 'photography presents a spatial continuum' (Kracauer 1995a: 49). Photography turns unbounded time into bounded space by virtue of photographing what is taking place within time and removing that from within time, and, thus, from time itself, whatever 'time' is; and, in consequence, the enigmatic mystery that is time is transformed into the more prosaic reality of space. In 'Photography', Kracauer explicitly uses the term 'duration' (*Dauer*) to indicate that photography is 'merely' a spatial 'representation of time' (*eine Darstellung der Zeit*), and not endowed with/not equipped with/cannot afford (*schenkte*) duration, and that, if the content of the photograph were to be so endowed, 'time would create its own images from that (*die Zeit schüfe aus ihnen sich Bilder*), images which would not be fixed in space. But this, of course, would be impossible in a still photograph (Kracauer 2017: 23). But would it be so in film? Kracauer does not expand on this, although, later in the 1927 piece, he does argue that film is closer to the ur-image than is photography, and this is, in part, because film is able to present movement, if not time itself. The idea that the moving film might be conceived of as sequences of 'images of time' which capture *Dauer*, also links Kracauer's 1927 piece to Lukács's writings concerning film and time in the 1913 'Thoughts towards an Aesthetic of the Cinema', and 1963's *The Specificity of the Aesthetic*. Beyond that, the idea that what we see in film is 'time', raises fundamental questions, some of which are addressed in the Introduction and Chapter 1 of this book, but which cannot be addressed more fully here.

In 'Photography', Kracauer also relates this transformation from fluid temporality into static spatial continuum in photography to what he calls 'historicist thinking' (Kracauer 1995a: 49), which, he claims, is 'concerned with [a false concept of] the photography of time' (50), and which, he goes on to contend, 'emerged at about the same time as modern photographic technology', implying that the two were linked to the same overarching historical context (as will be seen in the following chapter of this book, Kracauer makes the same point in *Theory of Film*: 49). According to Kracauer, 'historicism', a methodology which he associates, albeit equivocally, with the figure of

Dilthey, is characterised by a belief that a phenomenon can be explained 'purely in terms of its genesis', and where that genesis is conceived of as recoverable more or less in full. What Kracauer refers to here is an approach to history that consists in a belief that it is possible to:

> grasp historical reality by reconstructing the course of events in their temporal succession without any gaps. Photography presents a spatial continuum; historicism seeks to provide the temporal continuum. According to historicism, the complete mirroring of an intratemporal sequence simultaneously contains the meaning of all that occurred within that time. (49–50)

By the earlier cited phrase 'photography of time', Kracauer means the idea that what happened in time can be comprehensively understood and fixed, just as a photograph fixes a moment in the spatial continuum. The belief is that all possible relative materials can be collected, and then set out in a chronology that does not contain 'any gaps', and this would amount to a determinate succession of pieces of documentary evidences that would add up to a full clarification. What is invoked here, in terms of both photography and historicism, is an attempt to reconstruct and display everything, regardless of its quality, and an attempt that is also based on the premise that such an effort is possible. And yet, even if this were possible – and Kracauer thinks it is not – much of what would be reconstructed would be pedestrian, rather than significant. This is what Kracauer calls the 'photographer's perspective', and which he compares to that of historicism (49). This is at odds with the discriminating quest for significance and quality that characterises the 'opaque' and 'ambiguous' memory image that is proximate to the ur-image, the idea, and monogram: '*Memory* encompasses neither the entire spatial appearance of a state-of-affairs nor its entire temporal course. Compared to photography, memory's records are "full of gaps"' (50). Additionally, given what has already been said before, concerning the nature of time, the 'temporal continuum' that historicism purports to establish must be not only a pedestrian one but also a counterfeit one, because the actual temporal continuum is unbounded and indeterminate, and, accordingly, cannot be established. This is also what Kracauer means by the phrase 'intratemporal sequence', or 'intratemporal history' (*innerzeitlichen Verlaufs*): the idea that there is not one history but a succession of parallel histories (Kracauer 2017: 24).[7] That being the case, Kracauer concludes that the historicist project, perhaps like any based in empiricist objectivism, is fundamentally flawed. Kracauer's objections are, therefore, two-fold: he objects to the idea of a definite history built up from evidence to tell a definite story; and he objects to the mere collocation of materials into what he calls '*Das Herbarium/*a herbarium' (23). Historicism, and the 'photographer's perspective', erect an empiricism that is the inverse of the ur-image.

Kracauer does not mention any empiricist theorist of the time, such as, for example, those connected to the various schools of 'neo-positivism',[8] and so it is warrantable to conclude that his opposition is to empiricist historiography in general. He chooses an easy and relatively inconsequential target, however, when he mocks what he refers to as the 'philological' approach to the study of Goethe, based on the collection of all empirical evidence related to Goethe by the Goethe society, and he refers to this as akin to the fabrication of a superficial 'Herbarium' (a taxonomic collection and ordering of flora), which, of course, in terms of Goethe, would also amount to a specious chronological ordering of evidences (Goethe did this in August, and then this in September and so on). Kracauer takes particular exception to the Goethe Society Yearbooks, 'a series that in principle can never come to an end . . . ephemeral as the items it processes' (Kracauer 1995a: 49). As suggested, Kracauer does not think that such a chronological empirical historiography or collection of data can be productively applied to an authentic historical understanding of Goethe because Goethe was a figure in the life-world, experiencing the life-world as manifold, and carried along with the course of material reality as that moved through the passage of time. This is not so much a syntagmatic chronological movement as a paradigmatic movement full of intersections: 'intra-temporal', as Kracauer puts it. The empirical 'historicist' approach is based on the belief that, as mentioned, all relevant evidence related to a subject can be collected, and that, when all evidence is collected, and there are no more gaps in the record, the result will constitute proper, objective historiography. Kracauer ridicules this notion per se because of its naïve objectivism, but he also argues that what is considered 'relevant' about what is collected not only is based upon prosaic accumulations but is also often related to dominant discourses and systems of power and privilege. This, for example, is why he refers to the 'warehousing of nature' (*Einmagazinierung . . . der Natur*) that appears in photography as a 'secretion of the capitalist mode of production' (61). Empiricist historiography carries out another sort of 'warehousing', and one that, in its lack of theoretical conceptualisation and assembly of trivia, reinforces the established order.

The rejection of empiricist historicism in the 'Photography' essay is not particularly surprising, given the context of opposition to conservative empiricism, positivism and neo-positivism emanating from phenomenology, the Frankfurt School, and Marxism more generally, all of which influenced Kracauer at the time, and led him to criticise, *in particular*, a positivist approach that isolated technical and scientific developments from social and historical contexts, and also frequently adopted an uncritical posture towards the issue of the potential adverse impact of science and technology. As is clear from the 'Photography' essay, Kracauer wants to raise the issue of the potential detrimental impact of the technologies which had produced what he called the 'assault' and 'blizzard' of mass-produced photography, and was in agreement with his friend, Walter Benjamin, who warned against the dangers inherent in technologies which would generate an extent of objects and information that would come to 'outstrip human needs' (Benjamin, cited in Leslie 2000: 134). In this sense, in the 'Photography' essay, Kracauer largely adheres to the Frankfurt School's position on the mass 'culture industry' as problematic, although, and as will be seen, towards the end of his essay, he also points to the 'redemptive' aspects of photography to an extent. (The idea of 'redemption' is a key concept in Kracauer, and, as will be shown in later chapters of this book, links his German to his American writings.) Kracauer does not talk directly about the relationship between historicism and the ruling capitalist order in 'Photography' because historicism is not his main concern. He does, however, refer to the relation between photography and that order.

Kracauer argues that the deployment of comprehensive inclusivity in photography suits the needs of capitalist modernity because it distracts with trivia, contains no critical element and presents what is then taken to be the case: 'the aim of the illustrated newspapers is the complete reproduction of the world accessible to the photographic apparatus', and the term 'complete' here does not refer to a meaningful totality but to an indiscriminate reproduction that lacks inclusive meaning as a consequence, so that this 'blizzard of photographs betrays an indifference toward what the things mean', an indifference that serves and is intended to serve the reinforcement of the existing relations of power and authority through the diminution of meaning that might become antithetical and non-compliant (Kracauer 1995a: 57–8). Photography, according to Kracauer, is a product of capitalism, and, just as capitalism seeks to extract value from experience, so also 'the foundation of nature devoid of meaning arises with modern photography' (61). The 'mere nature' seen in photographs characterises the modern experience, and its reproduction is encouraged by the ruling capitalist class because that abridged experience poses no threat to it (61). Here, photography has created an inhuman '*general inventory* of a nature that cannot be further reduced'. Photography produces a 'catalogue of manifestations', and a 'barren self-presentation of spatial and temporal elements [that] belongs to a social order which regulates itself according to economic laws of nature', rather than human-oriented laws (61). Photography is, therefore, of considerable import for the go-for-broke game of history because it reinforces the existing alienation until the point may be reached when a 'mute nature' emerges through representation that is entirely separated from authentic human consciousness. When that point is reached, when an already compromised 'mere nature' relapses further into 'mute nature', the world will lack meaning, and photography will have become one of the instruments of such disenchantment. On the other hand – and here Kracauer offers more positive hope – photography could also serve to illuminate the reality of alienation and, in consequence, foster the rebirth of a 'liberated consciousness' (61).

One of Kracauer's key concepts regarding the mass culture of Weimar, and one that underpins his essay 'The Cult of Distraction' (1926), is that of 'distraction'. Distraction has both negative and positive aspects. In terms of the negative, Kracauer argues that the modern subject's relation to the world is a 'distracted' one, in which an unfocused mode of being prevails that has led to a superficial and relatively empty encounter between the self and the world (Aitken 2001: 169: 115). At the same time, however, the 'culture of distraction' contains positive elements capable of combating the prevailing abstraction, and, here, 'ideal' categories such as the 'infinite' and the 'eternal' re-emerge in a different form in genres such as dance and travel: genres which, in embodying such categories, serve to take consciousness back into an encounter with authenticity, and the 'world' (Frisby 1986: 184). In addition, the culture of distraction in general may be perceived as superficial, leading to insight into the nature of a depleted modern condition. Kracauer does not particularly mention the veiled, ideal dimension of mass culture in the 'Photography' essay, but he does argue that the culture of distraction offers the possibility for the sort of insight just referred to, in that the modern subject might come to acknowledge the predominance of superficiality in that culture (Kracauer 1995a: 61). So, for example, Kracauer argues that the distractive jumble of photographic content can generate such an outcome because such content discloses the extent to which the meaning of the world has become dissipated: 'For the first time in history, photography brings to light the entire natural cocoon; for the first time the inert world presents itself in its independence from human beings' (61–2). Here, the inert world of photography is so inert that a sense of its difference from authentic consciousness become evident, so that 'the reflection of the reality that has slipped away from it [consciousness]' can be examined (62). Now, 'it is the task of photography to disclose this previously unexamined foundation of nature' (61–2) (unseen foundation of nature/*ungesichtete Naturfundament*) (Kracauer 2017: 38). This is, essentially, the same argument over the role of distraction that is used in 'The Cult of Distraction' and other Weimar essays. Kracauer now has some positive things to say about photography, but he also has encouraging things to say about film.

When talking about the photograph of the grandmother referred to earlier, Kracauer argues that, in the photograph, seen much later by her grandchildren, 'likeness' has taken over from meaning because of the passage of time, and that a depersonalisation occurs, as the ur-image fades, and 'a person's history is buried as if under a layer of snow' (Kracauer 1995a: 51). That history – the ur-image, or what Kracauer also calls the 'last image' (*Das letzte Bild*) (Kracauer 2017: 25), which 'preserves the unforgettable' – is lost to photography, which 'appears as a jumble that consists partly of garbage' (Kracauer 1995a: 51). This is what occurs in the private realm of the photograph viewed in the context of the family photograph album and viewed by a relatively small number of family members. However, the case of the photograph of the film diva is different to this in various respects. First, the image is close to the ur-image because the diva still 'numbers among the living, and the cover of the illustrated magazine functions as a reminder of her corporeality' (54). Second, the diva is a public figure, with a public who are fascinated by her and want to know as much as possible about her: 'Everyone recognises her with delight' (47). The ur-image of the diva is shared inter-subjectively, and, although it is not the real ur-image of the person, because it is a manufactured persona – 'our demonic diva' – the viewers feel that they 'know' her well, that, in Kracauer's terms, they know her 'monogram', although, of course, they are mistaken. Here, the photographic image of the diva retains some 'transparency', and a 'transparency' that 'increases to the extent that insights thin out the vegetation of the soul and limit the compulsion of nature' (51) (places limits upon the prominence of the natural image/ *Naturzwang begrenzen*) (Kracauer 2017: 25).

However, Kracauer also maintains that the moving image of film is able to embody more of the monogram than a photograph because those moving images are more life-like, and, as such, more able to stimulate both recollection and associated knowledge because of the greater amount of phenomenal information they contain (Kracauer 1995a: 54). This is also a '*function of the flow of time*', because that information is given through a span of temporal duration, and it is that duration that enables the greater amount of information to be portrayed beyond that of which a still photograph would be capable (54). A person (a fan) in the 1920s, looking at the photograph of the diva, would experience some of the truth content of the memory image beneath the 'likeness'. Some of the memory image 'breaks through the wall of likeness into the photograph and thereby lends the latter a modicum of transparency' (54). If such a person were to watch a film featuring the diva, however, the potential for such transparency to occur, for the ur-image to come more into view across the flow of temporal duration, is augmented. The implication here, therefore, is that, through its ability to replicate phenomenal appearing across both space and time, there is less of a decrease in what Kracauer calls the 'semiotic value' of the memory image in film than there is in photography (55). Of course, Kracauer is, to repeat, talking about 'phenomena familiar to *contemporary* consciousness' here (54). Presumably, however, the same would apply to older works: if the photograph of the grandmother was viewed, and then a home movie of the grandmother was viewed, the latter would afford more transparency because it is closer to phenomenal appearing in presenting the passage of time.[9] Nevertheless, Kracauer's commitment to the importance of the memory image as 'last image' in 'Photography' leads him to insist that neither photography nor film can equal the ability of the memory image to grasp what is personally significant, because the two mediums present a 'continuum' which encompass everything, even 'garbage', whereas 'memory images retain what is given only insofar as it has significance' (50–1). Having said that, Kracauer does, as argued, seem to state that film has the advantage over photography in being able to present a spatial *and* temporal continuum. What seems to be implied here is that film, as a kind of record, inherently impels the spectator into a greater intuition of human-oriented meaning, because of the similarity of the medium to perceptual experience. If this is what is implied, then a direct connection can be drawn between the 'Photography' article from 1927 and the 1960 *Theory of Film*, which, as will be shown in the next chapter of this book, develops this particular theme in considerable depth.

In addition to this, film can achieve two more things of note. The first relates to the photographic 'warehousing of nature'. In a realist modality, with a realist 'responsibility', and also with reference to what has just been said about the ability of the medium to enable an intuition of human-oriented meaning, film can attempt to reinstate the 'right order of the inventory of nature' (62), or 'stock of nature' (*der richtigen Ordnung des Naturbestands*) (Kracauer 2017: 39). The warehousing of nature created by the photographic mediums is not in the 'right order' because it is, precisely, an all-encompassing 'warehousing', and one that also reflects the imperatives of capitalist modernity and circumvents the imperatives of the memory image; it is the memory image that holds the right order of the stock of nature. The objective, therefore, is to create, within representation, an 'order' that connects consciousness with material reality in a way similar to the ur-image of memory. Such representation will be necessarily, substantially realist, because it must remain comparable to perceptual experience; the 'right order' must look much like reality for it to be understood as the 'original order' and 'the reality that has slipped away from . . . consciousness' (Kracauer 1995a: 62). Nevertheless, such representation will not be *entirely* mimetic, because the reinstatement of the right order would involve an inevitable degree of symbolic abstraction to conform to the character of the memory image. The right order is one created by consciousness, and this cannot correspond to the 'provisional status of all given configurations' produced by the photographic mediums: configurations which 'distance them from human proximity' (62). In this way, the 'habitual relationship amongst the elements of nature', one that, from a human perspective, connected those elements to authentic human meaning, would be restored (and this is a habitual relationship both because, for human beings, nature can be perceived only within human consciousness, and because such perception is *of* but does not subsume nature – and such a lack of complete incorporation is characteristic of the habitual relationship) (62). This is what Kracauer calls the realist 'responsibility' of film, and it means that the right order of the inventory of nature involves the realistic image, reinforced by symbolic means. In film, this would work just as it works in a painting by, say, Rembrandt. Kracauer does not invoke Rembrandt to make this point, but he does refer to the German impressionist–realist painter Wilhelm Trübner:

> There is cognition in the material of colours and contours; and the greater the artwork, the more it approaches the transparency of the final memory image, in which the features of 'history' converge. A man who had his painting painted by Trübner asked the artist not to forget the wrinkles and folds in his face. Trübner pointed out the window and said, 'Across the way there is a photographer. If you want to have wrinkles and folds, then you'd better hire him – he'll put them all in. Me, I paint history.' In order for history to present itself, the mere surface coherence offered by photography must be destroyed. For in the artwork the meaning of the object takes on spatial appearance, whereas in photography the spatial appearance of an object is its meaning. The two spatial appearances – the 'natural' one and that of the object permeated by cognition – are not identical. (52)

In Trübner's *Self Portrait* (1902) there are, indeed, no wrinkles or folds. The artist stares out of the painting at the viewer, and it is his gaze, with its mixture of surprise and unease, that Kracauer would say captures the memory image of the artist's 'history'. In many respects, Trübner's quest to find a modality that incorporated both realism and formalism – he was influenced by both the French realism of Gustave Courbet and Édouard Manet, and the avant-garde Berlin Secession movement – also reflected Kracauer's later writings on film, in which, as the following chapters of this book will show, the interaction between the 'realist' and 'formative' approaches is discussed in depth. With this in mind, we can return to what was said earlier concerning the ability of film to elicit and portray human-oriented meaning. The comparability of film to perceptual experience is an important factor in this regard, but it is not the only one, and the other factor relates to modifications of the film as record made in order to portray the 'right order'. Kracauer's 'realism' in 1927, in relation to film, based, as it is, on the symbolic work of the memory image, is not entirely grounded in a mimetic stance, and, once more, we have a direct link between the 'Photography' essay and *Theory of Film*.

In addition to what might be called this 'constructive' realist modality, however, film can also perform a deconstructive one. If there is no longer a 'right order' that complies with the imperatives of the memory image, film can reveal that absence by portraying a wrong order, or a disorder. In 'photographic technology', including film, it may be possible to see the 'reflection of the reality that has slipped away from ... consciousness' (62). Prior to the photographic image, the alienated nature of the modern condition remained masked, but now:

> the photographic archive assembles in effigy the last elements of a nature alienated from meaning . . . For the first time in history, photography brings to light the entire natural cocoon (62) ('natural totality/*ganze naturale*'), (Kracauer 2017: 38)
> for the first time, the inert world presents itself in its independence from human beings, (Kracauer 1995a: 62)
> 'the dead world/*die Totenwelt in iher Unabhängigkeit vom Menschen*. (Kracauer 2017: 38).

What consciousness, and representation, must, therefore, do, is reveal the mere 'provisional' status of the existing configurations, one grounded in fundamental disorder or 'wrong order', and, through that, even 'awaken an inkling of the right order of the inventory of nature' (62). This deconstructive modality is, therefore, revelatory, just as the realist modality is in another sense, although it would also, perhaps inevitably, be accompanied by a pessimistic tone of loss. Nevertheless, and as suggested, the deconstructive modality can be of value in deconstructing all provisional configurations, and, in doing so, revealing them precisely as provisional. Kracauer refers to the writings of Franz Kafka in this respect, works which 'scramble the fragments' of reality, reordering them in a way that is different from both the 'natural reality' and the realist modality referred to. In this approach, 'a liberated consciousness absolves itself of this realist responsibility' (61) and is able to 'stir up the elements of nature' so that the 'fragments of daily life become jumbled', and this then places question marks over the alienated images presented in photography, and also film (63). This formative 'game' shows, by implication, that the 'valid organisation of things remains unknown', although the realist modality would seek to reinstate that organisation and knowledge. Kracauer argues that film has a capacity to 'stir up the elements of nature' by creating 'strange constructs'; and this 'game that film plays with the pieces of disjointed nature' has radical potential (63). The use of the word 'game' here (*Das Spiel*), however, suggests that Kracauer's preference is for film to establish the 'valid order', rather than play the 'game' of anarchically scrambling the fragments of reality. In fact, the idea of scrambling the fragments of reality appears only at the very end of 'Photography', and is at odds with the primary consideration of the essay: to stress the importance of reconstituting the right order of the memory image as ur-image, a reconstitution that, in film, would be principally realist in timbre. In this final sense, therefore, the 'Photography' essay from 1927 looks forward to the 1960 chapter on 'Photography' in *Theory of Film*. As following chapters of this book will also show, the revelatory and realist capacities which Kracauer indicates in his 1927 'Photography' essay to be characteristic of film and photography – within an overall realist modality – also provide the foundation for the theoretical positions he adopts in *Theory of Film* and *History*, and this supports the contention that a continuity exists between Kracauer's Weimar writings and his later American writings.

CONCLUSIONS: KRACAUER, HISTORY AND MEMORY

Given the attempt to relate photography to social and historical context that takes place towards the end of the 'Photography' essay, it may seem surprising that Kracauer did not move earlier, during the critique of empiricist historicism that he begins the essay with, also to address such a relationship. The reason for the lack of address here lies in what Kracauer means by the term 'history', in 1927. In 'Photography', Kracauer principally uses the term in relation to memory, and his main concern is to focus on the qualitative and subjective 'history' that is constructed through the act of memory. As argued earlier, Kracauer had been influenced by the ideas of Husserl since the early 1920s, and it could be that he was influenced by the distinction that the latter made between philosophical ideas and their contexts, in which, whilst ideas may be influenced by various factors, the ideas themselves have their own existence and logical structure as ideas. The memory image constitutes a subjective history born of its own inner logic, and, although it is related to shared understandings of the person or place remembered, it has its own aspect, constructed out of that logic. The memory image as ur-image has a certain 'form' and modus operandi that is – like the structures of perception – immutable, and not subject to historical or contextual contingency. Kracauer is, consequently, concerned not so much with historical context, although that context is a constant, if indirect, undercurrent throughout the essay, but more with the idea of the memory image as the opposite of the photographic image, or 'natural' image. The influence of Husserl can only be speculated upon here, but what is incontestable is that 'Photography' is concerned mainly with concepts, rather than processes and contexts.

It is not clear exactly where Kracauer derived his model of the memory image from. It does not, for example, stem in any palpable sense from Husserl. Husserl's conception of memory is based on the notion of memory as consciousness of the past, and, as such, memory shares the same or similar structure as consciousness of the present. In the present we have consciousness of something, and, also, a 'horizon of retention' in which the background to what we are focusing on remains present in some manner. In the same way, when an event is recollected, say, that of experiencing Kracauer's diva, we relive that event in terms of a 'recollected now', in the foreground, and a recollected 'horizon of retention' in the background (Carr 1987: 251). This, however, is not quite the same as Kracauer's notion of the recollected memory image as encapsulating the meaningful 'history' of the diva: a history that goes beyond any singular recollection to comprehend the overall character and truth of the diva. Kracauer's idea is more intensely inclusive, and the idea of memory as a quest for historical essence does not really appear in Husserl. Husserl's notion of recollection as 'secondary memory', and an active form of memory, unlike primary memory, which is passive because it just occurs, brings us closer to Kracauer's model. Husserl's conception of memory as forming an idealised 'objective time', a 'stable continuum' in opposition to the 'streaming now', and something that consciousness is able to connect to from time to time, is close in some respects to Kracauer's notion of the memory image, but, at the same time, does not relate very closely to Kracauer's model of the memory image that fades over the course of time (Russell 1965: 136). There is no 'objective time' here, although there is, at least at the beginning, the subjective experience of objective truth.

There is also some resemblance between Husserl and Bergson here, in terms of Bergson's account of memory as the 'reality of the past', the past as existing subconsciously, but always, so that all a fleeting consciousness active in the present needs to do is 'withdraw a veil' in order to access it (Lacey 1993: 133). As with Husserl, however, this still does not fully equate to the Kracauerian idea of the memory image as significant subjectively invoked history that fades over the course of time. The fact that Kracauer calls memories 'memory images' (*Gedächtnisbild*) also suggests Bergson, because, for Bergson, memories are mainly images, and, in *Matter and Memory*, Bergson does use the phrase 'memory-image' (Bergson 1991: 88–9),[10] or, in the original French, '*image-souvenir*' (Bergson 2015b: 97–8). Kracauer does not mention Nietzsche in 'Photography', but he was familiar with Nietzsche's work and thought, and it could be argued that the notion of the memory image shares similarities with the Nietzschean idea of memory as a discriminating remembering and forgetting: a process which includes active, wilful selection. Here, what is chosen to be remembered is also correlated with an attempt to arrive at the essence or truth of what is remembered, and this fits Kracauer's model. The Nietzschean idea that memory and remembering are associated with what is psychologically painful also has a degree of correspondence with what Kracauer writes about in 'Photography' (the 'loss' of the grandmother, for example),[11] but the more pragmatic idea associated with that of Nietzsche – that we remember bad things so as to avoid them happening again – finds no parallel whatever in Kracauer's piece.

In his essay in *The Mass Ornament* entitled 'The Crisis of Science' (1923), Kracauer argues that the danger for historiography lies in both the 'boundless activity of interminable fact gathering', and subjectivism: the 'senseless amassing of material on the one hand and unavoidable relativism on the other' (Kracauer 1995a: 213). This is also the perspective on history that Kracauer adopts in 'Photography', in which he regards both empiricist and relativist historicism as two opposite extremes which must be rejected. Kracauer, in other words, seeks a middle ground in which to transcend both; that middle ground is the authentic memory image, which is both subjective and authentic, and, as argued, objective and immutable in its form and modus operandi. In 'The Crisis of Science', Kracauer explores how Ernst Troeltsch and Max Weber both, in their different ways, sought to overcome the danger posed to historical and sociological enquiry by relativism (empiricism is not mentioned particularly in the essay), but he concludes that both failed because they sought objective guidelines which are untenable, and this is because subjective value positions must inevitably always 'slip back in' (221). This equates with the model that Kracauer adopts in 'Photography', although, of course, Kracauer does not just allow value positions to 'slip back in', in 'Photography', but, rather, foregrounds them as constituting the essence of the memory image.

In his essay in *The Mass Ornament* entitled 'On the Writings of Walter Benjamin' (1928), Kracauer's exposition of Benjamin's method of analysis as based on constructing situations 'Where meanings come together under the sign of an idea, they jump to one another like electric sparks rather than being "sublated"[12] into a formal concept' (260) (the meanings lose their identity and are integrated into a formal concept/*in einem Formal begriff 'aufzuheben'*) (Kracauer 2017: 250) bears some resemblance to Kracauer's model of the intuitive trans-rational memory image, in which elements seek to adhere impressionistically to the ur-image over the course of time, rather than form a fixed conception, either in intention, outcome or both (260). According to Kracauer, Benjamin 'never allows essentialities to be subsumed under a general concept but instead insists only upon a dialectical synthesis which preserves their full concreteness', and this, again, is in accord with the notion of the transparent memory image (260). The 'truth' of the memory image is never something singular and determinate. However, in his chapter on Benjamin, Kracauer then goes on to relate Benjamin's methodology more closely to the Hegelian idea of sublation when he argues that the electric sparks that come together 'eventually also undergo dialectical separation, and each acquires a subsequent history of its own' (260). There is no resonance with the idea of the memory image here. Kracauer's exposition of Benjamin's methodology was also not in relation to memory, but to his, Benjamin's, analysis of the 'Baroque tragic drama'; and, whilst the principle of indeterminate unity may have been carried across to an extent, there remain two quite different subject areas here, and, in all probability, insufficient grounds for citing Benjamin as an influence on the notion of the memory image.[13]

It can, therefore, be concluded that, in 'Photography', Kracauer sought to find a central course between objectivism and relativism through focusing on the authentic memory image. However, the approach to history, photograph and film adopted in 'Photography' is not the same as that taken in either *Theory of Film*, or *History*, and this is because of the focus on the model of the memory image in 'Photography', a different model to the one that Kracauer would later go on to explore. In all the texts by Kracauer explored in this book, the term 'history' is central. In 'Photography', however, its definition in terms of the memory image, a definition pre-dating Kracauer's greater influence by the Husserlian notion of the *Lebenswelt*, turned out to be something of a cynosure.

NOTES

1. These films were made by small companies that did not survive the First World War, and subsequent hegemony of Hollywood. These films are referred to as 'scenic' because they display the landscapes and habitats of distant lands for the viewing pleasure of audiences, mostly based in the developed world. For a more detailed account of these films in relation to the example of Hong Kong, see my *Hong Kong Documentary Film*, Edinburgh: Edinburgh University Press, 2013.
2. The German term is '*Gedachtnisbilder*' (Kracauer 2017: 25).
3. Where I have chosen to depart from the 1995 English translation, I begin with my own translation, as here, and follow with the German from the 1963 work.
4. This issue of the 'transparency' or 'opacity' of the photographic image, whether in still photographs or film, was considered in the Introduction to this book. There, if the image is 'transparent', it acts like an opening on to a world, so that 'we see the world through them [it]' (Walton 1984: 251). In 'Photography', however, Kracauer takes a different view to this, arguing that the photographic image is transparent only if it is viewed close to the time of its taking.
5. The phrase 'natural self-consciousness' is my translation from the German. In the 1995 English translation this is given as 'natural contingency'.
6. 'Dangerously risky final confrontation with History' is my translation of the German.
7. This notion of parallel histories, or parallel historical worlds, is one that, as will be shown in the final chapter of this book, Kracauer returns to in his *History*, particularly in Chapter 6 of that book.
8. Logical positivism, logical empiricism, neo-positivism, which Kracauer would have encountered in the 1920s and 1930s, based, amongst other things, on the premise that only empirical observation provides the ground of knowledge, and that metaphysical approaches should be rejected.
9. Of course, in this case, there were no films, as, in 1864, the cinema had not yet been invented.
10. Bergson hyphenates the phrase.
11. In his American writings, a sense of world-weariness, and melancholy sadness, allied to a the feeling of exile, and to the idea of being a 'stranger', is often prominent.
12. Very briefly, the Hegelian concept of sublation relates to two categories which become integrated into a third, but which nevertheless retain their individual identities to some

extent. However, Kracauer does not use the term that is usually used in relation to the Hegelian concept of sublation: '*aufheben*'. He prefers the term '*aufzuheben*', which places more emphasis on things being set aside, or cancelled out. It seems, however, that Kracauer is, none the less, referring to the action of sublation within the Hegelian dialectic, as there seems no other way to interpret his words.
13. Walter Benjamin (1977), 'Origin of the German Tragic Drama', London: New Left Books.

CHAPTER 9

'Introduction: Photography' and 'Basic Concepts', from *Theory of Film* (Kracauer 1960)

'PHOTOGRAPHY'

The 'Introduction' to *Theory of Film* discusses issues related to photography as a preface to the later engagement with film that begins in 'Section I' of the book, entitled 'General Characteristics'. The issue of 'photography' is a crucial one for Kracauer and was first addressed in substance in his 1927 German essay 'Photography', and, later, in his 1968 *History: The Last Things Before the Last* (*History*). In each of these cases, as in the 'Introduction' to *Theory of Film* considered here, 'photography', and, from 1960, the 'photographic approach', are understood not only as possessing an aesthetic importance but also as constituting ways of transcending an alienation and disenchantment that Kracauer considers is endemic to modernity. Photography, and the photographic approach, are, therefore, of considerable consequence for him. Nevertheless, the 'photographic approach' is very different from the 'photographic perspective' that Kracauer discussed in his 1927 'Photography' essay. In that essay, and as mentioned in the previous chapter of this book, Kracauer entertained the hope that the regressive 'warehousing' of nature that took place within photography held out the prospect that the modern subject might become aware of the prevailing abstraction that such warehousing indicated, and he also argued that such awareness was even more likely to be the case with film, which possessed the capacity to resist becoming complicit in the construction of an 'inventory' of nature (Kracauer 1995a: 61). In *Theory of Film*, however, Kracauer views photography, and the photographic approach, not only as facilitating such enlightenment, but also as providing a more constructive and decisive 'redemption' from the prevailing abstraction.

Kracauer begins his 'Introduction' by questioning approaches to an understanding of photography that are characterised by an overdependence upon 'phenomenological description based on intuitive insight' (Kracauer 1997: 3). In accord with the views of the Frankfurt School, with which he was associated, Kracauer believes that such concentrated description eliminates context and other matters of substance. Kracauer thus appears to align himself with a representative philosophical critique of phenomenology whose principal charge was that the 'descriptive' methodology of the latter cannot form the basis for proper and full understanding because such understanding necessarily involves access to contextual information, and, additionally, the application of theoretical analysis.[1] Kracauer, therefore, argues from the outset that descriptive phenomenological method is insufficient to an understanding of photography, and he goes on to contend that what is required instead is a study of the 'historically given ideas and concepts' attendant to the evolution of the medium (3). Photography is a 'historical entity' involving technology, photographs, photographers, audiences and discourse about the medium. Kracauer, however, is not so much concerned with the technological or material aspect of that entity, or the broad character of its audience, but, rather, with the more intellectual 'principles and ideas' related to photography that have evolved over time, from 'inception' onwards (3). What is proposed, therefore, is a study of the complex of historically evolving concepts regarding photography.

That Kracauer was concerned with foundational concepts at this stage of his engagement with photography, and, shortly after, film, is hardly surprising, given that, during the 1920s and 1930s, his work as a whole is marked by the influence of certain key concepts emanating from that context, whether it be the Weberian concept of 'disenchantment', which directly influenced the core Kracauerian concepts of 'distraction', 'abstraction' and 'redemption'; Neo-Kantian conceptions of 'truth' and 'natural beauty' (*Naturschöne*); or Husserl's notion of the life-world (*Lebenswelt*), all of which influenced the content of *Theory of Film*. The concepts that Kracauer tends to focus on also have one thing in common: they are concerned with non-conceptual experience, and this, as one critic has argued, involves, amongst other things, 'the primacy of the visual over the conceptual' in Kracauer's thinking (Koch 2000: 109). Kracauer, it could be said, is concerned with concepts that focus on the non-conceptual. This approach links *Theory of Film* with Kracauer's earlier Weimar writings, and the 1968 *History* book. For example, in the chapter in *The Mass Ornament* on Georg Simmel, Kracauer argues that what is significant about Simmel's thought is its concern for 'the realm of elementary, nonspiritual/nonintellectual activity' (Kracauer 1995a: 226). In fact, Kracauer's Simmel essay sheds light on both Kracauer's rejection of a certain kind of phenomenological method in *Theory of Film*, and the sort of conceptual analysis of photography that he wishes to undertake in the book. Kracauer writes that, although Simmel pays attention to particular things, including individual 'thought processes, emotions', he:

nonetheless never makes them the object of separate theoretical investigation. Such a rejection of phenomenology in the narrow sense . . . [means that] . . . The philosopher's itinerary does not conclude with them but rather leads over and beyond them towards other ends. (226)

In *Theory of Film*, Kracauer rejects 'phenomenology in the narrow sense' because it, precisely, does – in theory at least – conclude with the object under investigation, and does not go beyond that object to understand how the object is embedded within a wider set of intermediate and abstract conditions. This also means that the intellectual discourse on photography that Kracauer desires to posit in *Theory of Film* is one that is similarly concerned with photography as a medium capable not only of representing particularity but also of evoking the intermediate and abstract. Nevertheless, and notwithstanding Kracauer's criticism of phenomenology, as with phenomenology, particularity remains the starting point, and, consequently, the discourse on photography that Kracauer wishes to infer encompasses what he refers to as a 'terrestrial philosophy' based on the exploration and evocation of the intermediate and abstract through the particular; and it is this empirically based approach, that also covers the abstract, which forms the basis of his theory of photography and film in *Theory of Film* (226). Such an empirically based composite approach necessarily places limits on the abstract, and the same kind of composite trope also reappears in *History*, in which Kracauer asserts that 'philosophical truths do not fully cover the particulars logically subsumable under them . . . [and] are limited in scope' in relation to them (Kracauer 1995b: 212).

Kracauer's rejection of 'phenomenology in the narrow sense' did not lead him to reject other aspects of Husserl's thought. As mentioned in the preceding chapter of this book, Kracauer had been familiar with that thought since the 1920s. The similarities between Husserl and the critical theory of the Frankfurt School that Kracauer was associated with during the inter-war period were many. Even although, like Kracauer, Frankfurt School theorists such as Max Horkheimer rejected the unalloyed descriptive aspect of phenomenology as inimical to the socially oriented mission of critical theory, all of the major members of the Frankfurt School, including the semi-detached Kracauer, encountered the writings of Husserl as part of a general engagement with contemporary thought, and shared an empathy with those writings to varying degrees (Held 1980: 23). One matter, in particular, that they shared with Husserl was the view that a society dominated by instrumental, technical rationality and scientific imperatives had led to a general subordination of everyday human experience, and Husserl's *The Crisis of European Sciences* (1936), in which this premise is set out, had a direct influence on Max Horkheimer, Theodor Adorno, Herbert Marcuse (the latter a student of Husserl; Held 1980: 166–7), and, also, Kracauer, when he came to write the first drafts of *Theory of Film* in 1940. This position also influenced Kracauer long before that, however. In his 'Philosophy as Rigorous Science' (1911) Husserl had warned against the danger being created by the escalating separation that was taking place between objective scientific knowledge and everyday experience within the *Lebenswelt* (Natanson 1973: 143–4), and, in his essay in *The Mass Ornament* entitled 'The Crisis of Science' (1923), Kracauer – although citing the thought of Max Weber, rather than Husserl – similarly refers to the 'disenchantment of the world brought about by science' (Kracauer 1995a: 219). This would also become a major theme in both *Theory of Film*, in which it is argued that the 'reign of science and technology' will 'eliminate the qualities of things' (Kracauer 1997: 300), and *History*, in which the distance between an abstract scientific world-view and experience of the *Lebenswelt* is referred to repeatedly. For example, in *History*, when discussing a presumed historiography of the *Lebenswelt*, Kracauer criticises 'the logical positivists' for advancing a scientific approach to historical method that is 'Impregnated with the awe of high abstractions', and he goes on to assert that the approach to history that he proposes, and, indeed, the 'historical universe' itself, 'has more in common with the *Lebenswelt* than with the reduced nature of the scientist's making' (Kracauer 1995b: 47–8).

Whilst the concept of the *Lebenswelt* is not referred to directly in *Theory of Film*, it is in *History*, in which Kracauer also directly cites *The Crisis of European Sciences*. For example, in a chapter of *History* entitled 'The Historical Approach', a title which is purposely intended to parallel the phrase 'the photographic approach' which he elaborates in *Theory of Film*, Kracauer evokes the same sort of 'historical reality' as the 'photographic reality' in the earlier book ('The Historical Approach' chapter will be considered in depth in the following chapter of this book):

> In addition, historical reality is virtually endless, issuing from a dark which is increasingly receding and extending into an open-ended future. And finally, it is indeterminate as to meaning. Its characteristics conform to the materials of which it is woven. The historian's universe is of much the same stuff as our everyday world – the very world which Husserl was the first to endow with philosophical dignity. At any rate this world is the nearest approximation to what he calls the *Lebenswelt*. (Kracauer 1995b: 45–6)
>
> Instead of proceeding from, or climaxing in, statements about the meaning, or, for that matter, meaninglessness, of history as such, it [history] is a distinctly empirical science which explores and interprets given historical reality in exactly the same manner as the photographic media render and penetrate the physical world about us (194).

When employing the term 'history' here, Kracauer is referring to the history of ordinary familiarity experienced within the *Lebenswelt*. The content of the *Lebenswelt* varies from period to period – as well as from culture to culture – and, therefore, has a 'history'. However, at a personal level, experience of the *Lebenswelt* also has a history based on the structure of the 'natural attitude' and personal belief in the reality of the world (Natanson 1973: 137–8).[2] Kracauer's 'basic dimension of daily life' must, consequently, also be premised upon the assumptions of individuals concerning what occurred in the past and expectations concerning what is likely to occur in the future, and, therefore, in a concrete historical consciousness of the *Lebenswelt*. As will also be clear, the conceptions of history found in *Theory of Film* and *History* are very different from that deployed in the 1927 'Photography' essay. In that essay, 'history' stands for the essential and authentic history, whereas, in the two later books, the term references the quotidian.

The influence of Husserl's conception of the *Lebenswelt* and of the role of the experience of history within the *Lebenswelt* is apparent in the quotation from *History* just cited. In *Theory of Film*, however, another Husserlian conception related to history also appears to be in evidence, and one that is not fully congruent with the fluid, continuous model of the *Lebenswelt*. This is the notion of the 'historical present', with its 'historical pasts . . . which proceed from one another, each, as a past present, being a tradition producing a tradition out of itself' (Husserl 1970: 374). What is indicated here is distinction and division, and the detachment of parts from each other, rather than an evolving integrative continuity, and this is not the same as either the idea of *Lebenswelt* itself or Kracauer's formulation in the quotation cited. The notion of a 'historical present', with its distinct but linked 'historical pasts', helps to explain why Kracauer did not develop a linear history of the intellectual discourse on photography, but, rather, chose to divide his history into distinct 'early' and 'current' periods (a 'historical past' and a 'historical present'), in which ideas present in the early period are returned to and reconsidered in the latter. This is not an evolution, but rather a mutation into a new state that then reflexively considers the former. Whilst Kracauer's model of the historical discourse of photography is founded upon a conception of progression, that conception is not a teleological one. As befits his opposition to Hegelian grand-narrative historicism, Kracauer's history of the photographic discourse is not concerned with the idea of history as possessing either a predestined direction or an appointed final destination, but, rather, with the premise that, once the 'idea' is formed, that idea will return in reflection (in the sense of both a return of the same and a reflection upon that same) as 'successive waves' (Kracauer 1997: 4). No teleology is implied here and, in fact, no sense that new elements will necessarily be added in the future. Kracauer's stance indicates that the intellectual discourse on photography may have come to a halt because of the newly perceived authentic relation that holds between the 'photographic media' and 'material reality'. Whilst that discourse may have come to a halt, however, the authentic relation that has now been grasped becomes something to be constantly pursued, by both photography, and the historiography of photography. Underlying Kracauer's stance, therefore, is a non-teleological universal category of the idea as the 'photographic approach'. The idea is taken from the medium itself, and then used to guide the development of the medium. Unlike in Hegelian historicism, the authentic relation already exists, both in the abstract, and in the concrete instance of the here and now. The concrete, and the idea, cannot be separated, because the idea is *about* the concrete.

Kracauer's non-linear history of photography, based on the model of the idea of what photography is, is a history of ideas; he is interested in the 'principles and ideas' which are central to a new 'historical entity' such as photography (3). The object of Kracauer's enquiry is, therefore, to draw these ideas, or, as he also refers to them, 'substantive conceptions', from the empirical medium, in its origins, and contemporary manifestations, and then to arrive at an understanding of *the* idea: the universal, that stands for an authentic state of affairs in the world in relation to that medium. (4). As will be argued, for Kracauer, the idea of what photography is becomes the premise that the medium must be used to reveal the world. Kracauer is not so much interested in photography per se, but in the ability of the medium to record and reveal the world. Kracauer writes that *Theory of Film* 'is not intended as a history of photography – nor of film, for that matter. So, it will suffice for our purposes to scrutinise only two sets of ideas about photography' (3). The establishment of 'two sets of ideas' means that, in practice, Kracauer always approaches the empirical manifold of photography, and the history of photography, via these two overarching theoretical formulations. In addition, only one of these, the one embedded in the 'photographic approach', has value in relation to the depiction of the world. There are only a few references to major theorists or philosophers in *Theory of Film*, and there is no reference to Hegel in the book. In addition, in both his earlier Weimar writings, and the 1968 *History*, Kracauer is opposed to the large-scale, teleological historicism associated with Hegel. And yet, there is a respect in which reference to Hegel serves to illuminate Kracauer's notion of the photographic approach the better. For Hegel, the 'Idea', the 'necessary truth' underlying the 'whole course of history', is that of freedom, and this understanding of historical progression as, ideally, constituted by a 'development of the consciousness of freedom . . . and of the consequent realisation of that freedom', also underlies Kracauer's quest, in *Theory of Film*, in which the 'redemption of physical reality' is a prerequisite for realising such freedom (Hegel, cited in Walsh 1958: 143). *Theory of Film* is driven by assumptions regarding the need for the 'development of ... [a certain] ... consciousness of freedom'. Given this, both the 'photographic approach', and, also, the 'historical approach' set out in *History*, may be considered sub-categories of the principal category or Idea of freedom. However, and as argued, the dissimilarity with Hegel is that the idea of freedom can be realised now, rather than at some distant point in the future.

If the photographic approach is a sub-category of the Idea of freedom, Kracauer does not begin *Theory of Film* with that idea, but with the notion of the 'record': the instrument for achieving freedom. Freedom is to be achieved by means of the authentic, concrete relation to the world that is disclosed within the filmic record. 'Origin' is the point at which something begins, and, at the level of the Idea, or 'principle', the first substantive archetypal notion concerning photography that Kracauer posits, the first vital conceptual *radix* that manifests itself within discourse in relation to the new historical entity, and which is derived from that entity, is the belief that the medium is able to 'record' 'physical reality', where the term physical reality means perceptually given reality (Kracauer 1997: 4). In France, and elsewhere, according to Kracauer, this ability to record perceptual experience was, and for different reasons, initially seen as of both scientific and aesthetic value, so that individuals in both spheres lauded the medium's 'mathematical exactness' and 'unimaginable precision' (cited in Kracauer 1997: 4). Accuracy and exactitude of detail is, however, only a component part of the broader notion of recording, and the more important parts relate to conceptions and representations of truth, time, space and memory. First, the notion of recording embodies an idea of accuracy that is necessarily linked to notions of truth and objectivity because anything truthful and objective must also be accurate: to be accurate is to be *veristic*. Second, the idea of recording implies a fusion of past, present and future, because a recording of the present moment becomes a documentation of what is past, and, also, always exists for future reference; and this means that the idea of recording is also linked to the idea and experience of time. Third, the fact that the idea of recording is linked to the idea and experience of time means that it is also linked to memory: to the interior representation of the past. Finally, although the idea of recording is linked to the experience of time, it also implies an empirical object (a document or photograph) that exists in space.

The notion of recording is, therefore, and for Kracauer, not a singular one, but, rather, an intellectual constellation encompassing foundational categories, and this must be borne in mind when considering why and how Kracauer defines it as the fountainhead concept and principle of photography. This intellectual constellation can also be related to the associated but also diverse background of French mid- to late nineteenth-century traditions of positivist, materialist, empiricist, realist, determinist and naturalist thought which Kracauer discusses in outline in *Theory of Film*. Photography was, thus, subsumed within this compound tradition of the period, and one that affected both the sciences and the arts. This overall tradition also included a relatively new, post-romantic aesthetic necessity concerning the work of art: that the work of art should attempt to record, rather than create. This meant that the photograph, as work of art, and work of art as photograph, must attempt to reproduce 'the objects before [the] lens'; and this aesthetic determination to replicate in turn meant that the artist, whether painter, writer or photographer, had to dispense with more traditional aesthetic imperatives, and, in particular, with a 'freedom' to reveal an 'inner vision' that had nothing to do with such imitation and was characteristic of an earlier romantic conception of art (4). Such remission obviously involved the scientific use of photography, but it also encompassed forms of aesthetic photography, and linked the medium to the general movement of realism at the time.

The second wellspring idea concerning the value of photography that Kracauer proposes relates to the medium's capacity to reveal, and this is also associated with the first. In achieving a quantity and exactness of detail in the reproduction of perceptual reality, the photograph reveals things that otherwise would escape attention. Now, 'no detail, "even if imperceptible," can escape' the gaze of the camera, and the preservation of that within the photographic image (Gay-Lussac, cited by Kracauer 1997: 4). The record not only fuses the veracity of the past, present and future across time and in space, bringing all of that to remembrance in memory in the process, it also has a revelatory function in unveiling that which was previously veiled. What is revealed in particular in the photograph is the small and the ephemeral, the 'minutiae' that routinely escape attention because they are either diminutive or 'evanescent and fleeting', or both; and such things are also revealed 'objectively' to the extent that the section of perceptual reality which they inhabit that is before the camera is recorded accurately from the point of view and perspective of that camera, and, also, from a point of view and perspective that are consonant with our perceptual experience (4–5). The 'objectivity' of the photograph is limited to that point of view and perspective, and is unable to transcend that in order to accommodate other points of view and perspectives, just as our perceptual experience cannot. The record not only links the past and present, and extends these into the future, across time and in space, bringing all of that to potential recollection in memory, it also makes known that which is often obscured by the grand narratives and purposeful preoccupations to which Kracauer objects. In *History*, Kracauer mentions the 'happiness' he felt upon 'unexpectedly' discovering that this concern to bring to significance that which had been previously obscured had always been an underlying aspect of his thinking:

> Lately I came across my piece on 'Photography' [the 1927 essay] . . . The discovery made me feel happy for two reasons: it unexpectedly confirmed the legitimacy and inner necessity of my historical pursuits; and . . . it justified . . . the years I had spent on *Theory of Film*. This book . . . [now] appears to me in its true light: as another attempt of mine to bring out the significance of areas whose claim to be acknowledged in their own right has not yet been recognised . . . a single pursuit: the rehabilitation of objectives and modes of being which still lack a name . . . a region of reality . . . [that is still] . . . *terra incognita*. (Kracauer 1995b: 4)

The primary mission of *Theory of Film*, is, then, to reveal and 'rehabilitate' that which, for various reasons, some more worrying than others, routinely escapes attention, and to do so through the composite category of the record. The 'areas to be acknowledged in their own right', which 'still lack a name', are the 'ante-room' areas, the everyday 'last things before the last', and, in *Theory of Film*, the path which film must take in order to represent these areas is the one that 'winds through the thicket of things' (Kracauer 1997: 309). In his essay entitled 'On the Writings of Walter Benjamin' (1928) in *The Mass Ornament*, Kracauer also uses the same phraseology to describe Benjamin's approach in relation to 'abstract thinking', arguing that

> The difference between traditional abstract thinking and Benjamin's manner of thinking is thus as follows: whereas the former drains objects of their concrete plenitude, the latter burrows into the material thicket in order to unfold the dialectic of the essentialities. (Kracauer 1995a: 250)

The idea of a 'dialectic of the essentialities' is characteristic of the conceptual orientation of many of Kracauer's writings of the 1920s, but the similarities in phrasing and idea here – burrowing into the material thicket (1928), and winding through the thicket of things (1960) – reveal a continuity based on the premise that what is to be explored is the 'material world' and 'physical data' (Kracauer 1997: 309): a world that, in *History*, would be designated as the *Lebenswelt*. There is a fundamental similitude and identity between the revealing capacity of photography and what might be called a mindful experience of existence within the *Lebenswelt*.

Recording and revealing, with their associated categories of truth, memory, space and time, constitute the foundational ideational *radix* of photography. As will also be made clear later, when the 'photographic approach' is discussed – the approach that utilises that *radix* – these categories of recording and revealing are active, rather than passive. Recording may appear to be a relatively inert manœuvre, but it nevertheless remains an *act*, and revealing involves an even more active performance of exploration and encounter. This association with intentional action also indicates that the photographer motivated by these categories has no need to suppress his or her subjectivity, as might be required by any putative naïve realist form or theory of objectivist representation. Kracauer does, nevertheless, still regard the upsurge of this recording and revealing role of the photograph as a response to the excessive focus on subjective interiority within the preceding romantic tradition, and, also, as the outcome of a felt need to reconnect to a greater extent with external reality. The intellectual *radix* associated with photography is, therefore, also associated with a meta-cultural shift to a new paradigm, and, whilst that paradigm is not primarily centred upon limiting the representation and expression of subjective interiority (although that is, as will be argued later, involved), it is primarily centred upon a return to the representation and experience of external, material reality, and to the relation of subjectivity to that.

In *Theory of Film*, Kracauer submits, directly, that photography, and, later, film, are associated with an archetype of praxis which encompasses the realist artistic movements of the nineteenth century. Indirectly, given what has been argued in this and previous chapters of this book, it can also be inferred that, for Kracauer, this archetype encompasses a theoretical and philosophical tradition that stretches from Kant through to Weber, the Frankfurt School, Simmel, Dilthey, Lukács, André Bazin and Kracauer; the phenomenology of Bergson and Husserl; and, in addition, the realist artistic movements of the twentieth century, including those movements of realist cinema that Kracauer writes about in *Theory of Film*. Despite its focus on the subjective memory image, the 1927 'Photography' essay also refers to such an archetype. In the essay, Kracauer deploys two conceptions of realism, one positive, one negative. The positive relates to the realist archetype and is one that presents interiority as well as exteriority. So, for example, and to return to the portraits of Trübner mentioned in the previous chapter of this book, whilst not all the 'wrinkles' and 'folds' in the sitter's face are depicted, some are, as those are required to account for the authentic 'history' of the person painted. Similarly, Kracauer gives this account of a conversation between the writers Johann Peter Eckermann and Johann Wolfgang von Goethe, about a painting by Peter Paul Rubens:[3]

> In his description of a Rubens landscape presented to him by Goethe, Eckermann[4] notices to his surprise that the light in the painting comes from two different directions, 'which is contrary to nature.' Goethe responds: 'This is how Rubens proves his greatness, and shows to the world that he stands *above* nature with a free spirit, fashioning it according to his higher purpose . . . art is not entirely subject to natural

necessity but rather has laws of its own.' A *portrait painter* who submitted entirely to 'natural necessity' would at best create photographs. (Kracauer 1995a: 51–2)[5]

In both cases here realism predominates, but not a photographic realism, as would be the case with the portrait painter who submitted entirely to natural necessity. Rubens might stand 'above' nature for Goethe, but there is still plenty of realist depiction in his landscape, still plenty of 'nature' present that is being 'fashioned', still much 'natural necessity'. This composite approach to realist art in 1927 is indistinguishable from the account of, and support for, the nineteenth-century artistic realist tradition outlined in the 1960 *Theory of Film*, in which realism is seen as coalescing formative and empirical impulses, and is not viewed in terms of naïve realism. However, the second conception of realism put forward in 'Photography' is quite different, and relates, precisely, to photographic realism, and a 'warehousing' of nature that takes place within the photograph that does submit entirely to natural necessity, and which, as deleterious consequence, also reinforces the negative forfeits of capitalist modernity. Indeed, in 1927, Kracauer only considers photography of value at all in lieu of its irregular capacity to disclose, indirectly and accidentally, the alienation that is pervasive within contemporary life. In *Theory of Film*, however, and under the greater influence of phenomenology, and lesser influence of romantic anti-capitalism and the Frankfurt School, Kracauer takes the view that the encounter with phenomenal empirical material in photography 'reveals' the world to us, and not just an alienated world; and such revelation of the external through photography is now elevated above the subjective 'history' that is occasioned by the 'memory image' in 'Photography'. In that essay, Kracauer does not relate the medium of photography to contemporaneous artistic movements taking place either in the 1920s or in the nineteenth century. In *Theory of Film*, however, he associates photography directly with the realist artistic movements of the latter half of the nineteenth century, and the realist film movements of the twentieth century.

In relating photography to realist artistic movements in the nineteenth century, Kracauer also links realism to issues and movements of political reform: to 'the revolution temporally defeated in 1848', by which he may mean both the 'February Revolution' of 1848 in France, and other attempted revolutions which broke out in Europe in 1848. Kracauer cites the realist painter Gustave Courbet's declaration that he, Courbet, was both 'a partisan of revolution' and a 'sincere friend of real truth': that is, of artistic realism (Kracauer 1997: 5). However, Kracauer's reference to revolutionary politics is somewhat cosmetic, and he appears to be more interested in the issue of artistic 'truth' than political 'revolution', just as he was more focused on the claims for truth that photography was associated with, claims emanating from 'leading scientists, artists and critics', rather than any possible relation of photography to political radicalism, even though it is clear that photography could – self-evidently – play a role in such a politics, by documenting poverty, inequality, repression and so on (5). Although Courbet, like the writer Émile Zola, whom Kracauer also mentions in *Theory of Film*, was a political radical and activist, it is the fact that, leaving politics aside, both were preoccupied with a method based in inductive description, and one that also correlated with the photographic medium, that was of chief interest to Kracauer.[6] Courbet's *Burial at Ornans* (1850), which led the 'turn to realism in art' in the mid-nineteenth century in France (5), is not particularly significant for Kracauer because it embodied a 'pictorial democracy, a compositional egalitarianism seen as a paradigm for the quarante-huitard [1848] ideal itself' (Nochlin 1971: 48), but because it stimulated a movement which brought 'photography into focus' as 'an ideal means of reproducing and penetrating nature without any distortions' (Kracauer 1997: 5). It could be argued that Kracauer was less politically conscious in 1960 than he was in 1927, but the truth is that Kracauer's politics were always situated at an epochal level: that of the romantic anti-capitalist critique of modernity, and which formed a continuity across his thought, from the 1920s to the 1960s. Kracauer was also an observer of the political situation rather than a participant within it. As Walter Benjamin put it, when reviewing Kracauer's 1929 work, *The Salaried Masses: Duty and Distraction in Weimar Germany*,[7] Kracauer's sociological study of the German salariat: Kracauer is primarily concerned with the reality of false consciousness, rather than the reality which that consciousness obscures. False consciousness reproduces the interests of the upper classes, but is also taken as true by the lower classes, and Kracauer's self-ordained task is not to overturn the social order, but to 'liberate them [the lower classes] from the spell of ideologies that fetter them' (Benjamin, in Kracauer 1998: 110).[8] Benjamin sees Kracauer as a harbinger of revolution, 'a ragpicker at daybreak – in the dawn of the day of revolution'. In 1929, Kracauer is a 'malcontent' and a 'spoilsport' (114), and his task is to deconstruct the veils of false consciousness, without necessarily promoting an alternative to those. In 1960, however, Kracauer has a rejoinder to false consciousness: the redemption of physical reality.

It is important to bear in mind that, by the term truth, Kracauer does not mean scientific truth, and the archetype of realist praxis that he identifies, stretching from the nineteenth to the twentieth centuries, is only marginally connected to a science that had led to the disenchantment of the world. When discussing Courbet and Zola's relation to the scientific method, Kracauer is only presenting what he takes to be something of a historical idiosyncrasy, as he does not think that the work of either can be truly equated with scientific abstraction. Similarly, when he refers to the understandings of photographic truth held by 'leading scientists', Kracauer mainly does so in order to outline the historical background, and he is not interested in the abstract notions of truth that Weber, Husserl and others have argued now dominate science. Indeed, Kracauer directly criticises such scientific abstraction in *Theory of Film*. What Kracauer means by 'truth' is, above all, phenomenal truth: perceptual experience and its rendition; the philosophical *radix* of photography; the foundational ideas of 'recording' and 'revealing' – ideas which are also directly related to the phenomenological critique of science. As will be argued later, all of Kracauer's foundational concepts are phenomenal–empirical in character, again, leading away from a science that, according to phenomenology, always seeks to penetrate beneath empirical, perceptual reality, and, in the process, reduces the latter to that of a secondary status. Whilst Kracauer's conception of truth can be related to the general realist archetype that spread across diverse intellectual political and other spectrums during and after the nineteenth century, it is more precisely related to this phenomenological critique of scientific abstraction: a critique which insists upon the importance of the *Lebenswelt* and experience of the *Lebenswelt*.

Another important distinction also has to be made between the focus on the phenomenal–empirical in *Theory of Film*, one informed by the notion of the *Lebenswelt*, *and* the focus on small things and human being found in both *Theory of Film* and the 'Photography' essay. In 'Photography', Kracauer concerns himself with such small things as, for example, the contents of family photograph albums, and *The Mass Ornament* in general has been described as following a 'phenomenological procedure' in focusing on 'individual manifestations of daily life and dwelling upon them reflectively' (Schlüpmann 1987: 98). The difference between *The Mass Ornament* and *Theory of Film* is that the former is more human-centred ('Photography', for example, is concerned with human essence and being; this is the basis of the 'memory image'), whilst the latter, influenced more by the idea of *Lebenswelt*, insists on situating the human within a context of material reality. Both these involve 'small things', but there is, as argued, a greater emphasis on the concrete relation to perceptual reality in *Theory of Film*. This difference is exemplified in the following two quotations: the first from the essay in *The Mass Ornament* entitled 'Those Who Wait' (1922), the second from *Theory of Film*. In the following quotation Kracauer describes an attitude and posture of 'waiting' that may be adopted towards the alienation that characterises contemporary existence, and, here, 'waiting' involves temporally putting aside the assumption of easy solutions to the need to 'find fulfilment' in the hope that something more auspicious will eventually transpire (Kracauer 1995a: 138):

> What can at best be said, in any case, is that what is at stake for the people under discussion here is an attempt to shift the focus from the theoretical self to the self of the entire human being, and to move out

of the atomized unreal world of shapeless powers and figures devoid of meaning and into the world of reality and the domains it encompasses. The overburdening of theoretical thinking has led us, to a horrifying degree, to become distanced from reality – a reality that is filled with incarnate things and people and that therefore demands to be seen concretely. Anyone who tries to attune himself to this reality and to befriend it will not, of course, automatically come upon the meaning that constitutes this reality or upon an existence in faith. (139–40)

And here is Kracauer, in a section entitled 'The Tragic', in *Theory of Film*, discussing Vittorio De Sica's 1952 film *Umberto D*. In this quotation, Kracauer believes that De Sica has avoided making his film unnecessarily person-centred in order to link his characters more forcefully to their environment:

Actually however, the theme of alienation never claims priority; the many passages bearing on it are the most raw material for a tragedy, but not the tragedy proper. If De Sica had seen fit to build from the pertinent moods and incidents to which he confines himself a full-fledged tragedy, his *Umberto D* would have undoubtedly lost its episodic character and developed into a theatrical film pure and simple. (Kracauer 1997: 148)

In 'Those Who Wait', what is 'to be seen concretely' is the 'self of the entire human being', and reality is defined as being 'filled with incarnate things and people' (the term 'incarnate' implying some inner, essential spirit that is embodied in those things and people). The emphasis here, therefore, as in the 'Photography' essay, is on human being. On the other hand, in 'The Tragic', Kracauer endorses the way that the depiction of human being is restricted through the 'episodic character' of *Umberto D*, an episodic character that diffuses the portrayal of human being into the surrounding environment.

In *Theory of Film*, Kracauer proposes that the intellectual *radix* of photography, the foundational concepts of recording and revealing, were associated with a meta-cultural shift to a new paradigm. That paradigm was centred upon a return to the representation and experience of external, material reality, and arose in opposition to the previous archetype of interiority associated with romanticism. Kracauer's abstract foundational categories of recording and revealing are informed by his understanding of the significance of this paradigm, and such understanding governs his account of photography. His general theory oversees engagement with particularity, even though it is the latter engagement that is endorsed repeatedly in *Theory of Film*. Whilst Kracauer cannot be accused of technological determinism, because it is clear that it is the paradigm, and not technology that creates photography, he remains open to the accusation of inadvertently demoting the particular under the general in a way that he seems to repudiate openly (Schlüpmann 1987: 98). Kracauer does incorporate particularities under general categories, as most theorists do. However, Kracauer's categories are empirical and indeterminate in character, and all the intermediate categories that flow from these are similarly so. There is a congruence of identity between the general categories and particularities incorporated within them. There is also no fundamental difference between Kracauer's writings of the 1920s and *Theory of Film* in relation to the role of particularity. In 'Photography', Kracauer argues that capitalist modernity constructs a culture of valueless surface detail, as with the photographic 'general inventory' of nature. However, in addition to his focus on small things in his essay (such as family photograph albums), the essay ends by proposing critical *attention to* such surface detail and that inventory in order to grasp better both the nature of alienation and alternatives to that. There is, therefore, no substantive difference between the approach taken in 1927 and the focus on the empirical prevalent in *Theory of Film*. The real difference between the two is one of degree only, and the return to particularity is emphasised more in *Theory of Film*.

In *Theory of Film* Kracauer sets out the emergence of the 'photographic' and 'formative' approaches to photography during the nineteenth century. The photographic approach embraces the realist archetype referred to earlier and celebrates photography's ability to record. The formative approach, on the other hand, seeks to adopt the aura of 'Fine Art', and considers realist photography to be an unauthored 'plagiarism of nature' (Kracauer 1997: 6). In addition to relating the formative approach to existing predispositions towards high art, Kracauer also links that approach to the advancing forces of capitalist industry and the 'lower depths of commercial photography' that those forces engender (6). Implicit here, therefore, is the notion that the formative approach may be easily subsumed within the imperatives and practices of capitalism, whilst the realist approach may be less so. The formative approach, both at the level of presumptive 'art',[9] and at work in the lower depths of commercial photography, 'met the needs of the market' (6), whilst the '"dictionary" of nature' perceptible within realist photographs did not, or not to the same extent (7).[10]

Kracauer's account of the nineteenth-century discourse on photography is based on a dichotomy that he draws between 'truth', and 'beauty': between a desire for objectivity and accuracy on the one hand (the photographic approach), and a wish to use every '"dodge, trick, and conjuration" to elicit beauty from the photographic raw material' on the other (the formative approach) (7).[11] Despite his clear preference here, Kracauer, nevertheless, also believes that both these conceptions of truth and beauty were misguided, and that neither of these nineteenth-century positions succeeds in 'penetrating the essence of a medium which is neither imitation nor art in the traditional sense', because both stances were premised upon a misleading 'naïve realism': the realists believed that the recording ability of photography had a genuinely 'objective' basis to it, and that this basis should constitute the basic parameters of the medium; the formalists believed that such an ability, whilst genuine, was yet only a foundation to be transcended in order to express interiority. In both cases, the ability of photography to represent reality in a veridical manner was taken as a given (7). When, however, Kracauer turns to the twentieth century, in a section entitled 'Current views and trends', he finds that this opposition between beauty and truth, based, in part, on a shared conception of naïve realism, continues to persist, but now alongside another historically given central idea that *does* succeed in 'penetrating the essence of [the] medium': the idea that 'reality is as we see it' (8). The record fuses the truth of the past, present and future across time and in space, bringing that to recollection in memory, and also revealing that which was previously unknown, but 'truth', now, is seen in relative and phenomenological terms, as 'reality . . . as we see it'. The intellectual discourse on photography has now expanded in a manner 'unforeseeable in its earlier stages of development', as a belief in the objectivity of the photograph is replaced with one that focuses on the relativity of phenomenal and cultural experience, and, through that, representation (8).

Nevertheless, a dialectic between objectivity and relativity can be ascertained in the pages of *Theory of Film*, one which may stem from the influence of the cultural historicism of figures such as Dilthey, and from Husserl's engagement with the latter. In 'Philosophy as Rigorous Science' (1910), Husserl quotes Dilthey, asserting that the theory of historical development 'is necessarily linked to the knowledge of the relativity proper to the historical life form . . . thus the formation of a historical consciousness destroys . . . a belief in the universal validity of any of the philosophies' (Husserl, cited in Natanson 1973: 51). Husserl accepts this account of historical relativism, but he also insists that ideas have their own status as ideas, and that the character of ideas can be legitimately considered outside of relative historical context. This binary approach to the idea accords with Kracauer's history of photography, in which the wellspring ideas of recording and revealing have their own ideational distinctness, as well as historical context and genesis. Kracauer would return to Dilthey, and the problematic of historical relativism, later, in *History*. However, the main influence on Kracauer's concern for relativism in *Theory of Film* is surely Husserl's conception of the *Lebenswelt*. It will be recalled from Chapter 6 of this book that the *Lebenswelt* can be divided into two dimensions, the 'perceptual' and the 'cultural', where the term 'cultural' is used in a broad sense of 'world-view' which includes a historical dimension. Whilst the perceptual *Lebenswelt* is immutable, the cultural *Lebenswelt* is relative. The *Lebenswelt*, at the cultural level, is 'essentially a reflection of the culture [which members of the same community] have in common' (Bell 1990: 229). As Husserl himself put it, in a formulation replete with the expectations and understandings of his own cultural *Lebenswelt*, 'when we are thrown into an alien social sphere, that of the Negroes of the Congo . . . the facts that for them are fixed . . . are by no means the same as ours' (Husserl, cited in Bell 1990: 231).

When *The Crisis of European Sciences* appeared in 1936, the relativist implications of the notion of the cultural *Lebenswelt* posited within the work created a substantial critical debate, reignited after Husserl's death in 1938. Kracauer, influenced by this context, takes this relativist stance on the cultural/historical *Lebenswelt* into *Theory of Film* when he argues that the expansion of the intellectual discourse on photography was based upon a response that was dual in character. It was a response, first, to the experience of material relativity, and, second, to that of ideological relativity. Once, before the onset of capitalist modernity, people generally stayed in one place and had a relatively fixed perspective on and about that place. Given 'man's situation in a technological age', however, and particularly following the growth of corporate capitalism that affected developed countries in the late nineteenth and early twentieth centuries so much, people no longer stay in one place to the same extent and so no longer have a relatively fixed perspective on and about that place. One outcome of this is that, as people move from place to place, they are inevitably compelled to compare their original habitat with others, and those original provinces then lose their sense of 'absoluteness' (8–9). Here, 'stable impressions yield to ever-changing ones', so that 'not one single object has retained a fixed, definitely recognizable appearance' (9). Along with this comes a diminution of a sense of primary and fundamental experience that occurs with our experience of 'images' – visual representations – of material reality and 'nature': images that had remained constant 'for long stretches of the past' (8).

In place of 'absoluteness' we now have a mindset tuned towards viewing experience comparatively, and, therefore, no experience is able to retain a sense of being primary or fundamental. Kracauer evokes the view – presumably from a hypothetical aeroplane – in which 'bird's eye views of terrestrial landscapes' constantly change so that nothing remains fixed (9). This means that the photograph is the photograph of a partial 'appearance' of the object, not the object per se, because the object can be viewed from a variety of perspectives and never from just one point of view. This is not just a matter of different subjective perspectives on the object either; any one object is now less of a permanent feature within our life-worlds, given that, as we traverse those life-worlds, one object becomes unrelentingly replaced by many others. But photographs of such appearances of objects, in which a sense of the relativity of object-appearance is invoked or expressed, must, almost by definition, be taken at a distance from the object, so that only the general character – the macro-aspects – of the object is/are visible, and not its micro-aspects. For Kracauer, there is a double-edged sword in the recognition of the relativity of experience. On the one hand, such recognition corresponds better to the actual situation. On the other hand, such acknowledgement carries the risk that the prevailing abstraction within modernity will be correspondingly accepted and enhanced. There is, none the less, a way to combat such acquiescence and enhancement, and that is by focusing on the micro-aspects of things by peering closer into the depths of the object through the process of recording and revealing.

In a process that involves relativity, the meta-categories of recording and revealing take on additional significance. If the record fuses the 'truth' of the past, present and future across time and in space, bringing that to recollection in memory, revealing that which was previously unknown in the process, and all of this takes place within a course suffused by relativity, where the record is taken close to the object, the relativity of experience is attenuated. The prevailing abstraction of contemporary experience, which is linked to the relativity of that experience, can be experientially decelerated by a closer scrutiny of the constituent elements of the object. Such scrutiny is also more humanly authentic in that it conforms to our distinctive mode of being in the world: one that is of existence within the (almost) present moment, an existence whose limited perceptual horizon is focused, knowingly or unknowingly, on immediate detail. Whilst, therefore, Kracauer acknowledges the existence of relativity in order to disavow naïve realism, he also places constraints upon the scope of such relativity by virtue of his insistence on the value of the record that attenuates the felt relativity of experience: attenuation that works through enfolding more of an object within the subjective experience of temporal duration. There is also a parallel of sorts here with the distinction that Husserl makes between the perceptual and the cultural *Lebenswelt*: whilst cultural life-worlds may be varied, the perceptual life-world is a constant; and, in an analogous manner, scrutiny of the object from a distance increases its plurality, whilst closer scrutiny reduces that, and enhances the sense of constancy of the object viewed, and, at the same time, a sense of the lucidity of the world.

The same sense of the relativity of experience that undermines naïve realism also applies to 'phenomena on the ideological plane' (9). Whereas once we may have had a view of the world grounded in absolute and a-historical certainties concerning the veracity of that world and world view, now, in the – that is, Kracauer's – age of twentieth-century nascent globalisation, the mass media and mass communication bring a wide range of differing and competing world-views and value systems to our attention, 'thereby of course weakening their claims to absoluteness' (9). Now, the core beliefs of our primary *Zeitgeist* increasingly lose their primacy as they are overlain with 'mental configurations which we are free to interpret at will. Each is iridescent with meanings, while the great beliefs or ideas from which they issue grow paler' (9). And yet the same qualification that applies to limitations on material relativism also applies to such on ideological relativism, although in another respect. If we are faced with a surfeit of world-views and value systems, the end result is not ideological diversity, because powerful institutional and self-serving forces of ideology are at work in the world; and, as argued previously, the 'closed system' of ideology that Kracauer refers to, and which such forces rely on, is also designed to prescribe and delimit, rather than open meaning out (265–6). There may be cases where the existence of a perception of ideological relativism promotes a free pluralism of outlook, other cases where such a perception accentuates the prevailing sense of abstraction and meaninglessness, and cases where ideology seeks to encapsulate and delimit meaning within fixed parameters legislated by the powers that be. It is possible that an authentic pluralism of outlook may promote emancipation, but Kracauer believes that such deliverance is more likely to come from active engagement with our fundamental mode of being in the world: an existence within the present moment that can occur only through direct engagement with physical reality; an engagement which, in terms of representation, is also associated with the categories of recording and revealing.

How, then, do photography, and the discourse on photography, respond to this dual material and ideological experience of the relativity of things and loss of absoluteness, and, also, with the limitations on that loss enabled by the focus on the immediate context of phenomenal experience? As with other writers on aesthetic realism,[12] Kracauer argues that photography may respond to the diminution of material absoluteness, with its associated set order of things, by emphasising that diminution through disregarding accepted canons of aesthetic composition and perspective, and presenting an indeterminate, relatively extemporaneous and unregulated image of the world. In doing so, photography also 'synchronize[s] our vision' to the material relativity and fluidity that characterises modern experience and enables us to 'perceive the world we actually live in' (9). This is, additionally, in opposition to 'the power of resistance inherent in habits of seeing . . . the predilection which many people show today for wide vistas and panoramic views . . . [which] . . . go back to an era less dynamic than ours' (9). Such constant, persisting imagery does not connect to the 'ever-changing' reality of contemporary life under capitalist modernity, a reality that must be captured by mutable, unstructured 'appearance' (9). Thus, modern photography may 'explode perceptual traditions', and do so both unintentionally, at the level of commercial/everyday photography, and, perhaps, intentionally, at the level of intellectual realist photography (although Kracauer does not give examples of the latter) (9). As argued, however, this is also constrained by the realist imperative. Modern photography may express mutable unstructured experience and avoid dwelling on 'wide vistas and panoramic views', but it also, in addition, records and reveals things in attempting to foreground the basis of existence in immediate experience of phenomenal reality. There is, therefore, a dialectic to be achieved between rendering the mutability and immutability of experience of the world, and this is a dialectic that should also be intrinsic to the realist 'photographic approach'.

In addition to such a dialectic, the realist 'photographic approach' must also necessarily possess a relativist subjective dimension, and, as argued, Kracauer does not deny this. What he advocates in *Theory of Film*, however, and what distinguishes the photographic approach from the formative approach, is a realism of intent, based on a focus on recording and revealing that proceeds despite the recognition of the existence of subjectivism, and relativism. The formative approach is evident where the explorative 'visual conquests of realistically handled photography' are realigned in relation to the imperatives of internal aesthetic formulations, and in which photography aims at achieving 'art in the traditional sense': an achievement in which 'superfluous and disturbing details' are also suppressed for the sake of 'artistic simplification' (10). Kracauer is mainly referring to romantic art here, but his argument that, in the formative approach, aesthetic formulations override 'superfluous detail', also applies to modernist art. There is no categorical difference between realist and modernist photography in Kracauer's view, as both may engage in 'realistically handled' 'visual conquests' of reality. However, some types of modernism may also go beyond that in order to embrace formalism and leave reality behind. Kracauer's conclusion is that, in practice, twentieth-century photography, like its nineteenth-century predecessor, evidences a combination of a purist realism and an approach that sanctions the intrusions of the formative approach to varying degree. Kracauer, accordingly, asserts that contemporary photography is an 'arena of two tendencies', the photographic–realist and formative–artistic, with modernism falling into both camps (12). However, this partition, which may signal an obstructive fragmentation and irresolution, is not a state of affairs that Kracauer finds satisfactory, and this, in turn, leads him to investigate 'the basic aesthetic principle' of photography further (12).

The 'photographic approach' stems from the 'basic aesthetic principle' of photography, a principle that is in turn founded on a conception of aesthetic value based on a belief in the importance of adhering to medium specificity. When, therefore, Kracauer states that 'the achievements within a particular medium are all the more satisfying aesthetically if they build from the specific properties of that medium', he adopts a conception of aesthetic value based on a belief in the importance of medium specificity (12). It has been argued earlier in this chapter that claims that Kracauer adopted a 'normative' approach in *Theory of Film* can be disputed on grounds that the key concepts he puts forward in his book are all inherently indeterminate, and, therefore, non-normative. It can, however, be more legitimately claimed that Kracauer adopts a normative stance in defining aesthetic value in terms of medium specificity. This issue of Kracauer's dependence on 'medium-specificity theory' is important, and will be returned to in the following chapter of this book, when Kracauer's *History: The Last Things Before the Last* is considered, because, in that book, Kracauer relates the 'basic aesthetic principle' of photography to the 'basic principle' of historiography, thereby focusing on the principle itself, as well as the relation of that principle to a particular aesthetic medium, and, as a consequence, dealing with the matter in a more fundamental manner. A more detailed consideration of the general issue of medium specificity is, therefore, better addressed in that chapter. What needs to be considered in this present chapter is how the concept of medium specificity relates to the notions of recording and revealing set out in *Theory of Film*.

It has been argued in this chapter that the record fuses the supposed 'truth' of the past, present and future across time and in space, bringing that to recollection in memory, and revealing that which was previously unknown in the process. It has also been argued that this takes place within a course suffused by relativity, although a course that can be – within a realist approach – mediated by a focus on phenomenal reality that places limits upon the relativity of experience and the experience of relativity. The close focus on phenomenal reality *is* the 'realist approach', or a 'realism of intent', and is primarily enacted through the practices of recording and revealing, practices which are, therefore, closely connected to the representation of phenomenal reality. This means, in turn, that recording, and revealing, are aesthetically specific to photography and film, and, therefore, what the medium must 'build from' (12). The 'basic principle' states that an aesthetic medium must build from that which is specific to it as a medium. What is then supposed to be specific to the photographic mediums is their ability to record and reveal phenomenal reality. The photographic mediums should, consequently, focus on this, and, where this is the case, such mediums conform to the central supposition of aesthetic value: that of medium specificity.

Recording and revealing are basic properties of the photographic mediums, and, therefore, are associated with the basic aesthetic principle of medium specificity. The medium must build from these properties and that principle. Nevertheless, subjective and relative elements remain, because Kracauer rejects notions of naïve–realist objectivism. The photographic approach must, therefore, and as argued, also contain elements of subjectivism and relativism. Kracauer does not, accordingly, make an absolute distinction between the photographic–realist and formative approaches, and so does not adhere to an unalloyed notion of the basic principle. A medium must build from its basic properties, from what is medium-specific to it, but that does not mean that such building rules everything else out. Kracauer argues that, given the existence of subjectivity and relativity, these must form part of the photographic approach, but that, to be in line with the basic aesthetic principle of medium specificity, they must be subsidiary to the basic properties of the photographic approach. The photographic approach, therefore, involves both realist and formative elements, with priority given to the former. Kracauer also imagines a two-stage process here. In the first stage, recording and revealing take priority, whereas, in the second stage, the 'formative urges' are applied, but in a way that is still sensitive to the priority of the basic aesthetic principle and the primacy of recording and revealing. It has been argued in this chapter that one way of countermanding the relativity of experience and representation is to look closely at physical reality, and that relativity is increased when physical reality is looked at from a distance. And yet Kracauer also argues that 'distance' is important in another sense, because the 'photographic approach' is based on the photographer taking a neutral, and, therefore, 'distanced' stance towards that which is photographed: the photographer must look closely at the object, but from a psychological distance. In the first stage of the photographic approach, the realist stage, the photographer must attempt to observe, and, in doing so, must put aside part of their self, the part that wishes to organise things. In this first part of the process, the photographer must receive, rather than fabricate. Even here, however, 'reception' does not amount to anything like a pure objectivist neutrality.

Kracauer expands on this point by citing a passage from Marcel Proust's *The Guermantes Way*, the third volume of the seven-volume novel series *In Search of Lost Time/À la recherche du temps perdu* (1913–27), in which the narrator in the extract makes a reference to photography. In the quotation, the narrator asserts that the photographic image transcends the subjectivity of the photographer in presenting its objects literally, or in their physicality alone, outside of the 'transparent sheets of contiguous, overlapping memories ... We never see the people who are dear to us save in the animated system' of our value-laden subjectivity, although the photograph allows us to do so (cited in Kracauer 1997: 14).[13] Kracauer contends that Proust, via his narrator, compares the photographer 'to the witness, the observer, the stranger – three types supposed not to be entangled in the events they happen to watch' (14–15). This disentanglement is also enhanced by the ability of the photograph to capture a moment of time, so that such a moment, and its denoted content, can be observed in a disinterested manner. In a passage reminiscent of the position adopted in the 1927 'Photography' essay, Kracauer claims that Proust views the photograph as the opposite of what, in 1927, he called the 'memory image'. The photographer

> may perceive anything because nothing they see is pregnant with memories that would captivate them and limit their vision. The ideal photographer is the opposite of the unseeing lover. He resembles the indiscriminating mirror, he is identical with the camera lens. Photography, Proust has it, is the product of complete alienation. (15)

Kracauer, however, rejects what he takes to be Proust's account of photography, and, in doing so, also rejects the position on photography that he adopted in 1927: one in which photography *was* considered 'the product of complete alienation'. Now, in 1960, photography is no longer the opposite of the memory image, or subjectivity, and Kracauer contends that the idea of the photograph and photographer standing outside of subjectivity is one which would amount to the alienation of both from real life. Rather than photography being a 'mirror of nature' (this, again, reminiscent of the phrase 'natural image', which he applied to photography in 1927), he argues that

> there is no mirror at all . . . Photographs do not just copy nature but metamorphose it . . . Even Proust's alienated photographer spontaneously structures the inflowing impressions . . . And the activities in which he thus unconsciously engages are bound to condition the pictures he is taking. (15)

In addition to this, Kracauer argues that the spectator also engages in such 'structuring', and that, therefore, 'Objectivity' within the overall process is 'unattainable' (15). Kracauer thus moves away considerably from his position in 1927, in which photography was seen as a 'secretion of the capitalist mode of production', and the most extreme manifestation of the 'go-for-broke game of the historical process' (Kracauer 1995a: 62). In 1960, photography retains part of the 'animated system', and is not just a 'natural image', whilst the medium also offers the basis for the redemption of physical reality, although a redemption that can only fully take place within film.

Photography does not hold up 'a mirror to nature', but the 'conditioning' and 'unavoidable transformations' of nature that take place within the photograph still do not undermine the basic aesthetic principle of photography, because these mainly occur in the second, and less imperative, stage of the photographic approach. In the first stage, the photographer is receptive to information coming from physical reality, whilst still 'spontaneously' structuring the 'inflowing impressions'. Kracauer imagines this as the stage at which the photographer is observing the object and selecting the image, or images. In the second stage, the 'formative urges' are then brought into play so that the 'fuller self' and subjectivity of the photographer or film-maker can be brought into an act of interpretation. (This notion of a 'fuller self' will be discussed in more detail in the next chapter of this book, in relation to Kracauer's *History* book.) Kracauer imagines this as the stage at which the photographer is employing the panoply of techniques available to the medium, within the laboratory, to develop, modify and print the image. In an ideal realist modality, the photographer engages his 'formative faculties' during both first and second stages so that such engagement is 'governed by his determination to record and reveal reality', and, here, the 'formative tendency . . . does not have to conflict with the realistic tendency' (15–16). The attitude of the realist photographer should not, therefore, be one of complete disengagement, and, therefore, 'alienation', but, and especially during the first stage, one of a subjectively intentional empathy with external reality that evidences a 'real respect for that thing in front of him', with the expectation that, later, during the second stage, the 'thing in front of him' will be open to interpretation by the greater formative faculties through the same empathetic perspective (Paul Strand, cited in Kracauer 1997: 16). 'Empathy' is, therefore, a central aspect of the first stage of the realist 'photographic approach', but so also, according to Kracauer, is 'melancholy'.

The melancholic, like the empathetic, is especially related to the first, receptive, stage of the photographic approach, but, and like the empathetic, also carries on into the second to an extent. The melancholic photographer, drifting through the world, is estranged, perhaps intentionally so, from the more comfortable 'natural attitude' of knowledge of his surroundings: from an awareness of their utility, dependability and purpose for him. Kracauer turns to film, and to characters in film, now, to make this point, and, in a passage that bears some similarity with what Husserl says about the *epochē*, attests that:

> Now melancholy as an inner disposition not only makes elegiac objects seem attractive but carries still another, more important implication: it favours self-estrangement, which on its part entails identification with all kinds of objects. The dejected individual is likely to lose himself in the incidental configuration of his environment, absorbing them with a disinterested intensity no longer determined by his previous preferences . . . A recurrent film sequence runs as follows: the melancholy character is seen strolling about aimlessly: as he proceeds, his changing surroundings take shape in the form of numerous juxtaposed shots of house facades, neon lights, stray passers-by, and the like. (17)

This sequence and these shots, and the experience of them, now lack the sort of coherence and understanding that is related to the experience of the 'natural attitude', just as melancholia distances such knowledge from the melancholic, who experiences a world of disinterested or even unrelated impressions, and, as a consequence, a sense of self-estrangement. Kracauer evokes a number of films related to the 'city symphony' series of the 1920s in this regard, including *Rien que les heures* (Alberto Cavalcanti, 1926), with its portrayals of itinerant characters drifting through the unkind streets of Paris.[14] Even a film such as *Regen* (Joris Ivens, 1929), another film that Kracauer writes about, although not intentionally melancholic in the way that *Rien que les heures* is, is impregnated with a melancholic ethos because the streets of Amsterdam, in all their quiet beauty under the sweep of the rainstorm the film portrays, have now been lost to the past, in the 1920s, and so each shot in the film has the 'melancholy beauty of a vanished past', melancholy because the moment has gone from us. But each shot also has a 'dignity and depth of . . . perception' in this melancholic mode, one that implies a degree of gravity and weightiness; and, here, melancholia adds to the sense of empathy concomitant with the receiving phase of the photographic approach (Beaumont Newhall, cited in Kracauer 1997: 16).[15] All of this provides extra provision for the receptive modality of the photographic approach.

Associated also with the receptive phase of the photographic approach is Kracauer's argument that this approach should be based on the production of images that are found a posteriori, rather than posited a priori, and what is important to Kracauer is that what the photographer looks for and 'finds' is not something that he or she was already looking for, so that material reality is configured to such a priori intent, and, so, is 'covered', rather than revealed; and, in this case, nature is exploited 'for a pseudo-realistic statement of . . . vision' (Kracauer 1997: 18). Such a stance also violates the empathetic attitude required by the photographic approach, because empathy and exploitation are conflicting categories. What is required is a realist intent, in which those creating the photographs are 'devoted to the text of nature'. Kracauer even wishes to disclaim such 'pseudo-realism' as photographic, preferring to align such works with the 'graphic arts' instead. Thus, 'photomontage', in which the 'recorded raw material' is moulded to the a priori conceptual imperatives of the artist, should be considered as a 'special genre of the graphic arts', rather than as photography (18). Photomontage is, perhaps an extreme case, and Kracauer argues that, here, the status of the image as record is diminished, and, although fragments of record remain, those fragments have been placed together in an artificial way that violates the empathetic attitude required by the photographic approach, and fails to respect the 'text of nature' as in its natural order. More generally, however, Kracauer argues that the photographic image should emerge a posteriori through a realism of intent, and, if it does not, not only is it not a photograph, but also it is not a record in the sense in which that term has been defined earlier in this chapter. What is also striking here is how Kracauer's argument adheres closely to that set out in the 1927 'Photography' essay. In that essay, Kracauer also refers to photographs which 'stir up the elements of nature' and proceed by 'destroying natural reality and scrambling the fragments' (Kracauer 1995a: 62–3). In 1927, Kracauer does not designate such photographs as 'un-photographic', as he does in *Theory of Film*, in relation to photomontage, but he does make it clear that his preference is for photographs which do not do this, and which conform to the 'habitual relationship amongst the elements of Nature', in a way that enables the 'valid organisation of things' to emerge (62–3). There is, therefore, continuity on this point in Kracauer's thinking from 1927 to 1960. However, and as previously suggested, there is also a difference: by the phrase 'valid organisation of things', Kracauer does not just mean photographic realism, but a realism that embodies authentic 'history' and the 'animated system', and, it is the latter that is of the greater importance to him in 1927. In 1960, however, it is the world rendered in the first stage of the photographic approach that is of the greater importance to him.

To conclude this section of Kracauer's piece, we can say that, at the heart of Kracauer's model of photography is a conception of aesthetic value based on medium specificity. What is specific to the photographic mediums is the ability to record and reveal phenomenal experience. The photographic record fuses the truth of the past, present and future across time and in space, bringing all of that to recollection in memory, and, in doing so, reveals that which was previously unknown. This record is not objective, but relative and subjective. Nevertheless, it is also produced through the prism of the photographic approach, one based on a realism of intent, and one that requires an empathy with nature and determination to 'decipher' the 'book of nature' respectfully. The photographic approach may also, sometimes, require a melancholic attitude as respect for a present that has disappeared into the past or will shortly disappear into the past. Such melancholia provides a 'dignity and depth of perception' in tune with the empathetic attitude required of the photographic approach. And because the record, whilst fusing past, present and future, is essentially about the *past*, about what *has gone*, when the record brings the past to remembrance in memory, a sense of melancholy is appropriate, and, perhaps, inevitable. In addition, melancholy also aids the photographic approach because the melancholic artist, the 'dejected individual', aware that he is documenting that which will inevitably decay, adopts a 'kind of receptivity' to the objects he encounters that leads him outside Proust's animated sphere to observe the objects around him with a 'disinterested intensity' born of 'self-estrangement' (Kracauer 1997: 17). As the following chapter of this book will show, Kracauer also equates the realist photographer with himself. Kracauer, the exile, mourning the loss of his Weimar world, views his current existence in America from the perspective of the outsider: a perspective of estrangement that causes him, the 'curious explorer', to look at his world attentively (19).

Kracauer concludes his piece with an account of the 'affinities' and 'appeals' of the photographic mediums, all of which are in accord with the photographic approach. The first affinity is for 'unstaged reality': 'Pictures which strike us as intrinsically photographic seem intended to render nature in the raw, nature as it exists independently of us' (18). This affinity is, consequently, fundamentally realist in character, and conforms to the positions on 'metaphysical realism' and 'externalism' set out in the Introduction to this book.

Being unstaged, the world is also presented largely free of human intrusion, a presentation which can be associated with the notion of the 'outside world', or *Aussenwelt*, which is also set out in the Introduction to this book. However, this affinity for the unstaged is then related to the 'ephemeral': 'Now, nature is particularly unstageable if it manifests itself in ephemeral configurations which only the camera is able to capture' (18–19). The independently existing 'outside world' is characterised by a general condition of ephemerality and transience that the camera must seek to present. The image that is unstaged and transient promises a glimpse into a reality that we otherwise might never know: a revelation of the natural intricacies of the world that persist in a state of constant becoming, rather than persistent being. The ephemeral, by its very nature, *cannot* be staged, because it is in perpetual movement, in a continuous process of appearing and disappearing, and its indeterminate character is so complex that it cannot be replicated and placed before the camera as it exists in the world. An attempt at such a placing, however abridged, can, nevertheless, be attempted. Many things can be left unstaged, and 'captured' by the camera, but what the film camera can also do is capture things in flux. The ephemeral as flux is a core notion of phenomenology and is central to Husserl's notion of the *Lebenswelt* as 'experiential density' in flux (Natanson 1973: 127). Within the photographic approach, when applied to film, therefore, and under the superintendence of the cameraperson and spectator as 'imaginative reader or curious explorer', the objective is to observe unstaged ephemerality 'in its flux' (Kracauer 1997: 19). And, in this way, as Gilles Deleuze contends, film raises 'the question of attaining once more the world before man, before our dawn': the *Aussenwelt* (Deleuze, cited by Robnik 2015: 266).

The second, third and fourth affinities are really variations on, or subdivisions of, the first. The 'fortuitous', or 'random', is related to the ephemeral, but, additionally, emphasises the non-logical or non-purposeful connections between things. So, Kracauer emphasises the ability of photographs to render 'kaleidoscopic mingling . . . chance meetings, strange overlappings, and fabulous coincidences' (Kracauer 1997: 19). The third affinity is 'endlessness'. Here, and in a way that also suggests the influence of the concept of the *Lebenswelt*, Kracauer refers to the endless parameters of 'physical reality', to that which 'cannot be encompassed' and occurs in 'endless quantities', as the 'photographic approach' probes into 'an inexhaustible universe' (20). The fourth affinity is the 'indeterminate', where the photograph 'transmit[s] raw material without defining it' (20). Related to this is a focus on the individuality of the image, and the fact that this eliminates the 'general' or 'typical': 'It so radically isolates a momentary pose . . . that the function of this pose within the total structure . . . remains everybody's guess' (20). What underlies all this – the focus on the non-logical, the indeterminate and the vast interconnected aspects of the world, together with the ephemeral and the unstaged

– is the idea of *Lebenswelt*: an idea that indirectly influences *Theory of Film* and directly influences *History*.

The fourth affinity, the indeterminate, is the most potentially politically related of the four, in that it emphasises freedom from determination and insists upon the autonomy of the individual element by refusing to absorb that element within an overall totality. Significantly, Kracauer believes that this affinity is brought about in part by the deactivating force of technology. Kracauer does not deny that the realist photograph has 'structure and meaning to the extent to which . . . deliberate choices' are made, but he also thinks that such photographs still constitute a type of non-aligned record which results in the image always being 'surrounded with a fringe of indistinct multiple meanings' (20). Meaning and organisation are structured into the photograph, but the fringe of meaning and technological sovereignty that adheres to it counteracts this. Works of art such as paintings also generate a fringe of meaning for the spectator, but Kracauer argues that, because of its inhuman mechanical nature, the meanings generated by the photograph, and, therefore, film, are more indeterminate because:

> the latter is bound to convey unshaped nature itself, nature in its inscrutability. As compared with a photograph, any painting has a relatively definite significance. Accordingly, it makes sense to speak of multiple meanings, vague meaningfulness, and the like only in connection with camera work. (20)

Part of the reproduction of the photograph is carried out by mechanical and chemical processes, rather than by 'interpretable human intentions and circumstances [in which] the meanings inherent in it can virtually be ascertained', and this means that the former, inhuman as they are, can less easily be ascribed determinate intentionality and meaning (20). The political implications of this consist in that indeterminacy, partly sustained by a technology working on behalf of, or in accord with, physical material reality, rather than humanity, stands for, or empowers, a degree of freedom from manipulation and control by extant human systems and structures. Technology may be used to reinforce instrumental rationality and existing ideological systems, as Kracauer argues in his 1927 'Photography' essay, but, and particularly in the case of film, with its ability to show the world, it may also work to frustrate that by interposing a mechanism between human intent, and an intent to control, and the world. As Rudolf Arnheim put it, in his review of *Theory of Film*, Kracauer's 'aesthetic of unshaped matter', with its 'melancholy surrender' to a 'concrete reality' opened up to view by the mechanical apparatus of the camera, means that, in cinema, reality is redeemed from humanity's narrow, interest-oriented articulation of the real, and re-presented as a realm of freedom and indeterminacy that ultimately benefits humanity because that realm is necessary for humanity to flourish (Arnheim, cited by Robnik 2015: 266). Technology may be a source of alienation, but it may also be a product of an enlightened attempt to understand reality, and may also – at least to an extent – afford an unpremeditated comprehension of reality. The paradox inherent in the camera and resulting film sequence is that the inhuman may elevate the human. Kracauer's emphasis on the technological camera here should not, however, draw attention away from his overall stance, within which technology constitutes only part of the 'photographic approach': an approach that also involves human formative subjectivity.

In addition to the four affinities, Kracauer also argues that the realist photographic approach generates two 'appeals'. What Kracauer is referring to here is the binary opposition between 'truth' and 'beauty' that he established at the beginning of the introductory chapter of *Theory of Film*. So, for example, the first appeal is to truth, an appeal that resonates with the 'basic principle' of the medium and the 'photographic approach'. Kracauer, however, adds an extra dimension to the initial formulation of 'truthfulness to nature' associated with the aesthetic specificity of the medium by now arguing that this appeal to truth in a photograph also works in relation to memory, and, more specifically, to the diminution of memory that takes place over the course of time, and the concomitant gradual advent of the image as a denotatively revelatory record. To begin with, the photograph may function as a 'souvenir', a means of remembering or recalling a significant past event or person, with all the emotive signification associated with that. This would relate to the 'animated' connection with images referred to earlier in the cited passage from Proust, and Kracauer mentions the family photograph album in this regard, as a site of photographic souvenirs. As time moves on, however, and the varied recollections of the departed ones or places gradually fade, and particularly when the image is viewed by someone who did not possess the original memories, a 'significant change of meaning' occurs. Now, the chief importance of the photograph lies in its ability both to provide a denotative record of the person's likeness, and to reveal the – initially – subsidiary content of the image. Shorn of animated content, the image now makes possible certain incidental 'discoveries' as 'things emerge they [the spectators] would not have suspected in the original print – nor in reality itself for that matter . . . in fact we tend to look at them in the hope of detecting something new and unexpected' (21).

What occurs here is a 'significant *change* of meaning', not a reduction in meaning, as is the case with the photograph in the 1927 'Photography' essay. As memory and the animated system fade, realism, and the world, emerge, freed from the preferences of subjective intrusion. It is no longer the case that what is left in the photograph is only a 'warehousing of nature': a rendition of the superficial, of the 'general inventory of a nature that cannot be further reduced' (Kracauer 1995a: 61). Instead, the change that occurs is from the experience of the interior sphere through the image, to the experience of the exterior sphere through the image, and the image now 'redeems' the world for the modern subject who has been removed from it, and who is overly enchained within an interiority that is fashioned by trans-individual power and ideology. In 'Photography', Kracauer did talk about the 'valid organisation of things' and an 'original order of the stock of nature', but that order was always human-centred and oriented (61–3). In *Theory of Film*, on the other hand, the point is to link such orientation to the world, and, as animated contact with the image declines, this begins to occur. The appeal to truth here is not only to the truth of human being, but also to the relation of that to the world, and 'the aesthetic value of photographs would in a measure seem to be a function of their explorative powers' in relation to that (Kracauer 1997: 22).

If this first 'appeal' is to 'truth', the second, as mentioned, is to 'beauty'. This is, however, of little interest to Kracauer, and is interpreted as largely a subsidiary aspect of the 'desire for knowledge', and, therefore, is related to truth. Photographs are perceived as 'beautiful' because they 'satisfy that desire'. And when photographs satisfy that desire by 'penetrating . . . the recesses of matter', they can afford a particularly intense type of beauty that is indistinguishable from the knowledge of reality acquired (22). For Kracauer, then, photographic beauty is important in so far as it is connected to the 'desire for knowledge' of reality, and this leads on to his concluding remarks on the nature of photographic art. Kracauer wants to make a distinction between photographic art and the 'traditional arts'. The traditional arts, through formative means, 'overwhelm reality' in prioritising creativity and expression, whilst the 'formative effort' of the photographer is to 'represent significant aspects of physical reality without trying to overwhelm that reality' with creativity and expression (23). Kracauer proposes an 'extended' definition of the term 'art' here that would be appropriate for the medium of photography, one in which the photograph is deemed to possess both aesthetic formative qualities, and recording/revelatory ones, and in which the latter are more important than the former (23). Kracauer's conception of aesthetic beauty is determined by his conception of the 'basic aesthetic principle', one that is grounded in medium specificity, and one that, in relation to the photographic mediums, is based in an accuracy of recording and revealing of phenomenal reality. There is no fundamental distinction between truth and beauty to be made here; truth is truth to nature, or the world, and beauty consists in the presence and appreciation of that truth. In the photographic arts, aesthetic beauty is related to the satisfaction of a desire for knowledge of reality that is achieved when the specific disposition of the medium, one based in the qualities of recording and revealing of physical reality, is brought to bear and emphasised. When that happens, the reality that is presented is also one of indeterminate becoming, and this further emphasises the extent to which Kracauer's conception of filmic beauty differs from classical conceptions of the beautiful, which are often premised upon notions such as symmetry, and organised composition.

'BASIC CONCEPTS'

In the 'Basic Concepts' section of *Theory of Film*, Kracauer turns from photography to film. However, it is the earlier chapter, 'Introduction: Photography', that sets out the key conceptual issues that he uses to provide the theoretical armature for his book, and this chapter on film generally restates these issues in relation to film without fundamentally altering them. In this chapter, for example, Kracauer reaffirms the 'basic aesthetic principle': that is, that an aesthetic medium must build from its 'basic properties'. The basic properties of film, those of recording and revealing, are also identical to the basic properties of photography, and film, like photography, is, therefore, 'uniquely equipped to record and reveal physical reality, and hence gravitate towards it' (28). Kracauer also reaffirms his position that films which adhere to the basic aesthetic principle of medium specificity possess 'aesthetic validity', and, so, the domain of the 'aesthetic' is defined in those terms. Kracauer does not particularly place traditional aesthetic categories, such as expression, proportion or beauty, within that domain, but neither are these ruled out; it is just that he does not focus on them because he does not recognise them to be *central* to an aesthetic of film – one which is grounded in a medium specificity of recording and revealing of physical reality. Nevertheless they remain part of the film, and are brought to bear during the 'second stage' of the 'photographic approach'. As we have seen, Kracauer defines beauty, perhaps the most historically important aesthetic category of all, merely, and unusually, in terms of awareness of truthfulness: the beautiful as something that, at a fundamental level, provides truthful insight. Indeed, it could be argued that the only traditional aesthetic category Kracauer acknowledges as central to an aesthetic of film is that of truth.

In *Theory of Film* Kracauer also sets out an 'intuitionist' conception of truth based on the notion of reality as indeterminate becoming (Aitken 2001, 2006, 2017a). Here, the film reveals or illuminates aspects of indeterminate phenomenal reality by being structured in such a way that the spectator can intuit those aspects. When the basic aesthetic principle is applied to film, properties are mobilised that have as their principal objective the revelation of those aspects of reality. Kracauer argues that the various genres of film are valid and important, and for a variety of reasons. However, he also makes it clear that films should be considered aesthetically valid only if they build upon the basic aesthetic principle, and the revelatory conception of truth that this principle implies. Kracauer also argues that the basic aesthetic principle, when applied to film, marks film out from all the other arts, apart, presumably, from photography, because film is 'uniquely equipped to record and reveal physical reality' (28). This also means that film is different from 'art in the traditional sense': 'if film is an art at all, it certainly should not be confused with the traditional arts' (40). Kracauer often uses the term 'art' in an almost pejorative sense, to intimate a petit-bourgeois pseudo-romantic type of art and attitude towards art. This is most evident in his characterisation of nineteenth-century 'artistic' photography. On the other hand, Kracauer deploys the term 'aesthetic' in a more affirmative, and, also, modernist manner. Kracauer is opposed to romantic conceptions of art in which the expression of the vision of the artist is the key factor, and he is also opposed to the imposition of an ascendant 'romantic', or pseudo-romantic, attitude and style upon works of art. Kracauer's conception of the aesthetic is based on the idea that an artistic medium should investigate and work from its own aesthetically specific properties, and this approach is, essentially, modernist in character. Kracauer's rejection of romanticism is, however, based not only upon refutation of the idea that pre-existing 'romantic' aesthetic formats should be imposed upon film, or that the vision of the artist should be the predominate factor, but also on the premise that romanticism constituted a 'regressive' attempt to find a solution to the problems of modernity by looking backwards in time, 'as if we could set back the clock of history even if we wanted to!' Kracauer regards this as a 'romantic illusion', and, in its place, he advocates a realist–modernist focus on present 'experience and its material' (295–6). Kracauer's conception of the aesthetic, and the issue of the problem of modernity, is premised upon the deployment of aesthetic medium specificity in relation to what is present: on the existing world, not what happened in the past.

Film may be equipped to 'record and reveal physical reality', but that capacity is not realised in all films, only in realist films, or what Kracauer also calls 'cinematic' films (37). It is the films which build upon their aesthetic specificity – realist films, which 'incorporate aspects of physical reality with a view to making us experience them', and 'not the films reminiscent of traditional art works', or films which are too overlaid by categories such as formulaic composition and organisation – which are 'aesthetically valid' (40). When film holds to the basic aesthetic principle, and builds from its basic properties of recording and revealing, it is a unique branch and medium of the aesthetic, one created, or which emerges, in order to display and 'redeem' physical reality, and Kracauer regards such display and redemption as a valid aesthetic, although not necessarily new, aesthetic category.[16] Kracauer's distinction between realist film and both the 'traditional arts' and other types of film is, consequently, based on the conviction that the basic aesthetic principle, when applied to film, links the basic properties of the medium to conceptions of visual phenomenal truthfulness in a way that is different from the other arts, including what is none the less the foundation: photography. Kracauer's contention that film is a unique art form *in terms of the aesthetic* when it builds upon its basic properties also implies that it is not a unique art form in terms of the aesthetic when it does not, and, if it is not, then it is a different, though not necessarily *inferior*, type of film. Kracauer does not dismiss other types of film and insists that these have their own types of value and purpose, but not, for him, aesthetic value and purpose in his terms. The category of the aesthetic is, for him, based in the basic aesthetic principle of medium specificity, and, if a film does not hold to that, it cannot be considered to possess aesthetic value, as Kracauer defines that, although it may possess other sorts of value. Kracauer is not concerned to downgrade other types of film, only to upgrade a certain type of film, and this determination not to downgrade other types of film is also based upon his conception of ideology.

Kracauer believes that the realist film is different from the other arts and other sorts of films in respect of ideology. The notion of ideology is a central one in *Theory of Film*, and is defined, at a formal structural level, in terms of organised composition: the formal structure of ideology is a 'closed universe' of idea, concept and theme. Such a closed structure may be manipulative, but it is not necessarily so. The formal structure of ideology may be related to the general disenchantment of the human subject within modernity and is a component part of instrumental rationality and the sort of authoritarianism that caused Kracauer to flee Germany in the 1930s. It also stands against the kind of free experience of the open universe of the *Lebenswelt* that Kracauer wishes the realist film to inculcate, and films that do not inculcate such an experience may, like ideological structures in general, 'refer us from the material dimension back to that of ideology' (301). This, however, is not necessarily the case. Kracauer's conception of ideology is a composite one – one that does not lead him to the conclusion that either all ideological structures are entirely adverse, or that mainstream commercial cinema is – and this is primarily because his conception of ideology is influenced by the notion of the *Lebenswelt*. Ideological, explanatory structures or systems are not always undesirable, and some are legitimately explanatory. At one end of the scale there is manipulative ideology, and, at the other end, certain types of 'closed universes' which are humanly benevolent in intent and outcome. Kracauer is, consequently, not against explanatory structures, either per se, or in all films. He refers to the *Lebenswelt* here, in which such explanatory systems, or, in phenomenological terms, 'purposive projects', exist, but only as a lesser part of the *Lebenswelt*. Kracauer does not want to remove these explanatory structures from human experience, only ensure that they do not dominate human experience, and this position also applies to the cinema. Kracauer does not want to dismiss the vast amount of commercial and formative film-making that makes up the greater body of the cinema, but he does want to provide an alternative to it by proposing a different sort of film, one which would subsist alongside commercial cinema, and in which raw material predominates over organising structures. Kracauer argues that 'many a genre has a hold on the audience because it caters to widespread social and cultural demand; it is and remains popular for reasons which do not involve questions of aesthetic legitimacy' (38). The fact that these films are, in Kracauer's terms, not aesthetic is not pertinent, and does not detract from their value in responding meaningfully to 'widespread social and cultural demand'. Kracauer, however, leaves the study of these films to others. He, and his theory of film, one that is, unquestionably, based on a limited conception of the aesthetic, are concerned only with the group of films that fit that conception. As with the *Lebenswelt*, such films are, as argued, not required to dispense with ideological structures entirely.

What ideology does is organise things, and, so, there are two aspects involved: an organising structure, and that which is organised, the latter being the 'raw material' which the organising structure organises. If film conforms to the basic aesthetic principle, and builds upon its basic properties of recording and revealing within a general realist and cinematic approach, what is primarily foregrounded in this process is not the organising structure but the 'raw material' of film, which then exists as an 'element in its own right' (although Kracauer does not mean this in any naïve realist sense, but, rather, in the sense of the material having greater autonomy) (39). This raw material is the recorded substance of perceptual reality viewed through a subjectivity, and, in a realist film such as Joris Ivens's *Regen* (1929), a 'documentary capturing material phenomena for their own sake', that material is organised in such a way that the 'right balance' between realist–explorative and formative–organising tendencies is achieved (39). Kracauer did not adhere to a pure account of the basic properties of the film medium, and accepted that the 'formative urges', the organising structure, must play a role. But he also argued that the realisation of the basic properties of the medium must play the leading role. Kracauer, now, returns to this conception of the 'right balance' to be achieved between realist and formative tendencies that he addressed during the previous chapter of *Theory of Film* by famously – and controversially – opposing the figures of French film-makers Louis Lumière and Georges Méliès. Kracauer recognises that films often use narratives (organising structures), and that this requires a 'staging' or shaping of event and situation that is not fully compatible with a cinematic approach based on recording and revealing. In the latter case, in the films of Lumière, the world is set before the spectator 'for no other purpose than to present it', whereas, where staging is used, as in the films of Méliès, a fabricated world, and, moreover, one that is, at least to an extent, structured along the same lines as ideology, is created to serve a variety of conditional purposes (31).

Such staging will, however, conform to the basic aesthetic principle of the medium if it reinforces or allows attempts elsewhere in the film to present 'the given raw material itself' (34). The 'formative energies' involved must, therefore, at least, seek to evoke the 'impression of reality', from time to time, so that some of the events pictured feel as though they 'might have occurred in real life and have been photographed on the spot' (34). When writing about *Un Chien andalou* elsewhere in *Theory of Film*, Kracauer talks about how the plot of the film might have been – he does not think that it was – interrupted by shots of physical reality; and this form of intermission, in which shots are 'integrated into contexts suggestive of camera-reality and the flow of life', is one of the ways in which staging and organisation can appear alongside images of physical reality (190). It is also possible that staging can offer a stronger illusion of reality than if the film images had 'been captured directly by the camera'. Whilst accepting this, however, Kracauer does not believe that, in general, staging can fully capture the complex and elusive 'emanations' that radiate from perceptual experience of physical reality, and which may be recorded on film (35). There are also far more opportunities for the formative tendencies to exhibit themselves in film than in photography because film includes a genre such as the fantasy film, a genre which requires extensive staging, organised composition, and great intricacies of plot and characterisation. Kracauer also places documentary films in which the film images serve only to illustrate the commentary in this category of films in which the formative energies predominate (36). Here, although the documentary film contains recorded 'raw material', that material has been processed and packaged according to the needs of an abstract intellectual programme. Such a film may correspond to Kracauer's conception of ideological structure that is potentially adverse, even if its intent is to be openly communicative, and, if people in contemporary society are now 'ideologically shelterless', and not adequately defended from overwhelming ideological imposition, documentary films such as these, despite their good intentions, will only worsen that condition by adding to the overall burden of ideology (288).

The reason that Kracauer adopts the position that he does over the issue of cinematic realism is that he believes that modernity is characterised by increasing abstraction and that the imperative response to that should be based upon a return to the concrete *Lebenswelt*. Kracauer's 'photographic approach', 'cinematic approach', 'basic aesthetic principle' and 'basic properties of the medium' (and also, in another medium, the 'historical approach') are all means by which such a return might be effected through the medium of film. Kracauer's final position is undoubtedly, in some respects, essentialist and normative. In his defence, however, it could be said that he felt impelled to adopt that position by virtue of what he took to be the crucial struggle of his time, between disenchantment and the search for human meaningfulness in relation to the world, or 'physical reality'. The inheritor of the German intellectual tradition on the problems of modernity, Kracauer felt that the modern subject was faced with a 'very immediate, very urgent challenge' to counteract the prevailing abstraction and alienation of life by means of a return to the *Lebenswelt*, and to an understanding of the fact that 'we can experience only the reality still at our disposal'; and this is why he championed realist films (296–7).

NOTES

1. For this critique of the 'descriptive' aspect of phenomenology, and the way phenomenology falls short of a full-blown 'theory', see Chapter 4 of this book.
2. See Chapter 6 of this book.
3. Sir Peter Paul Rubens (1577–1640), Flemish artist of the Baroque tradition, particularly famed for his landscape paintings.
4. Johann Peter Eckermann (1792–1854), German poet and author, best known for his work *Conversations with Goethe* (1838–48). He was also Goethe's private secretary, and the discussion with Goethe is cited as having taken place on 18 April 1827 (information referenced in Kracauer 1995a: 355).
5. It is not clear to what painting the two are referring, but Eckermann's surprise might be partly to do with the fact that, in general, in a landscape painting by Rubens, the light normally comes from one direction. But this merely reinforces Kracauer's general point that realism should prevail.
6. Referring to the film *Gervaise* (René Clément, 1956), an adaptation of Zola's novel *L'Assommoir* (1877), Kracauer calls the film 'pure Zola and pure cinema to boot'. Clément described his film as a 'naturalistic documentary', and Kracauer argues that its 'truth to the medium goes together with loyalty to the novel', a novel which also possesses 'indestructible cinematic substance' (241).
7. First published as *Die Angestellten. Aus dem neusten Deutschland*, in serial publication in the *Frankfurter Zeitung* newspaper in 1929; first published in book form in 1930 by Societas-Verlag, Frankfurt am Main.
8. This review from Benjamin is cited in the 1998 translation of *The Salaried Masses* by Quintin Hoare, published by Verso, as 'An Outsider Attracts Attention: The Salaried Masses, by S. Kracauer' (pp. 109–14). However, the original source for the review is not cited.
9. Kracauer is talking about photographs with an affectation to be 'art' here, and not more authentic works of photographic art, which he may think did not exist at that point in time.
10. Kracauer is quoting the painter Eugène Delacroix, cited in Gisèle Freund (1936), *La Photographie en France au dix-neuvième siècle*, pp. 117–19, published in France. The publisher is not given
11. Kracauer does not cite where the interior quotation is taken from.
12. See for example, Linda Nochlin (1971), *Realism: Style and Civilisation*, Harmondsworth: Penguin; and Erich Auerbach (1968), *Mimesis: The Representation of Reality in Western Literature*, Princeton, NJ: Princeton University Press.

13. The quotation is from *The Guermantes Way*, vol. 3 of *In Search of Lost Time*, otherwise titled *Remembrance of Things Past*, p. 814. Kracauer cites this as volume 1 of the series, but this is incorrect, as it is volume 3.
14. For more on this film see Aitken (2001), *Alberto Cavalcanti*, Trowbridge: Flicks Books.
15. Beaumont Newhall (1949), *The History of Photography from 1839 to the Present Day*, New York. Publisher not cited.
16. Nevertheless, Kracauer does not expand on the prehistory – if any – of such a category.

CHAPTER 10

'The Historical Approach' and 'The Historian's Journey', from *History: The Last Things Before the Last* (Kracauer 1968)

'THE HISTORICAL APPROACH'

There is a continuity of theme between the chapters 'Introduction: Photography' and 'Basic Concepts' in *Theory of Film*, and 'The Historical Approach' ('Approach') in *History: The Last Things Before the Last* (*History*), even to the extent of replicating the language contained in the earlier book. So, for example, and in terms of both linguistic and thematic continuity, in 'Approach', Kracauer restates his position concerning the historical development of photography in the nineteenth century, declaring that the invention of the daguerreotype around 1840, at about the same time that schools of empiricist historiography emerged, was no coincidence, but, on the contrary, part of the general '*Zeitgeist*' of a turn from romanticism to empiricist, positivist and realist approaches (Kracauer 1995b: 49). Kracauer also reiterates his earlier account of the conflict over 'realist' and 'artistic' photography in the nineteenth century, but now makes the stronger assertion that it was 'recognised from the outset that photography was uniquely equipped to follow the realistic tendency to an extent unattainable in the related traditional arts' (59). Similarly, Kracauer repeats his point that photography cannot be considered as a mode of naïve realist objectivism, and, paraphrasing the language used in *Theory of Film*, claims that

> Naïve realism has long since gone; and nobody would dream of calling the camera a mirror. Actually, there is no mirror at all . . . no earthly reason why the photographer should suppress his formative urges in the interest of the necessarily futile attempt to achieve objectivity. (52)

As will be argued later, in 'Approach', Kracauer does modify his notion of the 'formative' urge further, but not in a way that differs in substance from the account laid out in *Theory of Film*.

History is a book about history. Nevertheless, there is also a continued engagement with the 'photographic mediums' in the book that is influenced by the account given of these mediums in *Theory of Film* and is premised upon the assumption that 'camera reality' and 'historical reality' may share certain similarities. This leads Kracauer to employ the definitions of photography and film found in *Theory of Film* in order to map out the basis of the 'historical approach'. The 'historical approach' is, as mentioned in the previous chapter of this book, equivalent to the 'photographic approach' set out in *Theory of Film*, and the similarity of phrasing is deliberate; Kracauer insists that photography does or should do with the present what historiography does or should do with the past. For example, Kracauer argues that 'camera reality parallels historical reality in terms of its structure and general constitution' (58), and that both have a similar subject-matter – the 'contingent', the 'random', 'transient impressions and unforeseeable encounters', the 'accidental'; all of this together means that 'the analogy between historiography and the photographic media . . . results from the solid fact that work in the two areas hinges on identical conditions: both crafts are committed to concern themselves with given worlds of comparable structure' (60). But what links these two worlds of comparable structure most is the extent to which they are inherently associated with the fundamental notion of *Lebenswelt*.

One major difference between *Theory of Film* and 'Approach', and between the former book and *History* as a whole, is that, in the latter cases, the notion of the *Lebenswelt* is clearly and repeatedly foregrounded. For example, the 'historical universe' is defined as having 'more in common with the *Lebenswelt* than with the reduced nature of the scientist's making' (48). That 'universe' is defined as 'indeterminate', a 'conglomerate of particular events, developments and situations of the human past' (45), and as dealing with 'the kind of life that falls into the orbit of everyday experience . . . inchoate, heterogeneous, obscure . . . an opaque mass of facts' (46). Kracauer also quotes directly from *The Crisis of European Sciences*, when Husserl defines the sciences as 'hovering' abstractly, 'as if in empty space, above the *Lebenswelt*' (46).[1] Kracauer then takes his cue from this to argue that the historical universe 'hovers' in a similar way, but at a lower level of abstraction, above the *Lebenswelt*, and is, therefore, closer to the *Lebenswelt* than are both the sciences and a philosophy that typically deals with absolutes and universals. Kracauer goes on to proclaim that 'The historian's universe is of much the same stuff as our everyday world – the very world which Husserl was first to endow with philosophical dignity' (45–6). That 'endowment' came in the form of the notion of *Lebenswelt*, and, although the *Lebenswelt* is not declared as such in *Theory of Film*, Kracauer was familiar with the notion when writing his book, and it could be argued that the idea of the *Lebenswelt* as the world of perceptual experience underlies the conception of physical reality set out in the 1960 work.

In his 1927 'Photography' essay, Kracauer makes a distinction between the two mediums of photography and film when he argues that film is more able to embody history – the 'history', that is, of the 'memory image' – than is the photograph, due to the closer relation of the film to perceptual experience. Here, the 'animated sphere', the sphere of human meaning that is embodied in memory, transcends the alienating 'photographic sphere' of the 'inventory' and 'warehousing of nature' found in the photograph, and appears more fully in the film (Kracauer 1995a: 61–2). In 'Approach', however, a chapter in a book about history, Kracauer is less concerned with the distinction between photography and film, groups both under the rubric of the 'photographic media' and relates that more evidently to historiography (Kracauer 1995b: 60). Even given the differences between the two mediums that Kracauer continues to allude to from time to time in *History*, what is of central importance to him is that both can be directly related to the idea of the *Lebenswelt*. So, for example, photography and film are necessarily indeterminate because of the considerable amount of empirical material they contain; because they are thereby 'surrounded by a fringe of indistinct multiple meanings' that 'delimits without defining' (60); and because the two mediums 'suggest life in its flux' (55). Film and photography are clearly different from each other. In *History*, however, Kracauer is concerned not so much with such difference as with connecting what both have in common with historiography in relation to the *Lebenswelt*; and what all three have in common in relation to that are 'intrinsic contingencies which obstruct calculability' and which are, consequently, 'indeterminate as to meaning' (45).

In *Theory of Film*, Kracauer sets out a history of the discourse on photography that is separated into two parts: 'Early views and trends', and 'Current views and trends'; he does so, it was argued in the previous chapter of this book, in part, because he was influenced by Husserl's conceptions of the 'historical presents and pasts', and *Lebenswelt*, both of which have pronounced contrastive and relativist aspects. In *History*, the influence of these and other concepts leads Kracauer to adopt a similarly 'differentiated' and relativistic conception of history. In a chapter of *History* entitled 'Ahasuerus, or the Riddle of Time',[2] Kracauer expands on the conceptions of 'differentiated historical time', 'relative time in history', 'shaped time' and relative spatial location that he employs in his book, citing the following from the historian Wolfgang von Leyden,[3] who writes on a model of time put forward by the eighteenth-century German philosopher Johann Gottfried Herder:[4]

> It is significant that Herder also held the view that everything carries within itself its own measure of time, or rather the measure of *its own time*; a measure that exists even if there is no other measure beside it . . . For, he argued, two different things will never have the same measure of time and therefore innumerable times may exist in the universe 'at the

same time'... the idea of a measure common to all times, just as the idea of infinite space which 'was' the sum total of all places in the universe, is something introduced by the intellect: both absolute space and absolute time are, properly speaking, a mere phantom. (146–7)

History can never, therefore, be reconstructed as a 'logical course of chronological time', but only as a 'discontinuous world of ruptures' and continuum (Koch 2000: 115).

In *History*, Kracauer cites Marx frequently, but generally to refute him, and he also takes the opportunity to do so over the issue of 'chronological time', at the same time linking Marx, tendentiously, to the French nineteenth-century positivist philosopher, Auguste Comte:

> Since Comte and Marx think of human history in terms of natural history, they take it all the more for granted that, like any physical process, history unfolds in measurable chronological time. With them, the historical process is tantamount to a linear movement – a necessary and meaningful succession of periods along a time continuum indefinitely extending into the temporal future. In other words, they unquestioningly confide in the magic of chronology. But what if... calendric time is not the all-powerful medium they suppose it to be but also an empty, indifferent flow which takes along with it a conglomerate of unconnected events... Then the historical process evolving in chronological time assumes an ambiguous character. (38)

Kracauer refutes notions of linear chronology and employs the notions of 'shaped time' and relative spatial location to refer to the differentiated spheres or 'areas' of time and spatial location that exist within a historical period. There is no 'infinite time' or 'absolute space' in history, only 'shaped' periods of spacetime. Kracauer also takes issue with the notion of the 'historical period' itself, arguing that, within such a supposed discontinuance, there is no overall and delimited span of time and space, because, as argued, events occur in different 'areas' that also have their own measure of time and related locations, and no two events will have the same measure of time or occur at the same point in space. The notion of 'historical period', together with that of linear chronology, embodies a sense of spatio-temporal fixity and linear development that works against the idea of the relativity of spacetime, and, consequently, the fundamental idea of the *Lebenswelt*. Kracauer also modifies the earlier statement on Marx here, arguing that Marx did not have an entirely linear conception of history:

> Let us, then, take a look at the period. Any period, whether 'found' or established in retrospect, consists of incoherent events or groups of

events – a well known phenomena which accounts, among other things, for the occurrence of events relatively unaffected by the Zeitgeist ... The typical period, that phase of the historical process, is a mixture of inconsistent elements ... Marx speaks of the *Ungleichzeitigkeit* (non-simultaneousness) of the ideological superstructure ... Dilthey stresses not only the unified context of the life of a period but also the existence of opposing forces which turn against the one-sidedness of the Zeitgeist, often continuing older ideas or anticipating the future. (Kracauer 1995b: 147–8)

Kracauer also makes the same point in the chapter from *History* entitled 'The Historian's Journey', which will be considered later in this chapter, when presented with an ad hoc historical assessment of the Weimar period that he had lived through. This analysis 'was true to fact', whilst, on the other hand, 'nothing had happened' the way it had been related, and Kracauer feared that:

All that was a matter of fluctuating opinions, agonizing doubts, and spontaneous decisions during the twenties would freeze into a more or less rigid pattern of trends, cross-currents, majority and minority attitudes, and the like ... I wondered at the incommensurable relationship between the picture he [the historian who presented this account to Kracauer] was about to draw and the reality which it was designed to cover. He did not represent the events as I knew them – events in flux and amenable to change – but conceived of them as elements of a period which was now definitely a *fait accompli*. (86–7)

Kracauer takes his model of relative spatio-temporal historical 'periods' from that of the trans-spatial and trans-temporal *Lebenswelt*, and, for him, the historical period is no period at all, but, rather, a historical continuum, in which events are in flux and amenable to change, and in which those events also possess their own internal 'measures of time' and areas of special location. For Kracauer, the historical universe is like the *Lebenswelt* because that universe spreads out through space and time more than it proceeds through space and time, and because it is full of inconsistencies and *Ungleichzeitigkeit*. The German term here implies that events do not happen at the same time, and that the perception that they do is mistaken. Events 'happen', but not at the 'same time', because, when they happen, they are part of different chains of temporal progression. History is not even a 'process' in the sense of one linked and ordered succession:

history is no process at all but a hodge-podge of kaleidoscopic changes – something like clouds that gather and disperse at random ... There is no flow of time. What does exist is a discontinuous, non-causal succession of situations or worlds, or periods . . . It is understood that these different worlds or situations reach fullness and fade away in times of different shapes. (160)

In 'Approach', Kracauer also redefines two issues that were central to *Theory of Film*: the notion of the 'basic aesthetic principle' of film and photography; and the distinction between the 'realist' and 'formative' tendencies. In the chapter on photography in *Theory of Film* Kracauer talks about the 'basic aesthetic principle of photography', and, in the following chapter, entitled 'Basic Concepts', he refers to the 'basic aesthetic principle' of film. The basic aesthetic principle is that an aesthetic medium should build from its 'basic' properties. When photography does this, it adopts the 'photographic approach', and when film does the same, it adopts the 'cinematic approach'; for both mediums, the basic properties involved are those of an ability to 'record and reveal physical reality' (Kracauer 1997: 28). Photography and film are aesthetic mediums, and, plainly, historiography is not. As argued in the previous chapter of this book, Kracauer's notion of the 'basic aesthetic principle' is based upon a conception of aesthetic value related to medium specificity, and, so, the 'basic aesthetic principle', when applied to non-aesthetic mediums such as historiography, becomes abridged to just the 'basic principle' that all mediums must build from their basic properties. As Kracauer puts it, 'the products of a medium with specific characteristics are the more satisfactory if they build from these characteristics' (Kracauer 1995b: 54).

In *History*, Kracauer attempts to define the basic properties and specific characteristics of historiography as he attempted to do for photography and film in *Theory of Film*, and, in his view, the basic properties and characteristics of both the 'photographic media' and historiography are the same. The intellectual constellation of recording and revealing is now extended to historiography, which, like film and photography, must similarly engage in 'recording and penetrating' reality, a reality that is now historical, and, consequently, non-corporeal (54). As with the photographic mediums, historiography must embrace the 'realist tendency' because this conforms to the medium specificity of the practice. Consequently, the historian must operate as an explorer who 'roams yet unconquered spaces' (this is also a paraphrase from *Theory of Film*) (55). This attachment of the 'basic principle' of medium specificity to historiography then leads Kracauer to define further two crucial themes that were addressed in *Theory of Film* and which also permeate *History*; and, once more, the continuity with what is argued in *Theory of Film* is clear. These themes are those of the 'realist' and 'formative' approaches.

In 'Approach', as, indeed, in *Theory of Film*, Kracauer does not oppose the realist and formative tendencies but sees them as two inseparable component parts of one overall process and wishes them to come into the 'right' alignment. That alignment must, none the less, favour the realist over the formative tendency. Kracauer talks about a two-fold stage in the historiographical process. First, there is the 'passive' stage, or, as he also puts it, the 'active–passive' stage. Here, the historian must actively open themselves up to the flow of evidence and 'establish the relevant evidence' (47). The historian, like the realist photographer, does not have the 'freedom' that the artist has, to express him- or herself (55), and, like the realist photographer, must attempt and achieve an 'empathic absorption' in the evidence (56). The parallels with *Theory of Film* here, in relation to the need for 'empathy' with the materials, are evident. The 'realist phase', the 'active–passive' phase of the historiographical process, is dominated by openness to and reception of the evidence/material, and, as has been argued more fully in the preceding chapter of this book, this phase is active–passive, rather than just passive, because it requires formative activity of a kind in order to fulfil the requirements of this phase. But then there is a later 'formative' phase, in which the historian must interpret the material, and the term formative here refers to the more active role played by the 'fuller self' in this process.

As in *Theory of Film*, so also in 'Approach', Kracauer rejects the idea of naïve realism, an idea that might lead to the hegemony of the 'active–passive' receptive phase of the historical approach on the grounds that objective knowledge is possible, and he paraphrases his earlier book by asserting, via a quotation from the historian Lewis Namier, that the historian does not seek an illusory 'objectivity', but, instead, seeks 'to discover and set forth, to single out and stress that which is of the nature of the thing, and not reproduce indiscriminately all that meets the eye' (51).[5] This singling-out of the nature of things is, nevertheless, by no means a return to the sort of full-blooded subjective 'animated' history referred to in the 1927 'Photography' essay. Rather, Kracauer sets out a sliding scale of historiographical methodology, beginning with the 'straightforward' technical record at one end and a history constituted by 'highly subjective statements' at the other (52). Echoing *Theory of Film* once more, he asserts that the 'right balance' must be struck between the realist and formative phases within this sliding scale, and that what must be achieved as a result is a situation 'in which spontaneity [creative interpretation] and receptivity are in a state of equilibrium' (56–7). The term 'equilibrium' is somewhat puzzling here, and what Kracauer really means (he can mean nothing else, given the general tenor of his argument) is that a relation between the two tendencies must be established in which interpretation shapes the evidence but does not overwhelm it in doing so. Kracauer, for example, speaks more accurately elsewhere in his chapter about interpretation 'moulding' the raw materials rather than 'consuming' them; here, the term 'moulding' implies a process in which the materials are amended and shaped without being fundamentally transformed. In this process, both the realist–receptive faculty and formative–interpretative faculty of the historian come into the 'right balance', although one that is not a 'balance' at all in the literal sense of that term. Kracauer, therefore, insists that the historian should abide by the 'basic historical principle' because that principle is medium-specific to historiography, that historiography must proceed from and privilege the active–passive receptive faculty in order to record and reveal, and that, where that happens, the subject-matter of historiography, like the 'camera-reality' of photography and film, will inevitably display 'all the earmarks of the *Lebenswelt*'. Although such historiography, like 'camera-reality', will be 'partly patterned, partly amorphous' (partly formative, partly realist), it will be the latter that should take precedence (58), and, like realist photography, such historiography will also dispense with 'an air of completeness' (54).

The previous two chapters of this book looked at two essays on photography by Kracauer, one published in 1927, the other in 1960 as a chapter in *Theory of Film*. However, in 1951, Kracauer also published an essay entitled 'The Photographic Approach'. This short piece was later enlarged and appeared as the longer chapter in *Theory of Film* entitled 'Introduction: Photography'. The contents of the 1951 paper are, however, virtually indistinguishable from the contents of that longer chapter, with, perhaps, one exception, related to the notion of 'completeness' mentioned above. In the 1951 paper Kracauer argues that a photograph should not appear to be or be regarded as 'complete' because 'its frame marks a provisional limit'; its content refers to other contents outside the frame, and it, therefore, 'denotes something that cannot be encompassed – physical existence' (von Moltke and Rawson 2012: 191). As argued, Kracauer makes something like the same point about historiography and history. Just as 'camera reality' is a reality whose frame marks only a 'provisional limit', because that reality extends beyond the frame, and, therefore, cannot be 'complete' within the frame, the frame of any historiographical enquiry also has its own provisional limit because historical reality, or what Kracauer also refers to as the 'historical universe', extends beyond that limit (Kracauer 1995b: 104). We thus see continuity in Kracauer's thought from at least 1951 to 1960, and then on to the posthumously published *History*, in 1968.

In 'The Historical Approach', of 1968, Kracauer builds on many of the key concepts found in *Theory of Film*. The major difference between the two works, however, is that, whilst the idea of the *Lebenswelt* underlies much of what is written in *Theory of Film*, that idea comes to the foreground in 'The Historical Approach', and in *History* as a whole. It is also clear that Kracauer focuses on the trans-spatial and trans-temporal aspects of the *Lebenswelt*, the way that the *Lebenswelt* extends through space and time in a lateral manner, and that this is emphasised above the way that the *Lebenswelt* extends through space and time in a linear fashion. Kracauer also takes these ideas forward in the second piece to be considered in this chapter, 'The Historian's Journey'. One difference between the two chapters, however, and as will be argued later, is that the latter chapter returns far more to the notion of the 'idea' that constitutes the intellectual *radix* of the account of photography found in *Theory of Film*.

'THE HISTORIAN'S JOURNEY' (1968)

Although, in *Theory of Film*, Kracauer argues that the 'basic aesthetic principle' of the 'photographic approach' is to build from the intrinsic, medium-specific properties of film and photography, the properties of recording and revealing, he also asserts that this remains a 'minimum requirement': the essential foundation upon which the interpretations and 'formative energies' of the photographer can later be further developed. In 'The Historian's Journey' ('Journey'), Chapter 4 of *History*, Kracauer also asserts that the 'basic principle' of the 'historical approach' is to build from the basic, medium-specific properties of historiography – essentially, those of recording and revealing – as a 'minimum requirement' upon which the later interpretations of the historian can be based (Kracauer 1995b: 90). Here, meeting the minimum requirement means beginning the process of enquiry with detailed observation, after which the historian may (or may not) progressively open themselves up to the information projecting back from the object of study until the end of the first, realist, phase of the historical approach is reached, and prior to the fuller engagement of the formative energies. The minimum requirement for film and photography, therefore, is that the initial and continuing intervention should be focused on recording and revealing, whilst the minimum requirement for historiography is, in similar vein, 'taking stock of "local and concrete things"' (90).[6] It is also important to appreciate that, in terms of both film and photography, and historiography, the phrase 'minimum requirement' means that the requirement must be met; it does not mean that the realist phase of these mediums should end at that minimum requirement. Consequently, the minimum requirement for historiography differentially encompasses the entire first phase of the historical approach and is operative along a sliding scale, with elementary 'bare and noncommittal' observation of 'concrete things' at one end, and more exhaustive, reflective 'self-forgetting immersion' at the other (89–90). When referring to work that occupies the initial part of this scale, Kracauer also makes a distinction between largely unpremeditated attempts to observe and assimilate materials, whose meaning would then be assessed a posteriori, and 'predatory raids into the past', which are intended to find data to support theses formulated a priori to such interventions (89). This, of course, echoes what is said in *Theory of Film*. There, Kracauer argues that the photographic approach should be based on the selection and production of images that are found a posteriori, rather than posited a priori, and that, when material reality is configured to prior intent, nature is exploited 'for a pseudo-realistic statement of . . . vision' (Kracauer 1997: 18). The images of physical reality posited or imagined a priori are the equivalent of non-corporeal, a priori arranged, 'predatory raids into the past' which are 'pseudo-realistic'.

What Kracauer alludes to is a process in which initial observation of primary data leads to a deepening meditation upon that data, a meditation in which subjectivity is involved, but where that subjectivity is focused upon perceiving and organising the data as well as possible whilst, for the time being, bracketing out abstract preconceptions and understandings concerning that data. In this sense, the practice of undertaking historiography is also analogous to the experience of *durée* or practice of *epochē* (see Chapters 1 and 6 of this book, respectively), as, in both cases, there is a focus on the singular and a bracketing out of the abstract. At the core of the historical approach is the principle of building from the fundamental, medium-specific properties of historiography as a minimum requirement, but, and as argued, the minimum requirement does not mark an end point, and is superseded by the basic principle of which it is a part; it is only an initiating safeguard for a principle that goes beyond it and which insists that minimum requirement evolves into overriding realist imperative. For Kracauer, the fundamental medium-specific property of historiography consists of a deep-rooted facility to meditate profoundly upon the primary data that are manifest: a facility that endows historiography with a capacity to record and reveal, just as the fundamental medium-specific property of film and photography is the same. In another sense, this facility of historiography is also analogous to a certain manner of watching a film. Just as, in the experience of *epochē*, *durée*, or engagement with the historical data, there is a meditation upon the singular, so also, in the viewing of a film, there is, or can be, a comparable meditation upon the concrete phenomenal substance of the film. *Epochē*, *durée*, film spectatorship, and the central property of the historical approach all, therefore, have the same thing in common: a capacity to contemplate what Kracauer calls the 'small, the monographic form' of things, where the term 'monographic' refers to the singular character and identity of that form (89). The term 'monographic' is also similar to the term '*monogram/Monogramm*' that Kracauer deploys in the 1927 'Photography' essay and means much the same thing: the meaningful coherent *identity* of something. So, in 'Photography', Kracauer asserts that the *monogram* 'condenses . . . [things into] . . . a single . . . figure' (Kracauer 1995a: 51), '*zu einem Linienzug verdichtet*' (Kracauer 2017: 26).[7] This is close to the 'small . . . monographic form' that Kracauer refers to in 'Journey', indicating yet another continuity of thought, although, it could be argued, the monographic form referred to in 'Journey' is more empirically based than the monogram of the memory image in 'Photography'.

Within the field of historiography, Kracauer finds the historical approach operating only at minimum-requirement level in what he refers to as 'technical histories': 'fact-oriented accounts exhibiting the immediate yield of detailed research . . . run-of-the-mill investigations' (Kracauer 1995b: 88–9). In the 1927 'Photography' essay Kracauer is dismissive of such histories, claiming that a collection of facts cannot provide a meaningful history and that such a collection would be little more than an 'ephemeral' 'herbarium' (Kracauer 1995a: 49). In 'Journey', he also cites the British historian and philosopher Herbert Butterfield describing such histories as constituting a 'limited and mundane realm of description and explanation' (Kracauer 1995ba: 89).[8] Nevertheless, such references are atypical of the overall stance adopted in 'Journey', and, as is implied by the central observatory property of the historical approach, in 'Journey', Kracauer generally discloses a more sanguine attitude to this sort of history (as he also does in terms of factual films in *Theory of Film*) because it conforms to the requirements of both that central observatory property and the basic principle of the historical approach. In addition, in 'Journey', Kracauer does not see such histories as of the same circumscribed type as may be implied by both his 1927 stance and his citation of Butterfield, and, instead, imagines histories which range from 'run-of-the-mill investigations . . . to inquiries which really involve self-forgetting immersion in the texts and remains' (89). In both cases, the same 'passive-objectivity' is required of the historian: an 'act of self-emptying', in which the self is 'still at a low pitch and moreover refuses to fully assert itself' (89). As the historian's journey proceeds within the framework of the historical approach, however, and a shift gradually takes place from the mundane investigation to the more introspective immersive enquiry that Kracauer refers to, the self asserts itself more, in order to activate those of its aspects that are concerned with understanding the immediate experience of the object and data as acutely as possible. This is the part of the process which involves the further meditation on and organisation of the data, where the historian must 'assimilate to himself the material collected, with the emphasis on his factual findings' (88). In 'Journey', consequently, Kracauer makes an imperative equation between the two phases of the photographic and historical approach – the realist and formative phases – and two dimensions of the self, thereby implying both that these approaches are fundamental to the self, and, following the general tenor of his stance in 'Journey', that the realist phase is the more fundamental.

Although, in 'Approach', Kracauer only touches upon the idea of the 'self', he attempts to develop that notion further in 'Journey'. What is involved in the first phase of the historical approach, and, to reiterate the position set out in 'Approach', is a certain 'state of passiveness' in which the 'sensitive historian' 'gathers the evidence' (89). This passivity on the part of the historian can be compared to the opening posture of the photographer in *Theory of Film*, where the photographer aims to 'represent significant aspects of physical reality without trying to overwhelm that reality – so that the raw material focused on is both left intact and made transparent' (Kracauer 1997: 23). There is, therefore, a degree of detachment shown here, so that the information embodied in the raw material can communicate its 'transparent' connotations, where the term 'transparent' indicates a relatively circumscribed array of connotations suggested by assignation with the raw material. Kracauer cites Schopenhauer in order to clarify further what he means by this stage of the historical approach when he writes that:

> Anybody looking at a picture [a painting], Schopenhauer claims, should behave as if he were in the presence of a prince and respectfully wait for what the picture may or may not wish to tell him, for were he to talk first he would only be listening to himself.[9] (Kracauer 1995b: 84)

As argued, the 'state of passiveness' involved here, the 'product of a reduced self', begins the historical approach, and is always, additionally, kept in place and active to an extent, even within the second, formative phase of the historical approach. However, as the historiographic journey proceeds through the first phase of the historical approach, this passivity becomes increasingly more reflective and attentive, and evolves into a more 'active passiveness' in which the historian may achieve full 'self-forgetting immersion in the texts and remains' at the finale of that first phase (89). The self-forgetting immersion that takes place here is an intentional one and constitutes a suspension of judgement similar to the *epochē*: a suspension of judgement whose purpose is to 'favour [and observe] the influx of minutiae' (89). The phrase 'self-forgetting immersion', therefore, implies the reduction of the psyche in order to become attentively immersed in the influx of minutiae.

The relationship of this to the act of viewing a painting, as in the Schopenhauer allusion just given, would be something like the following: the spectator may begin engagement with the painting by 'passively' perusing its phenomenal surface. Gradually, however, that will evolve into a more substantive and active engagement with the connotations conceived of as emanating from the painting, until a directed self-forgetting immersion in the experience takes place, and, here, as with the reduction of the psyche mentioned earlier, 'self-forgetting' does not mean a forgetting or 'reduction' of the entire self, but, rather, the formative aspect of the self, or those aspects of the self which characteristically form judgements (or, in terms of historiographic explanation, 'generalisations or macro-units') (89). The objective is to enable the realist, observing modality of the self to obtain as much knowledge from the source as possible. The emphasis, is, therefore, upon the acquisition of knowledge, rather than interpretation. It may be pointed out that the concept of 'transparency' introduced here by Kracauer is not the same as that employed by him in the 1927 'Photography' essay. In that essay, the term refers to the 'ur-image' (*Urbild*) redolent with meaning, whereas, in 'Journey', the term refers to a far more limited array of meaning, ranging from the empirical to a close network of associations and significations associated with that. Similarly, in 'Photography', Kracauer uses the term 'monogram' to refer to the authentic being of an individual, whereas, in *History*, he uses the term 'monographic form' to refer to a network of 'local and concrete things' (89). Kracauer has moved from a concern with the isolated, amplified, existential self, to one in which the relation holding between an intentionally reduced self and the world is of greater import; and from a belief in the impossibility of representing the memory image in an authentic manner, to one in which the physical and historical world can be validly represented. Nevertheless, here, authenticity does not mean objectivity, and Kracauer is not referring to any naïve–realist objectivism, but to a more accurate observation, and, eventually, depiction, of phenomenal experience that is necessarily, and none the less, given through subjectivity.

In order to clarify his idea of the self further, Kracauer also returns to the scene from Proust's *In Search of Lost Time* which is referred to in *Theory of Film*: the scene in which the narrator, Marcel, enters the rooms of his grandmother, and, in a detached frame of mind, sees her as she is, an elderly frail woman, rather than the family member with whom he had been so familiar. According to Kracauer, Proust invokes 'two different states of mind' here: the 'animated' and the 'photographic', with the animated standing for Marcel's 'memory image' of the grandmother, and the photographic for his detached consideration of the latter (83). In the 1927 'Photography' essay the initial chasm between these two mutually incompatible states is emphasised, as is the fact that, as time goes by, after, say, the death of the grandmother, the animated inevitably turns into the photographic. In *Theory of Film*, however, such fundamental opposition is disallowed, as Kracauer insists that there is no absolute distinction between these two states: no such thing as a photographic state that can exclude the 'animated' sphere of subjectivity and relativity, and no such thing as a pure animated state free of pragmatic or disinterested informational context. Instead of two states of mind, and, contra Proust, there is one state of mind that combines the animated with the non-animated, and subjectivity with observation.

In *Theory of Film*, the 1927 notion of the memory image, and memory itself, to a large extent, is replaced by a more general conception of the subjective involvement of the photographer within immediate experience and encounter, and, later, within the process of formative creation; this is also the stance adopted in both 'Approach' and 'Journey'. This shift from memory to immediate experience has the outcome that, in *Theory of Film*, Kracauer does not discuss the issue of the gradual loss of the animated in the photograph over the course of time, perhaps the major theme in the 1927 essay. Kracauer does, nevertheless, hold on to another key theme of the 1927 essay: the idea of the photograph as alienating, arguing that the photographic approach can be related to a 'state of alienation' (Kracauer 1997: 16). This is, however, not the undesirable state of alienation invoked in 1927, one provoked by the 'warehousing' of nature carried out by the photographic mediums. In the first, receptive stage of the photographic approach, the reduction of the self that is involved becomes a desirable state of alienation, because it allows greater cognisance of the 'external phenomena' to take place without the blurring impact of 'involuntary memories', and, additionally, provides a medium-specific foundation for the later engagement of the fuller self (15). In 'Journey' this state of alienation is also essentially redefined in the same way, as an intentional, temporary reduction of the self, that then leads on to a greater and more authentic expansion of the self through engagement with the materials first encountered in the receptive phase of the historian's journey.

In *Theory of Film*, Kracauer is less concerned with memory than with the encounter with immediate experience. In 'Journey', however, Kracauer returns to the issue of memory once more, and through the introduction of a wholly new concept: that of the 'palimpsest', in which the photographic mind is superimposed over the animated mind, which still, nevertheless, remains as a 'temporally effaced inscription' (Kracauer 1995b: 83). The dictionary definition of the term palimpsest is 'a manuscript or piece of writing on which later writing has been superimposed on effaced earlier writing', and something 'reused or altered but still bearing visible traces of its earlier form' (*Oxford English Dictionary*). It is in this sense of something that is superimposed on something that existed before it, of something altered that still bears the traces of its earlier being, that Kracauer employs the term palimpsest. Kracauer returns once more to the scene in Proust's novel when Marcel enters the rooms of his grandmother: 'No sooner does Marcel enter his grandmother's room than his mind becomes a palimpsest, with the stranger's observations being superimposed upon the lover's temporarily effaced inscription' (83). Here, the state of productive alienation invoked in *Theory of Film* seems less benign, and, as in 1927, the palimpsest represents the gradual descent into meaninglessness caused by the incremental loss of the memory image, as the stranger's observations efface the lover's inscription. This, however, is not entirely the case, because it is in the nature of the palimpsest that such effacement can be neither permanent nor complete.

Kracauer then compares this state of being, and state of mind, to his own situation as an 'exile' – the exile as palimpsest: 'sometimes life itself produces such palimpsests. I am thinking of the exile' (83). The exile's new, more abstract life – in Kracauer's case, his post-war life in America – is superimposed upon his old 'animated' life, his life in Weimar Germany, which none the less 'continues to smoulder beneath the person he is about to become'. As palimpsest, the identity of the exile must always be 'in a state of flux', so that he will 'never fully belong to the community to which he now in a way belongs'; the exile as palimpsest is a 'stranger', someone 'who does not belong to the house', and who is, therefore, destined to live always in the 'no-man's-land' of the photographic gaze, the no-man's-land that Marcel unexpectedly found himself occupying when he entered his grandmother's rooms. Nevertheless, as palimpsests, neither Marcel, nor the displaced historian, can be fully taken into the photographic gaze, because, for both, and as palimpsests, the 'natural self' must always remain 'smouldering beneath' that gaze (83–4). Being aware of the memory image, as Marcel is, and being in a condition of exile-hood, as Kracauer's expatriate is, affords at least some means of resisting the photographic gaze, and, perhaps, the abstract condition of capitalist modernity that nurtures that gaze: a condition that Kracauer refers to in both the 1927 'Photography' essay and *Theory of Film*.

As suggested, the concept of the palimpsest indicates a return to the memory image of the 1927 essay on photography. There, the irredeemable reduction of the memory image constituted an existential loss similar to the plight of the exile, as the exile looks back at his diminished 'natural self'. According to Kracauer:

> As he settles elsewhere, all those loyalties, expectations, and aspirations that comprise so large a part of his being are automatically cut off from their roots. His life history is disrupted, his 'natural self' relegated to the background of his mind. (83)

This also amounts to a reversal of the photographic and historical approaches. In both these approaches the 'no-man's-land' of the reduced self is intentionally adopted, can be more or less set aside as required, and is taken on at the *beginning* of both approaches. For the palimpsestic, however, and, consequently, for the memory image as palimpsest, the process *ends* in the no-man's-land of the photographic gaze, and a no-man's-land that cannot be fully set aside. Kracauer's notion of palimpsest also enables him to imagine two different types of historians. First, there are those – the non-palimpsestic – who are not cut off from their 'natural self', and who can adopt and then mainly set aside the photographic gaze, and who also begin the process with that gaze. Second, there are those – the palimpsestic – who *are* cut off from their natural self, who cannot mainly set aside the photographic gaze, and who are predestined always to end the historical approach with that gaze. In the latter case, the exiled historian, in a state of 'self-effacement, or homelessness', may, from a distance, gain insight into the alien historical environment that is studied. It is alien in two respects: because it is an environment in a foreign land (if it is the land in which the historian now lives, as palimpsest); and also because it is in the past, and therefore no longer 'exists'. Whilst it is true that, in a sense, all historians study a non-existent, alien environment, the historian who studies the historical environment of the land in which he lives as palimpsest is doubly alienated. The sense of alienation of the palimpsest will also continue to exist, as it does in part for Marcel, when he enters the rooms of his grandmother. In Proust's novel, the narrator, Marcel, does not, Kracauer argues, entirely turn into a photographer, because the animated sphere persists as a 'temporally effaced inscription' (83). It is true that Marcel, at least in this scene from the novel, never fully enters the 'no-man's-land' of the photographic gaze, but he also nevertheless remains within it as palimpsest; and there is a sense in which he will never be able to escape fully from that. For Marcel the palimpsest, his grandmother will forever remain largely outside the animated sphere, as an old, withered woman, whilst her lesser, animated self merely flickers beneath.

There is, however, another difference between Kracauer's account of the memory image and alienating photographic images in 1927, and his invocation of the palimpsestic exile in 1968. For those in the 1927 'Photography' essay who view the photograph of the late grandmother when she was a young girl, the loss of the animated sphere, and animated history, is not meaningful, because the grandmother was hardly known to them affectively and personally (let us imagine that she died when the grandchildren were very young); all that they can, therefore, ever see is the photographic 'inventory', and there is little or no sense of loss involved here, no sense of the melancholic palimpsestic. The two-fold palimpsestic gaze which once supported the memory image has been entirely replaced by an unaccompanied photographic gaze that merely observes the curious minutiae of the long-gone past, 'although the grandmother has disappeared, the crinoline has nonetheless remained' (Kracauer 1995a: 61). This disappearance of the animated is central to Kracauer's argument in the 1927 piece that photography contributes to an ongoing process of alienation that suits the purposes and interests of a dehumanising capitalist modernity, as he argues that 'The same mere nature that appears in photography flourishes in the reality of the society produced by this capitalist mode of production' (61). Painting, Kracauer contends, may retain the history of the memory image, but photography can bear its trace only whilst the spirit remains strong. However, this loss, this dehumanisation, is irrelevant for those who look at the photograph of the late grandmother as a young girl. They are, in addition, not aware that they are participating in a process designed increasingly to dehumanise them, and all that they experience is a meaningless world, now long gone, that stands in contrast to their own extant and animated one.

Existence in the no-man's-land of the photographic gaze is, however, meaningful to the meditating exile, such as Kracauer, who, unlike the viewers of the old photograph, is cognisant of the ineffectuality of his present existence because he retains an enduring melancholic sense of an animated, lost history. In this sense the exile is more aware than those who look at the photograph of the grandmother, and, although the exile's general mode of experience, of being alienated, might serve the interests of the larger forces of capitalist modernity, as though he was a kind of living photograph, providing, for example, historical reports that are void of all fervour, as a palimpsest the exile remains aware of the animated sphere and this means that he is also aware that he exists in the no-man's-land of the photographic gaze and can see beyond that land and gaze. And when the exile is a historian who experiences a permanent reduction of the self by virtue of being an exile and palimpsest, that can, as previously argued, be put to productive use, if the historian is able to extend his non-aligned photographic gaze to the historical world as well as to his present one, and view those worlds more tangibly, just as Marcel did when, in his present world, he entered the rooms of his grandmother (in this sense, the photographic gaze provides Marcel with *new* knowledge). The historian–exile can, therefore, take this sense of exile, this sense of reduction of the self through alienation, to his engagement with the sources, and observe them disinterestedly, and productively.

One of the key terms and concepts deployed by Kracauer in *History* is that of 'distance'. By distance Kracauer means two things. First, he refers to the distance from empirical historical reality created by large-scale narrative historiographies: 'macro-histories' that look at the past 'from a great distance' and subsume events under high levels of generality. Within such histories, 'all that is discernible . . . are vaguely contoured giant units, vast generalisations of uncertain reliability' (Kracauer 1995b: 118). Kracauer is referring here to the 'full-blown' teleological histories which emanate from the historicist tradition associated with Friedrich Schlegel, Hegel, Marx, Giambattista Vico and others. In such large-scale histories a considerable remoteness is created between theory and evidence, and the 'historian's formative urges get the better of his curiosity about the real course of events' (90). Kracauer, on the other hand, wishes to bring theory as close to evidence as possible, and this sets limits upon such theory. Unlike the 'technical' histories referred to earlier, such histories also fail to meet the minimum requirement of the historical approach. Second, by distance, and as previously argued, Kracauer means that the historical world is always distant to the historian because it is not *his/her* world: not the concrete *Lebenswelt*. The historical world has no physical existence, and, to access it, both historian, and historian as exile, the first voluntarily, the second necessarily, must approach that world from a dissociated sense of existential 'homelessness' (84). Historians may not have to be depressives, but they should have the facility to see the historical world as a stranger would.

In 'Journey', Kracauer also expands on the notion of the self-estrangement, or 'self-eradication', of the historian, by recourse to the place of such estrangement in the documentary film (Koch 2000: 114). So, for example, he refers to Joris Ivens and Henri Storck's 1934 film *Borinage*, a film about the living and working conditions of Belgian coalminers. Kracauer sees this film as the 'outspoken counterpart' of the technical histories that engage in a reduction of the self, and which, thus, try to avoid 'blurring the communications received' from the subject:

> Their most outspoken counterparts in the cinematic medium are documentary films designed to portray (physical) reality in a straightforward manner. Here you have again a case where a comparison between film and history proves rewarding. A few documentaries I know picture appalling living conditions with a matter-of-fact soberness which, as I have learned, results from the deliberate suspension of their authors' creative powers . . . the directors of these films proceed from the conviction that pictorial beauty and suggestive editing would interfere with their intention to let things be as they are. (Kracauer 1995b: 90)

Here, the self is constrained, and emotional involvement kept at a low level, in order that the film, and film-maker, may receive and take as much material as possible from the subject. The film-maker, like the historian and photographer, operates under the direction of a restrained, but receptive self. As argued earlier, the photographer/film-maker can then, later, add more of the 'full self' to this situation, although the historian cannot do so, or should not do so, to the same extent, given the professional disciplines and constraints of historiography; and the exile–historian even less so, as he/she is existentially unable to do so by virtue of being palimpsestic.

It is the first, mainly receptive phase of the historical approach that Kracauer is chiefly interested in, and, in 'Journey', he expands further on the nature of this phase through reference to the *Lebenswelt*. In effect, Kracauer argues that the historian should approach historical phenomena in the same way that engagement with the *Lebenswelt* normally takes place. The first phase of the historical approach owes its *raison d'être* to:

> a basic quality of historical phenomena which to ignore would be the death of history. Products of necessity as well as chance and freedom, these phenomena – immensely concrete and virtually inexhaustible phenomena – define, and fill, a universe which has many traits in common with the *Lebenswelt*. They stand out in it sphinx-like, as do their counterparts in the world we live in. And they would be impenetrable

to us did we not in our dealings with them proceed after the very manner in which we proceed in everyday life. (95)

The 'very manner in which we proceed in everyday life' is what Husserl refers to as the 'natural attitude'. It will be recalled that the natural attitude to the world is based on the belief that the *Lebenswelt* has a reality to which we are always committed as a matter of course (Carr 1987: 232). Whilst the natural attitude is, consequently, generally unreflective, it can, none the less, also include some 'reflection on its own activity', in that we can become conscious of things that often or normally occur without being noticed, and, as discussed in Chapter 6 of this book, this experience of 'noticing' is an ever-present possibility (Natanson 1973: 21). The given-ness of the *Lebenswelt* through the natural attitude also, none the less, includes a degree of ambiguity over the meaning of things and relationships between things, and is, consequently, accompanied by a 'fringe' of indeterminate meaning and 'undefined possibilities' (25). As we move through the *Lebenswelt*, these possibilities appear pertaining to what to do and what to become aware of. Indistinctness is, therefore, ever-present against the backdrop of the overall belief in the given-ness of the world. The natural attitude is also related to the perceptual and the 'cultural' *Lebenswelt*. That attitude is certainly 'one reality for all of us' at the level of the perceptual *Lebenswelt*. At the level of the cultural *Lebenswelt*, however, the natural attitude is related to the mores and beliefs native to a culture or society. The *Lebenswelt*, at the cultural level, is, 'essentially a reflection of the culture [which members of the same community] have in common' (Bell 1990: 229).[10] When, therefore, Kracauer says that the historical *Lebenswelt* should be engaged with in the same manner that the material *Lebenswelt* is, he means that the approach adopted with regard to that should be this combination of acceptance and reflection, of the perception of an indistinctness active against the background of given-ness.

If these notions of the natural attitude and the cultural *Lebenswelt* are applied to a historiography set within Kracauer's intellectual framework, it follows that what the historian must first try to do is 'understand'[11] the natural attitude of the historical–cultural *Lebenswelt* that they are bent on exploring. This means trying to be aware of what is taken as a matter of course and real within that historical world, as well as the indeterminacy and ambiguities which surround that, and what may be experienced as newly known. The historian must proceed in the same manner that they proceed though their own perceptual and cultural *Lebenswelt*, but with one important difference, and one which also bears upon the mission of the photographer/film-maker. Inhabitants of the material *Lebenswelt* would observe and experience what is taken for granted and what is experienced as new or different without bringing interpretation overly to bear on the matter. The historian should proceed in the same way in their exploration of the historical *Lebenswelt*, although the stance adopted in relation to that would, despite that, also be amended: in place of the generally – but not entirely – unreflective natural attitude, the historian would adopt the 'active–passive' mode of the realist approach, and, in addition to observation, this would also involve a constant building up of provisional interpretation – interpretation that is then held in abeyance as it progresses, and would also be more than that which would be normally expected in engagement with the material *Lebenswelt*. The historian, and particularly the palimpsestic historian, as explorer of the historical *Lebenswelt*, is, or should be, more reflective and inquisitive than the average inhabitant of the material *Lebenswelt*.

It is, consequently, the constellation of given-ness and its ambiguities that the historian must seek to fathom. The historian must look at the sources closely during the first phase of the historical approach in order to do this, and this will require the dialectical process of self-effacement and self-expansion previously referred to, in which there must be an initial surrender to the facts, and the adoption of what Kracauer calls an 'active passivity [that] is a necessary phase of the historian's work' (Kracauer 1995b: 85). The historian is 'distant' from the historical world they are investigating. An active attempt, one involving a combination of empathy and melancholy, must, accordingly, be made to obtain information about that world; and what is chiefly looked for is evidence of the way that the cultural *Lebenswelt* is engaged with in that world – what Kracauer refers to, in his remembrance of his experience of Weimar Germany, as the 'fluctuating opinions, agonising doubts and spontaneous decisions . . . events in flux and amenable to change', which circulated around the historical natural attitude (86–7). This historical reality is also further illuminated by comparing it to 'camera reality':

> the sort of reality on which the photographer, or film-maker, opens his lens – has all the earmarks of the *Lebenswelt*. It comprises inanimate objects, faces, crowds, people who intermingle, suffer and hope; its grand theme is life in its fullness, life as we commonly experience it. (58)

It is clear, therefore, that Kracauer's conception of the *Lebenswelt* consists of two principal parts: the first concerns the permanence of the natural attitude, 'life as we commonly experience it'; the second concerns the ambiguity surrounding that, and it could be argued that this dialectical conception, involving both definiteness and indeterminacy, lies at the very heart of Kracauer's understanding of photography, film and history. As a 'lens', both historiography and film/photography should open to the same reality. The photographer/film-maker and historian, are, thus, active *describers* of the *Lebenswelt*, charged with making the *Lebenswelt* evident to others.

This phase of active passivity in engagement with the sources constitutes the historian's 'journey' into the past, a journey which also leads to a 'change of identity' for the historian because the historian is altered by that journey. In the state of self-effacement, 'the phase in which he opens himself up to the suggestions of the sources', he finds what 'he did not know and could not know before', and this, consequently, leads on to a 'self-expansion', and, here, the self 'expands' 'in the wake of its near extinction', and in a manner influenced by what is encountered during its journey (91–2). The identity of the historian is, thus, altered by the journey into the past. It is, however, crucial that, in this process, and as argued previously, the 'formative' parts of the self are kept in check, and Kracauer argues that a 'productive absent-mindedness' of these parts should be cultivated by the historian (92). The journey into the past constitutes the first part of the historian's journey and his return to the present constitutes the second. The historian, or 'recipient', returns from the past 'enriched by the observations he has made during [the self's] temporary recession' within the phase of realism (92), and the historian now knows more about 'the very reality which was concealed from him by his ideas of it' (93). This is a reiteration of Kracauer's citation of Schopenhauer, given earlier, asserting that 'anybody looking at a picture . . . should . . . respectfully wait for what the picture may or may not wish to tell him, for were he to talk first he would only be listening to himself' (84). What the historian-recipient now knows more about is the 'historical phenomenon in their concreteness', and this is an experience of the concrete equivalent to immediate experience of the *Lebenswelt*. What Kracauer suggests here is also analogous to the Husserlian *epochē*, which brings about a temporary 'inhibiting' or 'putting out of play' of all positions taken toward the already-given Objective world . . . all existential positions'. This, however, 'does not leave us confronting nothing. On the contrary we gain possession of something by it' (Husserl, from *Cartesian Meditations*, cited in Natanson 1973: 59). That 'something' is what follows the *epochē*, and what the *epochē* makes possible, and, in terms of historiography, what is made possible is the mobilisation of the 'full self', as the historian begins to interpret the historical phenomena in their concreteness, and as the realist phase gives way to the formative phase of the historical approach.

For Kracauer, this latter process of interpretation, or 'understanding', or *Verstehen*, is broad-based, and, in the second phase of the historical approach, the full self employs both reason and intuition to that end. Understanding requires both because of the difficulties involved with 'unique encounters with opaque entities' (96) which are 'sphinx-like' in their impenetrability (95). Kracauer's reference to the 'understanding' here is surely derived from Kant's argument in *The Critique of Pure Reason* – a work which Kracauer knew well – that the 'faculty of understanding' performs an act of synthesis through a 'unique encounter' with a 'manifold of sensible intuitions', an act of synthesis carried out by a 'unified consciousness' which is aware that it is distinct from what it is aware of (Crowther 1991: 16). This reflexive 'unified consciousness' is what Kracauer refers to as the 'full self', in which the realist and formative spheres are purposefully combined in order to perform an act of synthesis – and, necessarily, abridgement – upon the manifold. In another chapter of *History*, entitled 'Nature',[12] Kracauer also expands further on this conception of the understanding, and, also, the 'desire' for understanding, through reference to Dilthey, and the assassination of President John F. Kennedy on Friday, 22 November 1963:

> When the assassination of President Kennedy became known in New York, people spontaneously formed little groups in the street and . . . talked . . . [about] . . . his youth, his way of living, his unfulfilled goals . . . a primitive instinct impelled them thus to evoke a past which had been the present a moment ago and to picture to themselves, and try to appraise, the full scope of what they – we – had . . . abruptly lost. In doing so they followed a desire which is at the bottom of all history writing: they wanted to 'understand'. One cannot speak of this desire without recalling Dilthey's persistent efforts to feature 'understanding' – the German *Verstehen* – as the main concern of the *Geisteswissenchaften* [human sciences].[13] 'Understanding' is a pivotal concept with him. Dilthey interprets it in terms which hold their own, despite their being grounded in a psychologising and somewhat foggy philosophy of life. He conceives of history as a life process, which, passing through us, involves our entire existence; and he argues that, in order to 'understand' the phenomenon comprising that process, we must experience them with the whole of our being, so that the life[14] that we are communes with theirs. From Ranke to Huizinga or Isaiah Berlin many a practicing historian similarly insists on the need for the historian's total involvement. (43–4)

There is some ambiguity here, in part, the result of Kracauer's tendency to speak in generalities (at no point in *History* does he engage with any specific historical context, just as he does not engage in analysis of any particular film in great detail in *Theory of Film*). The ambiguity is that he seems to be referring only to very recent history: 'a past that had been a present a moment ago', rather than less recent histories (what would be normally be understood by the term 'history'); and this is much like the attempt to understand a present situation as it slips into the past, much as an observer would engage with the material world during the practice of *epochē*, or experience of *durée*, or as, in the 1927 'Photography' essay, a viewer of a recently taken photograph would. Something like the 'memory image' from 1927 seems to re-emerge here, in this formulation of 'history'. It is only in this sense that it is possible to understand Kracauer's assertion that the main impulse behind history writing is the need to 'understand' how the present has just become a determined past, rather than one that will proceed into the future: or how a present that was expected to proceed into the future did not do so, and thus history writing becomes a despairing attempt to recover the totality of the meaning of that which would not, now, progress: the construction of history based on an unexpected need to 'understand' before the past claims all, like the attempt to perceive the memory image through a viewing of a recently taken photograph.

What Kracauer refers to, in discussing the response to the assassination of Kennedy, is this kind of experience taking place and shared within the inter-subjective *Lebenswelt*, and the need to construct a historical discourse concerning someone who has irredeemably passed from that *Lebenswelt*, a discourse concerning what that person was, did and intended to do, and this must be accomplished before the data and memory begin to dissipate through the force of the arrow of time. Here, the construction of 'history' is the product of a felt need to place oneself at the point in the past just before the present came to an end. Kracauer's history is a kind of wake: an exercise of remembrance that must be performed before memory fades. And this is, of course, not the only time that the issues of death, and remembrance, appear in his writings. However, what can then happen, in order to take this historiographical project further, is that a projection further back into the past can transpire through an act of imagination and empathy, as a less recent history is engaged with through a process of indirect insertion within an experience of that more remote, passed *Lebenswelt*.

Kracauer, nevertheless, then moves beyond the formulation of such an experience and projection: beyond a history which both greatly retains the memory image, and, also, conjures up the equivalent of the memory image through a process of empathetic imagination and incorporation, by criticising Dilthey's overall position because of the extent to which intuition and imagination are involved in that, an extent that is also, and unfortunately, as far as Kracauer is concerned, 'imbued with the spirit of [over-generalised] historicism' (44). Dilthey's stance is one that is advanced 'at the expense of scientific knowledge ... and unduly limits the territory to be explored' (44). Dilthey's approach, Kracauer contends, is too much at the expense of the 'formative stage' of the historical approach. 'Understanding' may encompass intuitive 'experience', but it must also be able to accommodate 'scientific knowledge', 'laws and regularities'; 'historical reality contains uniformities ... causal relationships ... A historian confining himself to "understanding", in Dilthey's sense, would miss a good deal' of that history, because the formative stage would not be sufficiently engaged with (44). This critique enables Kracauer to accommodate more remote histories the better through historiography, because both the receptive and formative stages of such a historiography are now not entirely dependent upon 'a past that had been the present a moment ago', or a conjuration of such through an act of empathetic imagination.

'Total involvement' in the construction of historical discourse, therefore, begins with the realist phase: with concrete identification with the 'life process' of history that 'pass[es] through us', and that involvement then expands to encompass our 'entire existence', one that includes more abstract aspects of that existence, and which is played out within the *Lebenswelt*. True or full *Verstehen* can occur only when the historian brings his or her experience of their own *Lebenswelt* into empathetic conjunction with study of the historical *Lebenswelt* under question: when the historical *Lebenswelt* is viewed through the perspective of the experience of the phenomenal *Lebenswelt*. After this, 'formative' 'scientific' procedure must be brought to bear. As mentioned earlier, however, this total involvement in the historical *Lebenswelt* also remains categorically different from the historian's involvement in his or her own material *Lebenswelt*, for two reasons. First, involvement in the material *Lebenswelt* is generally unreflective, whilst the historian's scrutiny of the historical *Lebenswelt* is marked by a greater degree of reflection, and, also, a greater degree of reflection than would have been common within experience of the historical *Lebenswelt* under scrutiny. Second, the idea of total involvement on the part of the historian is also mediated by the distance the historian is necessarily placed at; and this distance is further increased by the idea of the historian as exiled palimpsest, mentioned earlier.

By bringing up the Kantian concept of *Verstehen* Kracauer also points away from the historical phenomena in their concreteness and towards the 'principles' and 'ideas' that he concerned himself with in *Theory of Film*. In that work, Kracauer employs the indeterminate concepts of 'recording' and 'revealing' to constitute the intellectual constellation of the photographic mediums. These concepts are considered as medium-specific to the photographic mediums but are, none the less, not dealt with consequentially in the book, partly because Kracauer does not want to concern himself with philosophy but with material phenomena; philosophy is related to abstraction, precisely what Kracauer's 'redemption of physical reality' is meant to counter. Nevertheless, and as has been argued in the previous chapter of this book, the general notion of the foundational 'idea', or 'principle', underlies much of Kracauer's approach in *Theory of Film*, and this is because he is influenced by a range of thinkers, including Weber, Husserl and Kant, all of whom deploy abstract concepts. This influence also comes out more clearly in *History*, in which Kracauer refers to such figures directly, and, also, to the general notion of the 'Idea',[15] although, and as in *Theory of Film*, Kracauer is also at pains to distinguish that notion from philosophical ideas. Just as, in *Theory of Film*, Kracauer argues that film lies 'below' the philosophical Idea in terms of degree of abstraction, so, also, in *History*, he argues that the 'historical Idea' is less abstract than the philosophical Idea. Kracauer's conception of the Idea in *History* is central to that work, and such centrality, and shift towards a general consideration of the importance of the Idea, have implications, given his apparent overriding concern with phenomena in their concreteness.

In fact, the historian's journey ends with the historical Idea, and not with 'phenomena in their concreteness'. The historical Idea points beyond the material evidence to itself, as conceptual formulation, and, with the Idea, 'the historian's journey definitely reaches its close. Historical ideas mark its ultimate destination,' and, here, Kracauer brings *History* into accord with the history of photography that he set out more indirectly and obliquely in *Theory of Film* (97). As argued in the previous chapter of this book, however, this history is more historical than idealist. This is partly because, for Kracauer, as for both Kant and Husserl, the Idea is also linked to intuitive experience, as well as reason, and, so, Kracauer talks about the Idea stemming, in part, from 'insight' and a sense of revelation: 'we immediately realise that "something deep-set and fundamental that has lain unquestioned and in darkness, is suddenly illuminated"' (97–8).[16] The phrase 'immediately realise' implies some kind of intuitive, revelatory insight, and, as has been argued elsewhere, Kracauer's work, particularly in *Theory of Film*, but also in *History*, contains a strong intuitionist element, influenced mainly by Kantian concepts such as *Naturschöne*, in which an imaginative 're-enchantment' of experience occurs (Aitken 2017a: 20–1). The notion of a historical Idea does not, therefore, imply pure concept, or ratiocinative process, but, rather, a synthesis of empirical experience, reason and intuition.

Nevertheless, whilst the historical Idea may be synthetic, as opposed to mainly analytic in character, a distinction remains between the Idea itself and the material from which it is derived. The historical Idea is a conceptual 'generalisation', in the sense that it refers to and sums up a body of data, but it is also more than that, in that it is the product of an 'informed intuition' about those data that leads to an immediate realisation of something about those data. The Idea is, therefore, not only a generalisation from data, but a conceptual formulation, some of whose aspects are categorically different from generalisation. These Ideas 'quiver with connotations and meanings not found in the material occasioning them', and this takes the historical Idea beyond generality to constitute a 'universal . . . Based upon absorption in the facts, ideas have also other roots than the facts. They are genuine universals' (as will be argued shortly, however, they are not 'full-blown' universals) (98). The Idea is the outcome of a process of selection, with the self 'acting as a divining rod; it is a discovery, not an outward projection' (generalisation) (102–3). As such, the historical Idea cannot be arrived at only through 'an accumulation of detail. You will have to jump to capture it' (98–9). The 'detail' remains associated with the Idea, but part of the Idea is purely conceptual, just as any universal is associated with detail but is also distinct from such detail. Part of the Idea's conceptuality is a structure of signification formed from its own internal logic; the meanings and connotations which 'quiver' within them have their own being and must be 'discovered'. Kracauer uses somewhat misleading language here, such as 'discovering' or 'capturing' the Idea, as though these Ideas existed in some sort of Platonist world of 'Forms', waiting to be grasped. This, however, is not what he means. Kracauer is using a standard definition of the universal: many particulars can be subsumed under a universal, but, whilst the particulars can be pointed to in the empirical world, the universal cannot, and, consequently, the universal is categorically different from the particulars. The historical Idea, therefore, is one in which the historical data can be grouped under a universal whose central aspect is shared by or associated with those data, but where that central aspect also goes beyond the data to constitute something that exists-in-itself. That central aspect is also something to be investigated, and, accordingly, discovered. It is in this sense that Kracauer means that the Idea can be captured or discovered: it has a kind of existence, as any universal does, but not a material one, and it can, eventually, be formulated and used in conjunction with the data. Nevertheless, and as will be argued shortly, Kracauer's 'universals' are not complete universals in that they are not fully abstract and are not innate. Rather, they are what might be called 'concrete ideas', in that they are ideas that refer to and stem from things in the world. They are 'objects of the mind', in the sense that they exist in the imagination as entities, but are directed towards the world, and can, hypothetically, be modelled in the world in order to account for the data. A concrete idea of this sort can also be called a 'concrete object', or *concretum*, where the term 'object' refers to something, either physical or mental, at which thought is directed, and the term 'concrete' refers to material things. Kracauer's historical ideas are, accordingly, not 'abstract ideas', or 'abstract objects; they are imaginative configurations that are derived from and can be modelled in the world to one extent or another. Historical ideas, in Kracauer's characterisation, are *concretums* in this sense.

Kracauer gives two examples of such historical ideas:

> Burckhardt's notion of the awakening individual in the Renaissance is of this kind; and so is Marx's substructure–superstructure theory. The distinguishing feature of such explanations is that they seem to point beyond the material from which they are elicited. They introduce a new principle of explanation; they reveal – with one stroke, as it were – yet unsuspected contexts and relationships of a relatively wide scope; and they invariably involve matters of great import. These particular interpretations may be called 'ideas'. (97)

Marx may give examples of how ideas circulating in a society appear to complement the economic structure of that society, but the general thesis that the ideological superstructure of a society reflects the interests of those who control that economic sub-structure is not only a generalisation but also a conceptual formulation arrived at through its own internal logic. The historical Idea is a high-level conceptual explanation that is born of intuition and reason, and, as such, has its own structure apart from the material from which it has been elicited; and what is of interest here, as well, is how close Kracauer's argument is to Husserl's distinction between history and the Idea. Husserl maintained that, although social and historical factors may cause an Idea to emerge, that Idea still has its own 'normative as well as logical character', a character that constitutes the basis of its status as Idea (Natanson 1973: 53). Kracauer, however, does not go quite as far as Husserl, and wishes the Idea to remain solidly attached to the world as a *concretum*. The historian's journey within the historical approach leads to the historical Idea, but journey, approach and Idea remain close to the façade of the historical *Lebenswelt*. Of the three – journey, approach, and Idea – the last is furthest removed from the *Lebenswelt*, but not as far removed as the abstract idea, or *abstractum*. The terminology used by Kracauer here, of 'revealing with one stroke', also indicates further the intuitionist aspect of the historical Idea. Kracauer indicates the intellectual source of the historical Idea here. It is the German tradition of meta-concepts arising from Kant, Hegel, Marx, Weber, Husserl and others, and it is to this tradition that Kracauer's own meta-concepts can be related; concepts such as the 'go-for-broke game of history', 'recording', 'revealing', 'distraction', 'abstraction', 'redemption', the 'last things before the last' and the various 'historical Ideas'.

The historical Idea is not the same as the abstract Idea, and this leads Kracauer to make a further distinction between the historical Idea and the 'philosophical Idea', by which he basically means the abstract Idea, abstract object, or *abstractum*. The historical Idea is different from the philosophical Idea because it does not end in 'assumptions and norms' which 'claim effectively to control all of reality'. Instead, the historical idea has 'distinct boundaries', is intent on explaining or exploring 'this or that section of the past', and 'bears on a comparatively large section of historical reality', but not the whole of historical reality (Kracauer 1995b: 99). This is also one of the reasons why Kracauer criticises Marx so much in *History*: Kracauer believes that the base–superstructure thesis is too general and has moved beyond the proper ambit of the historical Idea. The historical Idea is not as general as the philosophical Idea because such generalities 'obscure rather than highlight conditions at a particular time and place' (99), and 'alter the distance to the subject' detrimentally (100). The historian's journey does not end at the ultimate philosophical Idea; it ends before that, 'at a lower level of abstraction'. That lower level of abstraction still implies a 'distance' from the sources, but that distance is not as great as with the philosophical pursuit of absolutes (102). Kracauer then closes 'Journey' by stressing the indeterminate nature of the historical Idea. The historical Idea can never be 'right' without also being 'wrong', and is more like an illumination, an 'image', or a 'nodal point'

> at which the concrete and the abstract meet and become one. Whenever this happens, the flow of indeterminate historical events is suddenly arrested and all that is then exposed to view is seen in the light of an image or conception which takes it out of the transient flow to relate it to one or another of the momentous problems and questions that are forever staring at us. (101)

The historical Idea 'hovers' above the historical *Lebenswelt* at a lower level than the philosophical Idea, and this means that it cannot encompass the entirety of a historical *Lebenswelt*. It is not a full universal but an intermediate one, that retains a contact with a segment of the flow of historical events. Nevertheless, the historical Idea, like the philosophical Idea, is also distinct from 'the flow of indeterminate historical events'. The *Lebenswelt* has a many-layered structure, and one which includes the historical Idea. The flow of indeterminate events is more concrete, and less abstract, than the historical Idea; and that level of abstraction also provides the historical Idea with a certain timelessness within the overall flow of temporality. The historical Idea *returns*, though in different configurations, and with a difference that is influenced by the flow of historical events. A 'great Idea', says Kracauer, quoting Alfred North Whitehead, 'is like a phantom ocean beating on the shores of human life in successive waves' (Kracauer 1997: 4).

AESTHETIC VALUE AND MEDIUM SPECIFICITY

One of the key aspects of Kracauer's stance, in both *Theory of Film* and *History*, and one that has been frequently criticised as 'normative', is his conception of aesthetic value as constituted by medium specificity. The emphasis that Kracauer places on medium specificity was derived from various influencing factors. One of these was the Kino Debate, the debate over the significance of the relatively new medium of film which took place in Germany and other countries between 1910 and 1931, and which was published in the pages of the *Frankfurter Zeitung* newspaper and other leading newspapers and journals (Levin 1987: 37–8). This debate included contributions from figures such as Georg Lukács, Ernst Bloch, Béla Balázs, Rudolf Arnheim, Bertolt Brecht, Kracauer and others (Kaes 1987b: 24). The Kino Debate encompassed a variety of positions but within that spectrum there was a certain attempt to try to understand the aesthetic specificity of the medium. So, for example, the idea that film was in some way more emblematic than other artistic mediums of the experience of modern culture and society evolved into a view, one also expressed by Kracauer in the 1927 'Photography' essay, that film was particularly capable of illuminating and transforming that experience (Blankenship 2001: 31). This perception was also influenced by the idea that film's primarily visual, gestural and non-cognitive identity was of importance in combating the pervasive influence of what Weber called 'instrumental rationality'; such a view can also be associated with a more general context of philosophical interest in non-verbal, gestural communication which influenced Central European cultural theory over 1890–30. Within this, aesthetic specificity was related to the philosophical meaning of the medium of film. In addition to this, however, attempts were also made to identify the technical aspects specific to the cinema.

Whilst the Kino Debate covered a wide spectrum of issues relating to film, including the different issues addressed by Kracauer in the papers eventually republished in *The Mass Ornament*, an interest in what was specific to film as an aesthetic medium was part of that debate, and this may have influenced Kracauer, although, in fact, that influence is not particularly present in the more sociologically oriented essays that make up *The Mass Ornament*. 'Film 1928' (1928), for example, is more concerned with the escapism offered by commercial cinema, and by the poor quality of films being made in Germany and reaching Germany from America:

> The American products that have made their way to us recently – with the exception of a few astonishingly fine achievements – would have done better never to have left. But the wretchedness of film production in Germany is of more immediate concern to us. (Kracauer 1995a: 308)

Similarly, 'The Little Shop Girls Go to the Movies'[17] (1927) focuses on how commercial films reproduce dominant ideologies of one sort or another, and on how the comfortable and conservative versions of reality presented in these films 'mirror the secret mechanisms of society' (292). Kracauer's point here has little to do with the specificity of the medium and is preoccupied with the role that film plays in displaying the 'societal will' of the 'members of the higher and next-to-higher classes' (292–3). In 'Photography' (1927), and 'The Cult of Distraction' (1926), however, one philosophical aspect of medium specificity does come to the fore: the ability of film to reveal the superficial and 'distracted' nature of the modern condition, and alternatives to that. The notion of 'distraction' in 'The Cult of Distraction' is one of Kracauer's key concepts, and is concerned with the way that films which are designed to be distractive can also, by dint of displaying such distraction, reveal the more meaningful alternatives to that; such distraction may, therefore, inadvertently reveal the 'actual state of disintegration . . . and expose . . . disintegration rather than masking it' (328). It has been argued that the German term for distraction, *Zerstreuung*, can also mean something like 'dispersal', and this can suggest a 'disintegration' of the actual, institutionally given, under the pressure of everyday experience (Mülder-Bach 2015: 284). In addition to such a revelatory function, distraction can, perhaps more typically, refer to a posture of taking-one's-mind-away from the deadening reality of everyday life. There is a kind of notion of medium specificity here, based on the ability of film, beyond that of any other medium, to reveal the reality of 'medium specificity' distracted, dispersed condition; and there is also a degree of industry-level medium specificity in the assertion that the 'movie theatres' should distinguish themselves from the 'bygone culture' of traditional theatrical theatres in order to function as a fitting vehicles for a cinema that would reveal distraction and dispersal (Kracauer 1995a: 328). Nevertheless, the references to medium specificity within *The Mass Ornament* do not amount to anything like the central place that medium specificity occupies in *Theory of Film* and *History*, and this is also a reason why some critics prefer *The Mass Ornament*.

Beyond Weimar Germany, conceptions of aesthetic value based in medium specificity were evident elsewhere, up to the point at which Kracauer left Europe for America in 1941, and these may have had an influence on his developing ideas during the late 1930s, when he was thinking about the future *Theory of Film*. In Russia, the formalist movement, which included figures such as Roman Jakobson, Viktor Shklovsky, Osip Brik, Vladimir Propp and others, attempted to identify the underlying laws and principles – or *litteraturnost* – which made literature 'literary', and which distinguished the medium from other aesthetic mediums (Mitchell 1974: 75). Russian formalism was also influenced by Husserl's argument in his *Logical Investigations* (1900) that each theoretical practice contained its own set of underlying axioms, and that these both distinguished a practice from others and determined the character of that practice. It was this that also influenced the later Russian formalist conception of *litteraturnost*. As we have seen, Kracauer was substantially influenced by Husserl. However, that influence is, again, not particularly apparent in the essays republished in *The Mass Ornament*. One other example of a stance towards medium specificity that may have influenced Kracauer was that adopted by Rudolf Arnheim. Arnheim contributed towards the Kino Debate in the 1920s by writing papers that were published in the *Frankfurter Zeitung* and he also published a book entitled *Film* in 1933, whilst Kracauer was in France (and contributed a review of *Theory of Film* in 1960). In his book, Arnheim was concerned to identify the specificity of cinematic representation, and argued that the 'special attributes of the medium should be clearly and cleanly laid bare', and that, 'In order that the film artist may create a work of art it is most important that he should consciously stress the peculiarities of the medium' (Arnheim 1933: 44–6). Whether the emphasis on medium specificity in Russian Formalism and Arnheim influenced Kracauer's developing ideas can only be speculated upon, although there are reasonable grounds for such speculation, including, as the above has shown, that a concern with medium specificity was widespread at the time. What is perhaps a clearer influence on Kracauer's conception of aesthetic value as medium specificity, however, was that of Kant.

In both *Theory of Film* and *History*, Kracauer defines filmic and historical value respectively in terms of medium specificity. Both mediums, he claims, must build from their basic properties, and both also share the same basic properties of recording and revealing physical (film) and historical (history) reality. In both cases there is also a primary stage based on receiving information and a secondary 'formative' phase in which the information is organised. Both the 'photographic' and 'historical' approaches are based on this two-stage model of the receptive and then formative stages, but it is the first stage which is the more important, because this stage produces new knowledge about reality, whilst the second merely organises that knowledge. It is also this first stage which is – largely – the medium-specific one. There are certain links to Kant here, and, it will be also argued later, to the interpretation of Kant by the art historian Clement Greenberg, who was influential in America from the 1940s through to beyond Kracauer's death in 1966. Kracauer's two-stage approach can be related to Kant's account of perception as the direction of the faculties towards a formless manifold. First, there is the manifold, the 'raw material', and the direction of attention to that. Second, there is the organising of the manifold into a form – a diversity that the faculties organise – and the faculties must, in the first instance, therefore, be open and receptive to the existence of the formless manifold. Kant called this the 'attribution of form to a formless manifold' (Gasché 2003: 87). Of course, this is not quite the same as Kracauer's two 'approaches' because Kant is talking about the basis of perception here: the organisation into perceptual material of signals coming from noumenal external reality. Nevertheless, the two-part model remains equivalent.

Kant's notion of the 'harmony of the faculties', in which the faculty of the 'Imagination' first absorbs the information coming to it from nature, and then organises that through the secondary stage of the 'Understanding', is also relevant. Here, once more, we have the two-part model, in which the manifold is observed by the faculty of the Imagination, and then a higher-order organisation is implemented by the faculty of Understanding. The faculty of Understanding is the 'formative' part of the process, whilst the initial, and 'receptive', part of the process, is carried out by the faculty of the Imagination. The model of the harmony of the faculties, in which aesthetic judgement arises from an auspicious interaction between the faculties of Understanding and Imagination, does not particularly favour one or the other of these two faculties (Aitken 2001: 171–2). However, another Kantian category that influenced Kracauer, that of *Naturschöne*, does. Here, the harmony of the faculties is achieved through the experience of nature. In *Naturschöne*, the empirical abundance of the natural environment enables the Imagination to explore freely diverse possible structures, formations and movements, and enables the Understanding to shape and regulate, and be affected by such regulation (Aitken 2017a: 20–1). *Naturschöne* is, therefore, closely related to the first stage of Kracauer's two 'approaches' because it is based upon the observation of nature. *Naturschöne* does involve a secondary, although limited, stage of organisation, in which the Understanding is brought to bear, but the emphasis is very much upon the primary stage of observation, and, in this sense, *Naturschöne* is close to Kracauer's conceptions of the first phase of the photographic and historical approaches. For Kracauer, film and historiography must hold to their basic properties because the 'basic principle', which is premised on a belief in the value of medium specificity, insists that the primary stage of the process, based on 'active–passive' reception, is specific and central to these mediums, whilst the following formative stage is not to the same extent. This two-stage process, with the emphasis on the first, points to the influence of the Kantian concept of *Naturschöne*.

A final, major influence on Kracauer's concern with medium specificity, certainly after he moved to America in 1940, may well have been that of the art theorist Clement Greenberg, an influential spokesman for the American abstract-expressionist movement in painting, the dominant movement in painting world-wide at the time, and someone whom Kracauer knew personally during the latter part of his life in America. Greenberg, of course, famously called Kant 'the first modernist' because 'he was the first to criticize the means of criticism' (Greenberg 1993: 85). Greenberg's understanding and appropriation of Kant have come under considerable question, but, leaving that aside, what he meant by the above statement is that Kant 'was the first' to focus on what 'criticism' (or, cognition) was, as well as on what that criticism was about (of course, this assertion is questionable, to say the least). What was important to Greenberg, however, was that, according to him, Kant focused on the means of representation and what was specific to that. From this, Greenberg used Kant to make something of a quantum leap, to argue, under the authority of Kant, that an artistic medium should remain true to its unique features and also investigate those features. For him, in terms of painting, that meant that painters should investigate issues raised by what was basic to a painting: the flatness and shape of the picture frame, and the application of paint to that; and this, in turn, meant that painters should not engage in a painterly illusionism that subverted or transformed that basis. The painting was a flat surface to which paint was applied, and so aesthetic questions and explorations should be restricted to the issues raised by and around that.

If interpreted through the lens of Kracauer's 'basic aesthetic principle', that an aesthetic medium must build from its basic properties, it can be said that the basic properties of the painting, the 'raw material' of the painting – paint, flat surface and frame (or edge) – should be explored using the available techniques of manipulating paint through line, shape, tone, colour and so on. Where that takes place, the artwork will be mainly constituted by the characteristic qualities of the raw material, and will, therefore, remain in identity with the aesthetic specificity of the medium. There is also a *kind* of two-stage process at work here. First, the artist must be open to the possibilities emerging from their exploration of applications of paint to the canvas (although that will also be guided by preconceptions, just as it is for Kracauer's photographer and historian). Second, the artist seeks to organise those possibilities within an ongoing framework primarily determined by them. In addition to Kant, Greenberg's conception of the importance of aesthetic specificity was influenced by Gotthold Ephraim Lessing's *Laocoon* (1767), just as Kracauer was in *Theory of Film*, and this led Greenberg to write 'Towards a Newer Laocoon' (1940), in which he attempted to define the medium specificity of painting, arguing that painting had qualities inherent to it, and that these 'basic qualities' (to use Kracauer's terms) should be adhered to.

At one level, and as argued previously, Kracauer's realism is fully compatible with a particular kind of modernist approach (though not the fully abstract one that Greenberg championed), as is evidenced by his praise for Joris Ivens's *Regen*; and, as has been maintained, an impressionistic, indeterminate form of modernism, as in *Regen*, conforms to both the model of the *Lebenswelt*, and the basic medium-specific property of film as the recording and revealing of physical reality. Kracauer could also be considered a 'formalist' in the sense that Greenberg was, in that the former argued that artistic technique should remain closely related to the 'raw material', and should not move too far away from, cover or manipulate that material. This does amount to the advocacy of a certain form of film-making. Where Greenberg and Kracauer differ, of course, is in their conceptions of what that raw material is. For Kracauer, it is phenomenal perception as captured by the film image and sequence, whereas, for Greenberg, it is paint on a flat, edged surface. The difference here is crucial, as it makes clear that Kracauer's formalism went beyond the work of art to the world existing beyond the artist and the work of art: Kracauer's form of film-making looked beyond itself, not *into* itself. Kracauer's realist film would not, therefore, be about the internal formal arrangements of the film, as would Greenberg's ideal painting, but about its ability to use those arrangements to render the external, phenomenal world. If Kracauer is a formalist, then, in addition, his form is also closely related to his content, an attitude closely connected to classical Marxist theory, as elaborated by Engels, Lenin and then, at some length, by Georg Lukács. Once more, whether Kracauer was directly influenced by this Marxist argument can only be speculated upon. Nevertheless, the idea that artistic form should be determined by the content to be represented is central to Kracauer's stance, and such centrality cannot be disassociated from this classical Marxist argument. Finally, Kracauer must also be distinguished from Greenberg with respect to the radical character of the latter. Greenberg's conception of medium specificity was an uncompromising and absolute one, but Kracauer always tried to avoid absolutes, and, when he talked about a film building from its basic properties, he did not mean that in absolute terms, but, rather, that such building upon medium specificity should be the predominant aspect present:

> He was unconcerned with, and distrustful of, rigid systems and methods . . . Kracauer's distrust of fixed and definitive systems of thought is deep seated and conscious. He avoids theology altogether . . . He admires Husserl, but mainly for his appeal to the Lebenswelt. He admires Erasmus precisely because he refuses to formulate or endorse any fixed theological or philosophical positions . . . It is because he does not believe in our ability to grasp 'the last things' through philosophical or theological systems that Kracauer is so much concerned with a 'provisional insight into the last things before the last'. (Kristeller 1995b: xii–xiii)

To what extent Kracauer was influenced by Greenberg's influential conception of aesthetic medium specificity remains a matter of some – warranted – speculation. Greenberg was a well-known figure in intellectual circles in New York – where Kracauer was based – during the 1940s and 1950s; and Kracauer was involved in various ways with the group of intellectuals that included both Greenberg, and the New York-based members of the Frankfurt School, such as Theodor Adorno. Kracauer even submitted one paper, eventually titled 'Hollywood's Terror Films', to the journal *Commentary*, at a time when Greenberg was one of the journal's editors (von Moltke and Rawson 2012: 21–2). This, however, appears to have been an unhappy experience, as Greenberg criticised Kracauer's manuscript heavily, and it does not appear that Greenberg and Kracauer were personally close (Gemünden and von Moltke 2015: 35). American abstract expressionism, however, which Greenberg championed, was, as previously claimed, probably the major international art movement at the time, and Kracauer was aware of that. Greenberg's – controversial and disputed – invocation of Kant as an advocate or implicit supporter of aesthetic medium specificity would also have been of interest to Kracauer, as a close reader of the *Critique of Judgement* during the 1920s. What *can* be said with some confidence is that Greenberg's emphasis on aesthetic value based on medium specificity, which he claimed to derive from Kant, and the invocation of Lessing in 'Towards a Newer Laocoon', is very close to Kracauer's approach in both *Theory of Film* and *History*. What was *not* close to that, however, was Greenberg's insistence on high culture and disregard for popular culture. Greenberg has been described as a figure who adopted an 'intransigent high-brow stance' in relation to culture and who called for the formation of an intellectual elite to repel the threat posed by mass and 'middle-brow' culture (von Moltke 2016: 152, 156). This was far removed from the positive, 'humanist' coverage of 'middle-brow' film in *Theory of Film* and similarly humanist and principled study of the quotidian in *History*.

There is no doubt that Kracauer's insistence on linking aesthetic value to medium specificity was a normative one, and one that also ruled many different types of film out of consideration, a major reason for the critical dismissal of *Theory of Film*. However, Kracauer had what he felt were good reasons for adopting the position he did. To him, there were larger issues to hand, and high stakes to play for within a modern condition that was becoming increasingly abstract and distant from human experience, and in which a return to the 'basic properties' of film, and historiography, might lead to a 'redemption' of both physical and historical reality. As far as Kracauer was concerned, and as *Theory of Film* makes abundantly clear, the 'go-for-broke game of history' that he invoked in the 1920s was still very much to play for.

NOTES

1. Edmund Husserl, *The Crisis of European Sciences, and Transcendental Phenomenology*, pp. 150–2.
2. This refers to the fable of the 'Wandering Jew' ('Ahasuerus'), condemned to wander endlessly through history. This is Chapter 6 of *History*.
3. Wolfgang Marius von Leyden (1911–2004), 'History and the Concept of Relative Truth' (1963), *History and Theory*, 2: 3. Pagination given by Kracauer is 279–80.
4. Johann Gottfried (von) Herder (1744–1803), *Understanding and Experience: A Metacritique of the Critique of Pure Reason* (1799). The citation given by Kracauer is for a German publication: Pt 1, sec. 2, 84, in *Sämmtliche Werke*, Pt 16 (Cotta, 1830).
5. Lewis Namier (1952), *Avenues of History*, London: H. Hamilton, p. 8.
6. The source for this phrase within double quotation marks is not given.
7. In the English version of 'Photography' this is given as 'condenses into . . . a single graphic figure'. However, the term '*Grafik*' does not appear in the original German, where the phrase 'condenses into a figure/*zu einem Linienzug verdichtet*' brings the meaning closer to what is suggested in this paragraph.
8. Herbert Butterfield (1900–79) is chiefly known for his book *The Whig Interpretation of History* (1931), an account, and criticism, of the sort of positive, optimistic historicism of which Kracauer was also critical.
9. Schopenhauer (1949), *Saemtliche Werke*, Wiesbaden, vol. 2, 'Die Welt als Wille und Vorstellung/The World as Will and Idea', pp. 464–5.
10. For more on this, see Chapter 6 of this book.
11. The concept of 'understanding', or *Verstehen*, is an important one for Kracauer, and will be addressed in more depth later in this chapter.

12. Chapter 1, 'Nature', pp. 17–44.
13. *Geisteswissenchaften*, broadly translated as the 'sciences of mind', a conception of the human sciences, encompassing philosophy, history and literary studies and so on, that is comparable to the notion of 'humanities'.
14. The phrase 'the life that we are' is a little strange, but is what is written down. It probably means 'the life that we have'.
15. From this point on, and to avoid confusion, the term 'idea' will be capitalised as 'Idea'.
16. Kracauer is quoting from Isaiah Berlin's essay 'History and Theory' (1960), in the journal *History and Theory*, 1: 1, 24.
17. A better translation of this might be 'The Little Store Girls Go the Movies', as the German term 'Ladenmadchen' here refers to the department stores that Kracauer writes about.

Bibliography

Adorno, Theodor, W. (1991) [1964], 'The Curious Realist: On Siegfried Kracauer', in *New German Critique*, 54 (Autumn): 159–77.
— (1997) [1970], *Aesthetic Theory*, Minneapolis: University of Minnesota Press.
— (2007) [1966], *Negative Dialectics*, New York: Continuum.
Aitken, Ian (1998a), 'Kracauer and Surrealism', *Screen*, 39 (Summer): 2, 124–40.
— (1998b), *The Documentary Film Movement: An Anthology*, Edinburgh: Edinburgh University Press.
— (2001), *European Film Theory and Cinema: A Critical Introduction*, Edinburgh: Edinburgh University Press.
— (2006), *Realist Film Theory and Cinema: The Nineteenth-Century, Lukácsian and Intuitionist-Realist Traditions*, Manchester: Manchester University Press.
— (2007), 'Physical Reality: The Role of the Empirical in the Film Theory of Siegfried Kracauer, John Grierson, André Bazin and Georg Lukács', *Studies in Documentary Film*, 1: 2, 105–21.
— (2009), '"What is There Really in the World?" Forms of Theory, Evidence and Truth in *Fahrenheit 9/11*: A Philosophical and Intuitionist Realist Approach', in Warren Buckland (ed.), *Film Theory and Contemporary Hollywood Movies*, London and New York: Routledge, pp. 310–30.
— (2012), *Lukácsian Film Theory and Cinema: A Study of Georg Lukács's Writings on Film, 1913–71*, Manchester: Manchester University Press.
— (2013a), 'Georg Lukács's Late Aesthetic and Film Theory: A Study of the Chapter entitled "Film" in Lukács's *The Specificity of the Aesthetic/Die Eigenart des Ästhetischen* (1963)', *New Review of Film and Television Studies*, 2: 3, 314–33.
— (2013b) [1990], *Film and Reform: John Grierson and the Documentary Film Movement*, London: Routledge.

— (2016), 'The *Aesthetic* and *The Leopard*: A Lukácsian Analysis of *The Leopard/ Il Gattopardo*', *Moderna: Semestrale di teoria e critica della letteratura*, XVIII, 1: 2, 205–25.
— (2017a) [2016] (ed.), *The Major Realist Film Theorists: An Anthology*, Edinburgh: Edinburgh University Press.
— (2017b) [2016], 'Introduction', in Aitken (ed.), *The Major Realist Film Theorists: An Anthology*, pp. 1–40.
— (2017c [2016]), 'The "Naturalist" Treatment of Film in *The Specificity of the Aesthetic* (Georg Lukács, 1963), and *One Day in the Life of Ivan Denisovich* (Alexander Solzhenitsyn, 1962, Caspar Wrede, 1970)', in Aitken (ed.), *The Major Realist Film Theorists: An Anthology*, pp. 156–71.
Allen, Robert C., and Richard Gomery (1985), *Film History: Theory and Practice*, New York: Alfred A. Knopf.
Andrew, Dudley (1976), *The Major Film Theories: An Introduction*, Oxford: Oxford University Press.
— (1990), *André Bazin*, New York and Oxford: Columbia University Press.
Arato, Andrew (1971), 'Lukács's Path to Marxism, 1910–23', *Telos*, 7: 128–36.
Arnheim, Rudolf (1933), *Film*, London: Faber and Faber.
Bazin, André (1958–62), *Qu'est-ce que le cinéma? vols I–IV*, Paris: Éditions du Cerf.
— (1967), *What is Cinema? vol. I*, Berkeley and Los Angeles: University of California Press.
— (1972), *What Is Cinema? vol. II*, Berkeley and Los Angeles: University of California Press.
Beardsley, Monroe C. (1981), *Aesthetics: Problems in the Philosophy of Criticism*, Indianapolis: Hackett.
Bell, David (1990), *Husserl*, London and New York: Routledge.
Benjamin, Walter (1992a), *Illuminations*, London: Fontana Press.
— (1992b) [1936], 'The Work of Art in the Age of Mechanical Reproduction', in Benjamin, *Illuminations*, pp. 166–95.
— (1996) [1920], 'The Concept of Criticism in German Romanticism', in Marcus Bullock and Michael W. Jennings (eds), *Selected Writings, vol. 1: 1913–1926*, Cambridge, MA: Belknap Press of Harvard University.
— (1998) [1929], 'An Outsider Attracts Attention: The Salaried Masses, by S. Kracauer', in, Siegfried Kracauer, *The Salaried Masses: Duty and Distraction in Weimar Germany*, London and New York: Verso, pp. 109–14.
— (2011) [1931], *A Short History of Photography*, Oxford: Oxford University Press.
Bergson, Henri (1946) [1934], *The Creative Mind: An Introduction to Metaphysics*, New York: The Philosophical Library.
— (1983) [1907], *Creative Evolution*, New York: University Press of America.

— (1991) [1896], *Matter and Memory: An Essay on the Relations of Body and Spirit*, New York: Zone.
— (2013) [1889], *Essai sur les données immédiates de la conscience*, Brussels: Ultraletters.
— (2015a) [1889], *Time and Free Will: An Essay on the Immediate Data of Consciousness*, Eastford, CT: Martino.
— (2015b) [1896], *Matière et mémoire: Essai sur la relation du corps à l'esprit*, Paris: Ligaran.
— (2016) [1907], *L'Évolution créatrice*, Paris: Createspace.
Biemel, Walter (1977), 'Husserl's *Encyclopaedia Britannica* Article, and Heidegger's Remarks Theron', in Frederick Elliston and Peter McCormick (eds), *Husserl: Expositions and Appraisals*, Notre Dame, IN, and London: University of Notre Dame Press, pp. 286–303.
Blankenship, Janelle (2001), 'Futurist Fantasies: Lukács's Early Essay "Thoughts toward an Aesthetic of the Cinema"', *Polygraph*, 13, 21–36.
Bloomer, Carolyne, M. (1976), *Principles of Visual Perception*, New York: Van Nostrand Reinhold.
Bohm, David, and Basil J. Hiley (1993), *The Undivided Universe: An Ontological Interpretation of Quantum Theory*, London: Routledge.
Bordwell, David, and Noël Carroll (1996), *Post-Theory: Reconstructing Film Studies*, Madison, WI: University of Wisconsin Press.
Bradley, F. H. (1914), *Essays on Truth and Reality*, London: Clarendon Press.
Bratu Hansen, Miriam (1987), 'Benjamin, Cinema and Experience: "The Blue Flower in the Land of Technology"', *New German Critique*, 40 (Winter): 179–224.
— (1997), 'Introduction', in Siegfried Kracauer, *Theory of Film: The Redemption of Physical Reality*, Princeton, NJ: Princeton University Press, pp. vii–xIv.
— (2012), *Cinema and Experience: Siegfried Kracauer, Walter Benjamin and Theodor W. Adorno*, Berkeley: University of California Press.
— (2015), 'Kracauer's Photography Essay: Dot Matrix-General (An-) Archive-Film', in Gerd Gemünden and Johannes von Moltke (eds), *Culture in the Anteroom: The Legacies of Siegfried Kracauer*, Ann Arbor: University of Michigan Press, pp. 93–110.
Bruzina, Ronald (2000), 'There is More to the Phenomenology of Time than Meets the Eye', in John B. Brough and Lester Embree (eds), *The Many Faces of Time*, Dordrecht, Boston and London: Kluwer Academic, pp. 67–84.
Bunge, Mario (2006), *Chasing Reality: Strife over Realism*, Toronto, Buffalo and London: University of Toronto Press.

Čapek, Miliĉ (1971), *Bergson and Modern Physics: A Reinterpretation and Re-evaluation*, Dordrecht: Martinus Nijhoff.
Carr, David (1974), *Phenomenology and the Problem of History: A Study of Husserl's Transcendental Philosophy*, Evanston, IL: Northwestern University Press.
— (1977), 'Husserl's Problematic Concept of the Life-World', in Frederick Elliston and Peter McCormick (eds), *Husserl: Expositions and Appraisals*, Notre Dame, IN, and London: University of Notre Dame Press, pp. 202–12.
— (1987), *Interpreting Husserl: Critical and Comparative Studies*, Dordrecht, Boston and Lancaster: Martinus Nijhoff.
Casebier, Alan (1991), *Film and Phenomenology: Toward a Realist Theory of Cinematic Representation*, New York, Port Chester, Melbourne and Sydney: Cambridge University Press.
Casey, Edward S. (1977), 'Imagination and Phenomenological Method', in Frederick Elliston and Peter McCormick (eds), *Husserl: Expositions and Appraisals*, Notre Dame, IN, and London: University of Notre Dame Press, pp. 70–82.
Cavell, Stanley (1979), *The World Viewed: Reflections on the Ontology of Film*, London and Cambridge, MA: Harvard University Press.
Christensen, Carleton B. (2012), 'The World', in Sebastian Luft and Søren Overgaard (eds), *The Routledge Companion to Phenomenology*, London and New York: Routledge, pp. 211–21.
Collinson, Diane (1994), 'Aesthetic Experience', in Oswald Hanfling (ed.), *Philosophical Aesthetics: An Introduction*, Oxford: Blackwell, pp. 111–78.
Conant, James (1992), 'Introduction', in Hilary Putnam, *Realism with a Human Face*, Cambridge, MA, and London: Harvard University Press, pp. xv–lxxiv.
Costall, Alan, and Arthur Still (1987), *Cognitive Psychology Under Question*, London: Harvester.
Crowther, Paul (1991), *The Kantian Sublime: From Morality to Art*, Oxford: Clarendon.
Currie, Gregory (1995), *Image and Mind: Philosophy and Cognitive Science*, Cambridge: Cambridge University Press.
Deleuze, Gilles (2003) [1985], *Cinema 2: The Time-Image*, Minneapolis: University of Minnesota Press.
— (2011) [1966], *Bergsonism*, New York: Zone Books.
— (2018) [1983], *Cinema 1: The Movement-Image*, London: Bloomsbury Academic.
Depraz, Natalie (2000), 'Hyletic and Kinetic Facticity of the Absolute Flow and World Creation', in John B. Brough and Lester Embree (eds), *The Many Faces of Time*, Dordrecht, Boston and London: Kluwer Academic, pp. 25–36.

Desmond, William (1986), *Art and the Absolute: A Study of Hegel's Aesthetics*, New York: State University of New York Press.
Devitt, Michael (1997), *Realism and Truth*, Princeton, NJ: Princeton University Press.
Douglas, Paul (1999), 'Bergson and Cinema: Friends or Foes?', in John Mullarkey (ed.), *The New Bergson*, Manchester and New York: Manchester University Press, pp. 209–27.
Druarte, Thérèse-Anne (1999), 'The Timaeus Revisited', in Johannes M. Van Ophuijsen (ed.), *Plato and Platonism*, Washington, DC: Catholic University of America Press, pp. 163–78.
Elliston, Frederick, and Peter McCormick (1977) (eds), *Husserl: Expositions and Appraisals*, Notre Dame, IN, and London: University of Notre Dame Press.
Elsaesser, Thomas (2009), 'World Cinema: Realism, Evidence, Presence', in Lúcia Nagib and Cecilia Mello (eds), *Realism and the Audiovisual Media*, London: Palgrave Macmillan, pp. 3–19.
Elveton, R. O. (1970) (ed.), *The Phenomenology of Husserl*, Chicago: Quadrant.
Engels, Friedrich (1977) [1885], 'Letter to Minna Kautsky', in David Craig (ed.), *Marxists on Literature: An Anthology*, Aylesbury: Penguin, pp. 267–8.
Fink, Eugene (1970), 'The Phenomenological Philosophy of Edmund Husserl and Contemporary Criticism', in R. O. Elveton (ed.), *The Phenomenology of Husserl*, Chicago: Quadrant, pp. 73–147.
Frisby, David (1986), *Fragments of Modernity: Theories of Modernity in the Work of Simmel, Kracauer and Benjamin*, Cambridge, MA: MIT Press.
Gasché, Rodolphe (2003), *The Idea of Form: Rethinking Kant's Aesthetics*, Stanford, CA: Stanford University Press.
Gaut, Berys (2010), *A Philosophy of Cinematic Art*, Cambridge: Cambridge University Press.
Gemünden, Gerd, and Johannes von Moltke (2015) (eds), *Culture in the Ante-Room: The Legacies of Siegfried Kracauer*, Ann Arbor: University of Michigan Press.
Gerhardt, Christina (2015), 'On Natural History: Concepts of History in Kracauer and Adorno', in Gerd Gemünden and Johannes von Moltke, *Culture in the Ante-Room: The Legacies of Siegfried Kracauer*, Ann Arbor: University of Michigan Press, pp. 229–43.
Gibson, James J. (1972), 'A Theory of Direct Visual Perception', in J. Royce and W. Rozenboom (eds), *The Psychology of Knowing*, New York: Garden and Breach.
— (1986) [1966], *The Ecological Approach to Visual Perception*, New York: Psychology Press.

Ginsberg, Terri, and Kirsten Moana Thompson (1996) (eds), *Perspectives on German Cinema*, New York: G. K. Hall.
Goldmann, Lucian (1967), 'The Early Writings of Georg Lukács', *TriQuarterly*, 9 (Spring): 165–81.
— (1972), 'The Aesthetics of the Young Lukács', *New Hungarian Quarterly*, XIII: 47, 129–56.
— (1977), *Lukács and Heidegger: Towards a New Philosophy*, London: Routledge and Kegan Paul.
Gombrich, E. H. (1960), *Art and Visual Illusion: A Study on the Psychology of Pictorial Representation*, London: Phaidon.
Greenberg, Clement (1992), 'Avant Garde and Kitsch', in C. Harrison and P. Wood (eds), *Art in Theory, 1900–1990*, Oxford: Blackwell, pp. 529–41.
— (1993), 'Modernist Painting', in John O'Brian (ed.), *Clement Greenberg: The Collected Essays and Criticism, vol 4*. Chicago: University of Chicago Press, pp. 85–93.
Gregory, R. L. (1990), *Eye and Brain*, London: Weidenfeld and Nicolson.
— (1991), 'Putting Illusions in Their Place', *Perception*, 20: 2–4.
Guerlac, Suzanne (2006), *Thinking in Time: An Introduction to Henri Bergson*, Ithaca, NY, and London: Cornell University Press.
Guthrie, W. K. C. (1967), *The Greek Philosophers: From Thales to Aristotle*, London: Routledge.
Hake, Sabine (1987), 'Girls and Crisis: The Other Side of Diversion', *New German Critique*, 40 (Winter): 147–164.
— (1993) (ed), *The Cinema's Third Machine: Writing on Film in Germany, 1907–1933*, Lincoln: University of Nebraska Press.
Hallam, Julia, with Margaret Marshment (2000), *Realism and Popular Culture*, Manchester: Manchester University Press.
Halliwell, J. J., J. Pérez-Mercader and W. H. Zurek (1996), (eds), *Physical Origins of Time Asymmetry*, Cambridge: Cambridge University Press.
Hamlyn, D. W. (1990), *In and Out of the Black Box: On the Philosophy of Cognition*, Oxford: Basil Blackwell.
Hanfling, Oswald (1994), *Philosophical Aesthetics: An Introduction*, Oxford: Blackwell.
Harré, Rom (1986), *Varieties of Realism: A Rationale for the Natural Sciences*, Oxford: Blackwell.
— (1988), *The Philosophies of Science*, Oxford and New York: Oxford University Press.
— (2015), 'Aspects of a Social Philosophy of Science', <https://iphras.ru/uplfile/socep/conf_soc_ep_2015/Harre_Nov_2015.pdf> (last accessed 1 April 2019).
Hawking, Stephen (2016), *A Brief History of Time*, New York: Bantam Books.

Heil, John (1983), *Perception and Cognition*, Berkeley: University of California Press.
Held, David (1980), *Introduction to Critical Theory*, Berkeley and Los Angeles: University of California Press.
Heller, Agnes (1966), 'Lukács's Aesthetics', *The New Hungarian Quarterly*, VII: 24, 84–94.
— (1980), 'The Philosophy of the Late Lukács', *Philosophy and Social Criticism*, 6: 1, 147–63.
— (1983a) (ed.), *Lukács Revalued*, Oxford: Basil Blackwell.
— (1983b), *Lukács Reappraised*, New York: Columbia University Press.
— (1983c), 'Lukács's Later Philosophy', in Heller, *Lukács Reappraised*, pp. 177–90.
Herman, Arthur (2013), *The Cave and the Light: Plato Versus Aristotle, and the Struggle for the Soul of Western Civilisation*, New York: Random House Trade Paperbacks.
Hesse, Mary (1980), 'The New Empiricism', in Harold Marrick (ed.), *Challenges to Empiricism*, London: Methuen, pp. 208–29.
Hillier, J., and A. Lovell (1972), *Studies in Documentary*, London: Secker and Warburg.
Hirst, R. J. (1967), 'Realism', in Paul Edwards (ed.), *The Encyclopedia of Philosophy*, New York: Macmillan, pp. 77–83.
Hopkins, Burt C. (1997) (ed.), *Husserl in Contemporary Context: Prospects and Projects for Phenomenology*, Dordrecht: Kluwer Academic.
Hospers, John (1978), *An Introduction to Philosophical Analysis*, London: Routledge and Kegan Paul.
Husserl, Edmund (1931) [1913], *Ideas: A General Introduction to Phenomenology*, London: Allen & Unwin.
— (1954) [1931], *Cartesian Meditations: An Introduction to Phenomenology*, The Hague: Nijhoff Academic.
— (1965) [1911], 'Philosophy as Rigorous Science', in *Philosophy and the Crisis of Phenomenology*, New York: Harper Torchbooks, pp. 71–148.
— (1969) [1929], *Formal and Transcendental Logic*, The Hague: Martinus Nijhoff Academic.
— (1970) [1936], *The Crisis of European Sciences and Transcendental Phenomenology: An Introduction to Phenomenological Philosophy*, Evanston, IL: Northwestern University Press.
— (1982) [1913], *Ideas Pertaining to a Pure Phenomenology and a Phenomenological Philosophy: General Introduction to a Pure Phenomenology*, Dordrecht: Kluwer Academic (also known as *Ideas I*).
— (1989) [1913] *Ideas II: Ideas Pertaining to a Pure Phenomenology and a Phenomenological Philosophy: Studies in the Phenomenology of Constitution*, Dordrecht: Kluwer Academic.

— (2002) [1936], 'The Way into Phenomenological Transcendental Philosophy by Inquiring back from the Pregiven Life-World', in Dermot Moran and Timothy Mooney (eds), *The Phenomenology Reader*, London and New York: Routledge, pp. 151–74.
Ilyenkov, E. V. (2008), *The Dialectics of the Abstract and Concrete in Marx's Capital*, Delhi: Aakar Books.
Jackson, F. and P. Petit (1988), 'Functionalism and Broad Content', *Mind*, 97: 387, 381–400.
Jay, Martin (2010), 'Magical Nominalism: Photography and the Re-enchantment of the World', in Neal Curtis (ed.), *The Pictorial Turn*, London and New York: Routledge, pp. 69–87.
— (2012), 'Afterword: Kracauer the Magical Nominalist', in Johannes von Moltke and Kristy Rawson (eds), *Siegfried Kracauer's American Writings: Essays on Film and Popular Culture*, Berkeley and Los Angeles: University of California Press, pp. 227–35.
Joós, Ernst (1987) (ed.), *Georg Lukács and his World: A Reassessment*, New York and Paris: Peter Lang.
Kadarkay, Arpad (1991), *Georg Lukács: Life, Thought and Politics*, Cambridge, MA: Basil Blackwell.
— (1995) (ed.), *The Lukács Reader*, Oxford: Blackwell.
Kaes, Anton (1987), 'The Debate about Cinema: Charting a Controversy (1909–1929)', *New German Critique*, 40 (Winter), 7–33. Translated by David J. Levin.
Kant, Immanuel (1973) [1790], *Critique of Judgement*, Oxford: Oxford University Press.
— (2007) [1781], *Critique of Pure Reason*, London: Penguin.
Keat, R., and J. Urry (1975), *Social Theory as Science*, London: Routledge.
Keeps, David (1918), *Bergson, Complexity and Creative Emergence*, London: Palgrave Macmillan.
Koch, Gertrud (1987), 'Béla Balázs: The Physiognomy of Things', *New German Critique*, 40 (Winter): 167–177.
— (1991), 'Exile, Memory and Image in Kracauer's Conception of History', *New German Critique*, 54 (Fall): 95–109.
— (2000), *Siegfried Kracauer: An Introduction*, Princeton, NJ: Princeton University Press.
Kockelmans, Joseph, K. (1977), 'Husserl and Kant on the Pure Ego', in Frederick Elliston and Peter McCormick (eds), *Husserl: Expositions and Appraisals*, Notre Dame, IN, and London: University of Notre Dame Press, pp. 269–85.
Kolakowski, Leszek (1978), *Main Currents of Marxism, vol. 3: The Breakdown*, Oxford: Clarendon Press.
Körner, Stephan (1955), *Kant*, New Haven, CT, and London: Yale University Press.

Kracauer, Siegfried (1974) [1946], *From Caligari to Hitler: A Psychological History of the German Film*, Princeton, NJ: Princeton University Press.

— (1985) [1964], *Theorie des Films: Die Errettung der äußeren*, Frankfurt am Main: Suhrkamp.

— (1995a), *The Mass Ornament, Weimar Essays*, Cambridge, MA, and London: Harvard University Press.

— (1995b) [1968], *History: The Last Things Before the Last*, Princeton, NJ: Markus Wiener.

— (1997) [1960], *Theory of Film: The Redemption of Physical Reality*, Princeton, NJ: Princeton University Press.

— (1998) [1929/1930], *The Salaried Masses: Duty and Distraction in Weimar Germany*, London and New York: Verso.

— (2017) [1963], *Das Ornament der Masse*, Frankfurt am Main: Suhrkamp.

Kristeller, Paul Oskar (1995), 'Preface', in Siegfried Kracauer, *History: The Last Things Before the Last*, Princeton, NJ: Markus Wiener, pp. v–ix.

Lacey, A. R. (1993), *Bergson*, London: Routledge.

Larkin, Maurice (1977), *Man and Society in Nineteenth-Century France: Determinism and Ideology*, New York: Macmillan.

Larrabee, Harold A. (1949), *Selections from Bergson*, New York: Appleton-Century-Crofts.

Larrabee, Mary Jeanne (2000), 'There's No Time like the Present: How to Mind the Now', in John B. Brough and Lester Embree (eds), *The Many Faces of Time*, Dordrecht, Boston and London: Kluwer Academic, pp. 85–112.

Leigh, Jacob (2009), 'Ontology, Film and the Case of Eric Rohmer', in Lúcia Nagib and Cecilia Mello (eds), *Realism and the Audiovisual Media*, London: Palgrave Macmillan, pp. 164–74.

Lenin, V. I. (1972), *Materialism and Empirio-Criticism: Critical Comments on a Reactionary Philosophy*, Peking: Foreign Language Press.

Leslie, Esther (2000), *Walter Benjamin: Overpowering Conformism*, London: Pluto Press.

Lessing, Gotthold Ephraim (1984) [1767], *Laocoon: Or, On the Limits of Painting and Poetry*, Baltimore and London: Johns Hopkins University Press.

Levin, Tom (1987), 'From Dialectical to Normative Specificity: Reading Lukács on Film', *New German Critique*, 40 (Winter): 35–64.

Lovell, Terry (1983), *Pictures of Reality: Aesthetics, Politics and Pleasure*, London: British Film Institute.

Löwy, Michael (1979), *Georg Lukács: From Romanticism to Bolshevism*, London: New Left Books.

— (1989), 'Naphta or Settembrini: Lukács and Romantic Anti-Capitalism', in Judith Marcus and Zoltán Tarr (eds), *Georg Lukács: Theory, Culture and Politics*, New Brunswick: Transaction, pp. 189–206.

Lukács, Georg (1913), 'Thoughts towards an Aesthetic of the Cinema', Frankfurt: *Frankfurter Zeitung und Handelsblatt*, 10 September.
— (1971a) [1920], *The Theory of the Novel*, Cambridge, MA: MIT Press.
— (1971b) [1969], *Solzhenitsyn*, Cambridge, MA: MIT Press.
— (1972) [1914], 'On the Phenomenology of the Creative Process', *The Philosophical Forum: A Quarterly* (Spring–Summer): 3–4, 314–25.
— (1974) [1911], *Soul and Form*, London: Merlin Press.
— (1976), *The Historical Novel*, Harmondsworth: Peregrine.
— (1981) [1963], *Die Eigenart des Ästhetischen/ The Specificity of the Aesthetic*, Berlin and Weimar: Aufbau.
— (1982), *The Ontology of Social Being, vol. 1: Hegel*, London: Merlin Press.
— (1990) [1923], *History and Class Consciousness: Studies in Marxist Dialectics*, London: Merlin Press.
— (1995a) [1910], 'Aesthetic Culture', in Arpad Kadarkay (ed.), *The Lukács Reader*, Oxford: Blackwell, pp. 146–59.
— (1995b) [1909], 'My Socratic Mask', in Arpad Kadarkay (ed.), *The Lukács Reader*, Oxford: Blackwell, pp. 57–62.
— (2002), *Studies in European Realism*. New York: Howard Fertig.
— (2005a) [1954], 'Art and Objective Truth', in Lukács, *Writer and Critic, and Other Essays*, Lincoln, NE: iUniverse, pp. 25–60.
— (2005b) [1936], 'Narrate or Describe?', in Lukács, *Writer and Critic, and Other Essays*, Lincoln, NE: iUniverse, pp. 110–48.
— (2015), *Die Theorie des Romans*, London: FB&c.
— (2018), *Die Seele und Die Formen*, London: FB&c.
McGinn, Colin (1991), *The Problem of Consciousness*, Oxford: Blackwell.
McGregor, Rafe (2018), 'Cinematic Realism: A Defence from Plato to Gaut', *British Journal of Aesthetics*, 58: 3, 225–39.
McIver Lopes, Dominic (2006), 'The Aesthetics of Photographic Transparency', in Noël Carroll and Jinhee Choi (eds), *Philosophy of Film and Motion Pictures*, Oxford: Blackwell, pp. 35–43.
Marcus, Judith, and Zoltán Tarr (1989) (eds), *Georg Lukács: Theory, Culture and Politics*, New Brunswick, NJ: Transaction.
Margulies, Ivone (ed.) (2003), *Rites of Realism: Essays on Corporeal Cinema*, Durham, NC, and London: Duke University Press.
Markosian, Ned (2001), 'Time, Space and the Nature of Physical Objects', in L. Nathan Oaklander (ed.), *The Importance of Time*, Dordrecht, Boston and London: Kluwer Academic, pp. 227–42.
Márkus, György (1983), 'Life and Soul: The Young Lukács and the Problem of Culture', in Agnes Heller (ed.), *Lukács Revalued*, Oxford: Basil Blackwell, pp. 1–26.
Matthews, Eric (2007), *Merleau-Ponty: A Guide for the Perplexed*, London and New York: Continuum.

Melling, David (1987), *Understanding Plato*, New York and Oxford: Oxford University Press.
Merleau-Ponty, Maurice (1962), *The Phenomenology of Perception*, London: Routledge & Kegan Paul.
Meunier, Jean-Guy (1987), 'Form Structure and Concept in the Young Lukács', in Ernst Joós (ed.), *Georg Lukács and his World: A Reassessment*, New York and Paris: Peter Lang, pp. 165–80.
Mickunus, Algis (1997), 'Life-World and History', in Burt C. Hopkins (ed.), *Husserl in Contemporary Context: Prospects and Projects for Phenomenology*, Dordrecht: Kluwer Academic, pp. 189–208.
Mitchell, Stanley (1974), 'From Shklovsky to Brecht: Some Preliminary Remarks towards a History of the Politicisation of Russian Formalism', *Screen*, Summer, 15: 2, pp. 74–81.
Moran, Dermot, and Timothy Mooney (eds) (2002), *The Phenomenology Reader*, London and New York: Routledge.
Morick, Harold (ed.) (1980), *Challenges to Empiricism*, London: Methuen.
Mülder-Bach, Inka (1991), 'History as Autobiography: *The Last Things Before the Last*', *New German Critique*, 54 (Fall): 139–57.
— (1998), 'Introduction', in Siegfried Kracauer, *The Salaried Masses*, London and New York: Verso, pp. 3–22.
— (2015), 'The Exile of Modernity: Kracauer's Configuration of the Stranger', in Gerd Gemünden and Johannes von Moltke (eds), *Culture in the Anteroom: The Legacies of Siegfried Kracauer*, Ann Arbor: University of Michigan Press, pp. 276–92.
Mullarkey, John (2007) (ed.), *The New Bergson*, Manchester and New York: Manchester University Press.
Murphy, Timothy S. (2007), 'Beneath Relativity: Bergson and Bohm on Absolute Time', in John Mullarkey (ed.), *The New Bergson*, Manchester and New York: Manchester University Press, pp. 66–81.
Nagib, Lúcia (2011), *World Cinema and the Ethics of Realism*, London: Continuum.
Nagib, Lúcia, and Cecilia Mello (2009) (eds), *Realism and the Audiovisual Media*, London: Palgrave Macmillan.
Natanson, Maurice (1973), *Edmund Husserl: Philosopher of Infinite Tasks*, Evanston, IL: Northwestern University Press.
Newhall, Beaumont (1949), *The History of Photography from 1839 to the Present Day*, New York: no publisher cited.
Nochlin, Linda (1979), *Realism: Style and Civilisation*, Harmondsworth: Penguin.
Noë, A. (2004), *Action in Perception*, Cambridge, MA: MIT Press.
Oaklander, Nathan L. (ed.) (2001), *The Importance of Time*, Dordrecht, London and Boston: Kluwer Academic.

Ophuijsen, Johannes, M. Van (1999) (ed.), *Plato and Platonism*, Washington, DC: Catholic University Press of America.
Parkinson, G. R. H (1970a) (ed.), *Georg Lukács: The Man, His Work and His Ideas*, New York: Random House.
— (1970b), 'Lukács on the Central Category of Aesthetics', in Parkinson (ed.), *Georg Lukács: The Man, His Work and His Ideas*, pp. 109–46.
Pascal, Roy (1970), 'Georg Lukacs: The Concept of Totality', in G. R. H. Parkinson (ed.), *Georg Lukács: The Man, His Work and His Ideas*, New York: Random House, pp. 147–71.
Passmore, John (1967), *A Hundred Years of Philosophy*, Harmondsworth: Penguin.
— (1985), *Recent Philosophers: A Supplement to A Hundred Years of Philosophy*, London: Duckworth.
Petro, Patrice (1996), 'Kracauer's Epistemological Shift', in Terri Ginsberg and Kirsten Moana Thompson (eds), *Perspectives on German Cinema*, New York: G. K. Hall, pp. 93–104
Pinkus, Theo (1975), *Conversations with Lukács*, Cambridge, MA: MIT Press.
Ponech, Trevor (1999), *What is Non-Fiction? (Thinking Through Cinema)*, London: Routledge.
— (2006), 'External Realism about Cinematic Motion', *British Journal of Aesthetics*, 354: 349–68.
Proust, Marcel (1913–27), *In Search of Lost Time/À la recherche du temps perdu*, London: Penguin, 2003.
Pullman, Bernard (1998), *The Atom in the History of Human Thought*, Oxford: Oxford University Press.
Putnam, Hilary (1987), *The Many Faces of Realism*, New York: Open Court.
— (1992a), *Reason, Truth and History*, Cambridge: Cambridge University Press.
— (1992b), *Realism with a Human Face*, Cambridge, MA, and London: Harvard University Press.
Radnoti, Sandor (1975), 'Balázs and Lukács: Two Radical Critics in a "God-forsaken World"', *Telos*, 155–64.
Rancière, Jacques (2006) [2001], *Film Fables*, London: Bloomsbury Revelations.
— (2011), 'Do Pictures Really Want to Live?' in Neal Curtis (ed.), *The Pictorial Turn*, London and New York: Routledge, pp. 27–36.
Rescher, N. (1973), *Conceptual Idealism*, Oxford: Blackwell.
Ricœur, Paul (1996), *A Key to Edmund Husserl's Ideas I*, Milwaukee: Marquette University Press.
Robnik, Drebli (2015), 'Among Other Things – a Miraculous Realist: Political Perspectives on the Theoretical Entanglements of Cinema and History', in Gerd Gemünden and Johannes von Moltke (eds), *Culture in the Anteroom:*

The Legacies of Siegfried Kracauer, Ann Arbor: University of Michigan Press, pp. 258–75.
Rosen, Philip (2003), 'History of Image, Image of History: Subject and Ontology in Bazin', in Ivone Margulies (ed.), *Rites of Realism: Essays on Corporeal Cinema*, Durham, NC, and London: Duke University Press, pp. 42–79.
Rothman, William, and Marian Keane (2000), *Reading Cavell's 'The World Viewed': A Philosophical Perspective*, Detroit: Wayne State University Press.
Rowlands, Mark (2003), *Externalism: Putting Mind and World Back Together Again*, Montreal: McGill University Press.
Ruggerone, Lucia (2012), 'Science and Life-World: Husserl, Schutz, Garfinkel', Springer Science + Business Media, B.V., 12 September, doi 10.1007/s10746-012-9249-6 (last accessed 1 February 2019).
Rushton, Richard (2011), *The Reality of Film: Theories of Filmic Reality*, Manchester: Manchester University Press.
Russell, Bertrand (1965), *A History of Western Philosophy*, London: George Allen and Unwin.
Russell, Matheson (2007), *Husserl: A Guide for the Perplexed*, New York: Continuum.
Sayers, Sean (1985), *Reality and Reason: Dialectic and the Theory of Knowledge*, Oxford: Basil Blackwell.
Schlüpmann, Heide (1987), 'Kracauer's Phenomenology of Film', *New German Critique*, 40 (Winter): 97–114.
Schmidt, James (1985), *Maurice Merleau-Ponty: Between Phenomenology and Structuralism*, London: Macmillan.
Schmitt, Frederick, F. (1995), *Truth: A Primer*, Boulder, CO, San Francisco and London: Westview Press.
Scruton, Roger (2006), 'Photography and Representation', in Noël Carroll and Jinhee Choi (eds), *Philosophy of Film and Motion Pictures*, Oxford: Blackwell, pp. 19–34.
Searle, John (1989), *Minds, Brains and Science*, Harmondsworth: Penguin.
Seel, Martin (2008), 'Realism and Anti-Realism in Film Theory', *Critical Horizons*, 9: 2, pp. 157–75.
Shields, Christopher (2007), *Aristotle*, London: Routledge.
Sobchack, Vivian (1992), *The Address of the Eye: A Phenomenology of Film Experience*, Princeton, NJ: Princeton University Press.
Stam, R., and S. Flitterman-Lewis (1992), *New Vocabularies in Film Semiotics: Structuralism, Post-structuralism and Beyond*, London and New York: Routledge.
Stewart, David, and Algis Mickunas (1974), *Exploring Phenomenology: A Guide to the Field and its Literature*, Athens, OH: Ohio University Press.

Thompson, E. P. (1978), *The Poverty of Theory and Other Essays*, London: Merlin.
Trigg, Roger (1989), *Reality at Risk: A Defence of Realism in Philosophy and the Sciences*, New York and London: Harvester Wheatsheaf.
van Langenhove, Luk (2010), *Rom Harré and the Exploration of the Human Umwelt*, London: Routledge.
Vandevelde, Pol (1996), 'Paul Ricœur: Narrative and Phenomenon', in Vandevelde (ed.), *Paul Ricœur: A Key to Edmund Husserl's Ideas I*, Milwaukee: Marquette University Press, pp. 7–31.
von Moltke, Johannes (2016), *The Curious Humanist: Siegfried Kracauer in America*, Berkeley: University of California Press.
von Moltke, Johannes, and Kristy Rawson (2012) (eds), *Siegfried Kracauer's American Writings: Essays on Film and Popular Culture*, Berkeley and Los Angeles: University of California Press.
Walsh, W. H. (1958), *Philosophy of History: An Introduction*, New York and Evanston, IL: Harper Torchbooks.
Walton, Kendall (1984), 'Transparent Pictures: On the Nature of Photographic Realism', *Critical Inquiry*, II: 246–77.
Wiles, Anne M. (1999), 'Forms and Predications in the Later Dialogues', in Johannes M. Ophuijsen (ed.), *Plato and Platonism*, Washington, DC: Catholic University Press of America, pp. 179–97.
Zamitto, John (1992), *The Genesis of Kant's* Critique of Judgement, Chicago: University of Chicago Press.

Index

absolute present, 115–18, 127, 145
absolute time, 65
absorption, 42
abstraction, 185
Abstractum, 280
accelerating extension, 7
active-passivity, 273–4
Adorno, Theodor, 181, 193, 219, 287
aesthetic, 247–50
aesthetic culture, 89
aesthetic regime, 42
aesthetic specificity, 248
aesthetics of transparency, 36
affect/affection, 50–4, 163–4
affective sensations, 66
affinities, 242–4
alienation, 239–40, 257, 267–70
allegory of the cave, 39
annihilation of the world, 162–5
Ansichsein, 146
anthropocentric reality, 7
anthropomorphism/de-anthropomorphism, 9, 145, 148
Antonioni, Michelangelo, 183, 186
apparent motion, 31
appeals, 242, 245–6

appearance, 178
apperception, 9, 176–7
appresentation, 176–7
Aristotle/Aristotelian, 72–81, 86–7, 102, 110, 149, 168
Arnheim, Rudolf, 191, 244, 281, 283–4
Arrivée d'un train en gare de la Ciotat, La/The Arrival of a Train at the Station of Ciotat, 119
Aussenwelt, 144, 243
Avventura, L'/The Adventure 183, 186

Balázs, Béla, 126, 191, 281
base-superstructure theory, 280
basic aesthetic principle, 236–9, 247–51, 259, 286
basic historical principle, 261–2
basic principle, 259, 262, 285
Battleship Potemkin, 121–2
beauty, 245–7
Beauty Itself, 73–4, 79, 82
Benjamin, Walter, 191–3, 206, 228
Bergson/Bergsonian, 1, 22, 26, 32–5, 45–71, 95, 99, 104–6, 109, 112, 115, 117, 122, 128–9, 136, 151–2, 203, 213

Berkeley, Bishop, 47
Berlin: die Symphonie der Großstadt/ Berlin: Symphony of a Great City, 188
Besonderheit/speciality, 141, 153
Bhaskar, Roy, 42
Bicycle Thieves, 36–7
Bloch, Ernst, 281
body, 50–2, 66
Borinage, 271
Brecht, Bertolt, 281
Burial at Ornans, 228
Burkhardt, Jacob, 279

Cabinet of Doctor Caligari, The, 149
camera reality, 255, 261, 273
Casebier, Allan, 27–9, 41
Cartesian dualism, 20
Cavell, Stanley, 42–3
Cervantes, Miguel de, 200
Chaplin, Charles, 139, 151, 189
Chien Andalou, Un/An Andalusian Dog, 183, 251
Chronos, 65
cinematic approach, 251, 259
cinematic experience, 30, 40
cinematographic conception of perception, 55, 152
cinematographic illusion, 32
Cinema Nuovo, 143–4
Cinema 1: The Movement-Image, 30
coding, 29
cognitivism, 16, 19, 26, 32
Commentary, 287
Comte, Auguste, 257
conceptual relativism, 174
concrete idea, 279
concrete universal, 140
Concretum, 279
confused multiplicity, 60, 67, 69, 152–3
conventionalism, 26–7

correspondence theory of truth, 8–9, 12
Courbet, Gustave, 227–8
Crisis of European Sciences, The, 161, 166, 168, 170, 173, 175–6, 178, 194, 219, 233, 255
Creative Evolution, 55
'Crisis of Science, The', 213–14
Critique of Judgment, The, 153, 287
Critique of Pure Reason, The, 274
'Cult of Distraction, The', 207 282

De Sica, Vittorio, 36, 186
Deleuze, Gilles, 30, 32–5, 65, 243
Dieser, 140–1
dialectical materialism, 154
Dilthey, Wilhelm, 193, 199, 204, 232, 258, 275–6
Ding an sich/thing-in-itself, 140, 181
disenchantment, 218
distance, 270, 273, 276, 281
distinct multiplicity, 67
distraction, 207, 218, 280, 282–3
Don Quixote de la Mancha, 200
Dostoevsky, Fyodor, 91–2
double reflection/*doppelter Widerspiegelung*, 135–6, 145, 149
Dulac, Germaine, 187
duration/*durée*, 34, 48, 55, 59–60, 63, 69, 99, 203, 263, 275

eidetic reduction, 158–61
eidos, 72–3, 158
Einstein, Albert, 63, 67
Einzelheit/singularity, 141
Eisenstein, Sergei, 121
élan vital, 57
empathy, 240–1, 260, 276–7
Encounters at the End of the World, 183

Engels, Friedrich, 140–1, 286
entity, 36
entropy, 64–5
epistemological depth, 12, 42
epochē, 157–79, 187, 240, 263, 265, 274–5
Epstein, Jean, 187
Erscheinung, 103–5, 135–6, 143, 149–51, 153–4
Erscheinungsformen/forms of appearance, 147–8
exile, 267–71
externalism, 2, 6–8, 13–15, 28, 30, 38, 40, 43, 154, 242

Fellini, Federico, 186
Film, 283
Film and Phenomenology, 27–8
Film History: Theory and Practice, 42
first domain of the soul, 79
form, 72, 74–80, 91–100, 110, 130, 168
formative approach, 231, 236
Frankfurt School, 193–4, 205–6, 218–19
Frankfurter Zeitung, 191, 205, 281, 283
freedom, 222–3, 245, 260
fuller self, 239, 260, 271, 274–5

Gattungswesen, 133–4
General Thesis of the Natural Attitude, 172
Geradesosein/just-being-so, 139–42, 150
Gibson, James G., 13–22, 31, 36, 38–9, 43
God's-Eye-View, 7–8
Goethe, Johann, Wolfgang, von, 100, 205, 226–7
Good Itself, The, 73–4, 77

Great Kinds of Forms, 73, 75, 77 81, 100,101
great moment, 90–1, 117–18, 131, 138, 145
Greenberg, Clement, 284–8
Guermantes Way, The, 238

Harmony of the Faculties, 180–1, 184, 284
Harré, Rom, 7, 20, 38, 42
Hegel, G.W. F./Hegelian, 140–1, 221–3, 280
Herder, Johann, Gottfried, 256
Herzog, Werner, 183
'Historian's Journey, The', 258, 262
'Historical Approach, The', 254–9, 261–2, 273, 280, 285
historical approach, 220, 242, 264–5
Historical Idea, 278, 279–81
historical reality, 285
historicism, 204–6, 205, 222, 276
History: The Last Things Before the Last, 191, 194–5, 217, 219–32, 237, 244, 254–9, 261–6, 270, 275–8, 280, 283–4, 288
'Hollywood's Terror Films', 287
Husserl, Edmund, 26–8, 41, 58, 106, 136, 142, 157–80, 186, 193–4, 212–13, 219–20, 229, 232–3, 240, 255, 272, 277, 280, 283
hyle, 168
hyletic content, 168
hyletic data, 168–9
hylomorphic, 75

idea, 276–80
ideology, 249–51
illusion, 31–3
image, 45–55, 152
image world, 67
Imagination, The, 180–1
immediate experience, 66

immobile section, 30, 32–4
indeterminacy, 243–4, 246–7, 255–6, 281
indirect seeing, 35–7
instrumental rationality, 282
internal realism, 7–1
internalism, 7, 9–10, 23
intuition/intuitionist, 247, 276, 278, 280
Ivens, Joris, 186, 250, 271, 286

Kafka, Franz, 211
Kant, Immanuel, 86–7, 112, 153, 168, 180–1, 185–6, 277, 280, 285
Kennedy, John, F., 275–6
Kierkegaard, Søren, 81, 85
Kino Debate, 126, 191, 281, 283
Kracauer, Siegfried/Kracauerian, 36, 62, 109, 160, 169, 179–215, 217–89

Laocoon, 286–7
Laplace, Pierre-Simon, 48
law of specificity, 38
Lebendigkeit, 122, 129, 136–7, 147
Lebensnähe, 135–7, 150
Lebenswelt/life-world, 34, 98–100, 108, 136, 157, 170–9, 184, 186, 188–9, 194, 215, 218, 220–34, 243–4, 249–52, 255–6, 258, 261, 270–4, 276–7, 280–1, 286
Lenin, Vladimir, 134, 137, 141, 148, 151, 286
Lessing, Gotthold, Ephraim, 286–7
'Letter to Minna Kautsky', 141
Limelight, 189
Logical Investigations, 283
logos, 142–3
Lukács, Georg, 26, 39, 62, 72–156, 191, 198–9, 281, 286
Lumière Brothers, 122, 250

Man With a Movie Camera, The, 188
Mass Ornament, The/Ornament der Mass, Das, 191, 192, 194–213, 218, 220, 225, 229, 282–3
Marx/Marxism, 43, 141, 151, 153–4, 195, 205, 257–8, 270, 279–80, 286–7
Matter and Memory, 45, 49, 51
medium specificity, 236–7, 242, 247–8, 259, 261–3, 276, 281–8
melancholy, 240, 242, 270
Méliès, Georges, 250
memory, 194–8, 200–1, 205, 207–9, 223, 266–7
memory image, 196–8, 200–2, 209, 215, 227, 238–9, 263, 266–9, 275–6
memory-image, 49–50
Merleau-Ponty, Maurice, 168–9, 173, 175
Mészáros, István, 143
metaphysical realism, 2, 8–9, 242
'Metaphysics of Tragedy, The', 127, 130–2
Moment der Gegenwart, 141
monogram, 200–2, 204, 208, 263, 266
movement-image, 30, 40–2

Namier, Lewis, 260
natural attitude, 27, 106–7, 143, 150, 157–79, 193, 221, 240, 272
naturalism, 137–9
nature, 285
Naturschöne, 180–3, 185–7, 189, 218, 278–9, 285
neo-positivism, 205
New Objectivity, 192
Newton, First Law of Motion, 64
Newton, Sir Isaac, 64
Nietzsche/Nietzschean, 79, 85, 213
noema/noetic/noematic, 27, 169

non-objectified form, 80
North Whitehead, Alfred, 281
novella, 135, 144

object, 28–30, 36, 40, 63, 98, 233–4
objectified form, 80
objectification, 94, 97–8, 105–6, 108, 146
Oedipus Rex, 106–7, 114
'On *Besonderheit* as a Category of the Aesthetic', 133, 143, 146
'On the Nature and Form of the Essay: A Letter to Leo Popper', 82
'On the Phenomenology of the Creative Process', 78, 92–113, 133–4, 146
'On the Writings of Walter Benjamin', 214, 225
One Day in the Life of Ivan Denisovich, 138–9, 151
ontological depth, 12
ontological turn, 26
Ontology of Social Being, The 153
open system, 42
optic array, 14–22, 25, 35, 37–8

palimpsest/palimpsestic, 267–9, 270–1, 273, 276
Peirce, Charles Sanders, 10–12, 43
persistence of vision, 24
Phaedrus, 78
phenomenalism, 26–7
phenomenological description, 218
phenomenological reduction, 158
phenomenology, 26–7, 94–112, 227, 229
Phenomenology of Spirit, The, 140
Philosophical Idea, 278, 280
philosophical realism, 5, 8–9, 12–13
'Philosophy as a Rigorous Science', 232

photographic approach, 217, 220, 222, 225, 231, 236, 238–45, 247, 251, 259, 262
'Photographic Approach, The', 261, 267
photographic conception of perception/reality, 53–4, 152
'Photography/*Die Photographie*', 191–215, 217, 221, 226, 229–31, 238, 244–6, 256, 263–4, 268, 275, 282, 285
photomontage, 241
Plato/Platonism/Neo-Platonism, 39, 72–84, 86–7, 89, 90–1, 95–6, 100–3, 109–12, 119, 127, 130–1, 279
Plenum, 171–2, 174
Popper, Leo, 85–6
Portrait of Saskia, 146
pragmatism, 7–9, 12, 26, 43
present image, 34, 37, 46–55, 59, 151
present moment, 116, 118–19, 131, 234
'productive absent-mindness', 274
programme analogy, 16–17
protension, 177–8
Proust, Marcel, 197, 238–9, 242, 245, 266–7, 269
psychological reduction, 161
pure duration, 48, 60, 69–70
pure heterogeneity, 60
Putnam, Hillary, 6–12, 43

quantitative multiplicity, 66–7
quantum theory, 64, 67

Rancière, Jacques, 42
raw material, 250, 286
reality effect, 26
record/recording, 223–5, 232–7, 240, 242, 246–8, 259, 262, 276, 280

redemption, 217, 222, 228, 246, 276, 286, 288
reflection/*Widerspiegelung*, 134, 141, 148–9, 151–2, 154
reflective experience, 66
réflexion, 52–3
Regen/Rain, 186–9, 240, 250, 286
Règle de jeu, La/Rules of the Game, The, 98, 107, 109
relativity, 232–4
Relativity, General Theory of, 63
Rembrandt van Rign, 146–7, 198, 210
Remembrance of Things Past/In Search of Lost Time, 238, 266
Repräsentation, 27–8
representational realism, 2–3
representational regime, 42
representationalism, 28–9, 35, 42, 97, 167–8
representative sensations, 66
represented image, 34, 46–55, 59, 151
retention, 177–8, 212
reveal/revealing, 224–5, 232–7, 240, 242, 246–8, 259, 262, 276, 280
Rien que les heures, 240
romantic anti-capitalism, 83
Romanticism, 247–8, 254
Rossellini, Roberto, 98
Rubens, Peter Paul, 226
Russian formalism, 283–4

Salaried Masses, The, 228
Sartre, Jean-Paul, 175
Schopenhauer, Arthur, 265, 274
second domain of the soul, 79
Second Law of Thermodynamics, 64
self, 264, 271, 274
screen, 55
shaped time, 257

'Short History of Photography, A', 192–3
Simmel, Georg, 106, 193–4, 199, 218
simple reflection/*einfachen Widerspiegelung*, 148
Socrates/Socratic, 78–9, 81, 87
Solzhenitsyn, Alexander, 138, 151
Sophocles/Sophoclean, 82, 84, 88, 106, 114, 129, 135
soul, 72–83, 91, 106, 110
Soul and Form, 72, 80–6, 90–2, 95–6, 100–3, 110, 112–13, 118, 124–5, 127, 130, 132–3, 135, 138, 158, 198
spacetime, 63, 65, 257
Specificity of the Aesthetic, The, 83, 91, 103, 127, 132, 133–56, 203
sphere of ownness, 160
Stalin/Stalinism, 138
Stimmung, 139
Storck, Henri, 271
Strada, La/The Street, 186, 188–9
stranger, 268, 270
stroboscopic effect, 24, 31
substance, 72–5, 102
surrealism, 183–5

temporality/time, 56–66, 83–91, 113, 115, 116–32, 135–6, 139, 141, 154, 191–216, 223–4, 225, 257–60
theatrical, 42
Theory of Film, 181–2, 184–5, 187, 189, 191, 193–6, 203, 209–12, 217–36, 244–7, 249–51, 254–6, 259–62, 264–6, 267–9, 277–8, 281, 283–4, 286–8
Theory of Forms, 39, 73–4, 81, 84, 102, 279
Theory of the Novel, The, 79–80, 83–4, 90–2, 95, 118, 125, 132–3, 135, 199–200

'Those Who Wait', 229
'Thoughts towards an Aesthetic of the Cinema', 89, 92, 112–33, 135–7, 139, 145, 147, 151, 154, 203
Time and Free Will, 67, 128–9
time of becoming, 53–5
Tolstoy, Leo, 91
total relevance factor, 29
Totalitäts der Gegenstandlichkeit, 142
totality, 99–100, 127, 144
tragic, the, 230
transcendental being, 164
'Towards a Newer Laocoon', 286–7
traditional arts, 246
transcendental idealism, 162
transcendental phenomenology, 162
transcendental reduction, 160–9
transcendental subjectivity, 160–9
transparency thesis, 35–7, 40–1
Trübner, Wilhelm, 210, 226
truth, 245–6
twin earth thesis, 6

Umberto D., 186, 230
Umwelt, 7, 20–1, 30–1, 34

Understanding, The, 180–1, 285
Ungleichzeitigkeit, 258
ur-image/*Urbild*, 196–8, 200, 202, 204, 208–9, 266

vehicle externalism, 13
veil of perception, 2–3
Verstehen/understanding 274–5, 277
Voyage to Italy, 98

Weber, Max, 193, 214, 229, 276, 280
Weimar, 273
Wesen, 103–5, 135–6, 138–9, 143, 149–50
'Work of Art in the Age of Mechanical Reproduction, The', 192
world, 166–8, 171, 178–9, 199, 242, 279
world consciousness, 166–7

Zerstreuung, 283
Zhdanov, Andrei, 137
Zola, Émile, 238
zones of indetermination, 53–5

EU representative:
Easy Access System Europe
Mustamäe tee 50, 10621 Tallinn, Estonia
Gpsr.requests@easproject.com